# PALESTINE.

PART OF JERUSALEM, WITH THE CHURCH OF THE HOLY SEPULCHRE.

# PALESTINE,

OR THE

# HOLY LAND;

FROM

**THE EARLIEST PERIOD TO THE PRESENT TIME.**

---

BY THE REV. MICHAEL RUSSELL, LL.D.

Author of "View of Ancient and Modern Egypt," "Nubia and Abyssinia,"
"History and Present Condition of the Barbary States," &c.

---

With a Map and Nine Engravings.

**FOURTH EDITION, ENLARGED.**

---

LONDON:

DARF PUBLISHERS LIMITED

1985

First Published 1837
New Impression 1985

ISBN 1 85077 053 0

Reprinted by A. Wheaton & Co. Ltd, Exeter

# PREFACE

## TO THE FOURTH EDITION.

In giving an account of the Holy Land, an author, upon examining his materials, finds himself presented with the choice either of simple history on the one hand, or of merely local description on the other; and the character of his book will of course be determined by the selection which he shall make of the first or the second of these departments. The volumes on Palestine hitherto laid before the public, will accordingly be found to contain either a bare abridgment of the annals of the Jewish people, or a topographical delineation of the country, with the cities and towns which they inhabited, from the era of their triumphs under Joshua, down to the period of their dispersion by Titus and Adrian. Several able works have recently appeared on each of these subjects, and have been, almost without exception, rewarded with the popularity which is seldom refused to learning and eloquence. But it occurred to the writer of the following pages, that the expectations of the general reader would be more fully answered, were the two plans to be united; combining an account of the constitution, the antiquities, the religion, the literature, and even the statistics of the Hebrews, with a narrative of their rise and fall in the sacred land bestowed upon their fathers.

In following out this scheme, he has made it his study to leave no source of information unexplored, which might supply the means of illustrating the political condition of the Twelve Tribes immediately after they settled on the banks of the Jordan. The principles which entered into the constitution of their commonwealth are extremely interesting, both as they afford a fine example of the progress of society in one of its earliest stages, when the migratory shepherd gradually assumes the habits of the agriculturist ; and also as they confirm the results of experience, in other cases, with regard to the change which usually follows in the form of civil government, and in the concentration of power in the hands of an individual.

The chapter on the Literature and Religion of the Ancient Hebrews cannot boast of a great variety of materials, because what of the subject is not known to the youngest reader of the Bible must be sought in the writings of Rabbinical authors, who have unfortunately directed the largest share of their attention to the minutest parts of their Law, and expended the labour of elucidation on those points which are least interesting to the rest of the world. It is deeply to be regretted, that so little is known respecting the Schools of the Prophets,—those seminaries which sent forth not only the ordinary ministers of the Temple and the Synagogue, but also that more distinguished order of men who were employed as instruments for revealing the future intentions of Providence. But the Author hesitates not to say, that he has availed himself of all the materials which the research of modern times has brought to light, while he has carefully rejected all such speculations or conjectures as might gratify the curiosity of learning without tending to edify the youthful mind. The account which is given of the Feasts and Fasts of the Jews, both before and after the Babylonian Captivity, will, it is hoped, prove useful to the reader, more especially by pointing out to him appropriate subjects of reflection while perusing the Sacred Records.

The history of Palestine, prior to the Fall of Jerusalem, rests upon the authority of the inspired writers, or of those annalists, such as Josephus and Tacitus, who flourished at the period the events of which they describe. The narrative, which brings down the fortunes of that remarkable country to the present day, is much more various both in its subject and references; more especially where it embraces the exploits of the Crusaders, those renowned devotees of religion, romance, and chivalry. The reader will find in a narrow compass the substance of the extensive works of Fuller, Wilken, Michaud, Mills, and Hogg. In the more modern part of this historical outline, in which the affairs of Palestine are intimately connected with those of Egypt, it was thought unnecessary to repeat facts already mentioned at some length in that volume of our series which is devoted to the latter country.

The topographical description of the Holy Land is drawn from the works of the numerous travellers and pilgrims, who, since the time of the faithful Doubdan, have visited the interesting scenes where the Christian Faith had its origin and completion. On this subject Maundrell is still a principal authority; for, while we have the best reason to believe that he recorded nothing but what he saw, we can trust implicitly to the accuracy of his details in describing every thing which fell under his observation. The same high character is due to Pococke and Sandys, writers whose simplicity of style and thought afford a voucher for the truth of their narratives. Nor are Thevenot, Paul Lucas, and Careri, though less frequently consulted, at all unworthy of confidence as depositories of historical facts. In more modern times we meet with equal fidelity, recommended by an exalted tone of feeling, in the volumes of Chateaubriand and Dr Richardson. Clarke, Burckhardt, Buckingham, Legh, Henniker, Jowett, Light, Macworth, Irby, Mangles, Carne, Wilson, Madden, Madox, Spence Hardy, the author of "Three Weeks in Palestine," Delamartine, and Bové, have not only contributed valuable materials, but also lent the aid of their names to correct or to confirm the statements of some of the more apocryphal among their predecessors.

The chapter on Natural History has no pretensions to scientific arrangement or technical precision in its details. It is calculated solely for the use of the common reader, who would soon be fatigued with the formal notation of the botanist, and could not understand the learned terms in which the student of zoology too often finds the knowledge of animal nature concealed. Its main object is to illustrate the Scriptures, by giving an account of the Quadrupeds, Birds, Serpents, Plants, and Fruits, which are mentioned from time to time by the inspired writers of either Testament.

The Map is recommended to the notice of the reader as containing a most accurate delineation of the country, as well as a good selection of ancient and modern names.

EDINBURGH, *July* 1837.

# CONTENTS.

## CHAPTER I.

### INTRODUCTORY OBSERVATIONS.

Interest attached to the History of Palestine—Remarkable Character of the Hebrew People—Their small Beginning and astonishing Increase—The Variety of Fortune they underwent—Their constant Attachment to the Promised Land—The Subject presents an interesting Problem to the Historian and Politician—The Connexion with Christianity—Effect of this Religion on the Progress of Society—Importance of the Subject to the pious Reader—Holy Paces—Pilgrims—Grounds for believing the ancient Traditions on this Head—Constantine and the Empress Helena—Relics—Naural Scenery—Extent of Canaan—Fertility—Geographical Distribution—Countries Eastward of the Jordan—Galilee—Samara—Bethlehem—Jericho—The Dead Sea—Tables representing the Possessions of the Twelve Tribes, ................Page 17

## CHAPTER II.

### HISTORY OF THE HEBREW COMMONWEALTH.

Form of Government after the Death of Joshua—In Egypt—In the Wilderness—Princes of Tribes and Heads of Families—Impatience to take Possession of Promised Land—The Effects of it—Renewal of War—Extent of Holy Land—Opinions of Fleury,

Spanheim, Reland, and Lowman—Principle of Distribution—Each Tribe confined to a separate Locality—Property unalienable—Conditions of Tenure—Population of the Tribes—Number of principal Families—A General Government or National Council—The Judges—Nature of their Authority—Not Ordinary Magistrates—Different from Kings, Consuls, and Dictators—Judicial Establishments—Judges and Officers—Described by Josephus—Equality of Condition among the Hebrews—Their Inclination for a pastoral Life—Freebooters like the Arabs—Abimelech, Jephthah, and David—Simplicity of the Times—Boaz and Ruth—Perpetuity of their Customs—Tribe of Levi—Object of their Separation—The Learned Professions Hereditary, after the Manner of the Egyptians—The Levitical Cities—Their Number and Uses—Opinion of Michaelis—Summary View of the Times and Character of the Hebrew Judges,...............Page 41

## CHAPTER III.

### HISTORICAL OUTLINE FROM THE ACCESSION OF SAUL TO THE DESTRUCTION OF JERUSALEM.

Weakness of Republican Government—Jealousy of the several Tribes—Resolution to have a King—Rules for Regal Government—Character of Saul—Of David—Troubles of his Reign—Accession of Solomon—Erection of the Temple—Commerce—Murmurs of the People—Rehoboam—Division of the Tribes—Kings of Israel—Kingdom of Judah—Siege of Jerusalem—Captivity—Kings of Judah—Return from Babylon—Second Temple—Canon of Scripture—Struggles between Egypt and Syria—Conquest of Palestine by Antiochus—Persecution of Jews—Resistance by the Family of Maccabæus—Victories of Judas—He courts the Alliance of the Romans—Succeeded by Jonathan—Origin of the Asmonean Princes—John Hyrcanus—Aristobulus—Alexander Jannæus—Appeal to Pompey—Jerusalem taken by Romans—Herod created King by the Romans—He repairs the Temple—Archelaus succeeds him, and Antipas is nominated to Galilee—Quirinius Prefect of Syria—Pontius Pilate—Elevation of Herod Agrippa—Disgrace of Herod Philip—Judea again a Province—Troubles—Accession of Young Agrippa—Felix—Festus—Florus—Command given to Vespasian—War—Siege of Jerusalem by Titus, .................................................................Page 70

## CHAPTER IV.

### LITERATURE AND RELIGIOUS USAGES OF THE ANCIENT HEBREWS.

Obscurity of the Subject—Learning issued from the Levitical Colleges—Schools of the Prophets—Music and Poetry—Meaning of the Term Prophesy—Illustrated by References to the Old Testament and to the New—The Power of Prediction not confined to those bred in the Schools—Race of False Prophets—Their Malignity and Deceit—Micaiah and Ahab—Charge against Jeremiah the Prophet—Criterion to distinguish True from False Prophets—The Canonical Writings of the Prophets—Literature of Prophets—Sublime Nature of their Compositions—Examples from Psalms and Prophetical Writings—Humane and liberal Spirit—Care used to keep alive the Knowledge of the Law—Evils arising from the Division of Israel and Judah—Ezra collects the Ancient Books—Schools of Prophets similar to Convents—Sciences—Astronomy—Division of Time, Days, Months, and Years—Sabbaths and New Moons—Jewish Festivals—Passover—Pentecost—Feast of Tabernacles—Of Trumpets—Jubilee—Daughters of Zelophedad—Feast of Dedication—Minor Anniversaries—Solemn Character of Hebrew Learning—Its easy Adaptation to Christianity—Superior to the Literature of all other Ancient Nations, ..................................................................103

## CHAPTER V.

#### DESCRIPTION OF JERUSALEM.

Pilgrimages to the Holy Land—Arculfus—Willibald—Bernard—Effect of Crusades—William de Bouldesell—Bertrandon de la Broquiere—State of Damascus—Breidenbach—Baumgarten—Bartholemeo Georgewitz—Aldersey—Sandys—Doubdan—Cheron—Thevenot—Gonzales—Morison—Maundrell—Pococke—Road from Jaffa to Jerusalem—Plain of Sharon—Rama or Ramla—Condition of the Peasantry—Vale of Jeremiah—Abou-Goosh—Jerusalem—Remark of Chateaubriand—Impressions of different Travellers—Dr Clarke—Tasso—Volney—Henniker—Mosque of Omar described—Mysterious Stone—Church of Holy Sepulchre—Ceremonies of Good Friday—Easter—The Sacred Fire—Grounds for Scepticism—Folly of the Priests—Emotion upon entering the Holy Tomb—Description of Chateaubriand—Holy Places in City—On Mount Sion—Pool of Siloam—Fountain of the Virgin—Valley of Jehoshaphat—Mount of Offence—The Tombs of Zechariah, of Jehoshaphat, and of Absalom—Jewish Architecture—Dr Clarke's Opinion on the Topography of Ancient Jerusalem—Opposed by other Writers—The Inexpediency of such Discussions, ..............................................................Page 132

## CHAPTER VI.

#### DESCRIPTION OF THE COUNTRY SOUTH AND EAST OF JERUSALEM.

Garden of Gethsemane—Tomb of Virgin Mary—Grottos on Mount of Olives—View of the City—Extent and Boundaries—View of Bethany and Dead Sea—Bethlehem—Convent Church of the Nativity described—Paintings—Music—Population of Bethlehem—Pools of Solomon—Dwelling of Simon the Leper—Of Mary Magdalene—Tower of Simeon—Tomb of Rachel—Convent of St John—Fine Church—Tekoa—Bethulia—Hebron—Sepulchre of Patriarchs—Al-baid—Kerek—Extremity of Dead Sea—Discoveries of Bankes, Legh, Irby, and Mangles—Convent of St Saba—Valley of Jordan—Mountains—Description of Lake Asphaltites—Remains of ancient Cities in its Basin—Quality of its Waters—Apples of Sodom—Tacitus, Seetzen, Hasselquist, Chateaubriand—Width of River Jordan—Jericho—Village of Rihhah—Balsam—Fountain of Elisha—Mount of Temptation—Place of Blood—Anecdote of Sir F. Henniker—Fountain of the Apostles—Return to Jerusalem—Markets—Costume—Science—Arts—Language—Jews—Present Condition of that People,...Page 189

## CHAPTER VII.

### DESCRIPTION OF THE COUNTRY NORTHWARD OF JERUSALEM.

Grotto of Jeremiah—Sepulchres of the Kings—Singular Doors—Village of Leban—Jacob's Well—Valley of Shechem—Nablous—Samaritans—Sebaste—Jennin—Gilead—Geraza or Djerash—Description of Ruins—Gergasha of the Hebrews—Rich Scenery of Gilead—River Jabbok—Souf—Ruins of Gamala—Magnificent Theatre—Gadara—Capernaum or Talhewm—Sea of Galilee—Bethsaida and Chorazin—Tarachea—Sumuk—Tiberias—Description of modern Town—House of St Peter—Baths—University—Mount Tor or Tabor—Description by Pococke, Maundrell, Burckhardt, and Doubdan—View from the Top—Great Plain—Nazareth—Church of Annunciation—Workshop of Joseph—Mount of Precipitation—Table of Christ—Cana or Kefer Kenna—Water-pots of Stone—Saphet or Szaffad—University—French—Sidney Smith—Dan—Sepphoris—Church of St Anne—Description by Dr Clarke—Baalbec—Temple of Aphaca—Vale of Zabulon—Vicinity of Acre,..............................233

## CHAPTER VIII.

#### THE HISTORY OF PALESTINE FROM THE FALL OF JERUSALEM TO THE PRESENT TIME.

State of Judea after Fall of Jerusalem—Revolt under Trajan—Barcochab—Adrian repairs Jerusalem—Schools at Babylon and Tiberias—The attempt of Julian to rebuild the Temple—Invasion of Chosroes—Sack of Jerusalem—Rise of Islamism—Wars of the Caliphs—First Crusade—Jerusalem delivered—Policy of Crusades—Victory at Ascalon—Baldwin King—Second Crusade—Saladin—His success at Tiberias—He recovers Jerusalem—The Third Crusade—Richard Cœur de Lion—Siege and Capture of Acre—Plans of Richard—His Return to Europe—Death of Saladin—Fourth Crusade—Battle of Jaffa—Fifth Crusade—Fall of Constantinople—Sixth Crusade—Damietta taken—Reverses—Frederick the Second made King of Jerusalem—Seventh Crusade—Christians admitted into the Holy City—Inroad of Karismians—Eighth Crusade under Louis IX.—He takes Damietta—His Losses and Return to Europe—Ninth Crusade—Louis IX. and Edward I.—Death of Louis—Successes of Edward—Treaty with Sultan—Final Discomfiture of the Franks in Palestine, and Loss of Acre—State of Palestine under the Turks—Increased Toleration—Bonaparte invades Syria—Siege of Acre and Defeat of French—Rupture between the Porte and the Viceroy of Egypt—Successes of Ibrahim—Crosses Mount Taurus—His Victory at Koniah—Actual State of the Holy Land—Number, Condition, and Character of the Jews,..............................Page 294

## CHAPTER IX.

#### THE NATURAL HISTORY OF PALESTINE.

Travellers too much neglect Natural History—Maundrell, Hasselquist, Clarke—GEOLOGY—Syrian Chain—Libanus—Calcareous

Rocks—Granite—Trap—Volcanic Remains—Earthquakes and Volcanic Eruptions in Syria and Southern Italy—Chalk—Marine Exuvia—Precious Stones—METEOROLOGY—Climate of Palestine—Winds—Thunder—Clouds—Waterspouts—Ignis Fatuus—ZOOLOGY—Scripture Animals—The Hart—The Roebuck—Fallow-deer—Wild-goat—Pygarg—Wild-ox—Chamois—Unicorn—Wild-ass—Wild-goats of the Rock—Saphan, or Coney—Mouse—Porcupine—Jerboa—Mole—Bat—BIRDS—Eagle—Ossifrage—Ospray—Vulture—Kite—Raven—Owl—Night-hawk—Cuckoo—Hawk—Little Owl—Cormorant—Great Owl—Swan—Pelican—Gier Eagle—Stork—Heron—Lapwing—Hoopoe—AMPHIBIA AND REPTILES—Serpents known to the Hebrews—Ephe—Chephir—Acshub—Pethen—Tzeboa—Tzimmaon—Tzepho—Kippos—Shephiphon—Shachal—Saraph, the Flying-serpent—Cockatrice Eggs—The Scorpion—Sea-monsters, or Seals—FRUITS AND PLANTS—Vegetable Productions of Palestine—The Fig-tree—Palm—Olive—Cedars of Libanus—Wild-grapes—Balsam of Aaron—Thorn of Christ,......Page 362

# ENGRAVINGS.

Map of Palestine,................................*To face the Vignette.*
Vignette—Part of Jerusalem, with the Church of the Holy Sepulchre.
View of Jerusalem from the Mount of Olives, ..............*Page* 149
Fountain of Siloam,..........................................................180
Tomb of Absalom,............................................................184
Village of Bethany, and Dead Sea,....................................194
Subterranean Church of Bethlehem,..................................197
River Jabbok, and Hills of Bashan,...................................251
Sea of Galilee, Town of Tiberias, and Baths of Emmaus,........259
Mount Tabor, ..................................................................267

# PALESTINE,

OR

# THE HOLY LAND.

## CHAPTER I.

*Introductory Observations.*

Interest attached to the History of Palestine—Remarkable Character of the Hebrew People—Their small Beginning and astonishing Increase—The Variety of Fortune they underwent—Their constant Attachment to the Promised Land—The Subject presents an interesting Problem to the Historian and Politician—The Connexion with Christianity—Effect of this Religion on the Progress of Society—Importance of the Subject to the pious Reader—Holy Places—Pilgrims—Grounds for believing the ancient Traditions on this Head—Constantine and the Empress Helena—Relics—Natural Scenery—Extent of Canaan—Fertility—Geographical Distribution—Countries Eastward of the Jordan—Galilee—Samaria—Bethlehem—Jericho—The Dead Sea—Tables representing the Possessions of the Twelve Tribes.

THE country to which the name of Palestine is given by the moderns, is that portion of the Turkish empire in Asia which is comprehended within the 31st and 34th degrees of north latitude, and extends from the Mediterranean to the Syrian Desert, eastward of the river Jordan and the Dead Sea. Whether viewed as the source of our religious faith, or as the most ancient fountain of our historical knowledge, this singular spot of earth has at all times been regarded with feelings of the deepest interest and curiosity. Inhabited for many ages by a people entitled above all others to the distinction of peculiar, it presents a record of events such as have not come to pass in any other land ; monuments of a belief denied to all other nations ; hopes not elsewhere cherished, but which, nevertheless, are connected with the destiny of the whole human race, and stretch forward to the consummation of all terrestrial things.

To the eye of mere philosophy nothing can appear more striking than the effects produced upon the world at large by the opinions and events which originated among the Jewish people. A pastoral family, neither so numerous, so warlike, nor so well instructed in the arts of civilized life as many others in the same quarter of the globe, gradually increased into a powerful community ; became distinguished by a system of doctrines and usages different from those of all the surrounding tribes ; retaining it, too, amid the numerous changes of fortune to which they were subjected, and finally impressing its leading principles upon the most enlightened nations of Asia and of Europe. At a remote era Abraham crosses the Euphrates, a solitary traveller, not knowing whither he went, but obeying a divine voice, which called him from among idolaters to become the father of a new people and of a purer faith, at a distance from his native country. His grandson, Jacob, a "Syrian ready to perish," goes down into Egypt with a few individuals, where his descendants, although evil entreated and afflicted, became a "nation, great, mighty, and populous," and whence they were delivered by the special interposition of Heaven. In prosperity and adversity they were still the objects of the same vigilant Providence which reserved them for a great purpose to be accomplished in the latter days ; while the Israelites themselves, as if conscious that their election was to be crowned with momentous results, still kept their thoughts fixed on Palestine as the theatre of their glory not less than as the possession of their tribes.

We accordingly see them at one period in bondage, the victims of a relentless tyranny, and menaced with complete extirpation : but the hope of enjoying the land promised to their fathers never ceased to animate their hearts ; for they trusted that God would surely visit them in the house of their affliction, and in his appointed time carry them into the inheritance of peace and rest. At a later epoch we behold them swept away as captives by the hands of idolaters, who used all the motives which spring from fear and from interest to secure their compliance with a foreign worship. But, rejecting all such inducements, they still continued a separate people, steadily resisting the operation of those causes which, in almost every other instance, have been found sufficient to melt down a vanquished horde into the population and habits of their masters. At length they appear as the instruments of a dispensation which embraces the dearest interests of all the sons of Adam ; and which, in happier circumstances than ever fell to their own lot, has already modified and greatly exalted the character, the institutions, and the prospects of the most improved portion of mankind in both hemispheres of the globe.

Connected with Christianity, indeed, the history of the Hebrews rises before the reflecting mind in a very singular point of view ; for, in opposition to their own wishes, they laid the foundations of a religion which has not only superseded their peculiar rites, but is rapidly advancing towards that universal acceptation which they were wont to anticipate in favour of their own ancient law. In spite of themselves they have acted as the little leaven which was destined to leaven the whole lump ; and, in performing this office, they have proceeded with nearly the same absence of intention and consciousness as the latent principle of fermentation to which the metaphor bears allusion. They aimed at one thing, and have accomplished another ; but while we compare the means with the end, whether in their physical or moral relations, it must be admitted that we therein examine one of the most remarkable events recorded in the annals of the human race.

Abstracting his thoughts from all the considerations of supernatural agency which are suggested by the inspired narrative, a candid man will nevertheless feel himself compelled to acknowledge that the course of events which constitutes the history of ancient Palestine has no parallel in any other part of the world. Fixing his eye on the small district of Judea, he calls to mind that, eighteen hundred years ago, there dwelt in that little region a singular and rather retired people, who, however, differed from the rest of mankind in the very important circumstance of not being idolaters. He looks around upon every other country of the earth at the same era, where he discovers superstitions of the most hateful and degrading kind, darkening all the prospects of the human being, and corrupting his moral nature in its very source. He observes that some of these nations are far advanced in many intellectual accomplishments, yet, being unable to shake off the tremendous load of error by which they are pressed down, are extremely irregular and capricious, both in the exercise of their reason and in the application of their affections. He learns, moreover, that this little spot called Palestine is despised and scorned by those proud kingdoms, whose wise men will not for a moment allow themselves to imagine that any speculation or tenet, arising from so ignoble a quarter, ought to have the slightest influence upon their belief, or could affect, in the most minute degree, the general character of their social institutions.

But, behold, while he yet muses over this interesting scene, a Teacher springs up from among the lower orders of the Hebrew people,—himself not less contemned by his countrymen than they were by the warlike Romans and the philosophic Greeks,—whose doctrines, notwithstanding, continue to gain ground on every hand, till at last the proud monuments of pagan superstition, consecrated by the worship of a thousand years, and supported by the authority of the most powerful monarchies in the world, fall one after another at the approach of his disciples, and before the prevailing efficacy of the new faith. A little stone becomes a mountain, and fills the whole earth. Judea swells in its dimensions till it covers half the globe, carrying captivity captive, not by force of arms, but by the progress of opinion and the power of truth. All the nations of Europe, in successive ages,—Greek, Roman, Barbarian, —glory in the name of the humble Galilean; armies, greater than those which Persia in the pride of her ambition led forth to conquest, are seen swarming into Asia, with the sole view of getting possession of his sepulchre; while the East and the West combine to adorn with their treasures the stable in which he was born, and the sacred mount on which he surrendered his precious life.\*

On these grounds there is presented to the historian and politician a problem of the most interesting nature, and which is not to be solved by any reference to the ordinary principles whence mankind are induced to act or to suffer. The effects, too, produced on society, exceed all calculation. It is in vain that we attempt to compare them to those more common revolutions which have changed for a time the face of nations, or given a new dynasty to ancient empires. The impression made by such events soon passes away: the troubled surface quickly resumes its equilibrium, and displays its wonted tranquillity; and hence we may assert, that the present condition of the world is not much different from what it would have been, though Alexander had never been born, and Julius Cæsar had died in his cradle. But the occurrences that enter into the history of Palestine possess an influence on human affairs which has no other limits than the existence of the species, and which will

---

\* See Dialogues on Natural and Revealed Religion, by the Rev. Robert Morehead, D. D., p. 241,—an able and interesting work.

be every where more deeply felt in proportion as society shall advance in knowledge and refinement. The greatest nations upon earth trace their happiness and civilisation to the benign principles and lofty sanctions of the faith to which it gave birth. Science, freedom, and security, attend its progress among all conditions of men; raising the low, befriending the unfortunate, giving strength to the arm of law, and breaking the rod of the oppressor.

Nor is the subject of less interest to the pious Christian, who confines his thoughts to the momentous facts which illustrate the early annals of his religion. His affections are bound to Palestine by the strongest associations; and every portion of its varied territory, its mountains, its lakes,—and even its deserts,—are consecrated in his eyes as the scene of some mighty occurrence. His fancy clothes with qualities almost celestial that holy land,

> " Over whose acres walked those blessed feet,
> Which eighteen hundred years ago were nail'd
> For our advantage to the blessed cross."*

In a former age, when devotional feelings were wont to assume a more poetical form than suits the taste of the present times, an undue importance was placed on the mere localities of Judea,—viewed as the theatre on which the great events of Christianity were realized,—and more especially on those relics which were considered as identifying particular spots, honoured by the sufferings or triumph of its Divine Author. The zealous pilgrim, who had travelled many thousand miles amid the most appalling dangers, required a solace to his faith in the contemplation of the Cross, or in being permitted to kiss the threshold of the tomb in which the body of his Redeemer was laid. To such an individual no description could be too minute, no details could be too particular. Forgetful of the ravages inflicted on Jerusalem by the hand of the Romans, and by the more furious anger of her own children within her,—fulfilling

---

* Shakspeare, Henry IV. Part I. Act. 1.

unintentionally that tremendous doom which was pronounced from the Mount of Olives,—the simple worshipper expected to enter the hall of judgment, the house of Pilate, and the palace of the high priest, and to be able to trace through the streets and lanes of the holy city the path which led his Saviour to Calvary. This natural desire to awaken piety through the medium of the senses, and to banish all unbelief, by touching with the hand, and seeing with the eye, the memorials of the Crucifixion, has, there is reason to apprehend, been sometimes abused by fraud as well as by ignorance.*

But it is nevertheless worthy of remark, that, from the very situation of Jerusalem, so well defined by natural limits which it cannot have passed, there is less difficulty in determining places with a certain degree of precision than would be experienced in any other ancient town. Nor can it be reasonably doubted, that the primitive Christians would mark with peculiar care the principal localities distinguished by the deeds or by the afflictions of their Divine Master. It is even natural to suppose, as M. Chateaubriand well observes, that the apostles and relatives of our Saviour, who composed his first church upon earth, were perfectly acquainted with all the circumstances attending his life, his ministry, and his death ; and as Golgotha and the Mount of Olives were not enclosed within the walls of the city, they would encounter less restraint in performing their devotions in the places which were sanctified by his more frequent presence and miracles. Besides, the knowledge of these scenes was soon extended to a very wide circle. The triumph of Pentecost increased vastly the number of believers ; and hence a regular congregation appears to have been formed in Jerusalem before the expiry of the third year from that memorable epoch. If it be

---

* Ces traditions, plus ou moins fidèles, plus ou moins altérées par le besoin pieux de credulité populaire, ou par le desir naturel à tous ces moines possesseurs d'une si précieuse relique d'en augmenter l intérêt en multipliant les détails, ont ajouté, peut-être, quelques inventions bénévoles au puissant souvenir du lieu.—Lamartine, Voyage en Orient, tome i. p. 209.

admitted that the early Christians were allowed to erect monuments in connexion with their religious worship, or even to select houses for their periodical assemblies, the probability will not be questioned that they fixed upon those interesting spots which had been distinguished by the wonders of their faith.

At the commencement of the troubles in Judea, during the reign of Vespasian, the believers at Jerusalem withdrew to Pella, whence, as soon as their metropolis was demolished, they returned to dwell among its ruins. In the space of a few months they could not have forgotten the position of their sanctuaries, which, generally speaking, being situated outside the walls, could not have suffered so much from the fury of the siege as the more lofty edifices within. That the holy places were known to all men in the time of Adrian is demonstrated by an undeniable fact. This emperor, when he rebuilt the city, erected a statue of Venus on Mount Calvary, and one of Jupiter on the sacred sepulchre. The grotto of Bethlehem was given up to the rites of Adonis; the jealousy of the idolaters thus publishing, by their abominable profanations, the sublime doctrines of the Cross, which it was their object to conceal or to calumniate.

But Adrian, although actuated by an ardent zeal in behalf of his own deities, did not persecute the Christians at large. His resentment seems to have been confined to the Nazarenes in Jerusalem, whom he could not help regarding as a portion of the Jewish nation,—the irreconcilable enemies of Rome. We perceive accordingly, that he had no sooner dispersed the church of the Circumcision established in the holy city, than he permitted within its walls the formation of a Christian community, composed of Gentile converts, whose political principles, he imagined, were less inimical to the sovereignty of the empire. At the same time he wrote to the governors of his Asiatic provinces, instructing them not to molest the believers in Christ merely on account of their creed, but to reserve all punishment for crimes committed against the laws and the public tranquillity. It has therefore been very generally admitted, that during this period of repose, and even down to the reign of Diocletian, the faithful at Jerusalem, now called Ælia Capitolina, celebrated the mysteries of their religion in public, and consequently had altars consecrated to their worship. Even if they were not allowed the possession of Calvary, the Holy Sepulchre, and of Bethlehem, where they might solemnize their sacred rites, it is not to be imagined that the memory of these holy sanctuaries could be effaced from their affectionate recollection. The very idols served to mark the places where the redemption of the world was begun and completed. Nay, the pagans themselves cherished the expectation that the temple of Venus, erected on the summit of Calvary, would not prevent the Christians from visiting that holy mount; rejoicing in the idea, as the historian Sozomen expresses it, that the Nazarenes, when they repaired to Golgotha to pray, would appear to the public eye to be offering up their adoration to the daughter of Jupiter. This is a striking proof that a perfect knowledge of the sacred places was retained by the church of Jerusalem in the middle of the second century. At a somewhat later period, when exposed to persecution, if they were not allowed to build their altars at the Sepulchre, or proceed without apprehension to the scene of the Nativity, they enjoyed at least the consolation of keeping alive the remembrance of the great events connected with these interesting monuments of their faith; anticipating, at the same time, the approaching ruin of that proud superstition by which they had been so long oppressed.

The conversion of Constantine gave a new vigour to these local reminiscences of the evangelical history. That celebrated ruler wrote to Macarius, bishop of Jerusalem, to cover the tomb of Jesus Christ with a magnificent church; while his mother, the Empress Helena, repaired in person to Palestine, in order to give a proper efficacy to the zeal which animated the throne, and to assist in searching for the venerable remains of the first age of the gospel. To this illustrious female is ascribed the glory of restoring to religion some of its most valued memorials. Not satisfied with the splendid temple erected at the Holy Sepulchre, she ordered two similar edifices to be constructed ; the one over the manger of the Messiah at Bethlehem, and the other on the Mount of Olives, to commemorate his Ascension into heaven. Chapels, altars, and houses of prayer, gradually marked all the places consecrated by the acts of the Son of Man ; the oral traditions were forthwith committed to writing, and thereby secured for ever from the treachery of individual recollection.*

These considerations give great probability to the conjectures of those pious persons, who, in the fourth century of our era, assisted the mother of Constantine in fixing the locality of holy scenes. From that period down to the present day, the devotion of the Christian and the avarice of the Mohammedan have sufficiently secured the remembrance both of the places and of the events with which they are associated. But no length of time can wear out the impression of deep reverence and respect, which are excited by an actual examination of those interesting spots that witnessed the stupendous occurrences recorded in the inspired volume. Or, if there be in existence any cause which could effectually counteract such natural and laudable feelings, it is the excessive minuteness of detail and fanciful description usually found to accompany the exhibition of sacred relics. The Christian traveller is, indeed, delighted when he obtains the first glance of Carmel, of Tabor, of Libanus, and of Olivet ; his heart opens to many touching recollections at the moment when the Jordan, the Lake of Tiberias, and even the waters of the Dead Sea spread themselves out before his eyes ; but neither his piety nor his belief is strengthened when he has presented to him a portion of the cross whereon our Saviour was suspended, the

---

* Chateaubriand, Itinéraire, tome i. p. 48, &c. Sozom. lib. iii. c. i. Euseb. Hist. Eccl. lib. vi. S. Cyril, Cat. xvi.

nails that pierced his hands and feet, the linen in which his body was wrapped, the stone on which his corpse reposed in the sepulchre, as well as that occupied by the ministering angel on the morning of the Resurrection. The scepticism with which such doubtful remains cannot fail to be examined is turned into positive disgust, when the guardians of the grotto at Bethlehem undertake to show the water wherein the infant Messiah was washed, the milk of the blessed Virgin his mother, the swaddling-clothes, the manger, and other particulars neither less minute nor less improbable.

But such abuses, the fruit of many ages of credulity and ignorance, do not materially diminish the force of the impression produced by scenes which no art can change, and hardly any description can disguise. The hills still stand round about Jerusalem as they stood in the days of David and of Solomon. The dew falls on Hermon; the cedars grow on Libanus; and Kishon, that ancient river, draws its stream from Tabor as in the times of old. The Sea of Galilee still presents the same natural accompaniments; the fig-tree springs up by the way-side, the sycamore spreads its branches, and the vines and olives still climb the sides of the mountains. The desolation which covered the Cities of the Plain is not less striking at the present hour than when Moses with an inspired pen recorded the judgment of God; the swellings of Jordan are not less regular in their rise than when the Hebrews first approached its banks; and he who goes down from Jerusalem to Jericho still incurs the greatest hazard of falling among thieves. There is, in fact, in the scenery and manners of Palestine, a perpetuity that accords well with the everlasting import of its historical records, and which enables us to identify with the utmost readiness the local imagery of every great transaction.

The extent of this remarkable country has varied at different times, according to the nature of the government which it has either enjoyed or been compelled to acknowledge. When it was first occupied by the Israelites, the Land of Canaan, properly so called, was confined between the shores of the Mediterranean and the western bank of the Jordan; the breadth at no part exceeding fifty miles, while the length hardly amounted to three times that space. At a later period, the arms of David and of his immediate successor carried the boundaries of the kingdom to the Euphrates and Orontes on the one hand, and in an opposite direction to the remotest confines of Edom and Moab. The population, as might be expected, has undergone a similar variation. It is true that no particular in ancient history is liable to a better-founded suspicion than the numerical statements which respect nations and armies; for pride and fear have, in their turn, contributed not a little to exaggerate, in rival countries, the amount of the persons capable of taking a share in the field of battle. Proceeding on the usual grounds of calculation, we must infer, from the number of warriors whom Moses conducted through the Desert, that the Hebrew people, when they crossed the Jordan, did not fall short of two millions; while, from facts recorded in the book of Samuel, we may conclude with greater confidence that the enrolment made, under the direction of Joab, must have returned a gross population of five millions and a half.

The present aspect of Palestine, under an administration where every thing decays and nothing is renewed, can afford no just criterion of the accuracy of such statements. Hasty observers have indeed pronounced that a hilly country destitute of great rivers could not, even under the most skilful management, supply food for so many mouths. But this precipitate conclusion has been vigorously combated by the most competent judges, who have taken pains to estimate the produce of the soil under the fertilizing influence of a sun which may be regarded as almost tropical, and of a well-regulated irrigation, which the Syrians knew how to practise with the greatest success. Canaan, it must be admitted, could not be compared to Egypt in respect of corn. There is no Nile to scatter the riches of an inexhaustible fecundity over its valleys and plains. Still it was not without reason that Moses described it as " a good land ; a land of brooks of water, of fountains, and depths that spring out of valleys and hills ; a land of wheat, and barley, and vines, and fig-trees, and pomegranates ; a land of oil-olive and honey ; a land wherein thou shalt eat bread without scarceness, thou shalt not lack any thing in it ; a land whose stones are iron, and out of whose hills thou mayest dig brass."*

The reports of the latest travellers confirm the accuracy of the picture drawn by this divine legislator. Near Jericho the wild olives continue to bear berries of a large size, which give the finest oil. In places subjected to irrigation, the same field, after a crop of wheat in May, produces pulse in autumn. Several of the trees are continually bearing flowers and fruit at the same time, in all their stages. The mulberry, planted in straight rows in the open field, is festooned by the tendrils of the vine. If this vegetation seems to languish or become extinct during the extreme heats, and if, in the mountains, it is at all seasons detached and interrupted,—such exceptions to the prevailing luxuriance are not to be ascribed simply to the general character of all hot climates, but also to the state of barbarism in which the great mass of the present population is immersed.

Even in our day, some remains are to be found of the walls which the ancient cultivators built to support the soil on the declivities of the mountains ; the form of the cisterns in which they collected the rain-water ; and traces of the canals by which this water was distributed over the fields. These labours necessarily created a prodigious fertility under an ardent sun, where a little moisture was the only thing requisite to revive the vegetable world. The accounts given by native writers respecting the productive qualities of Judea are not in any degree opposed even by the present aspect of the country. The case is exactly the same with some islands

---

* Deuteronomy, viii. 7, 8, 9.

in the Archipelago ; a tract from which in these days a hundred individuals can hardly draw a scanty subsistence formerly maintained thousands in affluence. Moses might justly say that Canaan abounded in milk and honey. The flocks of the Arab still find in it a luxuriant pasture, while the bees deposite in the holes of the rocks their delicious stores, which are sometimes seen flowing down the surface.

The opinions just stated with regard to the fertility of ancient Palestine receive an ample confirmation from the Roman historians, to whom, as a part of their extensive empire, it was intimately known. Tacitus, especially, in language which he appears to have formed for his own use, describes its natural qualities with the utmost precision, and, as is his manner, suggests rather than specifies a catalogue of productions, the accuracy of which is verified by the latest observations. The soil, says he, is rich, and the atmosphere dry ; the country yields all the fruits which are known in Italy, besides balm and dates.[*]

But it has never been denied that there is a remarkable difference between the two sides of the ridge which forms the central chain of Judea. On the western acclivity, the soil rises from the sea towards the elevated ground in four distinct terraces, which are covered with an unfading verdure. The shore is lined with mastic-trees, palms, and prickly pears. Higher up, the vines, the olives, and the sycamores, amply repay the labour of the cultivator ; natural groves arise, consisting of evergreen oaks, cypresses, andrachnés, and turpentines. The face of the earth is embellished with the rosemary, the cytisus, and the hyacinth. In a word, the vegetation of these mountains has been compared to that of Crete. European visiters have dined under the shade

---

[*] Terra finesque, quà ad Orientem vergunt, Arabia terminantur; a meridie Ægyptus objacet; ab occasû Phœnices et mare; septemtrionem a latere Syriæ longe prospectant. Corpora hominum salubria et ferentia laborem: rari imbres, uber solum : fruges nostrum ad morem ; præterque eas balsamum et palmæ. Hist. lib. v. c. 6.

of a lemon-tree as large as one of our strongest oaks, and have seen sycamores, the foliage of which was sufficient to cover thirty persons along with their horses and camels.*

On the eastern side, however, the scanty coating of mould yields a less magnificent crop. From the summit of the hills a desert stretches along to the Lake Asphaltites, presenting nothing but stones and ashes, and a few thorny shrubs. The sides of the mountains enlarge, and assume an aspect at once more grand and more barren. By little and little the scanty vegetation languishes and dies; even mosses disappear, and a red burning hue succeeds to the whiteness of the rocks. In the centre of this amphitheatre there is an arid basin enclosed on all sides with summits scattered over with a yellow-coloured pebble, and affording a single aperture to the east, through which the surface of the Dead Sea and the distant hills of Arabia present themselves to the eye. In the midst of this country of stones we perceive, encircled by a wall, extensive ruins, stunted cypresses, bushes of the aloe and prickly pear, while some huts of the meanest order, resembling whitewashed sepulchres, are spread over the desolated mass. This spot is Jerusalem.†

This melancholy delineation, which was suggested by the state of the Jewish metropolis in the third century, is not quite inapplicable at the present hour. The scenery of external nature is the same, and the

---

* On this subject M. de Lamartine writes as follows:—" Quand nous fûmes au revers de cette colline, la Terre Sainte, la terre de Chanaan, se montra tout entiere devant nous; l'impression fut grande, agréable et profonde; ce n'etait pas là cette terre nue, rocailleuse, sterile, cette ruche de montagnes basses et decharnées qu'on nous represente pour la terre promise, sur la foi de quelques ecrivains prévenus, ou de quelques voyageurs pressés d'arriver et d'écrire, qui n'ont vu, des domaines immenses et variés des douze tribes, que le sentier de roche qui mene, entre deux soleils, de Jaffa à Jérusalem."—Tome i. p. 197.

† Belon, Observations de Singularités, p. 140. Hasselquist's Travels, p. 56. Korte's Travels in Palestine. Chateaubriand, les Martyrs, vol. iii. p. 99. Schultze's Travels, vol. ii. p. 86.

general aspect of the venerable city is very little changed. But as beauty is strictly a relative term, and is every where greatly affected by association, we must not be surprised when we read in the works of eastern authors the high encomiums which are lavished upon the vicinity of the holy capital. Abulfeda, for example, maintains not only that Palestine is the most fertile part of Syria, but also that the neighbourhood of Jerusalem is one of the most fertile districts of Palestine. In his eye, the vines, the fig-trees, and the olive-groves, with which the limestone cliffs of Judea were once covered, appeared more valuable than the richest returns of agricultural skill, and more than compensated for the absence of those spreading fields waving with corn, which are necessary to excite in the mind of a European the ideas of fruitfulness, comfort, and abundance.

Following the enlightened narrative of Malte-Brun, the reader will find that, southward of Damascus, the point where the modern Palestine may be said to begin, are the countries called by the Romans Auranitis and Gaulonitis, consisting of one extensive plain, bounded on the north by Hermon or Djibel-el-Sheik, on the south-west by Djibel-Edjlan, and on the east by Haouran. In all these countries there is not a single stream which retains its water in summer; the most of the villages having their pond or reservoir, which they fill from one of the wadi, or brooks, during the rainy season. Of these fertile districts, Haouran is the most celebrated for the culture of wheat; and nothing can exceed in grandeur the extensive undulations of the fields, moving like the waves of the ocean in the wind. Bothin or Batinea, on the other hand, contains nothing except calcareous mountains, where there are vast caverns, in which the Arabian shepherds live like the ancient Troglodytes. Here a modern traveller, Dr Seetzen, discovered in the year 1816 the magnificent ruins of Gerasa, now called Djerash, where three temples, two superb amphitheatres of marble, and hundreds of columns, still remain among other monuments of Roman power. But by far the finest thing that he saw was a long street, bordered on each side with a splendid colonnade of Corinthian architecture, and terminating in an open space of a semicircular form surrounded with sixty Ionic pillars. In the same neighbourhood the ancient Gilead is distinguished by a forest of stately oaks, which supply wealth and employment to the inhabitants. Peræa presents on its numerous terraces a mixture of vines, olives, and pomegranates. Karak-Moab, the capital of a district corresponding to that of the primitive Moabites, still meets the eye, but is not to be confounded with another town of a similar name in the Stony Arabia.*

The countries now described lie on the eastern side of the river Jordan. But the same stream, in the upper part of its course, forms the boundary between Gaulonitis and the fertile Galilee, which is identical with the modern district of Szaffad. This town, which is remarkable for the beauty of its situation amid groves of myrtle, is supposed to be the ancient Bethulia, which was besieged by Holofernes. Tabaria, an insignificant place, occupies the site of Tiberias, which gave its name to the lake more generally known by that of Gennesareth, or the Sea of Galilee; but industry has now deserted its borders, and the fisherman with his skiff and his nets no longer animates the surface of its waters. Nazareth still retains some portion of its former consequence. Six miles farther south stands the hill of Tabor, sometimes denominated Itabyrius, presenting a pyramid of verdure crowned with olives and sycamores. From the top of this mountain, the modern Tor and scene of the Transfiguration, we look down on the river Jordan, the Lake of Gennesareth, and the Mediterranean Sea.†

Galilee, says a learned writer, would be a paradise were it inhabited by an industrious people under an enlightened government. Vine-stocks are to be seen here a foot and a half in diameter, forming, by their

---

* Seetzen, in Annales des Voyages, i. 398; and Correspondance de M. Zach, 425. † Maundrell, p. 60.

twining branches, vast arches and extensive ceilings of verdure. A cluster of grapes, two or three feet in length, will give an abundant supper to a whole family. The plains of Esdraëlon are occupied by Arab tribes, around whose brown tents the sheep and lambs gambol to the sound of the reed, which at night-fall calls them home.*

For some years this fine country has groaned and bled under the malignant genius of Turkish despotism. The fields are left without cultivation, and the towns and villages are reduced to beggary ; but the latest accounts from the Holy Land encourage us to entertain the hope, that a milder administration will soon change the aspect of affairs, and bestow upon the Syrian provinces at large some of the benefits which the more liberal policy of Mohammed Ali has conferred upon the pashalic of Egypt.

Proceeding from Galilee towards the metropolis, we enter the land of Samaria, comprehending the modern districts of Areta and Nablous. In the former we find the remains of Cesarea ; and on the Gulf of St Jean d'Acre stands the town of Caypha, where there is a good anchorage for ships. On the south-west of this gulf extends a chain of mountains, which terminates in the promontory of Carmel, a name famous in the annals of our religion. There Elijah proved by miracles the divinity of his mission ; and there, in the middle ages of the church, resided thousands of Christian devotees, who sought a refuge for their piety in the caves of the rocks. Then the mountain was wholly covered with chapels and gardens, whereas at the present day nothing is to be seen but scattered ruins amid forests of oak and olives, the bright verdure being only relieved by the whiteness of the calcareous cliffs over which they are suspended. The heights of Carmel, it has been frequently remarked, constantly enjoy a pure and enlivening atmosphere, while the lower grounds of Samaria and Galilee are occasionally obscured by the densest fogs.

---

* Chateaubriand, Itinéraire, ii. 123. Malte-Brun, vol. ii. 150—169. Edinburgh Edition.

The Shechem of the Scriptures, successively known by the names of Neapolis and Nablous, still contains a considerable population, although its dwellings are mean and its inhabitants poor. The ruins of Samaria itself are now covered with orchards; and the people of the district, who have forgotten their native dialect, as well perhaps as their angry disputes with the Jews, continue to worship the Deity on the verdant slopes of Gerizim.

Palestine, agreeably to the modern acceptation of the term, embraces also the country of the ancient Philistines, the most formidable enemies of the Hebrew tribes prior to the reign of David. Besides Gaza, the chief town, we recognise the celebrated port of Jaffa or Yaffa, corresponding to the Joppa mentioned in the Sacred Writings. Repeatedly fortified and dismantled, this famous harbour has presented such a variety of appearances, that the description given of it in one age has hardly ever been found to apply to its condition in the very next.

Bethlehem, where the divine Messias was born, is a large village inhabited promiscuously by Christians and Mussulmans, who agree in nothing but their detestation of the tyranny by which they are both unmercifully oppressed. The locality of the sacred manger is occupied by an elegant church, ornamented by the pious offerings of all the nations of Europe. But it is not our intention, in these introductory observations, to enter into a more minute discussion of the ancient traditions, by which the particular places rendered sacred by the Redeemer's presence are still marked out for the veneration of the faithful pilgrim. Suffice it to notice that they present much vagueness, mingled with no small portion of unquestionable truth. At all events, we must not regard them in the same light in which we are compelled to view the story that claims for Hebron the possession of Abraham's tomb, and attracts on this account the veneration both of Nazarenes and Moslems.

To the north-east of Jerusalem, in the large and fertile valley called El-Gaur, and watered by the Jordan, we find the village of Rah or Rahhah, the ancient Jericho, denominated by Moses the City of Palms. This is a name to which it is still entitled; but the groves of opobalsamum, or balm of Mecca, have long disappeared; nor is the neighbourhood any longer adorned with those singular flowers known among the Crusaders by the familiar appellation of Jericho roses. A little farther south two rough and barren chains of hills encompass with their dark steeps a long basin formed in a clay soil mixed with bitumen and rock-salt. The water contained in this hollow is impregnated with a solution of different saline substances, having lime, magnesia, and soda, for their base, partially neutralized with muriatic and sulphuric acid. The salt which it yields by evaporation is about one-fourth of its weight. The bituminous matter rises from time to time from the bottom of the lake, floats on the surface, and is thrown out on the shores, where it is gathered for various economical purposes. It is to be regretted that this inland sea has not yet been examined with the attention which it deserves. We are told, indeed, by the greater number of those who have visited it, that neither fish nor shells are to be found in its waters; that an unwholesome vapour is constantly emitted from its bosom; and that its banks, hideous and desolate in the extreme, are never cheered by the note of any bird. But it is admitted by the same travellers, that the inhabitants are not sensible of any noxious qualities in its exhalations; while the accounts formerly believed, that the winged tribes in attempting to fly over it fell down dead, are now generally regarded as fabulous. Tradition supports the narrative of Sacred Scripture so far as to teach that the channel of the Dead Sea was once a fertile valley, partly resting on a mass of subterranean water, and partly composed of a stratum of bitumen; and that, a fire from Heaven kindling these combustible materials, the rich soil sunk into the abyss beneath, and Sodom and Gomorrah were consumed in the tremendous conflagration.

This brief outline of the geographical limits and phy-

## INTRODUCTORY OBSERVATIONS. 37

sical characters of the Holy Land, may prove sufficient as an introduction to its ancient history. Details much more ample are to be found in numerous works, whose authors, fascinated by the interesting recollections which almost every object in Palestine was fitted to suggest, have endeavoured to transfer to the minds of their readers the profound impressions which they themselves experienced from a personal review of ancient scenes and monuments. But I purposely refrain at present from the minute description to which the subject so naturally invites, because, in a subsequent part of our undertaking, I shall be unavoidably led into a train of local particularities, while setting forth the actual condition of the country and of its venerable remains. Meantime, there are supplied, in the following table, the means of comparing the division or distribution of Canaan among the Twelve Tribes, with that which was adopted by the Romans during the first centuries of the Christian era.

| Ancient Canaanitish Division. | Israelitish Division. | Roman Division. |
|---|---|---|
| Sidonians, | Tribe of Asher (in Libanus), | Upper Galilee. |
| Unknown | Naphtali (north-west of the Lake of Gennesareth), | |
| Perizzites, | Zebulun (west of that lake), | Lower Galilee. |
| The same, | Issachar (Valley of Esdraëlon, Mount Tabor), | |
| Hivites, | Half-tribe of Manasseh (Dora and Cesarea), | Samaria. |
| The same, | Ephraim (Shechem, Samaria), | |
| Jebusites, | Benjamin (Jericho, Jerusalem), | Judea. |
| Amorites, Hittites, | Judah (Hebron, Judea Proper), | |
| Philistines, | Simeon (south-west of Judah), | |
| | Dan (Joppa), | |
| Moabites, | Reuben (Peræa, Heshbon), | Peræa. |
| Ammonites, Gilead, | Gad (Decapolis, Ammonitis), | |
| Kingdom of Bashan, | Half-tribe of Manasseh, Gaulonitis, Batanea, | |

## SUBDIVISION OF PALESTINE UNDER THE ROMANS IN THE FIRST THREE CENTURIES.

| | Subordinate Divisions. | Chief Towns. |
|---|---|---|
| Palæstina, | Galilæa Superior, | Cæsarea Philippi (v. Paneas). |
| | —— Inferior, | Tiberias. Nazareth. |
| | Samaria, | Samaria. Neapolis (v. Sichem). Cæsarea. |
| | Judæa. Judæa Propria, | Hierosolyma (Jerusalem). Jericho. Joppa. |
| | Pentapolis, s. Palæstina Propria, | Gaza. Asdod (v. Azotus). |
| | Idumea, | Hebron. |
| | Peræa. Trachonitis, | . . . . . . |
| | Gaulonitis, | (The present Tshaulân). |
| | Batanæa, | (The present Bothin). |
| | Auranitis, | Bostra. |
| | Ituræa | . . . . . . |
| | Decapolis, | Gerasa. Gadara. |
| | Peræa Propria, | Pella. Amathus. |
| | Ammonitis, | Philadelphia. |
| | Moabitis, | . . . . . . |

---

## DIVISION OF THE DIOCESE OF THE EAST, AS FAR AS RESPECTS PALESTINE (ESTABLISHED BY CONSTANTINE AND HIS SUCCESSORS, PARTLY ALSO BY TRAJAN).

| Provinces. | Chief Towns. | Corresponding Divisions. |
|---|---|---|
| Palæstina Prima, | Cæsarea (ad mare) *Jerusalem. | Samaria. Judæa Propria. Pentapolis, or the country of the Philistines. |
| Palæstina Secunda, | Scythopolis, (Bethsan). | Galilæa. Gaulonitis. Decapolis. |
| Palæstina Tertia, or Salutaris, | Petræa, | Idumæa. Arabia Petræa. |
| Phœnicia Prima, | Ptolemaïs, *Tyrus. | The Seacoast. |

## DIVISIONS OF THE KINGDOM OF JERUSALEM IN THE TWELFTH CENTURY, ACCORDING TO THE ABBE GUENEE.

*Feodal Divisions.*

| | |
|---|---|
| I. Royal Domains, | Jerusalem. <br> Nablous. <br> Acre. <br> Tyre, and their respective districts. |
| II. First Great Barony, | Country of Jaffa. <br> ———— of Ascalon. <br> Lordship of Rama. <br> ———— of Mirabel. <br> ———— of Ybelin. |
| III. Second Great Barony, | Principality of Galilee. |
| IV. Third Great Barony, | Lordship of Sidon. <br> ———— of Cesarea. <br> ———— of Bethsan. |
| V. Fourth Great Barony, | Lordship of Karak (Petra). <br> ———— of Hebron. <br> ———— of Montreal. |
| VI. County of Tripoli, | A dependent principality, but distinct from the kingdom of Jerusalem. |

*Ecclesiastical Divisions.*

| | |
|---|---|
| I. Patriarchs of Jerusalem, | Bishoprics of Bethlehem. <br> ———— of Lydda. <br> ———— of Hebron. |
| II. Archbishopric of Karak, | ———— of Mount Sinai. |
| III. Ditto of Cesarea, | ———— of Sebaste (Samaria). |
| IV. Ditto of Nazareth, | ———— of Tiberias. <br> Priory of Mount Tabor. |
| V. Ditto of Tyre, | Bishoprics of Beryta. <br> ———— of Sidon. <br> ———— of Paneas. <br> ———— of Ptolemaïs. |

---

## PRESENT DIVISIONS OF ANCIENT PALESTINE, ACCORDING TO BUSCHING, VOLNEY, AND OTHERS.

| | |
|---|---|
| I. El-Kods, | Jerusalem, Jericho, &c. The north-west of Judea. |
| II. El-Khalil, | Hebron, and the south of Judea. |
| III. Gaza or Palestine, | The Seacoast, with Jaffa, Gaza, &c. |

| | |
|---|---|
| IV. Ludd, .......................... | A district round the city of Ludd. |
| V. Nablous, ...................... | The city of this name, with the ancient country of Samaria. |
| VI. Areta, ........................ | Mount Carmel, with part of the Plain of Esdraëlon. |
| VII. Szaffad, .................... | Ancient Galilee, called also Belad-el-Bushra, or the country of the Gospel. |
| VIII. Belad Shekyf, ........... | Ancient Trachonitis, with Belad-Hauran, Auranitis, &c. |
| IX. El-Gaur (eastern), ........ | Ancient Peræa. One district is named Es-Szalth. |
| X. El-Sharrat, ................... | On the south and south-east of the Dead Sea, with El-Djibal, the ancient Gébalene. |

In a pastoral country, such as that beyond the river Jordan, especially where the Desert in most parts bordered upon the cultivated soil, the limits of the several possessions could not at all times be distinctly marked. It is well known, besides, that the native inhabitants were never entirely expelled by the victorious Hebrews, but that they retained, in some instances by force, and in others by treaty, a considerable portion of land within the borders of all the tribes,—a fact which is connected with many of the defections and troubles into which the Israelites subsequently fell.

## CHAPTER II.

### *History of the Hebrew Commonwealth.*

Form of Government after the Death of Joshua—In Egypt—In the Wilderness—Princes of Tribes and Heads of Families—Impatience to take Possession of Promised Land—The Effects of it—Renewal of War—Extent of Holy Land—Opinions of Fleury, Spanheim, Reland, and Lowman—Principle of Distribution—Each Tribe confined to a separate Locality—Property unalienable—Conditions of Tenure—Population of the Tribes—Number of principal Families—A General Government or National Council—The Judges—Nature of their Authority—Not Ordinary Magistrates—Different from Kings, Consuls, and Dictators—Judicial Establishments—Judges and Officers—Described by Josephus—Equality of Condition among the Hebrews—Their Inclination for a pastoral Life—Freebooters like the Arabs—Abimelech, Jephthah, and David—Simplicity of the Times—Boaz and Ruth—Perpetuity of their Customs—Tribe of Levi—Object of their Separation—The Learned Professions Hereditary, after the Manner of the Egyptians—The Levitical Cities—Their Number and Uses—Opinion of Michaelis—Summary View of the Times and Character of the Hebrew Judges.

LEARNED men have long exercised their ingenuity with the view of determining the precise form of the social condition which was assumed by the Israelites when they took possession of the Promised Land. The sacred writer contents himself with stating, that " it came to pass a long time after the Lord had given rest unto Israel from all their enemies round about, that Joshua waxed old and stricken in age ; and he called for all Israel, for their elders, and for their heads, and for their judges, and for their officers." The purport of the address he delivered on this occasion, and which is given at length in the twenty-third chapter of the book which bears his name, was solely to remind them of their religious obligations as the chosen people of Jehovah, and of the labours which they had yet to undergo in subduing the remainder of Canaan. Neither in this speech, nor in the exhortation with which he afterwards at Shechem endeavoured to animate the zeal and constancy of his followers, did he make any allusion to the form of government that it behoved them to adopt; declining even to direct their choice in the appointment of a chief, who might conduct their armies in the field, and preside in the deliberations of the national council.

The first events which occurred after the demise of Joshua appear to establish the fact, that to every tribe was committed the management of its own affairs, even to the extent of being entitled to wage war and make peace without the advice or sanction of the general senate. The only government to which the sons of Jacob had hitherto been accustomed was that most ancient system of rule which gives to the head of every family the direction and control of all its members. We find traces of this natural subordination among them, even under the pressure of Egyptian bondage. During the negotiations which preceded their deliverance under the ministry of Moses, the applications and messages were all addressed to the patriarchal rulers of the people. "Go gather the elders of Israel together" was the command of Jehovah to the son of Amram, when the latter received authority to rescue the descendants of Isaac from the tyranny of Pharaoh.

But during the pilgrimage in the Wilderness, and more particularly when the tribes approached the confines of the devoted nations of Canaan, the original jurisdiction of the family chiefs was rendered subordinate to the military power of their inspired leader, who, as the commander of the armies of Israel, was esteemed and obeyed by his followers as the lieutenant of the Lord of Hosts. In truth, the martial labours to which his office called him, placed the successor of Moses at the head of his countrymen in quality of a general, guiding them on their march or forming their array in the field of battle, rather than as a teacher of wisdom or the guardian of a peculiar faith and worship. Until the conquered lands were divided among the victorious tribes Joshua was a soldier and nothing more; while, on the other hand, the congregation of the Hebrews, who seconded so well his military plans, appear on the page of history in no other light than that of veteran troops, rendered hardy by long service in a parching climate, and formidable by the arts of discipline under a skilful and warlike leader.

From the exode, in short, till towards the end of Joshua's administration, we lose sight of that simple scheme of domestic superintendence which Jacob had established among his sons. The Princes of Tribes, and the Heads of Families, were converted into captains of thousands, of hundreds, and of fifties; regulating their movements by the sound of the trumpet, and passing their days of rest amid the vigilance and formality of a regular encampment. But no sooner did they convert their swords into ploughshares, and their spears into pruning-hooks, than they unanimously returned to their more ancient form of society. As soon as there appeared a sufficient quantity of land wrested from the Canaanites to afford to the tribes on the western side of the Jordan a competent inheritance, Joshua "sent the people away, and they departed;" and from that moment the military aspect their community had assumed gave way to the patriarchal model, to which in fact all their institutions bore an immediate reference, and to the restoration of which their strongest hopes and wishes were constantly directed.

Actuated by such views the Hebrews manifested perhaps an undue impatience to enjoy the fruits of their successful invasion. They had fought, it should seem, to obtain an inheritance in a rich and pleasant country, rather than to avenge the cause of pure religion or to punish the idolatrous practices of the children of Moab and Ammon. As soon therefore as the fear of their name and the power of their arms had scattered the inhabitants of the open countries, the Israelites began to sow and to plant; being more willing to make a covenant with the residue of the enemy, than to purchase the blessings of a permanent peace by enduring a little longer the fatigue and privations of war. Their eagerness to get possession of the land flowing with milk and honey, seems to have compelled Joshua to adopt a measure which at no distant period led to much guilt and suffering on the part of his people. He consented that they should occupy the vacant fields before the nations which they had been commissioned to displace were finally subdued; that they should cast lots for provinces which were still in the hands of the native Gentiles; and that they should distribute, by the line and the measuring-rod, many extensive hills and fair valleys which had not yet submitted to the dominion of their swords.

The effects of this injudicious policy soon rendered themselves apparent; and all the evils which were foreseen by the aged servant of God, when he addressed the congregation at Shechem, were realized in a little time to their fullest extent. The Hebrews did indeed find the remnant of the nations, among whom they consented to dwell, proving scourges in their sides and thorns in their eyes, and still able to dispute with them the possession of the good land which they had been taught to regard as a sacred inheritance, conferred upon them in virtue of a divine promise made to their fathers. For example, the author of the book of Judges relates, " the Amorites forced the children of Dan into the mountains, nor would they suffer them to come down to the valley." Hence we perceive the reason why the Israelites did not for several hundred years complete their conquest of Palestine. The Canaanites, recovering from the terror which had fallen upon them in the commencement of the Hebrew invasion, attempted not only to regain possession of their ancient territory, but even to obliterate all traces of their discomfiture. What movements were made by the petty sovereigns of the country, in order to effect this object, we are nowhere expressly told; though we find, from a consultation held by the southern tribes of Israel, soon after the death of Joshua, that the necessity of renewing military operations against the natives could no longer be postponed. It was resolved, accordingly, that Judah and Simeon should unite their arms and take the field, to prevent, in the first place, an inroad with which their borders were threatened, and, subsequently, to reduce to a state of entire subjection the cities and towns that stood within the limits of their respective districts. " And Judah said unto Simeon his brother, Come up with me into my lot, that we may fight against the Canaanites; and I likewise will go with thee into thy lot."*

But leaving these preliminary matters, we shall proceed to take a survey of the Hebrew commonwealth, as it appeared upon its first settlement under the successors of Joshua; endeavouring to ascertain the grounds upon which the federal union of the tribes was established; their relations towards one another in peace and in war; the resources of which they were possessed for conquest or self-defence; their civil rights and privileges as independent states; their laws and judicatories; and, above all, the nature and extent of their property, as well as the tenure on which it was held by families and individuals. Closely connected with this subject is a consideration of that agrarian law which was sanctioned by Moses and acted upon by Joshua, and which will be found not only to have determined but also to have secured the inheritance of every Israelite who entered the Promised Land.

The extent of that portion of Syria which was granted to the Hebrew nation has been variously estimated. On the authority of Hecatæus, a native of Abdera, who is quoted by Josephus, the limits of the territory possessed

---

* Judges, i. 3.

by the Jews are fixed at three millions of acres, supposing the *aroura* of the Greeks to correspond to the denomination of English measure just specified. Proceeding on this ground, the Abbé Fleury and other writers have undertaken to prove that the quantity of land mentioned by Hecatæus would maintain only three millions three hundred and seventy-five thousand men, —a computation which is liable to many objections, and has therefore not been generally received. It is obvious for instance that this author, who lived in the reign of Alexander the Great, and is said to have afterwards attached himself to the person of the first Grecian king of Egypt, described the country of the Jews as he saw it under the dominion of the Syrian princes of the Macedonian line. He accordingly beheld only the inheritance of the two tribes who had returned from the Babylonian captivity, and of consequence confined his estimate to the provinces they were permitted to enjoy; taking no account of those extensive districts formerly possessed by the Ten Tribes of Israel, and which, in his days, were in the hands of that mixed race of men who were descended from the Assyrian colonists whom Shalmaneser substituted in their place.\*

Confiding in the greater accuracy of Spanheim, Reland, and Lowman, I am inclined to compute the Hebrew territory at about fifteen millions of acres; assuming, with these writers, that the true boundaries of the Promised Land were Mount Libanus on the north, the Wilderness of Arabia on the south, and the Syrian Desert towards the east. On the west some of the tribes extended their possessions to the very waters of the Great Sea, though on other parts they found themselves restricted by the Philistines, whose rich domains comprehended the low lands and strong cities which stretched along the shore. It has been calculated by Spanheim, that the remotest points of the Holy Land, as possessed by King David, were situated at the distance of three

---

\* Joseph. contra Apion. cap. 1.   2 Kings, xvii. 24.

degrees of latitude, and as many degrees of longitude, including in all about twenty-six thousand square miles.*

If this computation be correct, there was in the possession of the Hebrew chiefs land sufficient to allow to every Israelite, capable of bearing arms, a lot of about twenty acres; reserving for public uses, as also for the cities of the Levites, about one-tenth of the whole. It is probable, however, if we make a suitable allowance for lakes, mountains, and unproductive tracts of ground, that the portion to every householder would not be so large as the estimate now stated. But even if reduced to one-half, the allotment would still supply ample means for plenty and frugal enjoyment. The Roman people under Romulus, and long after, could afford only two acres to every legionary soldier; and in the most flourishing days of the Commonwealth the allowance did not exceed four. Hence the *quatuor jugera*, or four acres, is an expression which proverbially indicated plebeian affluence and contentment,—a full remuneration for the toils of war, and a sufficient inducement at all times to take up arms in defence of the Republic.

The territory of the Hebrews was ordered to be equally divided among their tribes and families, according to their respective numbers; and the persons selected to superintend this national work were, Eleazer, the high-priest; Joshua, who acted in the character of judge; and the twelve Princes or Heads of Israel. The rule which they followed is expressed in these words,— " And ye shall divide the land by lot, for an inheritance among your families; and to the more ye shall give the more inheritance; and to the fewer ye shall give the less inheritance; every man's inheritance shall be in the place where his lot falleth; according to the tribes of your fathers ye shall inherit."

Every tribe was thus put in possession of a separate district or province, in which all the occupiers of the land were not only Israelites, but more particularly

* Reland. Palestina Illustrata, lib. ii. c. 5. Spanheim, Charta Terræ Israelis. Lowman on the Civil Government of the Hebrews.

sprung from the same stock, and descendants of the same patriarch. The several families, again, were placed in the same neighbourhood, receiving their inheritance in the same part or subdivision of the tribe ; or, to use the language of Lowman, each Tribe may be said to have lived together in one and the same County ; and each Family in one and the same Hundred ; so that every neighbourhood were relations to each other, and of the same families, as well as inhabitants of the same place.

To secure the permanence and mutual independence of the respective tribes, a law was enacted by the authority of Heaven, providing that the landed property of every Israelite should be unalienable. Whatever encumbrances might befall the owner of a field, and whatever might be the obligations under which he placed himself to his creditor, he was released from all claims at the year of jubilee. " Ye shall hallow," said the inspired legislator, " the fiftieth year, and proclaim liberty throughout all the land unto all the inhabitants thereof. It shall be a jubilee unto you, and ye shall return every man to his possession, and ye shall return every man unto his family. And the land shall not be sold for ever ; for the land is mine, saith the Lord ; for ye are strangers and sojourners with me."\*

The attentive reader of the Mosaical law will observe that, though a Hebrew could not divest himself of his land in perpetuity, he might dispose of it so far as to put another person in possession during a certain number of years ; reserving to himself and his relations the right of redeeming it should they ever acquire the means ; and having at all events the sure prospect of a reversion at the period of the jubilee. In the eye of the lawgiver this transaction was not regarded as a sale of the land, but merely of the crops for a stated number of seasons. It might indeed have been considered simply as a lease, had not the owner, as well as his nearest kinsman,

---

\* Levit. xxv. 23.

enjoyed the privilege of resuming occupation whenever they could repay the sum for which the temporary use of the land had been resigned.*

The houses built in fields or villages were, in regard to the principle of alienation, placed on the same footing as the lands themselves; being redeemable at all times, and destined to return to their original owners in the year of jubilee. But it is worthy of notice, that houses in cities and large towns were, when sold, redeemable only during one year; after which the sale was held binding for ever. There was indeed an exception even in this case in favour of the Levites, who could at any time redeem " the houses of the cities of their possession," and who, moreover, enjoyed the full advantage of the fiftieth year.

The Hebrews, like most other nations in a similar state of society, held their lands on the condition of military service. The grounds of exemption allowed by Moses prove clearly that every man of competent age was bound to bear arms in defence of his country,—a conclusion which is strikingly illustrated by the conduct of the Senate or Heads of Tribes, in the melancholy war undertaken by them against the children of Benjamin. Upon a muster of the army when assembled at Mizpeh, it was discovered that no man had been sent from Jabesh-gilead to join the camp; whereupon it was immediately resolved that 12,000 soldiers should be despatched to put all the inhabitants of that town to death. And the congregation commanded them, saying, " Go and smite Jabesh-gilead with the edge of the sword, with the women and children ;" and the only reason assigned for this severe order was, that " when the people were numbered, there were none of the men of Jabesh-gilead there."†

The reader will now be prepared to accompany me while I make a few remarks on the civil constitution of the Hebrews, both as it respected the government of the

---

\* Levit. xxv. 24-28. † Judges, xxi. 8-13.

tribes viewed as separate bodies, and as it applied to that of the whole nation as a confederated republic.

The tribes of Israel, strictly speaking, amounted only to twelve, descended from the twelve sons of Jacob. But as the posterity of Joseph was divided into two parts, distinguished respectively as the descendants of Ephraim and Manasseh, it follows that the host which entered the Land of Canaan under Joshua comprehended thirteen of these distinct genealogies. Viewed in reference to merely secular rights and duties, however, the offspring of Levi, having no part nor lot with their brethren, are not usually reckoned in the number; while on other grounds, and chiefly for their invincible propensity to idolatrous usages, the tribe of Dan at a later period was sometimes excluded from the list. In the twenty-sixth chapter of the book of Numbers, we have an account of the enrolment which was made on the plains of Moab; from which the numerical strength of the eleven ordinary tribes may be exhibited as follows :—

| | |
|---|---|
| Joseph (including Ephraim and Manasseh), | 85,200 |
| Judah, | 76,500 |
| Issachar, | 64,300 |
| Zebulun, | 60,500 |
| Asher, | 53,400 |
| Dan, | 46,400 |
| Benjamin, | 45,600 |
| Naphtali, | 45,400 |
| Reuben, | 43,730 |
| Gad, | 40,500 |
| Simeon, | 22,200 |

This catalogue comprehended all the men above twenty years of age, to which may be added 23,000 of the tribe of Levi, " all males from a month old and upward : for they were not numbered among the children of Israel, because there was no inheritance given them among the children of Israel." The whole amounted to six hundred and six thousand seven hundred.*

In every tribe there was a chief called the Prince of the Tribe, or the Head of Thousands; and under him

---

* Numbers, xxvi. 62.

were the Princes of Families, or Commanders of Hundreds. For example, we find, at the muster which was made of the Hebrews in the Wilderness of Sinai, that Nahshon, the son of Amminadab, was Prince of the Tribe of Judah. This tribe again, like all the others, was divided into several Families ; the term being used here not in its ordinary acceptation, to signify a mere household, but rather in the heraldic sense, to denote a lineage or kindred descended from a common ancestor, and constituting one of the main branches of an original stock. In this respect the Israelites were guided by the same principle which regulates precedency among the Arabs, as well as among our own countrymen in the Highlands of Scotland.

It appears, moreover, that a record of these Families, of the households in each, and even of the individuals belonging to every household, was placed in the hands of the chief ruler ; for it is related that, on the suspicion excited with regard to the spoils of Jericho and the discomfiture at Ai, " Joshua brought Israel by their tribes, and the tribe of Judah was taken : and he brought the family of Judah ; and he took the family of the Zarhites : and he brought the family of the Zarhites man by man ; and Zabdi was taken : and he brought his household man by man ; and Achan, the son of Carmi, the son of Zabdi, the son of Zerah, of the tribe of Judah, was taken."\*

We may collect, from the twenty-sixth chapter of the book of Numbers, that the Heads of Families, at the time the children of Israel encamped on the eastern bank of the Jordan, were in number fifty-seven. If to these we add the thirteen Princes, or Heads of Tribes, the sum of the two numbers will be seventy ; whence there is some ground for the conjecture of those who allege, that the council which Moses formed in the wilderness consisted of the patriarchal chiefs, who in right of birth were recognised as bearing an hereditary rule over the several sections of the people.

---

\* Joshua, vii. 16, 17, 18.

It is probable that the first-born of the senior family of each tribe was usually received as the prince of that tribe, and that the eldest son of every subordinate family succeeded his father in the honours and duties which belonged to the rank of a patriarch. But the details presented by the sacred narrative are much too scanty to permit us to form, with regard to this point, any general conclusion worthy of confidence. The case of Nahshon, besides, has been viewed as an instance quite irreconcilable with such an opinion; and it certainly seems to prove, that if the Prince of the Tribe was not elective, he was not always, at least, the direct descendant of the original chief. Nahshon, as has just been stated, was the son of Amminadab, the son of Ram, who was a younger son of Hezron, the son of Pharez, who was a younger son of Judah.*

From the particulars now stated, we find that every tribe had a Head who presided over its affairs, administered justice in all ordinary cases, and led the troops in time of war. He was assisted in these important duties by subordinate officers, the hereditary Chiefs of Families, who formed his council in such matters of policy as affected their particular district; supported his decisions in civil or criminal inquiries; and, finally, commanded under him in the field of battle.

But the polity established by the Jewish lawgiver was not confined to the constitution and government of the separate tribes. It likewise extended its regulations to the common welfare of the whole, as one kingdom under the special direction of Jehovah; and provided that, on all great occasions, they should have the means of readily uniting their councils, and combining their strength. Even during the less orderly period which

---

* 1 Chron. ii. 10, 11. In such cases a principle seems to have been applied similar to that in which *tanistry* was founded among the ancient Celtic kings of Scotland. Prior to the reign of Malcolm the Third, the throne was frequently filled by a brother of the deceased monarch, if there was any defect in the son, either from age or talent, which might render him unfit for the duties of royalty.

immediately followed the settlement of the Hebrews in the land of their inheritance, we find traces of such a general government; a national senate, whose deliberations guided the administration of affairs in all cases of difficulty or hazard; a judge, who was invested with a high degree of executive authority as the first magistrate of the commonwealth; and, lastly, the controlling voice of the congregation of Israel, whose concurrence appears to have been at all times necessary to give vigour and effect to the resolutions of their leaders. To these constituent parts of their ancient government we may add the Oracle or voice of Jehovah, without whose sanction, as revealed by Urim and Thummim, no measure of importance could be adopted either by the council or by the judge.

It has been justly remarked, at the same time, that however extensive the power might be which was committed to the supreme court of the nation, and how much soever the authority of a military judge among the Israelites resembled that of a Roman dictator, the privilege of making laws was at no period intrusted to any order of the Jewish state. As long as they were governed by a theocracy, this essential prerogative was retained by the Divine Head of the tribes. "Now therefore hearken, O Israel, unto the statutes, and unto the judgments, which I teach you, for to do them, that ye may live, and go in and possess the land which the Lord God of your fathers giveth you. Ye shall not add unto the word which I command you, neither shall ye diminish ought from it, that ye may keep the commandments of the Lord your God which I command you."*

It is the opinion of learned men, that the Council of Seventy, established by Moses in the wilderness, was only a temporary appointment, and did not continue after the people were settled in the land of Canaan. The only national convention of which we can discover

---

* Deut. iv. 1, 2; xii. 32. "Hoc igitur argumento maximo est—juris illius majestatis, quoad in legibus ferendis est positum, nihil quicquam penes hominem fuisse."—*Conringius de Repub. Heb.*

any trace subsequently to that event, is the occasional meeting of the Princes of Tribes and Chiefs of Families to transact business of great public importance. Thus, in the case of the war against Benjamin, already mentioned, we are informed, that the Heads " of all the tribes, even of all the tribes of Israel, presented themselves in the assembly of the people of God." On that memorable occasion, the interests and character of the whole commonwealth were at stake; for which reason the natural leaders of the tribes gathered themselves together at the head of their kinsmen and followers,— even four hundred thousand men that drew the sword, —in order to consult with one another, and to adopt such measures as might be deemed most suitable for punishing the atrocities which had been committed at Gibeah.

During the period to which this part of our narrative refers, the supreme power was occasionally exercised by Judges,—an order of magistrates to which nothing similar is to be found in any other country. The Carthaginians, indeed, had a class of rulers whose designation being derived from the same oriental term, appears to establish some resemblance in their office to that of the successors of Joshua. But it will be found upon a comparison of their authority, both in its origin and the purposes to which it was meant to be subservient, that the Hebrew Judges and the Suffetes of Carthage had very little in common. Nor do we find any closer analogy in the duties of a Grecian archon or of a Roman consul. These were ordinary magistrates, and periodically elected; whereas the Judge was never invested with power except when the exigencies of public affairs required the aid of extraordinary talents, or the weight of a supernatural appointment. On this account the Hebrew commander has been likened to the Roman dictator, who, when the republic was in danger, was intrusted with an authority almost unlimited, and with a jurisdiction which extended to the lives and fortunes of nearly all his countrymen. But in one important particular this similarity fails. The dictator laid down his office as soon as the crisis which called for its exercise had passed away; and in no circumstances was he entitled to retain such unwonted supremacy beyond a limited time. The Judge, on the other hand, remained invested with his high authority during the full period of his life; and is therefore usually described by the sacred historian as presiding to the end of his days over the tribes of Israel, amid the peace and security which his military skill, aided by the blessing of Heaven, had restored to their land.*

The Hebrew Judges, says Dupin, were not ordinary magistrates, but men raised up by God, on whom the Israelites bestowed the chief government, either because they had delivered them from the oppressions under which they groaned, or because of their prudence and equity. They ruled according to the law of Jehovah, commanded their armies, made treaties with the neighbouring princes, declared war and peace, and administered justice. They were different from kings,—

1. In that they were not established either by election or succession, but elevated to power in an extraordinary manner.

2. In that they refused to take upon them the title and quality of king.

3. In that they levied no taxes upon the people for the maintenance of government.

4. In their manner of living, which was very far from the pomp and ostentation of the regal state.

5. In that they could make no new laws, but governed according to the statutes contained in the Books of Moses.

6. In that the obedience paid to them by the people was voluntary and unforced; being at most no more than consuls and magistrates of free cities.†

But it is less difficult to determine what the Judges were not, than to ascertain with precision the various

---

\* Livii Hist. lib. xxviii. 37; lib. xxx. 7. Bochart. Geog. Sacra, pars ii. lib. ii. 24.

† Complete History of the Canon, b. i. c. 3.

parts of their complicated office. In war, they led the host of Israel to meet their enemies; and in peace, it is probable they presided in such courts of judicature as might be found necessary for deciding upon intricate points of law, or for hearing appeals from inferior tribunals. Those who went up to Deborah for judgment had, we may presume, brought their causes in the first instance before the judges of their respective cities; and it was only, perhaps, in cases where greater knowledge and a higher authority were required to give satisfaction to the litigants, that the chief magistrate of the republic, aided by certain members of the priesthood, was called upon to pronounce a final decision.

It belongs to this part of the subject to mention the provision made by Moses, and established by Joshua, for the due administration of justice throughout the land. " Judges and officers," said the former, " shalt thou make thee in all thy gates, which the Lord thy God giveth thee; and they shall judge the people with just judgment. Thou shalt not wrest judgment; thou shalt not respect persons, neither take a gift; for a gift doth blind the eyes of the wise, and pervert the words of the righteous." To the same purpose Josephus relates, in his account of the last address delivered by Moses to the chosen people, that this great legislator gave instructions to appoint seven judges in every city; men who had distinguished themselves by their good conduct and impartial feelings. Let those who judge, he adds, be permitted to determine according as they shall think right, unless any one can show that they have taken bribes to the perversion of justice, or can allege any other accusation against them.*

Between the " judges" and the " officers" nominated by the Jewish lawgiver, there was no doubt a marked distinction; though, from the remote antiquity of the appointment and the obscure commentaries of Rabbinical writers, it has become extremely difficult to define the

---

* Deut. xvi. 18, 19. Josephus' Antiquities, book iv. 8.

limits of their respective functions. Maimonides asserts, that in every city where the householders amounted to a hundred and twenty, there was a court consisting of twenty-three judges, who were empowered to determine in almost all cases both civil and criminal. This is unquestionably the same institution which is mentioned by Josephus in the fourth book of his Antiquities, and described by him as being composed of seven judges and fourteen subordinate officers or assistants, selected from among the Levites; for these, with the president and his deputy, make up the exact number of twenty-three specified by the native writers. In smaller towns the administration of law was intrusted to three judges, whose authority extended to the determination of all questions respecting debt, theft, rights of inheritance, restitution, and compensation. Though they could not inflict capital punishment, they had power to visit minor offences with scourging and fines, according to the nature of the delinquency and the amount of the injury sustained.*

Of the former of these judicial establishments, there were two fixed at Jerusalem, even during the period that the Sanhedrim was invested with the supreme authority over the lives and fortunes of their countrymen; one of which sat in the gate of Shusan, and the other in that of Nicanor. The place where these judges held their audience was, as Cardinal Fleury remarks, the gate of the city; for, as the Israelites were all husbandmen, who went out in the morning to their work and did not return till the evening, the gate of the city was the place where they most frequently met; and we must not be astonished to find that the people laboured in the fields and dwelt in the towns. These were not cities like our provincial capitals, which can hardly subsist on what is supplied to them by twenty or thirty leagues of the surrounding soil. They were the habitations for as many labourers as were necessary to cultivate the nearest

---

* Reland. Antiq. Sac. pars ii. c. 7.

fields; hence, as the country was very populous, the towns were very thickly scattered. For a similar reason, among the Greeks and Romans, the scene of meeting for all matters of business was the market-place or forum, because they were all merchants.* Among the Israelites, the judges took their seats immediately after morning prayers, and continued till the end of the sixth hour, or twelve o'clock; and their authority, though not in capital cases, continued to be respected by their countrymen, long after Jerusalem was levelled with the ground.†

With the aid of the particulars now stated, the reader may have been enabled to form some notion of the civil and political circumstances of the ancient Hebrews. They enjoyed the utmost degree of freedom which was consistent with the objects of regular society, acknowledging no authority but that of the laws as administered by the Elders of their Tribes, and the Heads of their Families. The equality of their property, too, and the sameness of their occupations, precluded the rise of those distinctions in social life, which, whatever may be their use in older nations, are opposed by all the habits of a people whose sole cares are yet devoted to the culture of their fields and the safety of their flocks. The form of government which suits best with such a distribution of wealth and employment, is unquestionably that which was established by Moses on the basis of the ancient patriarchal rule. But this model, so convenient in the earliest stage of social existence, was imperceptibly changed by the increasing power and intelligence of the people, until, as happened towards the close of Samuel's administration, the public voice made itself be heard, recommending an entire departure from obsolete notions. Thus we find, in the progress of the human race, that the simple authority of the family-chief passes through a species of oligarchy into a practical democracy, and

---

* Fleury, Mœurs des Israelites, xxv.
† Lewis, Orig. Heb. lib. i. 6.

ends at no very distant period in the nomination of an hereditary sovereign.

The epoch at which we now contemplate the Hebrew community is that very interesting one when the wandering shepherd settles down into the stationary husbandman. The progeny of Abraham, Isaac, and Jacob, who themselves were pastoral chiefs, appear to have retained a decided predilection for that ancient mode of life. Moses, even after he had brought the Twelve Tribes within sight of the Promised Land, found it necessary to indulge the families of Reuben, Gad, and Manasseh, so far as to give them the choice of a settlement on that side of Jordan, where they might devote themselves to the keeping of cattle. From the conduct also of the other tribes, who showed no small reluctance to divide the land and enter upon their several inheritances, it has been concluded, with considerable probability, that they too would have preferred the erratic habits of their ancestors to the more restricted pursuits which their great lawgiver had prepared for them, amid corn-fields, vineyards, and plantations of olives. " And Joshua said unto the children of Israel, How long are ye slack to go to possess the land which the Lord God of your fathers hath given you ?"*

Among the Arabs, even at the present day, the pastoral life is accounted more noble than that which leads to a residence in towns, or even in villages. They think it, as Arvieux remarks, more congenial to liberty ; because the man, who with his herds ranges the desert at large, will be far less likely to submit to oppression than people with houses and lands. This mode of thinking is of great antiquity in the eastern parts of the world. Diodorus Siculus, when speaking of the Nabathæans, relates, that they were by their laws prohibited from sowing, planting, drinking wine, and building houses ; every violation of the precept being punishable with

---

* Michaelis' Commentaries on the Laws of Moses, art. 44 ; and Joshua, xviii. 3.

death. They assign as a reason for this very singular rule the belief that those who possess such things will be easily brought into subjection by a tyrant; on which account they continue, says the historian, to traverse the desert, feeding their flocks, which consist partly of camels and partly of sheep.

The fact now stated receives a remarkable confirmation from the notice contained in the book of Jeremiah respecting the Rechabites; who, though they had for several ages been removed from Arabia into Palestine, persevered in a sacred obedience to the command of their ancestor; refusing to build houses, sow land, plant vineyards, or drink wine, but resolving to dwell in tents throughout all their generations.

With regard to these points, the Hebrews, in the early age at which we are now considering them, appear to have entertained sentiments not very different from those of the Arabs, from whose sandy plains they had just emerged. The life of a migratory shepherd, too, has a very close alliance with the habits of a freebooter; and the attentive reader of the ancient history of the Israelites will recollect many instances wherein the descendants of Isaac gave ample proof of their relationship to the posterity of Ishmael. The character of Abimelech, the son of Gideon, for example, cannot be viewed in any other light than that of a captain of marauders. The men of Shechem, whom he had hired to follow him, refused not to obey his commands, even when he added murder to robbery. Jephthah, in like manner, when he was thrust out by his brethren, became the chief of a similar band in the land of Tob. " And there were gathered vain men to Jephthah, and went out with him." But the elders of Gilead did not, on that account, regard their brave countryman as less worthy to assume the direction of their affairs, and to be head over all the inhabitants of their land,—an honour which he even hesitated to accept, when compared with the rank and emoluments of the situation which they requested him to relinquish.

Nor did David himself think it unsuitable to his high

prospects to have recourse for a time to a predatory life. When compelled to flee from the presence of Saul, he took refuge in the cave of Adullam ; " and every one that was in distress, and every one that was in debt, and every one that was discontented, gathered themselves unto him, and he became a captain over them." It has been suggested, indeed, that the son of the Bethlehemite employed his arms against such persons only as were enemies to the Hebrews. But there is no good ground for this distinction. His conduct to Nabal, whose possessions were in Carmel, proves that, when his camp was destitute of provisions, he deemed it no violation of honour to force a supply for the wants of his men even from the stores of a friendly house. We may judge, moreover, of the character of his followers, as well from the remonstrance made by the parsimonious rustic to whom he sent them, as from the effect which a refusal produced upon their ardent tempers. " Who is David ? and who is the son of Jesse ? There be many servants now-a-days that break away every man from his master. Shall I then take my bread, and my water, and my flesh that I have killed for my shearers, and give it unto men whom I know not whence they be ?—So David's young men turned their way, and went again, and came and told him all those sayings. And David said unto his men, Gird ye on every man his sword. And they girded on every man his sword, and David also girded on his sword ; and there went up after David about four hundred men, and two hundred abode by the stuff."*

It is manifest that, in the simple condition of society to which our attention is now directed, the profession of a freebooter was not in any sense accounted dishonourable. The courage and dexterity which such a life requires, stand high in the estimation of tribes who are almost constantly in a state of war ; and hence, in reading the history of the ancient Israelites, we must form an opinion of their manners and principles, not accord-

---

* 1 Samuel, xxv. 4-14.

ing to the maxims of an enlightened age, but agreeably to the habits, pursuits, and mental cultivation, which belonged to their own times.

It is farther worthy of remark, that during the period of the Hebrew Judges there is not the slightest trace of those distinctions of rank which spring from mere wealth, office, or profession. From the Princes of Judah down to the meanest family in Benjamin, all were agriculturists or shepherds; driving their own oxen, or attending in person to their sheep and their goats. The hospitable Ephraimite, who received into his house at Gibeah the Levite and his unfortunate companion, is described as " an old man coming from his work out of the field at even." Gideon, again, was thrashing his corn with his own hands, when the angel announced to him that he was selected by Divine Providence to be the deliverer of his people. Boaz was attending his reapers in the field, when his benevolence was awakened in favour of Ruth, the widow of his kinsman. When Saul received the news of the danger which threatened the inhabitants of Jabesh-gilead, he was in the act of " coming after the herd out of the field." Sovereign as he was, he thought it not inconsistent with his rank to drive a yoke of oxen. Every one knows that David was employed in keeping the sheep when he was summoned into the presence of Samuel to be anointed king over Israel; and even when he was upon the throne, and had by his military talent extended at once the power and the reputation of his countrymen among the neighbouring nations, the annual occupation of sheep-shearing called his sons and his daughters into the hill-country, to take their share in its toils and amusements. In point of blood and ancestry, too, every descendant of Jacob stood on the same footing; and the only ground of pre-eminence which one man could claim over another was connected with old age, wisdom, strength, or courage,—the qualities most respected in the original forms of civilized life.*

---

* Judges, vi. 12. 2 Samuel, xiii. 23, 24.

I have been the more careful to collect these fragments of personal history, because it is chiefly from them that the few rays of light are reflected which illustrate the state of society at the era of the Hebrew commonwealth. That the times in which the Judges ruled were barbarous and unsettled, is rendered manifest, not less by the general tenor of events, than by the qualities which predominated in the public mind during the long period between the death of Joshua and the reign of Solomon. These notices also convey to us some degree of information with regard to the political relations which subsisted among the Syrian tribes, prior to the commencement of the regal government at Jerusalem. The wars which were carried on at that remote epoch seem not to have been waged with any view to permanent conquest, or even to territorial aggrandizement, but merely to revenge an insult, to exact a ransom, or to capture slaves and cattle. The history of the Judges supplies no facts which would lead us to infer, that during any of the servitudes, which for their repeated transgressions were inflicted on the Hebrews, their lands were taken from them, or their cities destroyed by their conquerors. It was not till a later age that a more systematic plan of conquest was formed by the powerful princes who governed beyond the Euphrates and on the banks of the Nile; and who, not content with the uncertain submission of tributaries, resolved to reduce the Israelites for ever to the condition of subjects or of bondmen.

The effect of agricultural pursuits, as distinguished from the nomadic usages of the desert, is clearly illustrated in the progressive changes which the manners as well as the civil government of the Israelites underwent, after their settlement in Canaan. Their constitution passed through all the stages which in other countries have commonly marked the transition from the simplicity of pastoral life to the refinement and complicated institutions of a people who cultivate the soil, not only to supply their immediate wants, but also to procure the luxuries of foreign lands. The mere shepherd, whether in Tartary or in the Arabian Wilderness, experiences no alteration in his habits, and no change in his tastes. The flood of time rolls on, carrying with it to all others new views and desires; but century after century he remains the same.

A satisfactory proof of this statement will be found in the pages of every traveller who has set his foot into the desert which divides Palestine from Egypt and the Persian Gulf. He feels himself at once carried back to the age of the earliest patriarchs; and all the forms he sees present to him the picture of those ancient fathers with scarcely a single alteration. He may listen to their language, number their possessions, partake of their food, examine their dress, enter their tents, attend their ceremonies, and be introduced to their prince;—still all is the same. At the well they water their flocks; they sit at the door of the tent in the cool of the day; they take butter, and milk, and the calf that they have dressed, and set it before the stranger; and when the pasture is exhausted, they strike their tents and remove, as of old, in quest of an untouched valley, or a more abundant spring of water. Their treasures, too, as in the ancient days, consist of camels, kine, sheep, and goats, menservants and women-servants, and changes of raiment.*

The account which has been given of the political constitution of the ancient Jews would not be complete were we to omit all notice of the tribe of Levi, the duties and revenues of which were fixed by peculiar laws. It

---

* Notices of the Holy Land, &c. by the Rev. R. Spence Hardy. This author, who travelled about four years ago, remarks, " We may stand near one of their encampments, and as the aged men sit in dignity, or the young men and maidens drive past us their flocks, we are almost ready to ask if such a one be not Abraham, or Lot, or Jacob, or Job, or Bildad the Shuhite, or Rebekah, or Rachel, or the daughter of Jethro the Midianite; we seem to know them all. The mountains, and valleys, and streams, partake of the same unchangeableness : not a stone has been removed, not a barrier has been raised ; not a tree has been planted ; not a village has been collected together. The founder of the race might come to the earth, and he would recognise without effort his own people and his own land." P. 16.

may perhaps be thought by some readers that this institution rested on a basis altogether spiritual; but, upon suitable inquiry, it will be found that the Levitical offices comprehended a great variety of avocations much more closely connected with secular life than with the ministry of the tabernacle, or the services which were due to the priesthood. This sacred tribe, indeed, supplied to the whole nation of the Israelites their judges, lawyers, scribes, teachers, and physicians; for Moses, in imitation of the Egyptians, in whose wisdom he was early and deeply instructed, had thought proper to make the learned professions hereditary in the several families of Levi's descendants.

In the first chapter of the book of Numbers, a command is issued by the authority of Jehovah to separate the tribe now mentioned from the rest of their brethren, and not to enrol them among those who were to engage in war. It was determined, on similar grounds, that the Levites, who were to have no inheritance in the land like the other tribes, should receive from their kinsmen, in name of maintenance, a tenth part of the gross produce of their fields and vineyards. The occupations to which their time was consecrated were altogether incompatible with the pursuits of agriculture or the feeding of cattle. It was deemed expedient, therefore, that they should be relieved from the cares and toil connected with the possession of territorial estates, and devote their whole attention to the service of the altar and the instruction of the people.

To effect these wise purposes, it was necessary that the members of this learned body should not be confined to one particular district, but that they should be distributed among all the other tribes, according to the extent of their several inheritances and the amount of their population. With this view the law provided that a certain number of cities should be set apart for them, together with such a portion of soil as might seem requisite for their comfort and more immediate wants. " Command the children of Israel, that they give unto the Levites, of the inheritance of their possession, cities to dwell in; and ye shall give unto the Levites suburbs for the cities round about them. And ye shall measure from without the city, on the east side, two thousand cubits, and on the south side two thousand cubits, and on the west side two thousand cubits, and on the north side two thousand cubits; and the city shall be in the midst: this shall be to them the suburbs of the cities. So all the cities which ye shall give to the Levites shall be forty and eight cities: them shall ye give with their suburbs."*

But it was not till after the conquest and division of Canaan that the provisions of this enactment were practically fulfilled. When the other tribes were settled in their respective possessions, the children of Levi reminded Joshua of the arrangement made by his predecessor, and claimed cities to dwell in, and suburbs for their cattle. The justice of their appeal being admitted, the Levitical stations were distributed as follows:—

|   | Cities. |
|---|---|
| In the tribes of Judah, Simeon, and Benjamin, | 13 |
| In Ephraim, Dan, and the half-tribe of Manasseh, | 10 |
| In the other half-tribe of Manasseh, Issachar, Asher, and Naphtali, | 13 |
| In Zebulun, Reuben, and Gad, | 12 |
|   | 48 |

Every reader of the Bible is aware, that six of these cities were invested with the special right of affording protection to a certain class of criminals. The Jewish doctors maintain that this privilege, somewhat limited, belonged to all the forty-eight; for, being sacred, no act of revenge or mortal retaliation was permitted to take place within their gates. Into the six cities of refuge, properly so called, the manslayer could demand admittance, whether the Levites were disposed to receive him or not; and on the same ground he was entitled to gratuitous lodging and maintenance, until his cause should

---

* Numbers, xxxv. 2, 5, 7.

be determined by competent judges. It is added, that they could exercise a discretionary power as to the reception of a homicide into any of the other cities, and even with respect to the hire which they might demand for the house used by him during his temporary residence. But the institution of Moses, afterwards completed by Joshua, affords no countenance to these Rabbinical distinctions; and we have no reason whatever to believe that the benefit of asylum was granted to any Levitical town besides Hebron, Shechem, Ramoth, Bezer, Kedesh, and Golan.*

As learning and the several professions connected with the knowledge of letters were confined almost exclusively to the tribe of Levi, the distribution of its members throughout the whole of the Hebrew commonwealth was attended with many advantages. Every Levitical city became at once a school and a seat of justice. There the language, the traditions, the history, and the laws of their nations, were the constant subjects of study, pursued with that zeal and earnestness which can only arise from the feeling of a sacred obligation, combined with the impulse of an ardent patriotism. Within their walls were deposited copies of their religious, moral, and civil institutions; which it was their duty both to multiply and to preserve. They kept, besides, the genealogies of the tribes, in which they marked the lineage of every family which could trace its descent to the Father of the Faithful. Being carefully instructed in the law, and possessed of the annals of their people from the earliest days, they were well qualified to supply the courts with magistrates and scribes; men who were fitted not only to administer justice, but also to frame a record of all their decisions. It is perfectly clear that, in the reign of David and of the succeeding kings, the judges and other legal officers were selected from among the Levites; there being in those days not fewer than

---

* Joshua, xx. 7, 8. Numbers, xxxv. 6, 15. Deut. xix. 4, 10.

six thousand of this learned body who held such appointments.

Michaelis represents the Levitical order among the Hebrews in the light of a literary noblesse; enjoying such a degree of wealth and consideration as to enable them to act as a counterpoise to the influence of the aristocracy; while, on the other hand, they prevented the adoption of those hasty measures which were sometimes to be apprehended from the democratical nature of the general government. They were not merely a spiritual brotherhood, but professional members of all the different faculties; and by birth obliged to devote themselves to those branches of study, for the cultivation of which they were so liberally rewarded. Like the Egyptian priests, they occupied the whole field of literature and science; extending their inquiries to philosophy, theology, natural history, mathematics, jurisprudence, civil history, and even to medicine. Perhaps, too, observes the same author, it was in imitation of the sages of the Nile that the Hebrews made these pursuits hereditary in a consecrated tribe; whence flowed this obvious advantage, that the sons of the Levites, from the very dawn of reason, were introduced to scientific researches, and favoured with a regulated system of tuition suited to the occupation in which their lives were to be spent. In short, the institution bears upon it all the marks of that wisdom for which the Mosaical economy is so remarkably distinguished, when viewed as the basis of a government at once civil, religious, and political.*

In concluding this brief sketch of the Hebrew commonwealth, we may be permitted to remark, what, indeed, the youngest reader of the Sacred Volume cannot fail to have perceived, that the character and government of the Judges withdraw the attention from the ordinary course of human events, and fix it on the manifestations of a special providence. These personages were raised

---

* Michaelis' Commentaries on the Laws of Moses, vol. i. art. 52. Jablonsky, Panth. Ægypt. Prolegomena, 21, 41, 43.

up by the immediate interposition of God, to discharge the duties of an office which the peculiar circumstances of his People from time to time rendered necessary; and the various gifts with which they were endowed, as they constituted the main ground of vocation to their high employment, so they were suited to the difficulties they had to overcome, and also to the achievements they were called to perform. The sanctity of their manners did not, indeed, in all cases correspond to the dignity of their station; and the miracles which they wrought for the welfare of their country were not always accompanied with self-restraint and the due subordination of their passions. Their military exploits were worthy of the highest admiration; while, in some instances, their private conduct calls forth our surprise and regret. For examples of heroism and bravery, we can with confidence point to Gideon, to Samson, and to Jephthah; but there is not in their character any thing besides that a father could recommend to the imitation of his son, or which a lover of order and pureness of living would wish to see adopted in modern society. We observe, in the greater number of them, uncommon and even supernatural powers of body as well as of mind, united with the gross manners and fierce passions of barbarians. We applaud their patriotism, admire their courage and talent in the field, and even share in the delight which accompanied their triumphs; yet, when we return to their dwellings, we dare not inspect too narrowly the usages of their domestic day, nor examine into the indulgences with which they sometimes thought proper to remunerate the toils and cares of their public life. Divine Wisdom, stooping to the imperfection of human nature, employed the instruments that were best fitted for the gracious ends which, by their means, were about to be accomplished; though it does not appear to have been intended that mankind should ever resort to the history of the Judges for lessons of decorum, humanity, or virtue.

## CHAPTER III.

*Historical Outline from the Accession of Saul to the Destruction of Jerusalem.*

Weakness of Republican Government—Jealousy of the several Tribes—Resolution to have a King—Rules for Regal Government —Character of Saul—Of David—Troubles of his Reign—Accession of Solomon—Erection of the Temple—Commerce—Murmurs of the People—Rehoboam—Division of the Tribes—Kings of Israel—Kingdom of Judah—Siege of Jerusalem—Captivity—Kings of Judah—Return from Babylon—Second Temple—Canon of Scripture—Struggles between Egypt and Syria—Conquest of Palestine by Antiochus—Persecution of Jews—Resistance by the Family of Maccabæus—Victories of Judas—He courts the Alliance of the Romans—Succeeded by Jonathan—Origin of the Asmonean Princes—John Hyrcanus—Aristobulus—Alexander Jannæus—Appeal to Pompey—Jerusalem taken by Romans—Herod created King by the Romans—He repairs the Temple—Archelaus succeeds him, and Antipas is nominated to Galilee—Quirinius Prefect of Syria—Pontius Pilate—Elevation of Herod Agrippa— Disgrace of Herod Philip—Judea again a Province—Troubles— Accession of Young Agrippa—Felix—Festus—Florus—Command given to Vespasian—War—Siege of Jerusalem by Titus.

THE weakness and jealousy which seem inseparable from a government comprehending a number of independent states, had been deeply felt during the administration of Eli, and even under that of Samuel in his latter days. Established in different parts of the country, the several tribes were actuated by local interests and selfish views; those in the north, who were exempted from the hostile inroads of the Philistines and Ammonites, refusing to aid their brethren, the children of Simeon and Judah, whose territory was constantly exposed to the ravages of these warlike neighbours. In the time of the more recent Judges, indeed, the federal union on which the Hebrew commonwealth was founded appeared to be practically dissolved. Nay, a spirit of rivalry and dissension occasionally manifested itself among the kindred communities of which it was composed;—Ephraim, stimulated by envy, vexed Judah, and Judah vexed Ephraim.*

At a later period, several powerful kingdoms in the east, as well as the south, threatened the independence of the Twelve Tribes, especially those on the borders of the Desert. Assyria had turned her views towards the fertile lands which skirt the shores of the Mediterranean; and Egypt, in order to protect her rich valley from the aggressions of that rising empire, began to open her eyes to the expediency of securing for herself the frontier towns in the adjacent parts of Palestine. In a word, it was fast becoming manifest that the existence of the Hebrews, as a free and distinct people, could only be maintained by reviving the union which had originally subsisted among their leading families, under the form best calculated to combine their physical strength and patriotism in the support of a common cause. An aged priest, although he might with the utmost authority direct the solemnities of their national worship, and even administer the laws to which they were all bound to submit, could not command the secular obedience of rude clans, or, with any prospect of success, lead them to battle against an enemy practised in all the stratagems of war. The people, therefore, demanded the consent of Samuel to a change in the structure of their government, that they might have a king not only to preside over their civil affairs, but also to go out before them and fight their battles.†

The principal reason assigned by the elders of Israel for the innovation which they required at the hands of their ancient prophet was, that they might be "like all

---

\* Isaiah, xi. 13. † Samuel, viii. 4-21.

the nations;" evidently alluding to the advantages of monarchical power, when decisive measures become necessary to defend the interests of a state. It is remarkable that Moses had anticipated this natural result in the progress of society, and even laid down rules for the administration of the regal government. This wise legislator provided that the king of the Hebrews should not be a foreigner, lest he might be tempted to sacrifice the interests of his subjects to the policy of his native land, and perhaps to countenance the introduction of unauthorized rites into the worship of Jehovah. It was also stipulated that the sovereign of the Chosen People should not have a numerous cavalry, lest he might be carried by his ambition to make war in distant countries, and neglect the welfare of the sacred inheritance promised to the fathers of the Jewish nation.*

The qualities which recommended Saul to the choice of Samuel and the approbation of the Tribes, leave no room for doubt that it was chiefly as a military leader that the son of Kish was raised to the throne. Nor was their expectation disappointed in the young Benjamite, so far as courage and zeal were required in conducting the affairs of war. But the impetuosity of his character, and a certain indifference with regard to the claims of the national faith, paved the way for his downfal and the extinction of his family. The scene of Gilboa, which terminated the career of this monarch, exhibits a most affecting tragedy; in which the valour of a gallant chief, contrasted with his despair and sorrow, throws a deceitful lustre over an event which the reader feels that he ought to condemn.

David, to the skill of an experienced warrior, added a deep reverence for the institutions of his country and the forms of Divine worship; whence he procured the high distinction of being a man after God's own heart. To this celebrated king was reserved the honour of taking from the Jebusites a strong fortress on the borders

---

* Deut. xvii. 14 20.

of Judah and Benjamin, and of laying the foundations of Jerusalem, viewed, at least, as the metropolis of Palestine and the seat of the Hebrew government. On Mount Zion he built a suburb of considerable beauty and strength, which continued for many years to bear his name and to reflect the magnificence of his genius. Not satisfied with this acquisition, he extended his arms on all sides, till the borders of his kingdom touched the western bank of the Euphrates and the neighbourhood of Damascus. He likewise defeated the Philistines, those restless enemies of the southern tribes, and added their dominions to the crown of Israel. The Moabites, who had provoked his resentment, were subjected to military execution, and deprived of a large portion of their land; an example of severity which, so far from intimidating the children of Ammon, only incited them to try the fortune of war against the conqueror. David despatched an army under the command of the irascible Joab, who, after worsting them in the field, inflicted a tremendous chastisement upon the followers of Hanun, for having studiously insulted the ambassadors of his master.*

But the splendour of this reign was afterwards clouded by domestic guilt and treason; and the nation, which could now have defied the power of its bitterest enemies, was divided and rendered miserable by the foul passions that issued from the royal palace. Still, notwithstanding the rebellion of Absalom, and the defection of certain military leaders, David bequeathed to his successor a flourishing kingdom; rapidly advancing in the arts of civilized life, enjoying an advantageous commerce, the respect of neighbouring states, and a decided preponderance among the minor governments of Western Asia. His last years were spent in making preparations for the building of a temple at Jerusalem,—a work that he himself was not allowed to accomplish, because his hands were stained with blood, which, however justly shed,

---

* 2 Samuel, viii. 1, 2. 1 Chron. xviii. 1, 2; xix. 1-20.

rendered them unfit for erecting an edifice to the God of mercy and peace.*

The success which had attended the arms of his father rendered the accession of Solomon tranquil and secure, so far, at least, as we consider the designs of the surrounding nations. Accordingly, finding himself in possession of quiet as well as of an overflowing treasury, he proceeded to realize the pious intentions of his predecessor with regard to the House of God, and thereby to obey the last commands which had been imposed upon him before he received the crown. The chief glory of Solomon's administration is identified with the erection of the Temple. Nor were the advantages arising from this great undertaking confined to the spiritual objects to which it was principally subservient. On the contrary, the necessity of employing foreign artists, and of drawing part of his materials from a distance, suggested to the king the benefits of a regular trade; and as the plains of Syria produced more corn than the natives could consume, he supplied the merchants of Tyre with this valuable commodity, in return for the manufactured goods which his own subjects could not fabricate. It was in his reign that the Israelites first became a commercial people; and although considerable obscurity still hangs over the several tracks of navigation pursued by the mariners of Solomon, there is no reason to doubt that his ships were to be seen on the Mediterranean, the Red Sea, and the Persian Gulf.†

But the popularity of his government did not keep pace with the rapidity of his improvements or the magnificence of his works. Perhaps the vast extent of his undertakings may have led to unusual demands upon the industry of his people, and given occasion to those murmurs which could hardly be repressed even within the precincts of the court. Besides, he occasionally failed to illustrate, in his own conduct, the excellent precepts he propounded for the direction of others; and towards

---

* 1 Chron. xxii. 8.     † 2 Chron. ii. and ix. throughout.

the close of his life particularly, the wisdom of his moral lessons was strangely contrasted with the practical follies which stand recorded against him in the inspired narrative. He totally disregarded the leading principles of the constitution formed by Moses for the guidance of all Hebrew kings; not only maintaining a large body of horse, and marrying many wives who turned away his heart from the true faith, but proceeding so far as to countenance an idolatrous worship within sight of the very Temple which he had consecrated to Jehovah, the God of all the earth.*

It was in his reign that the limits of Jewish power attained their utmost reach, comprehending even the remarkable district of Palmyrene, a spacious and fertile province in the midst of a frightful desert. There were in it two principal towns, Thapsacus and Palmyra, from the latter of which the whole country took its name. Solomon, it is well known, took pleasure in adding to its beauty and strength, as being one of his main defences on the eastern border; and hence it is spoken of in Scripture as Tadmor in the wilderness. Josephus calls it Thadamor; the Seventy recognise it under the name of Theodmor and Thedmor; while the Arabs and Syrians at the present day keep alive the remembrance of its ancient glory as Tadmier and Tatmor. But of the labours of the Hebrew king not one vestige now remains. The inhabitants having revolted from the Emperor Aurelian, and pledged their faith to an adventurer called Antiochus, who had assumed the purple, this splendid town was attacked and razed to the ground. Repenting of his hasty determination, the Roman prince gave orders that Palmyra should be immediately rebuilt; but so inefficient were the measures which he adopted, or so imperfectly was he obeyed in their execution, that the city in the Desert has, during many centuries, been remarkable only for its ruins. The first object that now presents itself to the traveller who ap-

---

* 1 Kings, xi. 1-8.

proaches this forlorn place, is a castle of mean architecture and uncertain origin, about half an hour's walk from it on the north side. " From thence," says Mr Maundrell, " we descry Tadmor, enclosed on three sides by long ridges of mountains; but to the south is a vast plain which bounds the visible horizon. The barren soil presents nothing green but a few palm-trees. The city must have been of large extent, if we may judge from the space now taken up by the ruins; but as there are no traces of its walls, its real dimensions and form remain equally unknown. It is now a deplorable spectacle, inhabited by thirty or forty miserable families, who have built huts of mud within a spacious court which once enclosed a magnificent heathen temple."\*

The description now given, though written nearly a hundred and fifty years ago, applies with sufficient accuracy to its present state. It is inhabited by Syrian peasants, a race of men quite distinct from the Bedouins of the desert, and who earn a livelihood as well by cultivating the soil as by conducting a profitable trade in salt. Bruce, who visited this remarkable place, says, the ruins are " the most astonishing stupendous sight that perhaps ever appeared to mortal eyes. The whole plain, which is very extensive, is covered so thickly with magnificent buildings, that one seemed to touch the other, all of fine proportions, all of agreeable forms, all composed of white stones, which at a distance appeared like marble. At the end of it stood the palace of the sun, a building worthy to close so magnificent a scene.†

But the history of Palmyra, it must be confessed, does not afford to the reader a clear view, either of its origin, its advancement, or its decline; for though the prosperity it attained under Zenobia and its subversion by Aurelian are recorded in the pages of the Roman annalists, the period of its foundation and its fortunes after it was subjected by the imperial arms are involved in equal obscurity. The learned Hardouin even accuses those of

---

\* Maundrell's Journey from Aleppo to Jerusalem in 1697.
† Travels, vol. i. p. 60.

a manifest error who suppose the Palmyra mentioned in Scripture to be that described by Pliny. The authority, however, of the Greek and Latin versions of the Old Testament, the traditions of the inhabitants, and the vernacular name still preserved by the Arabs, all conspire to prove not only that Tadmor in the wilderness is the Palmyra of the classical writers, but also that Solomon was the founder of that remarkable city so conveniently placed as an emporium for the commerce of the eastern and the western world.*

Josephus relates that the Hebrew prince just named, "making an incursion into the desert which is above Syria, and taking possession of it, built a very large city there, at the distance of two days' journey from the Upper Syria, one from the Euphrates, and six from Babylon the Great. The reason of his building this town so far from the inhabited parts of Syria, was the total want of water in the country lower down, while springs and wells were found in that place alone." Pliny the elder, who was contemporary with the Jewish historian, confirms his account, and adds a gorgeous description both of the city and of the surrounding territory. It is distant, he says, from Seleucia, the Parthian capital, three hundred and thirty-eight miles; from Damascus, one hundred and seventy-six; and from the nearest part of the Syrian coast, two hundred and three.

Its intermediate position between Mesopotamia and Syria made it an excellent place for exchanging the commodities conveyed thither by the traders of the Mediterranean and the Indian Ocean; and the protection of its deserts long secured to it the enjoyment of independence, enabling the inhabitants to maintain a friendly intercourse with each of the rival empires of Parthia and Rome. It is probable that it was to this rivalry that its wealth and prosperity were principally due; for it appears to have first risen into notice at the time when the struggle between those great powers commenced. Palmyra is not mentioned by Strabo, who flourished only

---

* Plin. Hist. Nat. lib. v. c. 21.

half a century before Pliny and Josephus, whence it may be inferred that it had not yet assumed any importance as a commercial station. After the vengeance inflicted upon it by Aurelian, it seems to have regained some share of its former prosperity; and it figures accordingly as a place of importance, and an episcopal see, in the Imperial Catalogue of the eighth and even of the ninth century. The seat, however, of commerce, of arts, and of Zenobia, gradually sank into an obscure town, a trifling fortress, and at length a miserable village.*

The despotism exercised by Solomon created a strong reaction, which was immediately felt on the accession of his son Rehoboam. This prince, rejecting the advice of his aged counsellors, and following that of the younger and more violent, soon had the misfortune to see the greater part of his kingdom wrested from him. In reply to the address of his people, who entreated an alleviation of their burdens, he declared, that instead of requiring less at their hands he should demand more. "My father made your yoke heavy, I will add to your yoke; my father chastised you with whips, but I will chastise you with scorpions." Such a resolution, expressed in language at once so contemptuous and severe, alienated from his government ten tribes, who sought a more indulgent master in Jeroboam, a declared enemy of the house of David. Hence the origin of the kingdom of Israel, as distinguished from that of Judah; and hence, too, the disgraceful contentions between these kindred states, which acknowledged one religion, and professed to be guided by the same law. Arms and negotiation proved equally unavailing to reunite the Hebrews under one sceptre; till at length, about two hundred and seventy years after the death of Solomon, the younger people were subdued by Shalmaneser, the

---

* Dr Halley in the Philosophical Transactions has attempted a history of Palmyra, embodying all the facts which his industry could collect. (Lowthorp's Abridgment, vol. iii. p. 518.) The illustrations of Wood and Dawkins are known to every reader of taste, and leave nothing to be desired.

powerful monarch of Assyria, who carried them away captive into the remoter provinces of his vast empire.*

Our plan does not admit a minuter detail of the sacred history than may be readily found in the pages of the Old Testament. Suffice it therefore to observe, that Jerusalem soon ceased to be regarded by the Israelites as the centre of their religion, and the bond of union among the descendants of Abraham.

Jeroboam had erected in his kingdom the emblems of a less pure faith, to which he confined the attention of his subjects ; while the frequent wars that ensued, and the treaties formed on either side with the Gentile nations, soon completed the estrangement which ambition had begun. Little attached to the native line of princes, the Israelites placed on the throne of Samaria a number of adventurers, who had no qualities to recommend them besides military courage and an irreconcilable hatred towards the more legitimate claimants of the house of David. The following list will give a condensed view of the names, the order, and the length of the reigns which belong to these sovereigns, from the demise of Solomon down to the extinction of their kingdom by the arms of Assyria :

|     |                         | Years. | B. C. |
|-----|-------------------------|-------|------|
| 1.  | Jeroboam,               | 22    | 990  |
| 2.  | Nadad,                  | 2     | 968  |
| 3.  | Baasha,                 | 23    | 966  |
| 4.  | Ela,                    | 1     | 943  |
| 5.  | Zimri and Omri,         | 11    | 942  |
| 6.  | Ahab,                   | 22    | 931  |
| 7.  | Ahaziah,                | 2     | 909  |
| 8.  | Jehoram or Joram,       | 12    | 907  |
| 9.  | Jehu,                   | 28    | 895  |
| 10. | Jehoahaz,               | 17    | 867  |
| 11. | Jehoash or Joash,       | 16    | 850  |
| 12. | Jeroboam II.,           | 41    | 834  |
|     | 1st Interregnum,        | 22    | 793  |
| 13. | Zechariah and Shallum   | 1     | 771  |
| 14. | Menahem,                | 10    | 770  |
| 15. | Pekahiah,               | 2     | 760  |
| 16. | Pekah,                  | 20    | 758  |
|     | 2d Interregnum,         | 10    | 738  |
| 17. | Hoshea,                 | 9     | 728  |
|     | Samaria taken,          | 271   | 719  |

---

* 2 Kings, xvii. 1-7.

It appears to have escaped the notice of the greater number of commentators, that the separation of interests, which in the days of Rehoboam produced a permanent division of the tribes, had manifested itself at a much earlier period. In truth, it is extremely doubtful whether the union between the northern and the southern communities, which was meant to be accomplished by the institution of monarchy, were ever cordial or efficient. There is no doubt, at least, that the two parties differed essentially in their choice of a successor to Saul; for, when the people of Judah invited David to the supreme power as their anointed sovereign, the suffrages of Israel were unanimous in favour of Ishbosheth, the son of the deceased king. We may therefore conclude, that the exactions of Solomon were the pretext rather than the true cause of the unfortunate dismemberment of the Hebrew confederation, which in the end conducted both parties to defeat and captivity.

The kingdom of Judah, less distracted by the pretensions of usurpers, and confirmed in the principles of patriotism by a more rigid adherence to the law of Moses, continued during one hundred and thirty years to resist the encroachments of Egypt and Assyria, which now began to contend in earnest for the possession of Palestine. Several endeavours were made, even after the destruction of Samaria, to unite the energies of the Twelve Tribes, and thereby to secure the independence of the sacred territory a little longer. But a pitiful jealousy had succeeded to the aversion created by a long course of hostile aggression; while the overwhelming armies, which incessantly issued from the Euphrates and the Nile to decide their quarrels within the borders of Canaan, soon left to the feeble councils of Jerusalem no other choice than that of an Egyptian or an Assyrian master.

In the year six hundred and two before the Christian era, when Jehoiakim was on the throne of Judah, Nebuchadnezzar, who already shared the government with his father, advanced into Palestine at the head of a formidable host. A timely submission saved the city as well as the life of the pusillanimous monarch. But after a short period, finding the conqueror engaged in more important affairs, the Jewish prince made an effort to recover his dominions by throwing off the Babylonian yoke. The siege was renewed with greater vigour on the part of the invaders, in the course of which the king was killed, and his son Coniah raised to the supreme power. Scarcely, however, had the new sovereign taken the reins of government, when he found it necessary to open the gates of his capital to the Assyrians, who carried him, his principal nobility, and the most expert of his artisans, as prisoners to the banks of the Tigris.

The nominal authority was now confided to a brother or uncle of the captive ruler, whose original name, Mattaniah, was changed to Zedekiah by his lord paramount, who considered him merely as the governor of a province. Impatient of an office so subordinate, and instigated, it is probable, by the emissaries of Egypt, he resolved to hazard his life for the chance of reconquering the independence of his crown. This imprudent step brought Nebuchadnezzar once more before the walls of Jerusalem. A siege, which appears to have continued fifteen or sixteen months, terminated in the final reduction of the holy city, and in the captivity of Zedekiah, who was treated with the utmost severity. His two sons were executed in his presence, after which his eyes were put out; when, being loaded with fetters, he was carried to Babylon and thrown into prison.

The work of demolition was intrusted to Nebuzaradan, the captain of the guard, who " burnt the house of the Lord, and the king's house, and all the houses of Jerusalem, and every great man's house burnt he with fire. And the army of the Chaldees that were with the captain of the guard brake down the walls of Jerusalem round about. The rest of the people that were left in the city, and the fugitives that fell away to the King of Babylon, with the remnant of the multitude, did the captain of the guard carry away. But he left the poor of the land to be vine-dressers and husbandmen."*

The kings who reigned over Judah from the demise of Solomon to the destruction of the first Temple are as follows:—

|     |                         | Years. | B. C. |
| --- | ----------------------- | ------ | ----- |
| 1.  | Rehoboam,               | 17     | 990   |
| 2.  | Abijah,                 | 3      | 973   |
| 3.  | Asa,                    | 41     | 970   |
| 4.  | Jehoshaphat,            | 25     | 929   |
| 5.  | Jehoram or Joram,       | 8      | 904   |
| 6.  | Ahaziah,                | 1      | 896   |
| 7.  | Queen Athaliah,         | 6      | 895   |
| 8.  | Joash or Jehoash,       | 40     | 889   |
| 9.  | Amaziah,                | 29     | 849   |
|     | Interregnum,            | 11     | 820   |
| 10. | Uzziah or Azariah,      | 52     | 809   |
| 11. | Jotham,                 | 16     | 757   |
| 12. | Ahaz,                   | 16     | 741   |
| 13. | Hezekiah,               | 29     | 725   |
| 14. | Manasseh,               | 55     | 696   |
| 15. | Amor,                   | 2      | 641   |
| 16. | Josiah,                 | 31     | 639   |
| 17. | Jehoahaz,               | 3 months | |
| 18. | Jehoiakim,              | 11     | 608   |
| 19. | Coniah or Jehoiachin,   | 3 months | |
| 20. | Zedekiah,               | 11     | 597   |
|     | Jerusalem taken,        | 404    | 586   |

The desolation inflicted upon Jerusalem by the hands of her enemies excited the deepest sorrow, and gave rise to the most gloomy apprehensions with regard to the future. Considering themselves under the special protection of Jehovah, the inhabitants could not by any means be induced to believe that the throne of David would ever be overturned by the armies of the heathen. It was in vain that Jeremiah, at the imminent peril of his life, announced the approaching judgment, assuring the monarch and his princes that the King of Babylon would certainly lay waste their holy city, unless the evil were averted by an immediate change of manners. All his remonstrances were treated with contempt; and at length the prophet had to bewail the misery which

---

* 2 Kings, xxv. 4-13.

thus overtook his people, and the varied sufferings, the contumely, and the degradation, which they were doomed to endure in the land of their conquerors. " How doth the city sit solitary that was full of people! How is she become as a widow! She that was great among the nations, and princess among the provinces, is become tributary! She weepeth sore in the night, and her tears are on her cheeks! Judah is gone into captivity; she dwelleth among the heathen, she findeth no rest."\*

These sentiments, although applied to a later period, are beautifully expressed by a modern poet, to whom was granted no small share of the pathetic eloquence which distinguished the inspired writer whose words have just been quoted.

> " Reft of thy sons, amid thy foes forlorn,
> Mourn, widow'd Queen, forgotten Sion, mourn!
> Is this thy place, sad city, this thy throne,
> Where the wild desert rears its craggy stone,
> While suns unblest their angry lustre fling,
> And way-worn pilgrims seek the scanty spring?
> Where now thy pomp which kings with envy viewed?
> Where now thy might which all those kings subdued?
> No martial myriads muster in thy gate;
> No suppliant nations in thy Temple wait;
> No prophet-bards, thy glittering courts among,
> Wake the full lyre, and swell the tide of song;
> But lawless Force and meagre Want are there,
> And the quick darting eye of restless Fear;
> While cold Oblivion, 'mid thy ruins laid,
> Folds his dark wing beneath the ivy shade."†

The seventy years which were determined concerning Jerusalem, began, not at the demolition of the city by Nebuzar-adan, but at the date of the former invasion by his master, in the reign of Jehoiakim, when the Assyrians carried away some of the princes, and among others Daniel and his celebrated companions, as captives, or perhaps as hostages for the good conduct of the king. The event now alluded to took place exactly six centuries before the Christian era; and hence the return of

---

\* Lamentations, i. 1-4.   † Heber's Palestine.

the Jews to the Holy Land must have occurred about the year 530 prior to the same great epoch. But as their migration homeward was gradually accomplished under different leaders and with various objects in view, their historians have not thought it necessary to enter into particulars; and from this circumstance has arisen no small diversity in the calculations of divines respecting the commencement, the duration, and the end of the Babylonian captivity.

The tribes of Judah and Benjamin, who now constituted the whole Jewish nation, brought back with them to Palestine the ancient spirit of hostility towards the Israelitish kingdom, the people of which they were pleased to class under the general denomination of Samaritans,—an impure race, descended from the eastern colonists sent by Shalmaneser to replace the Hebrew captives whom he removed to Halah and Habor and the cities of the Medes. In this way they roused an opposition, and created difficulties, which otherwise they might not have experienced during their erection of the second temple. The countenance of the Persian court itself was occasionally withdrawn from men, who appeared to acknowledge no affinity with any other order of human beings, and who seemed determined to exclude from their country, as well as from their religious rites and privileges, all who could not establish an immaculate descent from the Father of the Faithful. For this reason, the sympathy which is so naturally excited in the breast of the reader in behalf of the weary exiles, who sat down and wept by the waters of Babylon with their thoughts fixed on Sion, is very apt to be extinguished when he contemplates the bitter enmity with which they rejected, amid the ruins of their metropolis, the kind offices of their ancient brethren.

The names of Zerubbabel, Nehemiah, and Ezra, occupy the most distinguished place among those worthies who were selected by Divine Providence to conduct the restoration of the chosen people. After much toil, interruption, and alarm, Jerusalem could once more boast of a Sanctuary, which, although destitute of the rich ornaments lavished upon that of Solomon, was at least of equal dimensions, and erected on the same consecrated ground. But the worshipper had to deplore the absence of the Ark, the symbolical Urim and Thummim, the Shechinah or Divine Presence, the spirit of prophecy, and the celestial fire which had maintained an unceasing flame upon the altar. Their Sacred Writings, too, had been dispersed, and their ancient language was fast becoming obsolete. To prevent the extension of so great an evil, the more valuable manuscripts were collected and arranged, containing the Law, the earlier Prophets, and the inspired hymns used for the purpose of devotion. Some compositions, however, which respected the remotest period of their commonwealth, especially the Book of Jasher and the Wars of the Lord, were irretrievably lost.

Under the Persian satraps, who directed the civil and military government of Syria, the Jews were permitted to acknowledge the authority of their own High Priest, to whom, in all things pertaining to the law of Moses, they rendered the obedience which was due to the head of their nation. Their prosperity, it is true, was occasionally diminished or increased by the personal character of the sovereigns who successively occupied the throne of Cyrus; but no material change in their circumstances took place until the victories of Alexander the Great had laid the foundations of the Syro-Macedonian kingdom in Western Asia, and also given a new dynasty to the crown of Egypt. The struggles which ensued between these powerful states frequently involved the interests of the Jews, and made new demands upon their allegiance; although it is admitted, that as each was desirous to conciliate a people who claimed Palestine for their unalienable heritage, the Hebrews at large were, during two centuries, treated with much liberality and favour. But this generosity or forbearance was interrupted in the reign of Antiochus Epiphanes, who, alarmed by the report of insurrections, and harassed by the events of an unsuccessful war in Egypt, directed his angry passions against the Jews. Marching at the head of a large force, he attacked their metropolis so suddenly that no means of defence could be used, and hardly any resistance attempted. Forty thousand of the inhabitants were put to death, and an equal number condemned to slavery. Not satisfied with this punishment, he proceeded to measures still more appalling in the eyes of a descendant of Abraham. He entered the temple, pillaged the treasury, seized all the sacred utensils, the golden candlestick, the table of shew-bread, and the altar of incense. He then commanded a great sow to be sacrificed on the altar of burnt-offerings, part of the flesh to be boiled, and the liquor from this unclean animal to be sprinkled over every part of the sacred edifice; thus polluting with the most odious defilement even the Holy of Holies, which no human eye, save that of the high priest, was ever permitted to behold.

A short time afterwards, being the year 168 before the epoch of Redemption, he issued an edict for the extermination of the whole Hebrew race, against whom he had again conceived a furious dislike. This commission was intrusted to Apollonius,—an instrument worthy of so sanguinary a tyrant,—who, waiting till the Sabbath, when the people were occupied in the peaceful duties of religion, let loose his soldiers upon the unresisting multitude, slew all the men, whose blood deluged the streets, and seized the women as captives. He first proceeded to plunder and then to dismantle the city, which he set on fire in many places. He threw down the walls, and built a strong fortress on the highest part of Mount Sion, which commanded the temple and all the adjoining parts of the town. From this garrison he harassed the inhabitants of the country, who, with fond attachment, stole in to visit the ruins, or to offer a hasty and perilous worship in the place where their sanctuary had stood. All the public services had ceased, and no voice of adoration was heard within the holy gates, except that of the profane heathen calling on their idols.*

But the persecution did not end even with these furious expedients. Antiochus next issued an order for uniformity of worship throughout all his dominions, and sent officers every where to enforce the strictest compliance. In the districts of Judea and Samaria, this invidious duty was intrusted to Athenæus, an old man, whose chief recommendation appears to have been his intimate acquaintance with the doctrines and usages of the Grecian religion. The Samaritans are said to have conformed without scruple, and even to have permitted their temple on Mount Gerizim to be regularly dedicated to Jupiter, in his character of the Stranger's Friend. Having so far succeeded, the royal envoy turned his steps to Jerusalem, where, at the point of the sword, he prohibited every observance connected with the true faith; compelling the people to profane the Sabbath, to eat swine's flesh, and to abstain, under a severe penalty, from the national rite of circumcision. The temple was consigned by consecration to the ceremonies of Jupiter Olympius; while the statue of that deity was erected on the altar of burnt-offerings, and sacrifice duly performed in his name. Two women, who had defied his authority so far as to have the initiatory ordinance enjoined by the Mosaical law performed on their children, were hanged in a conspicuous part of the city with their infants suspended round their necks; and many other cruelties were perpetrated, the very atrocity of which precludes them at once from popular belief and from the pages of history. Neither age, nor sex, nor profession, saved the proscribed Jew from the horrors of a violent death. From the capital, too, the persecution spread over the whole country; in every city the same barbarities were executed, and the same profanations introduced. As a last insult, the feasts of the Bacchanalia, the license of which, as they were celebrated in the later

---

* History of the Jews, vol. ii. p. 41.

ages of Greece, shocked the severe virtue of the older Romans, were substituted for the national festival of Tabernacles. The reluctant Hebrews were forced to join in these riotous orgies, and to carry the ivy, the insignia of the god. So nearly were the Jewish nation and the worship of Jehovah exterminated by the double weapons of superstition and violence!\*

But this savage intolerance produced in due time a formidable opposition. To a sincere believer death has always appeared a smaller evil than the relinquishment of his faith; and, in this respect, no people ancient or modern have shown more resolution than the posterity of Jacob. The severities of Antiochus, which had inflamed the resentment of the whole nation, called forth in a hostile attitude the brave family of the Maccabees, whose valour and perseverance enabled them to dispute with the powerful monarch of Syria the sovereignty of Palestine. Judas, the ablest and most gallant of five sons, put himself at the head of the insurgents, whose zeal, more than compensating for the smallness of their numbers, carried him to victory against large armies and experienced generals. Making every allowance for the enthusiastic description of an admiring countryman, who has recorded the exploits of the Maccabean chiefs, there will still remain the most ample evidence to satisfy every candid reader, that in nearly all the great conflicts the fortune of war followed the standard of the Jews.

But these victorious leaders, who had delivered their country from the oppression of foreigners, encountered a more formidable enemy in the factious spirit of their own people. Alcimus, a tool of the Syrians, assumed the title of High Priest, and in virtue of his office claimed the obedience of all who acknowledged the institutions of Moses. In this emergency Judas courted the alliance of the Romans, who willingly extended their protection to confederates so likely to aid their ambitious views in the East; but, before the Republic could interpose her

---

\* History of the Jews, vol. ii. p. 43.

arms in his behalf, the Hebrew general had fallen in the field of battle.

This distinguished patriot was succeeded by his brother Jonathan, who, though less celebrated as a warrior, had the good fortune to restore the drooping cause of the patriots, and even to establish their rights on the footing of independence. Profiting by a sanguinary competition for the throne of Syria, he consented to employ his power in favour of Alexander Balas, on condition that, in return for so seasonable an aid, he should be allowed to assume the pontifical robe as ruler of Judea. Hence the origin of the Asmonean princes, who, uniting civil with spiritual authority, governed Palestine during more than a hundred yéars.

But Jonathan at length fell the victim of that refined policy to which he was mainly indebted for his elevation. He left the sovereign priesthood to his brother Simon, who, wisely abstaining from all interference in the disputes which embroiled Egypt and Syria, directed his whole attention to the improvement of the Jewish commonwealth. To secure the tranquillity which had been so dearly purchased he cultivated a more intimate connexion with Rome ; sending, from time to time, such valuable tokens of his respect as could not fail to make an impression on the venal minds of those aspiring chiefs who already contended for the empire of the world in that celebrated capital. But a conspiracy, originating in his own house, and fomented by the agents of Antiochus, put an end to the life of Simon and of his eldest son, who had earned considerable reputation in the command of armies. The duty of avenging his death, and of governing a distracted country, devolved upon a younger brother, afterwards well known in history by the name of John Hyrcanus.

The unhappy circumstances under which he succeeded to power compelled him to submit for a time to the condition of vassalage ; but no sooner had Antiochus Sidetes fallen in the Parthian war, than he shook off the yoke of Syria, and exercised the rights of an independent sovereign. He even extended his sway beyond the Jordan, reducing several important towns to his obedience; though the achievement which most gratified his Jewish subjects was the capture of Shechem, followed by the demolition of the temple on Gerizim, so long regarded as the opprobrium of the Hebrew faith. At a later period he made himself master of Samaria and Galilee, when, to gratify still farther the vindictive grudge which yet rankled in the breasts of his people, he destroyed the capital of the former province, and debased it to the condition of a stagnant lake. Nor was his attention confined to foreign conquest. He strengthened the fortifications of Jerusalem, and built the castle of Baris within the walls that surrounded the hill of the Temple,—a stronghold which at a future period attracted no small degree of notice under the name of Antonia.

The government was enjoyed during a brief space by Aristobulus, the son of Hyrcanus, whose reign was distinguished only by the most painful domestic calamities. The throne was next occupied by Alexander Jannæus, a man of ignoble birth, but of a warlike and very ambitious temper. The distracted state of the neighbouring countries induced him to take the field, with the view of reducing several towns on the coast of the Mediterranean,—an undertaking which finally involved him in the troubled politics of Egypt and Cyprus. In process of time, the severity of his measures, or the meanness of his extraction, rendered him so unpopular at Jerusalem that the inhabitants expelled him by force of arms. A civil war of the most sanguinary nature raged several years, during which the insurgents invited the assistance of Demetrius Euchærus, one of the kings of Syria. This measure seems to have united a large party of Jews, who were equally hostile to the dominant faction within the city, and to the ally whom they had called to their aid. Alexander, after having repeatedly suffered the heaviest losses, saw himself again at the head of a powerful army, with which he resolved to march against the rebellious capital. He inflicted a signal punishment upon such of the unfortunate citizens as fell into his hands; ordering nearly a thousand of them to be crucified, and their wives and children to be butchered before their eyes.

Having fully re-established his power over the whole of Palestine, the victorious High Priest, now drawing towards the close of his days, gave instructions to his wife for the future government of the country. Alexandra, a woman of a vigorous mind, held the reins of civil power with great steadiness, while her eldest son, Hyrcanus the Second, was decorated with the sacred diadem as the head of the nation. But, unhappily, the commotions which had disturbed the reign of her husband were again excited, and once more divided the people into two furious parties. Aristobulus, the younger son of Jannæus, gave countenance to the faction who opposed his brother, and at length threw off his disguise so completely as to aspire to supreme power, in defiance as well of the rights of birth as of a legal investiture. Hyrcanus, who was far inferior to his ambitious relative in point of talent and resolution, would probably, after the death of their mother, have been unable to keep his seat on the throne, had he not received the powerful aid of Antipater, a son of Antipas, the governor of Idumea. Both sides were making preparation for an appeal to arms, when the Romans, who had already overrun the finest parts of Syria, advanced into Palestine, in the character at once of umpires and of allies.

Pompey readily listened to the claims of the two competitors, but deferred coming to an immediate decision; having resolved, as it afterwards appeared, that neither of the kinsmen should continue any longer to possess the civil and military command of Judea. Aristobulus, impatient of delay, and having no confidence in the goodness of his cause, had recourse to arms, and at length shut himself up in Jerusalem. The Roman general issued orders to his lieutenant, Gabinius, to invest the holy city; which, after a siege of three months, was taken by assault at a great expense of human life.

Many of the priests who were employed in the duties

of their office fell victims to the rage of the soldiers; while others, unable to witness the desecration of their temple by the presence of idolaters, threw themselves from the rock on which that building stood. Induced by curiosity, Pompey is said to have imitated the profane boldness of Antiochus; penetrating into the Holy of Holies, and examining all the instruments of a worship which differed so much from that of all other nations. But he was more politic, or more generous, than the Syrian monarch; for, although he found much treasure in the sanctuary, as well as many vessels of gold and silver, he carried nothing away. He expressed much astonishment that, in a fane so magnificent, and frequented by Jews from all parts of the earth, there should be no material form, whether statue or picture, to represent the Deity to whose honour it was erected. Having, in order to satisfy the scruples of the people, ordered a purification of the temple, he renewed the appointment of Hyrcanus to the high priesthood, but without any civil power; while, with respect to the more turbulent Aristobulus, he resolved to exercise the right of a conqueror, by sending him and his two sons to Rome, that they might swell the train of his approaching triumph.

The escape of one of these young men, and afterwards of the father himself, rekindled the flame of war in Palestine. But the Romans, under Gabinius and the celebrated Mark Antony, speedily subdued the hasty levies of Aristobulus, and completely re-established the ascendency of the Republic in all the revolted districts. In the civil war which ensued, Antipater, who still directed the affairs of the weak-minded Hyrcanus, paid his court so successfully to the dominant faction as to obtain for his master the protection of Cæsar, and for himself the procuratorship of Judea. Raised to this commanding eminence, he named Phasael, his eldest son, governor of Jerusalem, and confided to the younger, the artful and unscrupulous Herod, the charge of Galilee.

But there still remained an individual belonging to the family of Aristobulus, who, having found refuge among the Parthians, led a powerful army into Syria, and finally invested Jerusalem. The invaders, after obtaining possession of the city, deprived Hyrcanus of the priesthood and Phasael of his life; the barbarian soldiers, meantime, committing pillage on all classes, both within the walls and in the adjoining country. Herod, warned by his less fortunate relative in the capital, had fled to Rome, with the view, it is said, of recommending the interests of another Aristobulus, a grandson of Hyrcanus, and brother of the beautiful Mariamne, to whom he himself was already betrothed. Octavius and Antony, however, thought it more expedient for their rising empire that Herod should wear the vassal-crown of Judea in his own person, rather than see it placed on the head of an inexperienced youth; and as the son of Antipater was about to unite himself with a descendant of the Asmonean princes, it was considered that the claims of each family would be thereby fully satisfied.

The reign of Herod, who, to distinguish him from others of the same name, is usually called the Great, was no less remarkable for domestic calamity than for public peace and happiness. Urged by suspicion, he put to death his beloved wife,* her mother, brother, grand-

---

* The effects produced upon the mind of the king by the murder of Mariamne are powerfully described by two poetical writers, the author of the History of the Jews and the unfortunate Lord Byron. "All the passions," says the former, "which filled the stormy soul of Herod were alike without bound: from violent love and violent resentment he sank into as violent remorse and despair. Every where by day he was haunted by the image of the murdered Mariamne; he called upon her name; he perpetually burst into passionate tears. In vain he tried every diversion,—banquets, revels, the excitements of society. A sudden pestilence broke out, to which many of the noblest of his court, and of his own personal friends, fell a sacrifice; he recognised and trembled beneath the hand of the avenging Deity. On pretence of hunting, he sought out the most melancholy solitude, till the disorder of his mind brought on disorder of body, and he was seized with violent inflammation and pains in the back of his head, which led to temporary derangement."—Vol. ii. p. 107.

1.
  "Oh, Mariamne! now for thee
    The heart for which thou bledst is bleeding;
  Revenge is lost in agony,
    And wild remorse to rage succeeding.

father, uncle, and two sons. His palace was the scene of incessant intrigue, misery, and bloodshed; his nearest relations being ever the chief instruments of his worst sufferings and fears. It was, perhaps, to divert his apprehensions and remorse that he employed so much of his time in the labours of architecture. Besides a royal residence on Mount Sion, he built a number of citadels throughout the country, and laid the foundations of several splendid towns. Among these was Cesarea, a station well selected both for strength and commerce, and destined to become, under a different government, a place of considerable importance.

But the impurity of his blood as an Idumean, and his undisguised attachment to the religion of his Gentile masters, created an obstacle to a complete understanding with his subjects, which no degree of personal kindness, or of wisdom and munificence in the conduct of public affairs, could ever entirely remove. At length he determined on a measure which, he hoped, would at the same time employ the people and ingratiate himself with the higher classes,—the rebuilding of the temple

---

Oh, Mariamne! where art thou?
  Thou canst not hear my bitter pleading:
Ah, couldst thou—thou wouldst pardon now,
  Though Heaven were to my prayer unheeding.

2.

" And is she dead?—and did they dare
  Obey my phrensy's jealous raving?
My wrath but doom'd my own despair:
  The sword that smote her's o'er me waving.
But thou art cold, my murder'd love!
  And this dark heart is vainly craving
For her who soars alone above,
  And leaves my soul unworthy saving.

3.

" She's gone, who shared my diadem;
  She sunk, with her my joys entombing;
I swept that flower from Judah's stem
  Whose leaves for me alone were blooming;
And mine's the guilt, and mine the hell,
  This bosom's desolation dooming;
And I have earned those tortures well,
  Which unconsumed are still consuming."

*Hebrew Melodies.*

in its former splendour and greatness. The lapse of five hundred years, and the ravages of successive wars, had much impaired the structure of Zerubbabel. As it was necessary to remove the dilapidated parts of the edifice before the new building could be begun, the Jews looked on with a suspicious eye; apprehensive lest the king, under pretence of doing honour to their faith, should obliterate every vestige of their ancient altars. But the prudence of Herod calmed their fears; the work proceeded with the greatest regularity; and the nation saw, with the utmost joy, a fabric of stately architecture crowning the brow of Mount Moriah, with glittering masses of white marble and pinnacles of gold. Yet during this pious undertaking the Jewish monarch maintained his double character; presiding at the Olympic games, granting large donations for their support, and even allowing himself to be nominated president of this pagan festival.*

As he advanced towards old age his troubles multiplied, and his apprehensions were increased, till at length, about four years prior to the common era of Christianity, Herod sank under the pressure of a loathsome disease. He was permitted by the Romans so far to exercise the privileges of an independent prince as to distribute by will the inheritance of sovereignty among the more favoured of his children; and, in virtue of this indulgence, he assigned to Archelaus the government of Idumea, Samaria, and Judea, while he bestowed upon Antipas a similar authority over Peræa and Galilee.

But the young princes required the sanction of the Roman emperor, whom they both regarded as their liege lord; and with that view repaired to the capital of Italy. The will of the late king was acknowledged and confirmed by Augustus, who was moreover pleased to give to Herod Philip, their elder brother, the provinces of Auranitis, Trachonitis, Paneas, and Batanea. Archelaus, the metropolis of whose dominions was Jerusalem, ruled in quality of ethnarch about nine years;

---

* History of the Jews, vol. ii. p. 114.

but so little to the satisfaction either of his master at Rome, or of the people whom he was appointed to govern, that, at the end of this period, he was summoned to render an account of his administration at the imperial tribunal, when he was deprived of his power, and finally banished into Gaul. Judea was now reduced to a Roman province, dependent on the prefecture of Syria, though usually placed under the inspection of a subordinate officer, called the procurator or governor. Thus the sceptre passed away from Judah, and the lawgiver, sprung from the family of Jacob, ceased to enjoy power within the confines of the Promised Land.

No reader can require to be reminded, that it was at this epoch, in the last year of Herod's reign, the Messias was born, and conveyed into Egypt for security. The unjust and cruel government of Archelaus, for which, as has just been related, he was stripped of his authority by the head of the Empire, was probably the cause why the holy family did not again take up their residence in Judea, but preferred the milder rule of Antipas. When Joseph " heard that Archelaus did reign in Judea in the room of his father Herod, he was afraid to go thither: notwithstanding, being warned of God in a dream, he turned aside into the parts of Galilee : and he came and dwelt in a city called Nazareth."*

The first thirty years of the Christian era did not pass away without several insurrections on the part of the Jews, and repeated acts of severity and extortion

---

* Matth. ii. 22, 23. " Among the atrocities which disgraced the latter days of Herod, what is called the Massacre of the Innocents (which took place late in the year before, or early in the same year with the death of Herod) passed away unnoticed. The murder of a few children in a village near Jerusalem would excite little sensation among such a succession of dreadful events, except among the immediate sufferers. The jealousy of Herod against any one who should be born as *a king in Judea*,—the dread that the high religious spirit of the people might be re-excited by the hope of a real Messiah,—as well as the summary manner in which he endeavoured to rid himself of the object of his fears, are strictly in accordance with the relentlessness and decision of his character."—*History of the Jews*, vol. ii. p. 125.

inflicted upon them by their stern conquerors. The commotion excited by Judas, called the Galilean, is regarded by historians as one of the most important of those ebullitions which were constantly breaking forth among that inflammatory people, not only on account of its immediate consequences, but for the effects produced on the national mind with respect to their notions on the lawfulness of tribute and submission to a heathen government.

Upon the exile of Archelaus, the prefecture of Syria was committed to Publius Sulpicius Quirinius. This commander is mentioned in the Gospel of St Luke by the name of Cyrenius, and is described as the person under whom the taxing was first made in that province. We may hence conclude, that the enrolment which took place at the birth of our Saviour was merely a *census*, comprehending the numbers, and perhaps the wealth and station, of the several classes of the inhabitants.

It was about the twenty-sixth year of our epoch that Pontius Pilate was nominated to the government of Judea. Ignorant or indifferent as to the prejudices of the people, he roused amongst them a spirit of the most active resentment, by displaying the image of the emperor in their holy city, and by seizing part of their sacred treasure for the purposes of general improvement. As their fiery temper drove them, on most occasions, to acts of violence, he did not hesitate to employ force in return; and we find, accordingly, that his administration was dishonoured by several instances of military execution directed against Jews and Samaritans indiscriminately. His severity towards the latter people finally led to his recall and disgrace about the year 36, when Vitellius, the father of the future emperor of the same name, presided over the affairs of the Syrian province.

The plan of this work does not permit me to do more than allude to the great event which took place at Jerusalem under the auspices of Pilate. We may nevertheless observe, that the inspired narrative is in strict harmony with the character, not only of the time to which it refers, but also of the persons whose acts it describes. The expectation of the Jews when Jesus of Nazareth first appeared,—their subsequent disappointment and rage,—their hatred and impatience of the Roman government,—the perplexity of the military chief, and the motive which at length induced him to sacrifice the innocent person who was brought before him,—are facts which display the most perfect accordance with the tone of civil history at that remarkable period.

During the troubles which agitated Judea, the districts that owned the sovereignty of Antipas and Philip, namely, Galilee and the country beyond the Jordan, enjoyed comparative quiet. The former, who is the Herod described by our Saviour as " that fox," was a person of a cool and rather crafty disposition, and might have terminated his long reign in peace, had not Herodias, whom he seduced from his brother—the second prince just mentioned—irritated his ambition by pointing to the superior rank of his nephew, Herod Agrippa, whom Caligula had been pleased to raise to a provincial throne. Urged by his wife to solicit a similar elevation, he presented himself at Rome, and obtained an audience of the emperor; but the successor of Tiberius was so little pleased with his conduct on this occasion, that he divested him of the tetrarchy, and banished him into Gaul.

The death of Herod Philip, and the degradation of the Galilean tetrarch, paved the way for the advancement of Agrippa to all the honour and power which had belonged to the family of David. He was permitted to reign over the whole of Palestine, having under his direction the usual number of Roman troops, which experience had proved to be necessary for the peace of a province at once so remote and so turbulent. The only event that disturbed the tranquillity of his government, was an insane resolution expressed by Caligula to place his own statue in the temple of Jerusalem, as an object of respect, if not of positive and direct worship, to the whole Jewish nation. The prudence of the Syrian prefect, and the influence which Agrippa still possessed over the mind of his imperial friend, prevented the horrors that must have arisen from an attempt to desecrate, in this odious manner, a sanctuary deemed most holy by every child of Abraham.

But no position could be more difficult to hold with safety and reputation than that which was occupied by this Hebrew prince. He was assailed on the one hand by the jealousy of the Roman deputies, and on the other by the suspicion of his own countrymen, who could never divest themselves of the fear that his foreign education had rendered him indifferent to the rites of the Mosaical law. To satisfy the latter, he spared no expense in conferring magnificence on the daily service of the temple, while he put forth his hand to persecute the Christian church, in the persons of St Peter and James the brother of John. To remove every ground of disloyalty from the eyes of the political agents who were appointed by Claudius to watch his conduct, he ordered a splendid festival at Cesarea in honour of the new emperor; on which occasion, when arrayed in the most gorgeous attire, certain words of adulation reached his ear, not fit to be addressed to a Jewish monarch. The result will be best described in the words of Sacred Scripture :—" And upon a set day Herod, arrayed in royal apparel, sat upon his throne, and made an oration unto them. And the people gave a shout, saying, It is the voice of a god, and not of a man. And immediately the angel of the Lord smote him, because he gave not God the glory ; and he was eaten of worms, and gave up the ghost."[*] He left a son and three daughters, of whom Agrippa, Bernice, and Drusilla, make a conspicuous figure towards the close of the book of Acts. These events took place between the fortieth and the forty-fifth year of the Christian Faith.

The youth and inexperience of the prince dictated to the Roman government the propriety of assuming once more the entire direction of Jewish affairs. The pre-

---

[*] Acts, xii. 21-23.

fecture of Syria was confided to Cassius Longinus, under whom served, as procurator of Judea, Caspius Fadus, a stern though upright soldier. But the impatience and hatred of the people were now inflamed to such a degree, that gentleness and severity were equally unavailing to preserve the tranquillity of the country. Impostors appeared on every hand, proclaiming deliverance to the oppressed children of Jacob, and provoking the more impetuous among their brethren to take up arms against the Romans. Various conflicts ensued, in which the discipline of the legions hardly ever failed to disperse or destroy the tumultuary bands who, under such unhappy auspices, attempted to restore the kingdom to Israel. The holy city, which was from time to time beleaguered by both parties, sustained material injury from the furious assaults of pagan and Jew alternately. The predictions of its downfal, already circulated among the Christians, began to mingle with the shouts of its fanatical inhabitants; and already, even at the accession of Agrippa the Second to his limited sovereignty, every thing portended that miserable consummation which at no distant period closed the temporal scene of Hebrew hope and dominion.

Every succeeding day witnessed the progress of that ferocious sect, founded on the opinions of Judas the Gaulonite, who acknowledged no sovereign but Jehovah, and who constantly denounced as the greatest of all sins those payments or services by means of which a heathenish government was supported. In prosecuting their revolutionary schemes, they esteemed no man's life dear, and set as little value upon their own. Devoted to the principles of a frantic patriotism, they were content to sacrifice to its claims the clearest dictates of humanity and religion; being at all times ready to bind themselves by an oath that they would neither eat nor drink until they had slain the enemy of their nation or of their God. This was the school which supplied that execrable faction, who added tenfold to the miseries of Jerusalem in the day of her visitation; and who contributed more than all the legions of Rome to realize the bitterness of the curse which was poured upon her devoted head.

A succession of unprincipled governors, who were sent forth to enrich themselves on the spoils of the Syrian provinces, accelerated the crisis of Judea. About the middle of the first century, the notorious Felix was appointed to the government, who, in the administration of affairs, habitually combined violence with fraud, sending out his soldiers to inflict punishment on such as had not the means or the inclination to bribe his clemency. An equal stranger to righteousness and temperance, he presented a fine subject for the eloquence of St Paul; who, it is presumed, however, made the profligate governor tremble, without either affecting his religious principles or improving his moral conduct.

The short residence of Festus procured for the unhappy Jews a respite from oppression. He laboured successfully to put down the bands of insurgents, whose ravages were inflicted indiscriminately upon foreigners and their own countrymen; nor was he less active in checking the excesses of the military, so long accustomed to rapine and free quarter. Agrippa at the same time transferred the seat of his government to Jerusalem, where his presence served to moderate the rage of parties, and thereby to postpone the final rupture between the provincials and their imperial master. But this brief interval of repose was followed by an increased degree of irritation and fury. Florus, alike distinguished for his avarice and cruelty, and who saw in the contentions of the people the readiest means of filling his own coffers, connived at the mutual hostility which it was his duty to prevent. In this nefarious policy he received the countenance of Cestius Gallus the prefect of Syria, who, imitating the maxims of his lieutenant, studiously drove the natives to insurrection, in order that their cries for justice might be drowned amid the clash of arms.

But he forgot that there are limits to endurance even among the most humble and abject. Unable to support the weight of his tyranny, and galled by certain insults directed against their faith, the Jewish inhabitants of Cesarea set his power at defiance, and declared their resolution to repel his injuries by force. The capital was soon actuated by a similar spirit, and made preparations for defence. Cestius marched to the gates and demanded an entrance for the imperial cohorts, whose aid was required to support the garrison within. The citizens, having refused to comply, already anticipated the horrors of a siege; when, after a few days they saw, to their great surprise, the Syrian prefect in full retreat, carrying with him his formidable army. Sallying from the different outlets with arms in their hands, they pursued the fugitives with the usual fury of an incensed multitude; and, overtaking their enemy at the narrow pass of Bethhoron, they avenged the cause of independence by a considerable slaughter of the legionary soldiers, and by driving the remainder to an ignominious flight.

Nero received the intelligence of this defeat while amusing himself in Greece, and immediately sent Vespasian to assume the government, with instructions to restore the tranquillity of the province by moderate concessions or by the most vigorous warfare. It was in the sixty-seventh year of Christianity that this great commander entered Judea, accompanied by his son, the celebrated Titus. The result is too well known to require details. A series of sanguinary battles deprived the Jews of their principal towns one after another, until they were at length shut up in the capital; the siege and final reduction of which compose one of the most affecting stories that are any where recorded in the annals of the human race.

## CHAPTER IV.

*Literature and Religious Usages of the Ancient Hebrews.*

Obscurity of the Subject—Learning issued from the Levitical Colleges—Schools of the Prophets—Music and Poetry—Meaning of the Term Prophesy—Illustrated by References to the Old Testament and to the New—The Power of Prediction not confined to those bred in the Schools—Race of False Prophets—Their Malignity and Deceit—Micaiah and Ahab—Charge against Jeremiah the Prophet—Criterion to distinguish True from False Prophets—The Canonical Writings of the Prophets—Literature of Prophets—Sublime Nature of their Compositions—Examples from Psalms and Prophetical Writings—Humane and liberal Spirit—Care used to keep alive the Knowledge of the Law—Evils arising from the Division of Israel and Judah—Ezra collects the Ancient Books—Schools of Prophets similar to Convents—Sciences—Astronomy—Division of Time, Days, Months, and Years—Sabbaths and New Moons—Jewish Festivals—Passover—Pentecost—Feast of Tabernacles—Of Trumpets—Jubilee—Daughters of Zelophedad—Feast of Dedication—Minor Anniversaries—Solemn Character of Hebrew Learning—Its easy Adaptation to Christianity—Superior to the Literature of all other Ancient Nations.

THERE is no subject on which greater obscurity prevails than that of the learning and schools of the Hebrews, prior to the Babylonian captivity. The wise institution which provided for the maintenance of Levitical towns in all the tribes, secured at least a hereditary knowledge of the Law, including both its civil and its spiritual enactments. It is extremely probable, therefore, that all the varieties of literary attainment which might be deemed necessary, either for the discharge of professional duties or for the ornament of private life, were derived from those seminaries, and partook largely of their general character and spirit. An examination of the scanty remains of that remote period will justify, to a considerable extent, the conjecture now made. It will appear that the poetry, the ethics, the oratory, the music, and even the physical science, cultivated in the time of Samuel and David, bore a close relation to the original object of the Levitical colleges; being adapted to promote the principles of religion and morality, no less than of that singular patriotism which made the Jew delight in his separation from all the other nations of the earth.

Our attention is first attracted by the numerous allusions, scattered over the earlier books of the Old Testament, to the Schools of the Prophets. These were establishments, obviously intended to prepare young men for certain offices analogous to those which are discharged in our days by the different orders of the clergy; maintained in some degree at the public expense; and placed under the superintendence of persons distinguished for their gravity and high endowments. The principal studies appear to have been poetry and music, the elements of which were necessary to the young prophet when called to take a part in the worship of Jehovah. In the book of Samuel we find the pupils of one of those seminaries performing on psalteries, tabrets, and harps; and in the first book of Chronicles it is said that the sons of Asaph, of Heman, and of Jeduthun, prophesied with harps, with psalteries, and with cymbals. For the same reason Miriam the sister of Moses is called a prophetess. When preparing to chant her song of triumph, upon the destruction of the Egyptians at the Red Sea, " she took a timbrel in her hand, and all the women went out after her with timbrels and with dances."

On a similar ground is the expression to be interpreted when used by St Paul in the eleventh chapter of his First Epistle to the Corinthians: " Every woman praying or prophesying with her head uncovered, dishonoureth her head;" that is, every female who takes a part in the devotions of the Christian Church,—the supplications and the praises,—ought, according to the practice of eastern nations, to have her face concealed in a veil, as becoming the modesty of her sex in a mixed congregation. The term prophesy, in this instance, must be restricted to the use of psalmody, because exposition or exhortation in public was not permitted to women, who were not allowed to speak or even to ask a question in a place of worship. Nay, the same apostle applies the title of prophet to those persons among the heathen who composed or uttered songs in praise of their gods. In his Epistle to Titus, for example, he alludes to the people of Crete in these words, " one of themselves, even a prophet of their own, has said, the Cretans were always liars;" and every classical scholar is aware that, in the language of pagan antiquity, a poet and a prophet were synonymous terms.

But the function of the latter was not confined to the duty of praise and thanksgiving; it also implied the ability to expound and enforce the principles of the Mosaical Law. He was entitled to exhort and entreat; and we accordingly find that the greater portion of the prophetical writings consist of remonstrances, rebukes, threatenings, and expostulations. In order to be a prophet, in the Hebrew sense of the expression, it was not necessary to be endowed with the power of foreseeing future events. It is true that the holy men, through whom the Almighty thought meet to reveal his intentions relative to the church, were usually selected from the order of persons now described. But there were several exceptions, among whom stand pre-eminent the eloquent Daniel and the pathetic Amos. To prophesy, therefore, in the later times of the Jewish commonwealth, usually meant the explication and enforcement of Divine truth, —an import of the word which was very naturally extended into the era of the New Testament, when the more ancient and recondite sense of the phrase had been almost entirely laid aside.

In truth, it should seem that even before the days of Samuel the opinions, or rather perhaps the popular notions, connected with the name and offices of a prophet, had undergone some change, and began to point to higher objects. Saul, when employed in seeking his father's asses, had journeyed so far from home that he despaired of finding his way back; and when he was come to the land of Zuph he said to his servant, " Come, and let us return; lest my father leave caring for the asses, and take thought for us. And he said unto him, Behold now, there is in this city a man of God, and he is an honourable man; all that he saith cometh surely to pass: now let us go thither; peradventure he can show us our way that we should go. Then said Saul to his servant, But, behold, if we go, what shall we bring the man, for the bread is spent in our vessels, and there is not a present to bring to the man of God: what have we? And the servant answered Saul again, and said, Behold, I have here at hand the fourth part of a shekel of silver; that will I give to the man of God to tell us our way. (Beforetime in Israel, when a man went to inquire of God, thus he spake, Come, and let us go to the Seer: for he that is now called a Prophet, was beforetime called a Seer.) Then said Saul to his servant, Well said; come, let us go. So they went unto the city where the man of God was."*

The description of soothsayer whom Saul and his servant had resolved to consult, is very common in all lands at a certain stage of knowledge and civilisation,—a personage who, without much reliance on divine aid, could amuse the curiosity of a rustic, and perplex his ignorance with an ambiguous answer. But the age of Samuel required more solid qualifications in the prophets, and the term seer, accordingly, had already given way to that of expounder, or master of eloquence and wisdom. The expedient suggested by the attendant of the son of Kish was very natural, and quite consistent with his rank and

---

* 1 Samuel, ix. 5-11.

habits; while the easy acquiescence which he obtained from his master denotes the simplicity of ancient times, not less than the untutored state of mind in which the future king of Israel had left his father's dwelling. Before he mounted the throne, however, he was sent to acquire the elements of learning among the sons of the prophets; whom, in a short time, he accompanied in their pious exercises in a manner so elevated as to astonish every one who had formerly known the young Benjamite,— till then, it should seem, remarkable only for a mild disposition and great bodily strength.

The bias towards prediction, which is almost unavoidably acquired by the practice of elucidation and commentary on a dark text, soon showed itself in the Schools of the Prophets. Many of them, trusting to their own ingenuity rather than to the suggestion of the Spirit of truth, ventured to foretell the issue of events, and to delineate the future fortunes of nations, as well as of individuals. Hence the race of "false prophets" who brought so much obloquy upon the whole order, and not unfrequently barred against the approach of godly admonition the ears of those who were actually addressed by an inspired messenger. Nay, it appears that some of them arrogated the power of realizing the good or the evil they were pleased to prognosticate; allowing the people to believe that they were possessed with demons, which enabled them not only to foresee but to influence in no small measure the course of Providence. The impression on the mind of Ahab, with respect to Micaiah, leaves no room for doubt that the king imagined the prophet to be actuated by a malignant feeling towards him. "I hate him," he exclaimed, "for he doth not prophesy good concerning me, but evil." Nor was the conviction, that this ungracious soothsayer spoke from his own wishes rather than from a divine impulse, confined to the Israelitish monarch. The messenger who was sent to call Micaiah spake unto him, saying, "Behold now, the words of the prophets declare good unto the king with one mouth: let thy word, I pray thee, be like the word of one of them, and speak that which is good."*

When we consider the uncertainty which must have attended all predictions, where the wishes or feelings of the prophet could give a varied expression to the purposes of God, we cannot any longer be surprised at the neglect with which such announcements were frequently treated by those to whom they were directed. It is remarkable, too, that one prophet did not possess the gift of ascertaining the truth or sincerity of another who might declare that he spoke in the name of God; and hence there were no means of determining the good faith of this order of men, except the general evidence of a pious character, or the test of a successful experience. For example, the man of God who was sent to denounce the curse upon the altar at Bethel, could not penetrate the motives of the " old prophet," an inhabitant of that city, who, pretending the authority of an angel, induced him to violate all the injunctions which had been imposed upon him by the word of Jehovah. Again, when Jeremiah proclaimed the approaching fall of Jerusalem, the other prophets were among the first to oppose him, saying, " Thou shalt surely die: why hast thou prophesied in the name of the Lord that this house shall be like Shiloh, and this city shall be desolate without an inhabitant?" The Princes of Judah assembled in the Temple to hear the charge repeated against this fearless minister; when again " spake the priests and the prophets unto the princes, and to all the people, saying, This man is worthy to die; for he hath prophesied against this city, as ye have heard with your ears."

It is worthy of notice, too, that the prediction which gave so much offence was strictly conditional, and that Jeremiah thereby exposed himself to the hazard of suffering the severe punishment due to a false prophet; because if the people had turned from their sins, the fate of their capital and nation would have been protracted. " The

---

* 1 Kings, xxii. 8, 13.

Lord sent me to prophesy against this house, and against this city, all the words that ye have heard. Therefore now mend your ways and your doings, and obey the voice of the Lord your God; and the Lord will repent him of the evil that he hath pronounced against you. As for me, behold, I am in your hand; do with me as seemeth good and meet unto you: but know ye for certain, that, if ye put me to death, ye shall surely bring innocent blood upon yourselves, and upon this city, and upon the inhabitants thereof: for of a truth the Lord hath sent me unto you, to speak all these words in your ears."*

The decision of the princes was more equitable than the accusation adduced by the priests and prophets; for according to the law of Moses no man could be punished for predicting the most calamitous events, provided he persevered in the assertion that he spoke in the name of Jehovah. The Divine legislator only denounced the penalty of death against such prophets as should speak in the name of any false god, or who should speak in the name of Jehovah that which they were not commanded to speak; but, with regard to the latter offence, the guilt could only be substantiated by the failure of the prophecy. " And if thou say in thine heart, How shall we know the word which the Lord hath not spoken? When a prophet speaketh in the name of the Lord, if the thing follow not, nor come to pass, that is the thing which the Lord hath not spoken, but the prophet hath spoken it presumptuously."†

But it is obvious that, in all cases where a condition was implied, the fulfilment of the prediction could not be regarded as essential to the establishment of the prophetic character. The capture of Jerusalem produced the most undeniable testimony to the inspiration of Jeremiah, as well as to the sincerity of his expostulation; yet it is well known that his motives did not escape suspicion, and that his memory was loaded by

---

\* Jeremiah, xxvi. 8-16. † Deut. xviii. 21, 22.

many of his countrymen with the charge of having, by his discouraging addresses and evil auguries, promoted the views of the Chaldeans.

It may not appear out of place to inform the young reader that the prophets, whose writings are contained in the Old Testament, are in number sixteen, and usually divided into two classes, the greater and the minor, according to the extent of their works and the importance of their subject. Of the former, Isaiah, who may be regarded as the chief, began to prophesy under Uzziah, and continued till the first year of Manasseh. Jeremiah flourished a short time before the great captivity, and lived to witness the fulfilment of his own predictions. Ezekiel, who had been carried into the Babylonian territory some time prior to the ruin of his native country in the days of Zedekiah, began to perform his office among the Jewish captives in the fifth year after Jehoiakim was made prisoner. Daniel, the youngest of the four, was only twelve years of age when he was involved in the miseries of conquest, and reduced to the condition of a dependant at a foreign court.

Among the twelve minor prophets, Jonas, Hosea, Amos, and Micah, preceded the destruction of the kingdom of Israel. Nahum and Joel appeared between that catastrophe and the captivity of Judah. Habakkuk, Obadiah, and Zephaniah, lived at the time when Jerusalem was taken, and during part of the captivity. Haggai, Zecharias, and Malachi, the last of this sacred order prophesied after the return from Babylon.

But our business is rather with the literature of the prophets at large than with the special functions of the few individuals of their body who were commissioned by Heaven to reveal the secrets of future time. Of the fruits of their professional study we have fine examples preserved in the Psalms of David and the Proverbs of Solomon; the former, a collection of sacred lyrics composed for the worship of Jehovah; the latter, a compend of practical truth, suggested by Divine wisdom, and expressed in language equally striking for its vigour and its rare simplicity.

In early times the dictates of moral philosophy were enounced in short sentences, the result of much thought, and of which the effect was usually heightened by the introduction of a judicious antithesis both in the sentiment and the expression. The apothegms ascribed to the wise men of Greece belong to this kind of composition; being extremely valuable to a rude people, who can profit by the fruits of reasoning without being able to attend to its forms, and deposite in their minds a useful precept, unencumbered with the arguments by means of which its soundness might be proved. The books which bear the name of Solomon are distinguished above all others for the sage views they exhibit of human life, and for the sensible maxims addressed to all conditions of men who have to encounter its manifold perils,— proving a guide unto the feet and a lamp unto the path.

In no respect do the Hebrews appear to greater advantage than when viewed in the light of their sublime compositions. Nor ought this remark to be confined simply to the style or mechanism of their writings,— which is nevertheless allowed by the best judges to possess many merits,—but should be extended more especially to the exalted nature of their subjects, the works, the attributes, and the purposes of Jehovah. The poets of pagan antiquity, on the other hand, excite, by their descriptions of divine things, our ridicule or disgust; and even the most approved of their order suggest the grossest ideas in connexion with the principles and enjoyments which were supposed to prevail among the inhabitants of Olympus. But the contemporaries of David, inferior in many things to the ingenious people who listened to the strains of Homer and of Virgil, are remarkable for their elevated conceptions of the Supreme Being, as the Creator and Governor of the world, not less than for the suitable terms in which they give utterance to their exalted thoughts.

In no other country but Judea, at that early period,

were such sentiments as the following either expressed or felt. " O Jehovah, our Lord, how excellent is thy name in all the earth, thou that hast set thy glory above the heavens! When I consider thy heavens, the work of thy fingers, the moon and the stars which thou hast ordained ; what is man, that thou art mindful of him, or the son of man, that thou visitest him ! Bless Jehovah, O my soul. O Lord my God, thou art very great, and art clothed with honour and majesty! Thou coverest thyself with light as with a garment, and stretchest out the heavens like a curtain."—" Who layeth the beams of his chambers in the waters, who maketh the clouds his chariot, and walketh upon the wings of the wind."— " Bless Jehovah, O my soul, and all that is within me bless his holy name. Bless Jehovah, O my soul, and forget not all his benefits ; who forgiveth all thine iniquities ; who healeth all thy diseases ; who redeemeth thy life from destruction ; who crowneth thee with loving-kindness and tender mercies. Jehovah is merciful and gracious, slow to anger, and plenteous in mercy. He hath not dealt with us after our sins, neither rewarded us according to our iniquities. For as the heaven is high above the earth, so great is his mercy toward them that fear him. For he knoweth our frame ; he remembereth that we are dust."—" O Lord thou hast searched me and known me : thou knowest my down-sitting and mine uprising; thou understandest my thoughts long before. Thou art about my bed and about my path, and art acquainted with all my ways. Whither shall I go from thy Spirit, or whither shall I flee from thy presence? If I ascend up into heaven, thou art there ; if I go down to the dwelling of the departed, thou art there also. If I take the wings of the morning and abide in the uttermost parts of the sea, even there shall thy hand lead me, and thy right hand shall hold me. If I say, surely the darkness shall cover me, even the night shall be turned into day. Yea the darkness is no darkness with thee, but the night shineth as the day : the darkness and the light are both alike to thee."

A similar train of lofty conception pervades the writings of the prophets. " Who hath measured the waters in the hollow of his hand, and meted out the heavens with a span, and comprehended the dust of the earth in a measure, and weighed the mountains in scales, and the hills in a balance ? Behold, the nations are as a drop of a bucket, and are counted as the small dust of the balance ; he taketh up the isles as a very little thing. It is he that sitteth upon the circle of the earth, and the inhabitants thereof are as grashoppers. Lift up your eyes on high, and behold who hath created these things, who bringeth out their host by number : he calleth them all by names, by the greatness of his might, for that he is strong in power ; not one faileth. Hast thou not known, hast thou not heard, that the everlasting God, the Lord, the Creator of the ends of the earth, fainteth not, neither is weary ? There is no searching of his understanding."

The following quotation from the same inspired author is very striking, inasmuch as the truth contained in it is founded upon an enlarged view of the Divine government, and directly pointed against that insidious manicheism which, originating in the East, has gradually infected the religious opinions of a large portion of mankind. Light was imagined to proceed from one source, and darkness from another ; all good was traced to one Being, and all evil was ascribed to a hostile and antagonist Principle ; spirit, pure and happy, arose from the former, while matter, with its foul propensities and jarring elements, took its rise from the latter. But Isaiah, guided by an impulse which coincides with the inferences of the profoundest philosophy, thus speaks concerning the God of Israel :—" I am the Lord, and there is none else ; there is no God besides me. I form the light and create darkness ; I make peace and create evil ; I the Lord do all these things."

Nor is it only in such sublimity of language and exalted imagery that the literature of the Hebrews surpasses the writings of the most learned and ingenious portion of the heathen world. A distinction not less remarkable is to be found in the humane and compassionate spirit which animates even the earliest parts of the Sacred Volume, composed at a time when the manners of all nations were still unrefined, and the softer emotions were not held in honour. "Blessed is he who considereth the poor and needy; the Lord will deliver him in the time of trouble. The Lord will preserve him and keep him alive; he shall be blessed upon earth, and thou wilt not deliver him into the will of his enemies. The Lord will strengthen him upon the bed of languishing; thou wilt make all his bed in his sickness."

We shall in vain seek for instances of such a benign and liberal feeling in the works of the most enlightened of pagan writers, whether poets or orators. How beautifully does the following observation made by Solomon contrast with the contempt expressed by Horace for the great body of his countrymen! "He that despiseth his neighbour sinneth; but he that hath mercy on the poor, happy is he. He that oppresseth the poor reproacheth his Maker."

Among the Israelites there was no distinction as to literary privilege or philosophical sectarianism. There was no profane vulgar among the Chosen People; the stores of Divine knowledge were open to all alike. The descendant of Jacob beheld in every member of his tribe a brother and not a master; one who, in all the respects which give to man dignity and self-esteem, was his equal in the strictest sense of the term. In perfect harmony with this was the noble flame of patriotism which glowed in all their institutions before the people became corrupted by idolatry and a too frequent intercourse with the surrounding tribes; and the still more noble spirit of fraternal affection which breathed in their Law, their Devotional writers, and their Prophets.

In order to prevent any part of the sacred oracles from becoming obsolete or falling into oblivion, the inspired lawgiver left an injunction to read the books which bear his name in the hearing of all the people, at the end of every seven years at farthest. "And Moses wrote this law, and delivered it unto the priests, the sons of Levi which bare the ark of the covenant of the Lord, and unto all the elders of Israel. And Moses commanded them, saying, At the end of every seven years, in the solemnity of the year of release, in the feast of tabernacles, when all Israel is come to appear before the Lord thy God, in the place which he shall choose, thou shalt read this law before all Israel in their hearing. Gather the people together, men, and women, and children, and thy stranger that is within thy gates, that they may hear, and that they may learn, and fear the Lord your God, and observe to do all the words of this law ; and that their children, which have not known any thing, may hear and learn to fear the Lord your God, as long as ye live in the land whither ye go over Jordan to possess it."\*

The value of the Levitical institution, whence originated the schools of the prophets, will be the most highly appreciated by those readers who have noted the evils which arose from its suppression among the Ten Tribes, and, finally, in the kingdom of Judah itself. The separation of the Israelites under Jeroboam led, in the first instance, to a defection from the Mosaic ritual, and, in the end, to the establishment of a rival worship ; a revolution which compelled all the Levites, who remained attached to the primitive faith, to desert such of their cities as belonged to the revolted tribes, and to seek an asylum among their brethren who acknowledged the successor of Solomon. Hence the reign of idolatry, and that total neglect of the Law which disgraced the government of the new dynasty ; though, to the honour of the people, it ought to be mentioned that, with a view to perpetuate their relationship to the Father of the faithful, they preserved certain copies of the Pentateuch, even after the desolation of their land and the complete extinction of their political independence.

---

\* Deut. xxxi. 9-14.

It is more surprising to find that, even among the orthodox Hebrews at Jerusalem, the Law sank into a gradual oblivion; insomuch that, in the days of Jehoshaphat, the fifth from David, it was found necessary to appoint a special commission of Levites and priests, to revive the knowledge of its holy sanctions in all parts of the country. "And they taught in Judah, and had the book of the Law of the Lord with them, and went about throughout all the cities of Judah, and taught the people."*

At a later period, after the succession of several idolatrous princes, the neglect of the Mosaical writings became still more general, till at length the very manuscript, or book of the Law itself, which used to be read in the ears of the congregation, could nowhere be found. Josiah, celebrated for his piety and attention to the ceremonies of the national religion, gave orders to repair the Temple for the renewed worship of Jehovah; on which occasion, Hilkiah the high priest found the precious record in the house of the Lord, and sent it to the king.† A momentary zeal bound the people once more to the belief and usages of their ancestors; but the example of the profane or careless sovereigns who afterwards filled the throne plunged the country once more into guilt, obliterating all recollection of the Divine statutes, considered at least as a code of public law. The captivity throws a temporary cloud over the Hebrew annals, and prevents us from tracing beyond that point the progress of opinion on this interesting subject. But upon the return from Babylon a new era commences; and we now observe the same people, who in their prosperity were constantly deviating into the grossest superstitions and most contemptible idolatry, remarkable for a rigid adherence to the ritual of Moses, and for a severe intolerance towards all who questioned its heavenly origin or its universal obligation. Ezra is understood to have charged himself with the duty of col-

---

* 2 Chronicles, xvii. 9.  † 2 Kings, xxii. 8.

lecting and arranging the manuscripts which had survived the desolation inflicted upon his country by the arms of Assyria; at the same time substituting, for the more ancient characters usually known as the Samaritan, the Chaldean alphabet, to which his followers had now become accustomed. From these notices, however, which respect a later period, we return to the more primitive times immediately succeeding the era of the Commonwealth.

I have ascribed the cultivation of sacred knowledge to the schools of the prophets, without having been able to trace very distinctly the institution of these seminaries to the Levitical colleges, the proper fountains of the national literature. It would appear that, in the days of Samuel, the necessity of certain subordinate establishments was admitted, in order to supply a class of teachers qualified to instruct such of the people as lived at a distance from the cities of the Levites. The rule of the prophetical schools seems to have borne some resemblance to that of the better description of Christian convents in the primitive ages; enjoining abstinence and labour, together with an implicit obedience to the authority of their superiors. The clothing also, it may be presumed, was humble, and even somewhat particular. A rough garment fastened with a girdle round the loins is alluded to by Zechariah; while the impression made on the courtiers at Ramoth-gilead, by the appearance of one of the sons of the prophets sent thither by Elisha, would lead us to the same conclusion. "Wherefore," said they, "came this mad fellow to thee?" Nor is it without reason that some authors have attributed the conduct of the children who mocked Elisha himself to the uncouthness of his dress, and to the want of a covering for his head. Be this as it may, there is no doubt that from these societies sprang the most distinguished men who adorned the happiest era of the Jewish church.

Were we allowed to form a judgment from the few incidents recorded in the books of the Kings, we should conclude that the accomplishment of writing was not very general among the subjects of David and Solomon. It is ingeniously conjectured by Michaelis, that Joab the captain of the host, and sister's son of the inspired monarch himself, could not handle the pen; else he would not, for the purpose of concealing from the bearer the real object for which he was sent, have found it necessary to tax his ingenuity by putting the very suspicious detail of Uriah's death into the mouth of a messenger to be delivered verbally to the king. He would at once have written to him that the devoted man was killed.*

As to science in its higher branches, we cannot expect any proofs of eminence among a secluded people, devoted as the Hebrews were to the pursuits of agriculture and the feeding of cattle. Solomon, indeed, is said to have been acquainted with all the productions of nature, from the cedar of Libanus to the hyssop on the wall; and we may readily believe that the curiosity which marked his character would find some gratification in the researches of natural history,—the first study of the opening mind in the earliest stage of social life. But astronomy had not advanced farther than to present an interesting subject of contemplation to the thoughtful spirit of piety, which, however, could only regard the firmament as a smooth surface spread out like a curtain, or bearing some resemblance to the canopy of a spacious tent. The schools of the prophets, we may presume, were still strangers to those profound calculations which determine the distance, the magnitude, and the periodical revolutions of the heavenly bodies. Even the sages of Chaldea, who boast a more ancient civilisation than is claimed by the Jews, satisfied themselves with a few facts which they had not learned to generalize, and sometimes with conjectures which had hardly any relation to a fixed principle or a scientific object. Long after the reign of David, these wise men had not distinguished the study of the stars from the dreams of astrology.

---

* 2 Samuel, xi. 18, 22. Commentaries on Laws of Moses, vol. i. p. 257.

The first application of astronomical science is to the division of time, as marked out by the periodical movements of the heavenly bodies. The Israelites combined in their calculations a reference both to the sun and to the moon, so as to avail themselves of the natural measure supplied by each. Their year accordingly was lunisolar, consisting of twelve lunar months, with an intercalation to make the whole agree with the annual course of the sun. It was farther distinguished as being either common or ecclesiastical; the former beginning at the autumnal equinox, the season at which, as they imagined, the world was created; while the latter, by Divine appointment, commenced about six months earlier, the period when their fathers were delivered from the thraldom of Egypt. Their months always began with the new moon; and before the captivity they were merely named according to their order, the first, second, third, and so on, down to the twelfth. But upon their return they used the terms which they found employed in Babylon, according to the following series:—

| | |
|---|---|
| Nisan,* | March |
| Zif, or Ijar, | April |
| Sivan, | May |
| Tamuz, | June |
| Ab, | July |
| Elul, | August |
| Ethanim, or Tisri, | September |
| Bul, or Mareshuan, | October |
| Chisleu, | November |
| Tebeth, | December |
| Sebat, | January |
| Adar, | February |

One-half of these months consisted of thirty days, the other of twenty-nine, alternately, making in all three hundred and fifty-four. To supply the eleven days and six hours which were deficient, they introduced every second year an additional month of twenty-two days,

---

* Nisan was sometimes called Abib, as descriptive of the state of vegetation in that month,—the earing of the corn and the blooming of the fruit-trees.

and every fourth year one of twenty-three days; by which means they approached as nearly to the true measure as any other nation had attained till the establishment of the Gregorian calendar.

The space from sunrise to sunset was divided into twelve equal parts; and hence the hours of their day varied in length according to the season of the year. For example, when the sun rose at five and set at seven, an hour contained seventy minutes; but when it rose at seven and set at five, the hour was reduced to fifty minutes, and so on in proportion to the duration of the time that the sun was above the horizon. A similar rule applied to the night, which was likewise divided into twelve equal portions.

It must not be forgotten, however, that the observations now made apply rather to the acquirements of the Jews after their return from the East, than to the more simple condition in which they appear under their Judges and Prophets.

Next to the learning of this early period, the reader of the sacred history will have his curiosity excited with regard to the time, the place, and the manner of religious worship. When the Israelites had obtained possession of the Holy Land, and distributed the territory among their tribes, the tabernacle, or ambulatory temple, was placed at Shiloh, a town in the possession of Ephraim. To that sacred retreat they were wont to travel at the three great festivals, to accomplish the service enjoined by their law.

But it appears that a more ordinary kind of religious duty was performed at certain stations within the several tribes, in the intervals between the regular feasts appointed for the whole nation; having some reference, it is probable, to the periodical return of the Sabbath and new moons. For this purpose the people seem to have repaired to elevated grounds, where they might more readily perceive the lunar crescent, and give utterance to their customary expression of gratitude and joy. This species of adoration was connived at rather than authorized by the priests and Levites, who found it impossible to check altogether the propensity of the multitude to perform their worship on the high hill and under the green tree. Samuel, the prophet and judge, saw the expediency on one occasion of building an altar unto Jehovah on Ramah, which is called the High Place ; and in the reign of Solomon the same practice was continued, " because there was no house built unto the name of the Lord until those days."*

It is difficult to determine with precision at what epoch the Hebrews first formed those meetings or congregations which are called synagogues,—a name afterwards more frequently applied to the buildings in which they convened. The earliest allusion to them is found in the seventy-fourth psalm, where the writer, describing the havoc committed by the Assyrians, remarks, " they have burnt up all the synagogues of God in the land." We might infer, from this statement alone, that such edifices were common before the Babylonian captivity ; but we are supplied with a more direct proof in the words of St James, who informs us, that " Moses of old time hath in every city them that preach him, being read in the synagogues every Sabbath-day."†

The duty in these places, which was restricted to prayer and exposition, was performed by that section of the Levites who are usually denominated Scribes ; the higher office of sacrifice, the scene of which was first the Tabernacle and afterwards the Temple, being confined to the priests, the sons of Aaron. Perhaps in remote places, where the population was small, the inhabitants met in the house of the Levite,—a conjecture which derives some plausibility from an affecting incident mentioned in the second book of the Kings. When the son of the woman of Shunem died, " she called unto her husband and said, Send me, I pray thee, one of the young men, and one of the asses, that I may run to the man of God. And he said, Wherefore wilt thou go ; it is neither new

---

* 1 Kings, iii. 2. † Acts, xv. 21.

moon nor Sabbath." It is reasonable to conclude, that on such days it was customary to repair to the dwelling of the holy man for religious purposes.

It has been already stated, that soon after the settlement of the Israelites in the Promised Land, the tabernacle was established at Shiloh, a village in Ephraim, at that time the most numerous and powerful of all the tribes. The profanity or disobedience of the people in that district led to the removal of the Divine Presence, the symbols of which were commanded to be deposited in Jerusalem. "Go ye," says the prophet Jeremiah, "unto my place which was in Shiloh, where I set my name at the first; and see what I did to it for the wickedness of my people Israel." Hence the origin of the feud which subsisted so long between Ephraim and Judah, and afterwards between the Jews and Samaritans, with regard to the spot where Jehovah ought to be worshipped. Each laid claim to a Divine appointment; neither would yield to the other or hold the slightest intercourse in their adoration of the same great Being; and the question remained as far as ever from being determined, when the Romans, by their victorious arms, finally cut down all distinction between Gerizim and Moriah.

Though our limits will not permit us to indulge in a minute account of the Jewish festivals; yet, as the three great institutions, at which all the males of the Hebrew nation were commanded to appear before Jehovah, are frequently mentioned in the history of the Holy Land, it may be proper at least to specify their general objects. The Feast of the Passover, comprehending that of unleavened bread, commemorated, as is well known, the signal deliverance of this wonderful people from the tyranny of Pharaoh. It was appointed to be kept upon the fifteenth day of the first month, to last seven days, and to begin, as all their festivals began, in the evening or at the going down of the sun.

It is necessary to attend to the distinction just stated, respecting the beginning and end of their sacred days. The observance even of the ordinary Sabbath commenced on the evening of Friday, and terminated at the going down of the sun on Saturday. " From even unto even shall ye celebrate your Sabbaths." But the Jews, in the concluding period of their political existence, had innovated so far on the Mosaical institution as to prohibit the passover from being kept on Monday, Wednesday, or Friday, and to appoint the celebration of it on the following days. The year in which our Lord suffered death, this great annual feast fell on Friday—beginning, agreeably to the principle already stated, at sunset on Thursday evening—and the Redeemer accordingly, who came to fulfil all righteousness, ate the paschal supper with his disciples on the evening of Thursday. The Jews at large, as we find from the evangelical narrative, were not to observe that rite till the following evening; and hence, the early part of Friday being the preparation, they would not go into the judgment-hall " lest they should be defiled, but that they might eat the passover" after the going down of the sun. For the same reason they besought Pilate that the bodies might be removed; intimating that the day which was to begin at sunset was to them a high day, being in fact not only the Sabbath, but also the paschal feast,—both extremely solemn in the estimation of every true Israelite.

On the ground now stated is easily explained the apparent discrepancy between the account given by St John and that of the other Evangelists. They tell us that our Lord celebrated the passover on Thursday evening, the first day of the yearly festival; whereas the beloved disciple relates, that the next morning was still the " preparation" of that sacred ordinance which was to be observed by the whole nation the ensuing night. Both statements are perfectly correct: our Saviour adhered to the day fixed by the original institution, while the priests and lawyers followed the rule established by the Sanhedrim, which, as has been already noticed, threw the festival a day too late.

The proper Preparation, indeed, of every festival began only at three o'clock, called by the Hebrews the ninth hour, and continued till the close of the day, or the disappearance of the sun. It was at that hour, accordingly, that the Jews entreated the governor to take down the bodies from the cross; holding it extremely improper that any token of a curse, or capital punishment, should meet their eyes while making ready to eat the paschal lamb.

The Feast of Pentecost was an annual offering of gratitude to Jehovah for having blessed the land with increase. It took place fifty days after the passover, and hence the origin of its name in the Greek version of our Scriptures. Another appellation applied to it was—the Feast of Weeks—for the reason assigned by the inspired lawgiver. " Seven weeks shalt thou number unto thee ; beginning to number the seven weeks from such time as thou puttest the sickle to the corn. And thou shalt keep the feast of weeks unto the Lord thy God with a tribute of a free-will offering of thine hand, in the place which Jehovah shall choose to place his name there. And thou shalt remember that thou wast a bondman in Egypt."*

This was a very suitable observance in an agricultural society, where joy is always experienced upon gathering in the fruits of the earth. The Israelites were especially desired on that happy occasion to contrast their improved condition, as freemen reaping their own lands, with the miserable state from which they had been rescued by the good providence of Jehovah. The month of May witnessed the harvest-home of all Palestine in the days of Moses, as well as in the present times ; and no sooner was the pleasant toil of filling their barns completed, than all the males repaired to the holy city with the appointed tribute in their hands, and the song of praise in their mouths. Jewish antiquaries inform us, that there was combined with this eucharistical service a commemoration of the wonders which took place at Mount Sinai when the Lord condescended to pronounce his law in the ears of his people. The history of our own religion has

---

* Deut. xvi. 9-12.

supplied a greater event, which at once supersedes the pious recollections of the Hebrew, and touches the heart of the Christian worshipper with the feeling of a more enlightened gratitude.

The termination of the vintage was marked with a similar expression of thanksgiving, uttered by the assembled tribes in the place which had received the "Name of Jehovah;" that is, the visible manifestation of his presence and power. The precept for this observance is given in the following terms:—"On the fifteenth day of the seventh month, when ye have gathered in the fruit of the land, ye shall keep a feast unto the Lord seven days. And ye shall take unto you, on the first day, the boughs of goodly trees, branches of palm-trees, and the boughs of thick trees and willows of the brook; and ye shall rejoice before the Lord your God seven days. Ye shall dwell in booths seven days, that your generations may know that I made the children of Israel to dwell in booths when I brought them out of the land of Egypt."

This festival was of the most lively and animated description, celebrated with a joyous heart, and under the canopy of heaven in a most delightful season of the year. If more exquisite music and more graceful dances accompanied the gathering in of the grapes on the banks of the Cephisus, the tabret and the viol and the harp, which sounded around the walls of the sacred metropolis, were not wanting in sweetness and gayety; and, instead of the frantic riot of satyrs and bacchanals, the rejoicing was chastened by the solemn religious recollections with which it was associated, in a manner remarkably pleasing and picturesque.*

The Feast of Trumpets had a reference to the mode practised by many of the ancients for announcing the commencement of seasons and epochs. The beginning of every month was made known to the inhabitants of Jerusalem by the sound of musical instruments. "Blow up the trumpet in the new moon, in the time appointed,

---

* History of the Jews, vol. i. p. 115.

on our solemn feast-day : for this was a statute for Israel, a law of the God of Jacob." As the first day of the moon in September was the beginning of the civil year, the festivity was greater and more solemn than on other occasions. The voice of the trumpets waxed louder than usual, and the public mind was instructed by a grave assurance from the mouth of the proper officer that another year was added to the age of the world. " In the seventh month, in the first day of the month, shall ye have a Sabbath, a memorial of blowing of trumpets, an holy convocation. Ye shall do no servile work therein ; but ye shall offer an offering made by fire unto the Lord."\*

I have already alluded to the Jubilee, which occurred periodically after the lapse of forty-nine years. The benevolent uses of this most generous institution are known to every reader, more especially as they respected personal freedom and the restoration of lands and houses. Great care was taken by the Jewish legislator to prevent an accumulation of property in one individual, or even in one tribe. Nor was his anxiety less to prevent the alienation of land, either by sale, mortgage, or marriage. With this view we find him establishing a rule, suggested by the case of the daughters of Zelophedad—who had been allowed to become heirs to their father—of which the object was to perpetuate the possession of landed estates within the limits of each particular clan. The heads of the chief families of Manasseh, to which community the young women belonged, having come before Moses and the Princes of Israel, reminded these dignitaries of the fact just mentioned, and said, " If they be married to any of the sons of the other tribes, then shall their inheritance be taken from the inheritance of our fathers, and shall be put to the inheritance of the tribe whereunto they are received ; so shall it be taken from the lot of our inheritance. And when the jubilee of the children of Israel shall be, then shall their inheritance be put unto the inheritance of the tribe whereunto they

---

\* Levit. xxiii. 24, 25.

are received : so shall their inheritance be taken away from the inheritance of the tribe of our fathers."

To this judicious remonstrance Moses gave the following answer :—" This is the thing which the Lord doth command concerning the daughters of Zelophedad ; let them marry to whom they think best ; only to the family of the tribe of their father shall they marry. And every daughter that possesseth an inheritance shall be wife unto one of the family of the tribe of her father, that the children of Israel may enjoy every man the inheritance of his fathers. Neither shall the inheritance remove from one tribe to another tribe ; but every one of the tribes of the children of Israel shall keep himself to his own inheritance."*

Besides the anniversaries enjoined by Divine authority, the Hebrews observed several others which were meant to keep alive the remembrance of certain great events recorded in their history. Of these was the Feast of Dedication mentioned by St John, referring, it has been thought, to the purification of the altar by Judas Maccabæus, after it had been profaned by Antiochus, the king of Syria. When the ceremony was performed, " Judas and his brethren, with the whole congregation of Israel, ordained that the days of the dedication of the altar should be kept in their season, from year to year, by the space of eight days, from the five-and-twentieth day of the ninth month, with mirth and gladness."†

The restoration of the heavenly fire in the Temple, after the return from Babylon, was likewise commemorated every year. This sacred flame, which had been long extinct, was revived on the altar the day that Nehemiah performed sacrifice in the new building. For this reason the Jews of Palestine wrote to those in Egypt, recommending an annual festival in remembrance of an event so important to their national worship. They thought it necessary to certify them of the fact, that their brethren also might celebrate the " feast of the fire

---

\* Numbers, xxxvi. 1-10.  † St John, x. 22.

which was given us when Neemias offered sacrifice after that he had builded the Temple and the altar."*

It was likewise a custom among this singular people, that the young women " went yearly to lament the daughter of Jephthah, the Gileadite, four days in a year." A more joyous ceremony, on the fourteenth and fifteenth days of the month Adar, reminded the faithful Israelite of the triumph gained by his ancestors over the cruel and perfidious Haman, who had intended to extirpate their whole race. Besides these, we find in the book of Zecharias the prophet an allusion to the " fast of the fourth month, and the fast of the fifth, and the fast of the seventh, and the fast of the tenth ;" days of humiliation which probably recalled certain national calamities, such as, the destruction of their city and temple, and the era of their long captivity.

In concluding this chapter on the literature and religion of the ancient Hebrews, it may be remarked with regard to the system bequeathed to them by Moses, that it contains the only complete body of law which was ever given to a people at one time,—that it is the only entire body of law which has come down to our days,—that it is the only body of ancient law which still governs an existing people,—that, the nation to whom it was addressed being scattered over the face of the whole earth, it is the only body of law that is equally observed in the four quarters of the globe,—and, finally, that all the other codes of law of which history has preserved any recollection were given to communities who already possessed written statutes, but who wished to change their form or modify their application ; whereas, in this case, we behold a new society under the hands of a legislator who proceeds to lay its very foundations.†

It may be said of the Jews, that they had no profane literature, no works devoted to mere amusement or relaxation. As they admitted no image of any thing in

---

* 1 Maccab. iv. 36, &c. 2 Maccab. i. 18, 19.

† Croxall's Scripture Politics, pp. 60, 85. Histoire des Hébreux, par Rabelleau, tome i. p. 405. Esprit de l'Histoire, tome i. p. 28.

heaven or in earth, they consequently rejected the use of all those arts called imitative, and which supply so large a portion of the more refined enjoyment characteristic of civilized nations. In like manner, they seem to have viewed in the light of sacrilege every attempt to bring down the sublime language, in which they praised Jehovah and recorded his mighty works, to the more common and less hallowed purposes of fictitious narrative, or of amatory, dramatic, and lyrical composition. They have no epic poem to throw a lustre on the early annals of their literature. Even the Song of Songs is allowed to have a spiritual import, pointing to much higher themes than Solomon and his Egyptian bride. A solemn gravity pervades all their writings, befitting a people who were charged with the religious history of the world, and with the oracles of Divine truth. No smile appears to have ever brightened the countenance of a Jewish author,—no trifling thought to have passed through his mind,—no ludicrous association to have been formed in his fancy. In describing the flood of Deucalion, the Roman poet laughs at the grotesque misery which he himself exhibits, and purposely groups together objects with the intention of exciting in his readers the feeling of ridicule. But in no instance can we detect the faintest symptom of levity in the inspired penmen; their style, like their subject, is uniformly exalted, chaste, and severe; they wrote to men concerning the things of God, in a manner suitable to such a momentous communication; and they never ceased to remember that, in all their records, whether historical or prophetic, they were employed in propagating those glad tidings by which all the families of the earth were to be blessed.

There can be no stronger proof of the pure and sublime nature of Hebrew poetry than is supplied by the remarkable fact, that it has been introduced into the service of the Christian church, and found suitable for expressing those lofty sentiments with which the gospel inspires the heart of every true worshipper. No other nation of the ancient world has produced a single poem which could be used by an enlightened people in these days for the purposes of devotion.* Hesiod, although much esteemed for the moral tone of his compositions, presents, nevertheless, very few ideas capable of being accommodated to the theology of an improved age. In perusing the works of the greatest writers of paganism, we are struck with a monstrous incongruity in all their conceptions of the Supreme Being. The majesty with which the Israelites surrounded Jehovah is entirely wanting; the attributes belonging to the great Sovereign of the Universe are not appreciated; the providence of the Divine mind, united with benevolence, compassion, and mercy, is never found to enter into their descriptions of the Eternal First Cause; while their incessant deviations into polytheism outrage our religious feelings, and carry us back to the very rudest periods of human history.

In these respects the literature of the Jews is far

---

* The sentiment contained in the text is beautifully expressed in the following Ode by Lord Byron:—

1.

"The harp the monarch-minstrel swept,
　The King of men, the loved of Heaven,
Which Music hallow'd while she wept
　O'er tones her heart of hearts had given,
　Redoubled be her tears, its chords are riven!
It soften'd men of iron mould,
　It gave them virtues not their own;
No ear so dull, no soul so cold,
　That felt not, fired not to the tone,
　Till David's lyre grew mightier than his throne!

2.

"It told the triumphs of our King,
　It wafted glory to our God;
It made our gladden'd valleys ring,
　The cedars bow, the mountains nod;
　Its sound aspired to heaven and there abode!
Since then, though heard on earth no more,
　Devotion and her daughter Love
Still bid the bursting spirit soar
　To sounds that seem as from above,
　In dreams that day's broad light cannot remove."

exalted above that of every other nation of which history has preserved any traces. It must be acknowledged, that we remain ignorant of the learning and theological opinions cultivated among the Persians at the time when the progeny of Abraham were under their dominion, and cannot therefore determine the precise extent to which the dogmas of the captive tribes were affected by their intercourse with a race of men, who certainly taught the doctrine of the Divine Unity and abstained from idolatrous usages. But confining our judgment even to the oldest compositions of the Hebrews,—those, for example, which may be traced to the days of Moses, of Samuel, and of David,—we cannot hesitate to pronounce that they are distinguished by a remarkable peculiarity, indicating by the most unambiguous tokens, that, in all things pertaining to religious belief, the descendants of Jacob were placed under a special superintendence and direction.

## CHAPTER V.

*Description of Jerusalem.*

Pilgrimages to the Holy Land—Arculfus—Willibald—Bernard—Effect of Crusades—William de Bouldesell—Bertrandon de la Broquiere—State of Damascus—Breidenbach—Baumgarten—Bartholemeo Georgewitz—Aldersey—Sandys—Doubdan—Cheron—Thevenot—Gonzales—Morison—Maundrell—Pococke—Road from Jaffa to Jerusalem—Plain of Sharon—Rama or Ramla—Condition of the Peasantry—Vale of Jeremiah—Abou-Goosh—Jerusalem—Remark of Chateaubriand—Impressions of different Travellers—Dr Clarke—Tasso—Volney—Henniker—Mosque of Omar described—Mysterious Stone—Church of Holy Sepulchre—Ceremonies of Good Friday—Easter—The Sacred Fire—Grounds for Scepticism—Folly of the Priests—Emotion upon entering the Holy Tomb—Description of Chateaubriand—Holy Places in City—On Mount Sion—Pool of Siloam—Fountain of the Virgin—Valley of Jehoshaphat—Mount of Offence—The Tombs of Zechariah, of Jehoshaphat, and of Absalom—Jewish Architecture—Dr Clarke's Opinion on the Topography of Ancient Jerusalem—Opposed by other Writers—The Inexpediency of such Discussions.

HAVING described, as fully as the plan of this undertaking will admit, the constitution, history, learning, and religion of the ancient Hebrews, I now proceed to give an account of the present condition of the country which they inhabited nearly 1500 years, interrupted only by short intervals of captivity or oppression. The connexion which Christianity acknowledges with the people and soil of Judea, has, from the earliest times, given a deep interest to travels in the Holy Land. The curiosity natural to man with respect to things which have obtained celebrity, joined to the conviction, hardly less natural, that there is a certain merit in enduring privation and fatigue for the sake of religion, has in every age induced pilgrims to visit the scenes where our Divine Faith was originally established, and to communicate to their contemporaries the result of their investigations. It is to be regretted, indeed, that some of them from ignorance, and others from a feeling of the weakest bigotry, have omitted to notice those very objects which are esteemed the most interesting to the general reader; thinking it their duty, as one of them expresses it, to " quench all spirit of vain curiosity, lest they should return without any benefit to their souls."

About the year 705, Jerusalem and its holy places were visited by Arculfus, from whose report Adamnan composed a narrative, which was received with considerable approbation. He describes the Temple on Mount Calvary with some minuteness, mentioning its twelve pillars and eight gates. But his attention was more particularly attracted by relics, those objects which all Jerusalem flocked to handle and to kiss with the greatest reverence. He saw, or believed he saw, the cup used at the Last Supper,—the sponge on which the vinegar was poured,—the lance which pierced the side of our Lord,—the cloth in which he was wrapped,—also another cloth woven by the Virgin Mary, whereon were represented the figures of the Saviour and of the Twelve Apostles.

Eighty years later, Willibald, a Saxon, undertook the same journey, influenced by similar motives. From his infancy he had been distinguished by a sage and pious disposition; and, on emerging from boyhood, he was seized with an anxious desire to " try the unknown ways of peregrination—to pass over the huge wastes of ocean to the ends of the earth." To this erratic propensity he owed all the fame which a place in the Romish calendar and the authorship of an indifferent book can confer. In Jerusalem he saw all that Arculfus saw, and nothing more; but he had previously visited the Tomb of the Seven Sleepers, and the cave in which St John wrote the Apocalypse.

Bernard proceeded to Palestine in the year 878. He travelled first in Egypt, and from thence made his way across the Desert, the heat of which recalled vividly to his imagination the sloping hills of Campania when covered with snow. At Alexandria he was subjected to tribute by the avaricious governor, who paid no regard to the written orders of the sultan. The treatment which he received at Cairo was still more distressing. He was thrown into prison, and in this extremity he asked counsel of God, whereupon it was miraculously revealed to him that thirteen denari, such as he had presented to the other Mussulman, would produce here an equally favourable result. The celestial origin of this advice was proved by its complete success. The pilgrim was not only liberated, but obtained letters from the propitiated ruler which saved him from all farther exaction.

The Crusades threw open the holy places to the eyes of all Europe ; and accordingly, so long as a Christian king swayed his sceptre in the capital of Judea, the merit of individual pilgrimage was greatly diminished. But no sooner had the warlike Saracens recovered possession of Jerusalem, than the wonted difficulty and danger returned ; and, as might have been expected, the interest attached to the sacred buildings, which the eyes of " infidel dogs" were no longer worthy to behold, revived in greater vigour than formerly. In 1331, accordingly, William de Bouldesell adventured on an expedition into Arabia and Palestine, of which some account has been published. In the monastery of St Catherine, at the base of Mount Sinai, he was hospitably received by the monks, who showed him the bones of their patron reposing in a tomb, which, however, they appear not to have treated with much respect. By means of hard beating, we are told, they brought out from these remains of mortality a small portion of blood, which they presented to the pilgrim as a gift of singular value. A circumstance which particularly astonished this man of easy faith, would probably have produced no surprise in a less believing mind; the blood, he remarks, " had not the appearance of real blood, but rather of some thick oily substance;" nevertheless, the miracle was regarded by him as one of the greatest that had ever been witnessed in this world.

A hundred years afterwards, Bertrandon de la Broquiere sailed from Venice to Jaffa, where, according to the statistics of contrite pilgrims, the " pardons of the Holy Land begin." At Jerusalem he found the Christians reduced to a state of the most cruel thraldom. Such of them as engaged in trade were locked up in their shops every night by the Saracens, who opened the doors in the morning at such an hour as seemed to them most proper or convenient. At Damascus they were treated with equal severity. The two first persons whom he met in this city knocked him down,—an injury which he dared not resent for fear of immediately losing his life. About thirty years before the period of his visit, the destroying arms of Timur had laid a large portion of the Syrian capital in ruins, though the population had again increased to nearly one hundred thousand. During his stay he witnessed the arrival of a caravan consisting of more than three thousand camels, the entry of which required not less than two days and two nights; the Koran wrapped in silk being carried in front on the back of a dromedary, richly adorned with the same costly material. This part of the procession was surrounded by a number of persons brandishing naked swords, and playing on all sorts of musical instruments. The governor, with most of the inhabitants, went out to meet the holy cavalcade, and to do homage to the sacred ensign, which at once proclaimed their faith, and announced that the object of a pious mission had been successfully accomplished. Broquiere found the greatest respect paid to every one who had performed the pilgrimage to Mecca, and was gravely assured by an eminent moulah, that no such person could ever incur the hazard of everlasting damnation.

We merely mention the names of Breidenbach of Mentz, and of Martin Baumgarten, who in the beginning of the sixteenth century achieved a journey into the Holy Land. The latter of these, while passing through Egypt, was most barbarously treated by the Saracen boys, who pelted him with dirt, brickbats, stones, and rotten fruit. At Hebron he was shown the field " where it is said, or at least guessed, that Adam was made ;" but the reddish earth of which it is composed is now used in the manufacture of prayer-beads.

The work of Bartholemeo Georgewitz, who travelled in the same century, gives a melancholy account of the miseries endured by such Christians as were carried into slavery by the Turks in those evil days. The armies of that nation were followed by slave-dealers supplied with chains, by means of which fifty or sixty were bound in a row together, leaving only as much room between them as would allow the facility of walking. The hands were manacled during the day, and at night the feet also. The sufferings inflicted upon men of rank, and those belonging to the learned professions, were beyond description; extending not only to the lowest labours of the field, but even to the work of oxen, being sometimes yoked like these animals in the plough. Separated from home by great rivers and arms of the sea, it was extremely difficult for those who were sent into Asia to effect their escape; and hence, in many cases, the horrors of captivity had no other limits than those of the natural life. No wonder that Bartholemeo recommends to every one visiting those parts to make his will, " like one going not to the earthly, but to the heavenly Jerusalem."

Laurence Aldersey, who set out from London in 1581, was the first Protestant who encountered the perils of a voyage to Syria. In the Levant a Turkish galley hove in sight, and caused great alarm. The master, " being a wise fellow, began to devise how to escape the danger; but, while both he and all of us were in our dumps, God sent us a merrie gale of wind." As they approached Candia a violent storm came on, and the mariners began to reproach the Englishman as the cause, " and saide I was no good Christian, and wished I were in the middest of the sea, saying that they and the shippe were the worse for me." He replied, " I thinke myself the worst creature in the worlde, and do you consider yourselves also." These remonstrances were followed by a long sermon, the tenor of which was, " that they were not all good Christians, else it were not possible for them to have such weather." A gentleman on board informed Aldersey, that the suspicions respecting him originated in his refusal to join in the prayers to the Virgin Mary, —a charge which he parried, by remarking that " they who praied to so many goe a wrong way to worke." The friars, resolving to bring the matter to an issue, sent round the image of our Lady to kiss. On its approach the good Protestant endeavoured to avoid it by going another way ; but the bearer " fetched his course about," and presented it. The proffered salutation being then positively rejected, the affair might have become serious, had not two of the more respectable monks interceded in his behalf, and enforced a more charitable procedure.

Of the people of Cyprus he remarks, that they " be very rude, and like beasts, and no better : they eat their meat sitting upon the ground, with their legs acrosse like tailors." On the 8th of August they arrived at Joppa, but did not till the next day receive permission to land from the great pasha, " who sate upon a hill to see us sent away." Our countryman had mounted before the rest, which greatly displeased his highness, who sent a servant to pull him from the saddle and beat him ; " whereupon I made a long legge, saying, Grand mercye, Seignor." This timely submission seems to have secured forgiveness ; and accordingly, " being horsed upon little asses," they commenced their journey towards Jerusalem. Rama he describes as so " ruinated, that he took it to be rather a heape of stones than a towne ;" finding no house to receive them but such a one as they were compelled to enter by creeping upon their knees. The party were exposed to the usual violence and extortion of the Arabs ; " they that should have rescued us stood still, and durst doe nothing, which was to our cost." On reaching the holy city they knelt down and gave thanks; after which they were obliged to enter the gate on foot, no Christian at that period being allowed to appear within the walls mounted. The superior of the convent received the pilgrims courteously into his humble establishment, where, Aldersey tells us, " they were dieted of free cost, and fared reasonable well."*

The beginning of the seventeenth century witnessed a higher order of travellers, who, from such a mixture of motives as might actuate either a pilgrim or an antiquary, undertook the perilous tour of the Holy Land. Among these one of the most distinguished was George Sandys, who commenced his peregrinations in the year 1610. He was succeeded by Doubdan, Cheron, Thevenot, Gonzales, Morison, Maundrell, and Pococke; all of whom have contributed many valuable materials towards a complete knowledge of the localities, government, and actual condition of modern Palestine. In our own days the number of works on these important subjects has increased greatly; presenting to the historian of the Turkish provinces in Asia a nearer and more minute view of society than could be obtained by the earlier travellers, who, instead of yielding to the characteristic bigotry of the Moslem, usually opposed to it a prejudice not less determined and uncharitable. We must not hazard a catalogue of the enterprising authors to whom the European public are indebted for the information, now enjoyed by every class of readers, with regard to the most interesting of all ancient kingdoms, the country inhabited by Israel and Judah. In the description which I am about to give of the principal towns, the buildings, the antiquities, the manners, the opinions, and the religious forms which meet the observation of the intelligent tourist in the land of Canaan, I shall select the most striking facts from writers of all nations and sects; making no distinc-

---

* Murray's Historical Account of Discoveries and Travels in Asia, vol. iii. p. 130, &c.

tion but such as shall be dictated by a due estimation of the learning, candour, and talents which appear in their several volumes.

Palestine is usually approached either from the sea at the port of Jaffa, the ancient Joppa, or from Egypt by way of the intervening desert. In both cases the principal object is to obtain a safe and easy route to the capital, which even at the present hour cannot be reached without much danger, unless under the special protection of the native authorities. The power of Mohammed Ali, it is true, extends to the walls of Damascus; and wherever his government is acknowledged no violence can be committed with impunity on European travellers. But the Syrian pashas, equally deficient in inclination and vigour, still permit the grossest extortion, and sometimes connive at the most savage atrocities. Besides, there is a class of lawless Arabs who scour the borders of the Wilderness, holding at defiance all the restrictions which a civilized people impose or respect. Sir Frederick Henniker, who followed the unwonted track which leads from Mount Sinai to the southern shore of the Dead Sea, narrowly escaped assassination, after having been severely wounded, and repeatedly robbed, by one of the most savage hordes of Bedouins.

The history of the Crusades will draw our attention to Jaffa more minutely than would be suitable at the present stage of the narrative; we shall therefore proceed on the usual route to Jerusalem, collecting, as we go along, such notices as may prove interesting to the reader. At a short distance from this celebrated port, the pilgrim enters the plain of Sharon, celebrated in Scripture for its beautiful roses. The monk Neret informs us, that in his time it was covered with tulips, the variety of colours forming a lovely parterre. At present the eye of the traveller is delighted with a profusion of roses, the narcissus, the white and orange lily, the carnation, and a highly fragrant species of everlasting flower. This plain stretches along the coast, from Gaza in the south to Mount Carmel on the north, being bounded towards the east by the hills of Judea and Samaria. The whole of it is not upon the same level; it consists of four platforms separated from each other by a wall of naked stones. The soil is composed of a very fine sand, which, though mixed with gravel, appears extremely fertile; but, owing to the desolating spirit of Mohammedan despotism, nothing is seen in some of the richest fields except thistles and withered grass. Here and there, indeed, are scanty plantations of cotton, with a few patches of dhourra, barley, and wheat. The villages, which are commonly surrounded with olive-trees and sycamores, are for the most part in ruins; exhibiting a melancholy proof that, under a bad government, even the bounty of Heaven ceases to be a blessing.

The path by which the hilly barrier is penetrated is difficult, and in some places dangerous. But before you reach it, turning towards the east you perceive Rama or Ramla, the ancient Arimathea, distinguished by its charming situation, and well known as the residence of a Christian community. The convent, it is true, had been plundered five years before it was visited by Chateaubriand, and it was not without the most urgent solicitation that the friars were permitted to repair their building; as if it were a maxim among the Turks, that the progress of ruin and decay should never be arrested. Volney tells us, that when he was at Ramla, a commander resided there in a serai, the walls and floors of which were on the point of tumbling down. The Frenchman asked one of the inferior officers why his master did not at least pay some attention to his own apartment. The reply was, "If another shall obtain his place next year, who will repay the expense?"

In those days the aga maintained about one hundred horsemen and as many African soldiers, who were lodged in an old Christian church, the nave of which was converted into a stable, as also in an ancient khan, which was disputed with them by the scorpions. The adjacent country is planted with a superior description of olives; the greatest part of which are as large as the walnut-trees of France, though they are daily perishing through age and the ravages of contending factions. When a peasant is disposed to take revenge on his enemy, he goes by night and cuts his trees close to the ground, when the wound, which he carefully covers from the sight, drains off the sap like an issue. Amid these plantations are seen at every step dry wells, decayed cisterns, and immense vaulted reservoirs, which prove that, in ancient times, this town must have been upwards of four miles in circumference. At present it does not contain more than a hundred miserable families. The houses are only so many huts, sometimes detached, and sometimes ranged in the form of cells round a court, enclosed by a mud wall. In winter the inhabitants and their cattle may be said to live together; the part of the building allotted to themselves being raised only two feet above that in which they lodge their beasts. By this means the peasants are kept warm without burning wood,—a species of economy indispensable in a district absolutely destitute of fuel. As to the fire necessary for culinary purposes, they make it, as was the practice in the days of Ezekiel the prophet, of dung kneaded into cakes, which they dry in the sun, exposing them to its rays on the walls of their huts. In summer their lodging is more airy, but all their furniture consists of a single mat and a pitcher for carrying water. The immediate neighbourhood of the village is sown at the proper season with grain and water-melons; all the rest is a desert, and abandoned to the Bedouin Arabs, who feed their flocks in it. There are frequent remains of towers, dungeons, and even of castles with ramparts and ditches, in some of which are a few Barbary soldiers with nothing but a shirt and a musket. These ruins, however, are more commonly inhabited by owls, jackals, and scorpions.*

The only remarkable antiquity at Ramla is the minaret of a weather-worn mosque, which, by an Arabic inscrip-

---

* Chateaubriand, Itinéraire, tome i. p. 380. Volney's Travels, vol. ii. p. 335.

tion, appears to have been built by the Sultan of Egypt. From the summit, which is very lofty, the eye follows the whole chain of mountains, beginning at Nablous, and skirting the extremity of the plain till it loses itself in the south.*

A ride of two hours brings the traveller to the verge of the mountains, where the road opens through a rugged ravine, and is formed in the dry channel of a torrent. A scene of affecting solitude and desolation surrounds his steps as he pursues his journey, in what is so simply described in the gospel as the " hill country of Judea." He finds himself amidst a labyrinth of mountains, of a conical figure, all nearly alike, and connected with each other at their base. A naked rock presents strata or beds, resembling the seats of a Roman amphitheatre, or the walls which support the vineyards in the valleys of

---

* The latest travellers have not added much to our knowledge of this interesting town, the Rama of Jeremiah. The crusaders found here one of the principal cities of the country, and under their protection it continued to rise in importance, from its convenient situation at the foot of the hills along which winds the main road to Jerusalem. Robert, the reckless count of Normandy, was appointed bishop of this place; and St George, the patron saint of England, is supposed to have died here. There is still a Latin convent in possession of the Spaniards, and the ruins, which are extensive, bear marks of great strength.—*Notices of the Holy Land,* p. 130.

The author of " Three Weeks in Palestine" relates, that between Jaffa and Ramla there is an extensive grove of very large and aged olive-trees, which are said to have been planted by the crusaders. " While breakfast was preparing, we ascended the flat roof of the *hospitium* to take a survey of Ramla and its environs. The morning was lovely, and the sun just peeping over the mountains to the east. The fresh and brilliant colouring of dawn shed over the surrounding landscape a beauty that did not really belong to it. However, the immediate vicinity was pretty; the garden-hedges of prickly pear and other shrubs gave it a pleasing appearance of cultivation, and, to the south, above a mile distant, rose from behind a grove of magnificent olive-trees a lofty and handsome tower of the time of the crusades, now used as a minaret to the mosque below, which, viewed from where we stood, had much of the character of an English church-tower, and added greatly to the scene. Ramla itself is a wretched dilapidated place, but exhibits the marks of having once been a mo.e extensive and flourishing town than it is at present."—P. 14.

Savoy. Every recess is filled with dwarf oaks, box, and rose-laurels. From the bottom of the ravines olive-trees rear their heads, sometimes forming continuous woods on the sides of the hills. On reaching the most elevated summit of this chain, he looks back towards the south-west on the beautiful Valley of Sharon, bounded by the Great Sea; before him opens the Vale of St Jeremiah; and in the same direction, on the top of a rock, appears in the distance an ancient fortress called the Castle of the Maccabees. It is conjectured that the author of the Lamentations was born in the village which still retains his name, amidst these sombre mountains; so much is certain, at least, that the melancholy of this desolate scene appears to pervade the compositions of the prophet of sorrows.

The arms of Ibrahim Pasha have delivered this interesting retreat from the tyranny of Abou-Goosh, a fierce robber, who was wont to lay all travellers under contribution. He is mentioned by Lamartine, in whose favour his kindness or forbearance was purchased by Lady Hester Stanhope. "This man," says another pilgrim of the Holy Land, " once formed the daring scheme of seizing on Jerusalem, and of establishing himself there, and had well nigh succeeded in the attempt. His various acts at length roused the attention of the Porte, and a mandate was issued to Abdallah, pasha of Acre, to reduce him to better behaviour, which had been recently put in execution; consequently we were suffered to pass without molestation. Nevertheless, our guides, doubtful of this constrained honesty, and unwilling to put it to too severe a test, would not permit us to linger a moment, but hurried us through rapidly. The chief, surrounded by some twenty of his banditti, fine tall fellows armed to the teeth, was seated under a tree enjoying his pipe, and cast most covetous and sinister glances upon us as we passed: however not a word was said to us, although they were evidently making their remarks upon us. Up another valley to the right, at the distance of three or four miles, he possesses a hill fort, which appeared a strong position.* When the author of the Notices visited Syria, Abou-Goosh was a prisoner at Damascus.†

The unvarying manners of the East exhibit to the view of the stranger, at the present day, the same picture of rural innocence and simplicity which might have met the eye of the Redeemer's mother when she came into this pastoral country to salute her cousin Elizabeth. Herds of goats with pendent ears, sheep with large tails, and asses which remind you, by their beauty, of the onagra of Scripture, issue from the villages at the dawn of day. Arab women are seen bringing grapes to dry in the vineyards; others with their faces veiled, carrying pitchers of water on their heads, like the daughters of Midian.

From this valley the traveller towards Sion descends into that which bears the name of Turpentine, and is deeper and narrower than the other. Here are observed some vineyards, and a few patches of dhourra. He next arrives at the brook where the youthful David picked up the five smooth stones, with one of which he slew the gigantic Goliath. Having crossed the stream, he perceives the village of Heriet-Lefta on the bank of another dry channel, which resembles a dusty road. El Birê appears in the distance on the summit of a lofty hill on the way to Nablous, the Shechem of the Israelites and the Neapolis of the Herods. He now pursues his course through a desert, where wild fig-trees thinly scattered wave their embrowned leaves in the southern breeze. The ground, which had hitherto exhibited some verdure, becomes altogether bare; the sides of the mountains, expanding themselves, assume at once an appearance of greater grandeur and sterility. Presently all vegetation ceases; even the very mosses disappear. The confused amphitheatre of the mountains is tinged with a red and livid colour. In this dreary region he continues to ascend a whole hour in order to gain an elevated hill which

---

* Three Weeks in Palestine, p. 17.
† Notices of the Holy Land, p. 102.

he sees before him : after which he proceeds, during an equal space, across a naked plain strewed with loose stones. All at once, at the extremity of this plain, he perceives a line of Gothic walls flanked with square towers, and the tops of a few buildings peeping above them ;—he beholds Jerusalem, once the joy of the whole earth !

It has been remarked that the vicinity of this capital must have appeared extremely beautiful when its hills were terraced after the manner of the East, and verdant with the olive, the fig-tree, and the vine ; but that which was then its most captivating feature now adds to its deformity, and the bare and blasted rocks seem to say that Jehovah in his anger has passed by and cursed the city for its sins. There are rocks, but they have no sublimity; hills, but they have no beauty; fields and gardens, but they have no richness; valleys, but they have no fertility ; a wide spreading lake, but it is the Dead Sea.*

"I can now account," says M. Chateaubriand, "for the surprise expressed by the crusaders and pilgrims at the first sight of Jerusalem, according to the reports of historians and travellers. I can affirm that whoever has, like me, had the patience to read nearly two hundred modern accounts of the Holy Land, the Rabbinical compilations, and the passages in the ancient writers respecting Judea, still knows nothing at all about it. I paused with my eyes fixed on Jerusalem, measuring the height of its walls, reviewing at once all the recollections of history from the patriarch Abraham to Godfrey of Bouillon, reflecting on the total change accomplished in the world by the mission of the Son of Man, and in vain seeking that Temple, not one stone of which is left upon another. Were I to live a thousand years, never should I forget that desert, which yet seems to be pervaded by the greatness of Jehovah and the terrors of death."†

---

\* Notices of Holy Land, p. 183.
† Itinéraire, tome ii. p. 385. The first view of Jerusalem from the Jaffa road is at by far the least imposing point from which it can be seen : I own I felt wofully disappointed. The approach is over

On this occasion a camp of Turkish horse, with all the accompaniments of oriental pomp, was pitched under the walls. The tents in general were covered with black lamb-skins, while those belonging to persons of distinction were formed of striped cloth. The horses, saddled and bridled, were fastened to stakes. There were four pieces of horse-artillery, well mounted on carriages, which appeared to be of English manufacture. These fierce soldiers are stationed near the capital, as well for the purpose of checking the savage Bedouins, who acknowledge no master, as for enforcing the tribute demanded from all strangers who enter the holy city. The recollections of the Mussulman, no less than those of the Christian, inspire a reverential feeling for the town in which David dwelt; and accordingly, although the European pilgrim is oppressed by the present laws of Palestine, his motives are usually respected, and even praised.

The reader, who has perused with attention some of the more recent works on Palestine, must have been struck with the diversity, and even the apparent contradiction, which prevail in their descriptions of Jerusalem. According to one, the magnificence of its buildings rivals the most splendid edifices of modern times, while another could perceive nothing but filth and ruins, surmounted by a gaudy mosque and a few glittering minarets. The greater number, it must be acknowledged, have drawn from their own imagination the tints in which they have been pleased to exhibit the metropolis of Judea; trusting more to the impressions conveyed by the brilliant delineations of poetry, than to a minute

---

table land of some extent, and the wall on this side, standing on higher ground than the town itself, entirely conceals it: in fact nothing is visible but a battlemented wall with square towers at intervals. I had pushed on before the party, and upon arriving near the gate, dismounted and sat down upon a stone by the wayside to await their approach, ruminating upon the past, the present, and the future. I was quickly roused from my reverie by the whiz of a bullet close to my ear, which speedily put all my ideas to flight. Springing up with alacrity, I saw a Turkish soldier recovering his musket, and coolly walking off, no doubt esteeming it excellent sport to startle a giaour."—*Three Weeks in Palestine,* p. 20.

inspection of what they might have seen with their own eyes.*

Dr Clarke, for example, there is reason to suspect, has allowed his pen to be guided by the ardent muse of Tasso, rather than by the cool observation of an unbiassed traveller. " No sensation of fatigue or heat," says he, " could counterbalance the eagerness and zeal which animated all our party in the approach to Jerusalem ; every individual pressed forward, hoping first to announce the joyful intelligence of its appearance. We passed some insignificant ruins, either of ancient buildings or of modern villages ; but had they been of more importance they would have excited little notice at the time, so earnestly bent was every mind towards the main object of interest and curiosity. At length, after about two hours had been passed in this state of anxiety and suspense, ascending a hill towards the south—Hagiopolis! exclaimed a Greek in the van of our cavalcade ; and, instantly throwing himself from his horse, was seen upon his knees, bareheaded, facing the prospect he surveyed. Suddenly the sight burst upon us all. The effect produced was that of total silence throughout the whole company. Many of our party, by an immediate impulse, took off their hats as if entering a church, without being sensible of so doing. The Greeks and Catholics shed torrents of tears ; and, presently beginning to cross them-

---

* The following reflections on the destruction of Jerusalem are natural and affecting. Alluding to the prediction of our Lord, Mr Hardy remarks, " We know from undisputed authority that the prophecy was literally fulfilled at the siege by Titus ; and looking now at the city as it lies beneath our feet, we cannot point out one single building, or part of a building, not even so insignificant a ruin as two stones together, that the most zealous antiquarian can suppose to have existed at the time of Christ. Other cities have been sacked and partially destroyed, but the ruin has not been total. I have seen the Parthenon at Athens, the Colloseum at Rome, and there are temples still standing even at Thebes. Here rage hath done its worst ; and there is no present edifice over which the Jews can weep and say *our fathers reared these walls !* The sepulchres alone have come down to our time, but they are hewn out of the rock and not built, and it is only with the stone that contains them they can perish."—*Notices of Holy Land,* p. 182.

selves with unfeigned devotion, asked if they might be permitted to take off the covering from their feet, and proceed barefooted to the Holy Sepulchre. We had not been prepared for the grandeur of the spectacle which the city alone exhibited. Instead of a wretched and ruined town, by some described as the desolated remnant of Jerusalem, we beheld as it were a flourishing and stately metropolis, presenting a magnificent assemblage of domes, towers, palaces, churches, and monasteries; all of which, glittering in the sun's rays, shone with inconceivable splendour. As we drew nearer, our whole attention was engrossed by its noble and interesting appearance."*

The effect produced upon the Christian army when they obtained the first view of the holy city is beautifully described by the Italian poet,' thereby supplying, as we have suggested, the model which has been so faithfully copied by the English tourist.

> " Now from the golden East the zephyrs borne,
> Proclaim'd with balmy gales the approach of morn;
> And fair Aurora deck'd her radiant head
> With roses cropt from Eden's flowery bed;
> When from the sounding camp was heard afar
> The noise of troops preparing for the war;
> To this succeed the trumpet's loud alarms,
> And rouse, with shriller notes, the host to arms.
>
> " With holy zeal their swelling hearts abound,
> And their wing'd footsteps scarcely print the ground.
> When now the sun ascends the ethereal way,
> And strikes the dusty field with warmer ray;
> Behold, Jerusalem in prospect lies!
> Behold, Jerusalem salutes their eyes!
> At once a thousand tongues repeat the name,
> And hail Jerusalem with loud acclaim!
>
> " At first, transported with the pleasing sight,
> Each Christian bosom glow'd with full delight;
> But deep contrition soon their joy suppress'd,
> And holy sorrow sadden'd every breast;

---

* Travels, vol. iv. p. 289. To account in some degree for this impression, it must be mentioned that Dr Clarke approached Jerusalem from the north, and entered by the gate of Damascus. On that side the view is really imposing.

View of Jerusalem from the Mount of Olives.

Scarce dare their eyes the city walls survey,
Where clothed in flesh their dear Redeemer lay;
Whose sacred earth did once their Lord enclose,
And where triumphant from the grave he rose!

" Each faltering tongue imperfect speech supplies;
Each labouring bosom heaves with frequent sighs.
Each took the example as their chieftains led,
With naked feet the hallow'd soil they tread;
Each throws his martial ornaments aside,
The crested helmets with their plumy pride:
To humble thoughts their lofty hearts they bend,
And down their cheeks the pious tears descend."*

No city assuredly presents a more striking example of the vicissitude of human affairs than the capital of the Jews. When we behold its walls levelled, its ditches filled up, and all its buildings encumbered with ruins, we can scarcely believe we view that celebrated metropolis, which formerly withstood the efforts of the most powerful empires, and for a time resisted the arms of Rome itself; though, by a whimsical change of fortune, its mouldering edifices now receive her homage and reverence. In a word, we with difficulty recognise Jerusalem. Still more are we astonished at its ancient greatness, when we consider its situation, amid a rugged soil, destitute of water, and surrounded by the dry channels of torrents and steep hills. Remote from every great road, it seems not to have been calculated either for a considerable mart of commerce, or for the centre of a great consumption. It overcame, however, every obstacle, and may be adduced as a proof of what patriotism and religion can effect in the hands of a good government, or when favoured by happy circumstances from without. The same principles, in some degree modified, still preserve to this city its feeble existence.

---

* Hoole's Translation. The original presents one of the most animated and musical passages in the Gerusalemme Liberata:—

" Ma quando il sol gli aridi campi fiede
Con ragi assai fervente, a in alto sorge,
Ecco apparir Gerusalem si vede!
Ecco additar Gerusalem si scorge!
Ecco da mille voci unitamente,
Gerusalemme salutar si sente!"—Canto iii. stan. v. 2.

The renown of its miracles, perpetuated in the East, invites and retains a considerable number of inhabitants within its walls.*

As a contrast to the description of Dr Clarke, the reader may not be displeased to peruse the notes of Sir Frederick Henniker on the same subject :—" Jerusalem is called, even by the Mohammedans, the Blessed City, —the streets of it are narrow and deserted,—the houses dirty and ragged,—the shops few and forsaken,—and throughout the whole there is not one symptom of either commerce, comfort, or happiness. Is this the city that men call the Perfection of Beauty, the Joy of the whole earth ?—The town, which appears to me not worth possession, even without the trouble of conquest, is walled entirely round, is about a mile in length and half a mile in width, so that its circumference may be estimated at three miles. In three quarters of an hour I performed the circuit. It would be difficult to conceive how it could ever have been larger than it now is; for, independent of the ravines, the four outsides of the city are marked by the brook of Siloam, by a burial-place at either end, and by the Hill of Calvary ; and the Hill of Calvary is now within the town, so that it was formerly smaller than it is at present. The best view of it is from the Mount of Olives ; it commands the exact shape, and nearly every particular, namely, the Church of the Holy Sepulchre, the Armenian Con-

---

* Volney's Travels in Egypt and Syria, vol. ii. p. 303. " Jerusalem has lost its rank in political importance. It was once the head of a pashalik, and until lately the office of governor was considered to be a respectable situation, and was entered upon with great pomp; but it is now filled by a person from the immediate neighbourhood, and of comparatively low rank. It is difficult to state the population with any degree of certainty. From the observations I was enabled to make, though it was the busiest period of the year, and there were at least two thousand strangers present, I think that in the statements before the public the truth is exceeded. I should estimate the numbers in this proportion ; 6000 Jews, 3000 Mussulmans, and 3000 Christians. The Jews occupy a portion of the city that borders on the Temple. They are said to be principally old persons who come here to die."—*Notices of Holy Land*, p. 175.

vent, the Mosque of Omar, St Stephen's Gate, the round-topped houses, and the barren vacancies of the city. The Mosque of Omar is the St Peter's of Turkey. The building itself has a light pagoda appearance; the garden in which it stands occupies a considerable part of the city, and contrasted with the surrounding desert is beautiful; but it is forbidden ground, and Jew or Christian entering within its precincts must, if discovered, forfeit either his religion or his life."*

The observation made by Sir Frederick, with regard to the difficulty and danger of entering the Mosque of Omar, has been verified on more than one occasion. But the obstacles, apparently insurmountable, were overcome by Dr Richardson, who, in return for the successful exercise of his professional skill, was rewarded by a clandestine visit to the shrine of the Mussulman saint. The few details which we are about to select from his volume will render manifest that the veil of mystery does not conceal any thing really worth seeing. Like Pompey in the Temple, the Christian visiter, whose presence, in a similar manner, profanes the holy place, feels no other surprise than is occasioned by the fact, that men have agreed to excite curiosity by prohibiting an imaginary gratification.

" On our arrival at the door, a gentle knock brought up the sacristan, who, apprized of our intention, was within waiting to receive us. He demanded, rather sternly, who we were, and was answered by my black conductor in tones no less consequential than his own. The door immediately edged up to prevent as much as possible the light from shining out, and we squeezed ourselves in with a gentle and noiseless step, although there was no person near who could be alarmed by the loudest sound of our bare feet upon the marble floor. The door was no sooner shut than the sacristan, taking a couple of candles in his hand, showed us all over the interior of the building, pointing, in the pride of his heart, to the elegant marble walls, the beautifully gilded

---

* Notes on Egypt, &c. p. 274.

ceiling, the well where the true worshippers drink and wash,—with which we also blessed our palates and moistened our beards,—the paltry reading-desk with the ancient Koran, the handsome columns, and the green stone with the wonderful nails. As soon as we had completed this circuit, pulling a key from his girdle, he unlocked the door of the railing that separates the outer from the inner part of the mosque, which, with an elevation of two or three steps, led us into the sacred recess. Here he pointed out the patches of mosaic in the floor, the round flat stone which the Prophet carried on his arm in battle, directed us to introduce our hand through the hole in the wooden box, to feel the print of the Prophet's foot, and through the posts of the wooden rail, to feel as well as to see the marks of the angel Gabriel's fingers (into which I carefully put my own) in the sacred stone that occupies the centre of the mosque, and from which it derives the name of Sakhara or Locked-up, and over which is suspended a fine cloth of green and red satin. It was so covered with dust that, but for the information of my guide, I should not have been able to tell the composing colours. Finally, he pointed to the door that leads into the small cavern below, of which he had not the key.

" I looked up to the interior of the dome ; but, there being few lamps burning, the light was not sufficient to show me any of its beauty farther than a general glance. The columns and curiosities were counted over again and again, the arches were specially examined and enumerated, to be sure that I had not missed nor forgotten any of them. Writing would have been an ungracious behaviour, calculated to excite a thousand suspicions, that next day would have gone to swell the current of the city gossip, to the prejudice both of myself and of my friend. Having examined the adytum, we once more touched the footstep of the Prophet, and the fingerprints of the angel Gabriel, and descended the steps, over which the door was immediately secured."*

---

* Travels along the Mediterranean and Parts Adjacent, vol. ii. p. 285.

Dr Richardson was afterwards permitted to visit this splendid mosque during the day, when he found that the dimensions of the enclosure in which it stands is about fifteen hundred feet in length, and a thousand in breadth. In the sacred retirement of this charming spot the followers of the Prophet delight to saunter, or repose, as in the elysium of their devotions; and, arrayed in the gorgeous costume of the East, add much to the interest, the beauty, and solemn stillness of the scene, from which they seem loath to retire. The Sakhara itself is a regular octagon of about sixty feet a side, and is entered by four spacious doors, each of which is adorned with a porch projecting from the line of the building and rising considerably on the wall. All the sides of it are panelled. The centre stone of one panel is square, of another it is octagonal, and thus they alternate all round; the sides of each running down the angles like a plain pilaster, and giving an appearance as if the whole were set in a frame. The marble is white, with a considerable tinge of blue; square pieces of the latter colour being introduced in different places, so as to confer upon the exterior a very pleasing effect. The upper story is faced with small tiles painted of different colours, white, yellow, green, and blue; some of them are also covered with sentences from the Koran. At this height there are seven elegant windows on each side, except where the porches interfere, and then there are only six; the general appearance of the edifice being extremely light and beautiful, more especially from the mixture of the soft colours above and the delicate tints of the marble in the main body of the structure.

The interior fully corresponds to the magnificence and beauty just described. There are twenty-four marble columns, placed parallel to the eight sides of the building, three opposite to each, so as still to preserve the octagonal form. Eight of them are large plain pillars belonging to no particular order of architecture, and all standing opposite to the eight entering angles of the edifice, and deeply indented on the inner side; so that they furnish an acute termination to the octagonal lines within. Between every two of the square columns there are two of a round figure, well proportioned, and resting on a base. They are from eighteen to twenty feet high, with a sort of Corinthian capital. A large square plinth of marble extends from the top of the one column to the other, and above it there is constructed a number of arches all round, which support the inner end of the roof or ceiling, the outer end resting upon the walls of the building. This is composed of wood, or plaster, highly ornamented with a species of carving, and richly gilt.

But this gorgeous temple owes both its name and existence to a large irregular mass of stone, having an oblong shape, which still occupies the centre of the mosque. It is a portion of the calcareous rock on which the city is built, and which prevails in the other mountains in the neighbourhood of Jerusalem, having very much the appearance of being a part of the bed that might have been left when the foundation of the building was levelled. It rises highest towards the southwest corner, and falls abruptly at the end, where are the prints of the Prophet's foot. The upper surface is irregular, the same as when it was broken from the quarry. All round it is enclosed with a wooden rail about four feet high; and, as we have already mentioned, there is a cover or canopy of variously coloured silk suspended over it. Nothing, in short, can be held in higher veneration than the Hadjr-el-sakhara, or concealed stone.*

But this fragment of rock has more weighty pretensions to the veneration of the Moslem than the mere print of the angel Gabriel's fingers or of the Prophet's foot; for, like the Palladium of ancient Troy, it is said to have fallen from heaven on this very spot, at the time when prophecy commenced in Jerusalem. It was employed as a seat by the venerable men to whom that gift was communicated; and, as long as the spirit of

---

* Richardson's Travels, vol. ii. p. 301.

vaticination continued to enlighten their minds, the slab remained steady for their accommodation. But no sooner was the power of prophecy withdrawn, and the persecuted seers compelled to flee for safety to other lands, than the stone is declared to have manifested the profoundest sympathy in their fate, and even a desire to accompany them in their flight. On this occasion Gabriel the archangel interposed his authority, and prevented the departure of the prophetical chair. He grasped it with his mighty hand, and nailed it to its rocky bed till the arrival of Mohammed, who, horsed on the lightning's wing, flew thither from Mecca, joined the society of seventy thousand ministering spirits, and, having offered up his devotions to the throne of God, fixed the stone immovably in this holy site, around which the Caliph Omar erected his magnificent mosque.

Within the same enclosure there is another house of Prayer called El Aksa, which, though a fine building, is greatly inferior to the Mosque of Omar. Between the two there is a beautiful fountain, which takes its name from a clump of orange-trees overshadowing its water. The minor temple is composed of seven naves supported by pillars and columns, and at the head of the centre nave is a fine cupola. Two others branch off at right angles to the principal body of the edifice. Before it is a portico of seven arches in front and one in depth, supported by square pillars. Ali Bey, who in his character of Mussulman was permitted to examine the holy fane at leisure, describes the great central nave of the Aksa as about 162 feet long and 32 broad. It is supported on each side by seven arches lightly pointed, resting upon cylindrical pillars in the form of columns, but without any architectural proportion, and with foliaged capitals which do not belong to any order. The fourth pillar to the right of the entrance is octangular, and enormously thick. It is called the pillar of Sidi Omar. The walls rise thirteen feet above the tops of the arches, and contain two rows of twenty-one windows each. The roof is of timber, without being vaulted. The cupola is supported by four large arches resting upon four square pillars. It is spherical, with two rows of windows, and is ornamented with arabesque paintings and gilding of exquisite beauty. Its diameter is equal to that of the central nave.

Burckhardt describes the Holy House in Jerusalem as a union of several buildings erected at different periods of Islamism, bearing upon them demonstrative proofs of the prevailing taste of the various ages in which they were successively constructed. Hence it is not precisely one mosque, but a group of mosques. Its name in Arabic, El Haram, strictly signifies a place consecrated by the peculiar presence of the Divinity. The profane and the infidel are therefore forbidden to enter it. The Mussulman religion acknowledges but two temples, those, namely, of Mecca and of Jerusalem : both are called El Haram ; both are equally prohibited to Christians, Jews, and every other person who is not a believer in the Prophet. The mosques, on the other hand, are considered merely as places of meeting for certain acts of worship, and are not held so especially consecrated as to demand the total exclusion of all who do not profess the true faith. Entrance into them is not denied to the unbeliever by any statute of the Mohammedan law ; and hence it is not uncommon for Christians at Constantinople to receive from the government a written order to visit even the Mosque of St Sophia. But the sultan himself could not grant permission to an infidel either to pass into the territory of Mecca, or to enter the sacred edifice at Jerusalem. A firman granting such privileges would be regarded as a most horrid sacrilege : it would not be respected by the people ; and the favoured object would inevitably become the victim of his own imprudent boldness.*

In the interior of the rock whereon the Sakhara stands, there is a cave into which Dr Richardson could not obtain admittance. He was four times in the mosque,

---

* Travels of Ali Bey, vol. ii. p. 214.

and went twice thither under the express assurance that the doors of the mysterious crypt should be thrown open to him. But when he arrived the key was always wanting, and when the keeper of it was sought he could nowhere be found. M. Burckhardt, the fictitious Ali Bey, who encountered no obstacle, reveals all the mystery of this subterranean mansion. It is a room forming an irregular square of about eighteen feet surface, and eight feet high in the middle. The roof is that of a natural vault, quite rough and unequal. In descending the staircase, there is upon the right hand, near the bottom, a little tablet of marble, bearing the name of El Makam Souleman, the place of Solomon. A similar one upon the left is named El Makam Daoud, the Place of David. A cavity or niche on the south-west side of the rock is called El Makam Ibrahim, the Place of Abraham. A similar concave step at the north-west angle is described as El Makam Djibrila, the Place of Gabriel; and a sort of stone table at the north-east angle is denominated El Makam el Hoder, the Place of Elias. In the roof of the apartment, exactly in the middle, there is an aperture almost cylindrical through the whole thickness of the rock, about three feet in diameter. This is the Place of the Prophet.

The same author observed a copy of the Koran, the leaves of which were four feet long, and more than two feet and a half broad. Tradition reports that it belonged to the Caliph Omar; but Mr Burckhardt had already seen a similar one in the grand mosque at Cairo, and another at Mecca, to both of which the same origin was assigned. The drawings supplied by this enterprising traveller give a very distinct notion of the extent and magnificence of the great Mussulman temple,—the most prominent object in the modern Jerusalem, and occupying the site of the still more interesting edifice erected by Solomon in the proudest period of Jewish history.

But the Christian pilgrim, who walks about the holy city " to tell her towers and mark her bulwarks," is more readily attracted by less splendid objects,—the memorials of his own more humble faith. Among these the most remarkable is the Church of the Holy Sepulchre, which is built on the lower part of the sloping hill, distinguished by the name of Acra, near the place where it is joined to Mount Moriah. The Turkish government, aware of the veneration which all Christians entertain for relics in any way connected with the sufferings of the great Author of their religion, have converted this feeling into a source of revenue; every person not subject to the Sublime Porte, who visits the shrine of Jesus Christ, being compelled to pay a certain sum for admittance. The church, nevertheless, is opened only on particular days of the week, and cannot be seen at any other time without an order from the two convents, the Latin and the Greek, with the sanction of the governor of the city. On such occasions the pressure at the doors is very great; the zeal of the pilgrims, checked by the rudeness of the Turks, who delight to insult and disappoint their anxiety, leading sometimes to scenes of tumult not quite in harmony with their pious motives.

The mind, it has been remarked, is not withdrawn from the important concerns of this hallowed spot by any florid decorations or brilliant display of architecture in its plan or in its walls; but the religion of the place is allowed to take full possession of the soul, and the visiter feels as if he were passing into the presence of the great Jehovah. Having entered within these sacred walls, the attention is first directed to a large flat stone in the floor, a little within the door; it is surrounded by a rail, and several lamps hang suspended over it. The pilgrims approaching on their knees, touch and kiss it, and then offer up their prayers in holy adoration. This is the stone on which the body of our Lord is said to have been washed, and anointed, and prepared for the tomb. Turning to the left, and proceeding a little forward, the stranger finds himself in a circular space immediately under the dome, surrounded with sixteen large columns which support the gallery above. In the centre of this area stands the Holy Sepulchre; it is enclosed in an oblong house, rounded at one end with small arcades, or closets for prayer. These are for the Copts, the Abyssinians, the Maronites, and other Christians, who are not, like the Roman Catholics, the Greeks, and Armenians, provided with chapels in the body of the church. At the other end it is squared off and furnished with a platform in front, which is ascended by a flight of steps, having a small parapet on each hand, and floored with marble. In the middle stands a block of polished stone about a foot and a half square; on which sat the angel who announced the blessed tidings of the resurrection to Mary Magdalene, and Joanna, and Mary the mother of James. After laying aside his shoes and the covering of his head, the worshipper is allowed to enter by a low narrow door into this mansion of victory, where Christ triumphed over the grave, and disarmed Death of his terrors. Here the mind looks on Him who, though he knew no sin, yet entered the regions of mortality to redeem us from its power, and the prayers of a grateful heart ascend with a risen Saviour to the presence of God in heaven.*

The tomb exhibited is a sarcophagus of white marble, slightly tinged with blue, being fully six feet long, three feet broad, and two feet two inches deep. It is but indifferently polished, and seems as if it had at one time been exposed to the action of the atmosphere, by which it has been considerably affected. It is made in the Greek fashion, without any ornament, and not like the more ancient tombs of the Jews, which we see cut in the rock for the reception of the dead. There are seven lamps constantly burning over it, the gifts of different sovereigns in successive ages. It occupies in width about one-half of the sepulchral chamber, and extends from one end of it to the other. A space about three feet wide in front of it is all that remains for the accommodation of visiters, so that not more than four can be conveniently admitted at a time.

---

* Richardson's Travels, vol. ii. p. 321.

Leaving this hallowed spot, the pilgrim is conducted to the place where our Lord appeared to Mary Magdalene, and next to the Chapel of Apparition, where he presented himself to the Blessed Virgin. The Greeks have an oratory opposite to the Holy Sepulchre, in which is a globe, representing, as they are pleased to imagine, the centre of the earth ; thus transferring from Delphi to Jerusalem the absurd notion of the pagan priests relative to the figure of the habitable world. After this the visiter enters a dark narrow staircase, which, by eighteen steps, carries him to Mount Calvary. " This is the centre, the grand magnet of the Christian church ; from this proceed life and salvation ; thither all hearts tend and all eyes are directed ; here kings and queens cast down their crowns, and great men and women part with their ornaments ; at the foot of the cross all are on a level, equally needy and equally welcome."\*

On Calvary is shown the spot where the Redeemer was nailed to the cross, the hole into which the end of it was fixed, and the rent in the rock. All these are covered with marble, perforated in the proper places, so that they may be seen and touched. On solemn occasions a cross is erected on an elevated part of the ground, and a wooden body stretched upon it in the attitude of suffering. Descending from the Mount the traveller enters the Chapel of St Helena, the mother of Constantine, in which is the vault where the true cross is said to have been found,—an event that continues to be celebrated by an appropriate mass every year on the third of May. The place is large enough to contain about thirty or forty individuals, and on that anniversary it is usually crowded to the door.

The spirit in which these commemorations are sometimes made is by no means honourable to the Christian character. An ancient rivalry between the members of the Greek and those of the Roman communion continues

---

\* Dr Richardson's Travels, vol. ii. p. 325.

to imbitter their disputes with regard to their respective privileges. Maundrell informs us that in his time each fraternity had their own altar and sanctuary; at which they had a peculiar right to perform divine service, and to exclude all other nations. But that which has always been the great prize contended for by the several sects, is the command and appropriation of the Holy Sepulchre, —a distinction contested with so much unchristian fury and animosity, especially between the Greeks and Latins, that, in disputing which party should go in to celebrate their mass, they have sometimes proceeded to blows and wounds, even at the very door of the Sepulchre, mingling their own blood with their sacrifices. About the end of the seventeenth century the King of France interposed, and obtained an order from the grand vizier to put that holy place into the possession of the Western Church,—an arrangement which was accomplished in the year 1690, and secured to the Latins the exclusive right of saying mass in it. And though it be permitted to Christians of all nations to go into it for their private devotions, yet none other may solemnize any public office of religion there.*

The daily employment of these recluses is to trim the lamps, and to make stated visits and processions to the several sanctuaries in the church. Thus they spend their time, many of them for four or six years together; nay, so far are some transported with the pleasing contemplation in which they here indulge, that they will never come out to their dying day; burying themselves, as it were, alive in our Lord's grave.†

It was at the holy season of Easter that the traveller last named visited Jerusalem, when he witnessed the annual service performed by the monks; deformed, perhaps, by the introduction of too many minute details, intended to illustrate the great event to which it refers. "Their ceremony begins on Good Friday night, which is called by them the *Nox Tenebrosa*, and is observed

---

\* Maundrell's Journey from Aleppo to Jerusalem, p. 71.
† Ibid.

with such an extraordinary solemnity that I cannot omit to give a particular description of it :—As soon as it grew dark, all the friars and pilgrims were convened in the Chapel of the Apparition, in order to go in a procession round the church. But before they set out one of the friars preached a sermon in Italian. He began his discourse thus :—*In questa notte tenebrosa,*—at which words all the candles were instantly put out, to yield a livelier image of the occasion. And so we were held by the preacher for near half an hour very much in the dark. Sermon being ended, every person present had a large lighted taper put into his hand, as if it were to make amends for the former darkness ; and the crucifixes and other utensils were disposed in order for beginning the procession. Amongst the other crucifixes there was one of a very large size, which bore upon it the image of our Lord as big as the life. The image was fastened to it with great nails, crowned with thorns, and besmeared with blood ; and so exquisitely was it formed, that it represented, in a very lively manner, the lamentable spectacle of our Lord's body as it hung upon the cross. This figure was carried all along in the head of the procession ; after which the company followed to all the sanctuaries in the church, singing their appointed hymn at every one.

" The first place they visited was that of the Pillar of Flagellation, a large piece of which is kept in a little cell just at the door of the Chapel of the Apparition. There they sang their proper hymn ; and another friar entertained the company with a sermon in Spanish, touching the scourging of our Lord. From hence they proceeded in solemn order to the prison of Christ, where they pretend he was secured whilst the soldiers made things ready for his crucifixion ; here likewise they sang their hymn, and a third friar preached in French. From the prison they went to the altar of the Division of our Lord's garments, where they only sang their hymn without adding any sermon. Having done here, they advanced to the Chapel of the Division ; at which, after their hymn, they had a fourth sermon—as I remember —in French.

" From this place they went up to Calvary, leaving their shoes at the bottom of the stairs. Here are two altars to be visited; one where our Lord is supposed to have been nailed to the cross,—another where his cross was erected. At the former of these they laid down the great crucifix upon the floor, and acted a kind of resemblance of Christ's being nailed to the cross; and after the hymn another friar preached a sermon in Spanish upon the Crucifixion. From hence they removed to the adjoining altar, where the cross is supposed to have been erected, bearing the image of our Lord's body. At this altar is a hole in the natural rock, said to be the very same individual one in which the foot of our Lord's cross stood. Here they set up their cross with the bloody crucified image upon it; and leaving it in that posture, they first sang their hymn, and then the Father Guardian, sitting in a chair before it, preached a Passion-sermon in Italian.

" At about one yard and a half distant from the hole in which the foot of the cross was fixed is seen that memorable cleft in the rock, said to have been made by the earthquake which happened at the suffering of the God of nature; when, as St Matthew witnesseth, the rocks rent and the very graves were opened. This cleft, or what now appears of it, is about a span wide at its upper part, and two deep; after which it closes. But it opens again below, as you may see in another chapel contiguous to the side of Calvary, and runs down to an unknown depth in the earth. That this rent was made by the earthquake that happened at our Lord's Passion there is only tradition to prove; but that it is a natural and genuine breach, and not counterfeited by any art, the sense and reason of every one that sees it may convince him; for the sides of it fit like two tallies to each other, and yet it runs in such intricate windings as could not well be counterfeited by art, nor arrived at by any instruments.

" The ceremony of the Passion being over, and the Guardian's sermon ended, two friars, personating, the one Joseph of Arimathea, the other Nicodemus, approached the cross, and with a most solemn, concerned air, both of aspect and behaviour, drew out the great nails, and took down the feigned body from the cross. It was an *effigies* so contrived that its limbs were soft and flexible, as if they had been real flesh; and nothing could be more surprising than to see the two pretended mourners bend down the arms which were before extended, and dispose them upon the trunk in such a manner as is usual in corpses. The body being taken down from the cross was received in a fair large winding-sheet, and carried down from Calvary; the whole company attending as before to the Stone of Unction. This is taken for the very place where the precious body of our Lord was anointed and prepared for the burial. Here they laid down their imaginary corpse; and casting over it several sweet powders and spices, wrapped it up in the winding-sheet. Whilst this was doing they sang their proper hymn, and afterwards one of the friars preached in Arabic a funeral sermon. These obsequies being finished, they carried off their fancied corpse and laid it in the Sepulchre, shutting up the door till Easter morning. And now after so many sermons, and so long, not to say tedious, a ceremony, it may well be imagined that the weariness of the congregation, as well as the hour of the night, made it needful to go to rest."\*

Easter-eve passed without any remarkable observance, —a period of leisure which was employed by many of the pilgrims in having their arms marked with the usual ensigns of Jerusalem. " The artists who undertake the operation do it in this manner; they have stamps of wood of any figure that you desire, which they first print off upon your arm with powder of charcoal, then taking two very fine needles tied close together, and dipping them often, like a pen, in certain ink compounded, as I

---

\* Journey, p. 74.

was informed, of gunpowder and ox-gall, they make with them small punctures all along the lines of the figure which they have printed; and then, washing the part in wine, conclude the work. The punctures they make with great quickness and dexterity, and with scarce any smart, seldom piercing so deep as to draw blood. In the afternoon of this day the congregation was assembled in the area before the holy grave, where the friars spent some hours in singing over the Lamentations of Jeremiah, which function, with the usual procession to the holy places, was all the ceremony required by this ritual."

On Easter-day the scene was changed from gloom to the most lively congratulation. "The clouds of the former morning were cleared up; and the friars put on a face of joy and serenity, as if it had been the real juncture of our Lord's resurrection. Nor doubtless was this joy feigned, whatever their mourning might be; this being the day on which their Lenten disciplines expired, and they were now come to a full belly again. The mass was celebrated this morning just before the Holy Sepulchre, being the most eminent place in the church; where the Father Guardian had a throne erected, and being arrayed in Episcopal robes, with a mitre on his head, in the sight of the Turks he gave the Host to all that were disposed to receive it; not refusing it to children of seven or eight years old. This office being ended, we made our exit out of the Sepulchre, and returning to the convent, dined with the friars."*

The latest travellers in Palestine witnessed similar observances on the same solemn occasion, none of which were in the least degree calculated to edify an enlightened mind, and many of them such as could not be contemplated without feelings of just indignation, mingled with contempt.

A recent author, for example, writes on this subject as follows:—" Having despatched a hasty meal, we

---

* Journey, p. 76.

hurried off to the church of the Holy Sepulchre, to attend the service of the crucifixion. Oh! what a scene awaited us! What a Babel of unhallowed discord! The *religio loci*—the reverential awe—with which I was at first strongly impressed, was quickly dissipated by the mummeries that were enacted, and the thousand unchristian horrors that assailed us on every side. Well may the Moslem scoff, the Infidel point the finger of scorn at such Christianity as this! It resembles more the rites of Hindoo superstition than the solemn worship of a Christian temple ; and from all I saw and heard, I have much reason to fear that the precincts of an idol sanctuary seldom enclosed an assemblage of worse and more unholy passions than were then concentrated upon the very spot where Christ died. The most intense hatred and spirit of rivalry exist among the various sects of professing Christians, who take every opportunity of slandering each other. Each endeavours to bribe the Turk to oppress the other, and were it not for the iron hand which keeps them all down, they would tear one another to pieces. It was the Roman Catholic service that was performed this evening, to which those of other persuasions paid no attention whatever : on the contrary, they seemed bent on disturbance, talking, walking about, yelling, screaming, making every possible noise that could desecrate the spot. The lash, too, of the Turkish whip, laid on with no lenient hand by the Janissaries appointed to preserve order, perpetually resounded through the church."\*

There is no greater obstacle to the propagation of Christianity among the Syrian tribes, and more especially among the Turks and Jews, than the foolish exhibitions which disgrace the return of the principal festivals in the Holy Land. The mummeries already described could not fail to be sufficiently revolting to a people who allow not any image or representation of created things, even in the uses of ordinary life. Still the sincerity and

---

\* Three Weeks in Palestine, pp. 21, 22.

apparent devotion with which the ceremony of the Crucifixion was performed, might in some degree atone for the unseemly method adopted by the monks to commemorate an event at once so solemn and important. But what shall be said in defence of the manifest fraud which is annually practised in Jerusalem on Easter-eve by the Greek church, when the credulous multitude are taught to believe that fire descends from heaven into the Holy Sepulchre to kindle their lamps and torches?

Upon comparing the description given by Maundrell with the accounts of modern writers, we perceive that a century and a half have passed away without producing any improvement, and that the friars of the present age are probably not less ignorant or dishonest than their predecessors five hundred years ago. " They began their disorders by running round the Holy Sepulchre with all their might and swiftness, crying out as they went, *huia*, which signifies *this is he*, or *this is it*,—an expression by which they assert the verity of the Christian religion. After they had, by these religious circulations and clamours, turned their heads and inflamed their madness, they began to act the most antic tricks and postures in a thousand shapes of distraction. Sometimes they dragged one another along the floor, all round the Sepulchre; sometimes they set one man upright upon another's shoulders, and in this posture marched round; sometimes they tumbled round the Sepulchre after the manner of tumblers on the stage. In a word, nothing can be imagined more rude or extravagant than what was acted upon this occasion.*

" The Greeks first set out in a procession round the Holy Sepulchre, and immediately at their heels followed the Armenians. In this order they compassed the Holy Sepulchre thrice, having produced all their gallantry of standards, streamers, crucifixes, and embroidered habits. Toward the end of this procession there was a pigeon came fluttering into the cupola over the Sepulchre; at

---

* Maundrell's Journey, p. 94.

sight of which there was a greater shout and clamour than before. This bird, the Latins told us, was purposely let fly by the Greeks, to deceive the people into an opinion that it was a visible descent of the Holy Ghost. The procession being over, the suffragan of the Greek patriarch, and the principal Armenian bishop, approached to the door of the Sepulchre, and cutting the string with which it is fastened and sealed, entered in, shutting the door after them,—all the candles and lamps within having been before extinguished in the presence of the Turks and other witnesses. The exclamations were doubled as the miracle drew nearer to its accomplishment; and the people pressed with such vehemence towards the door of the Sepulchre that it was not in the power of the Turks to keep them off. The cause of their pressing in this manner is the great desire they have to light their candles at the holy flame as soon as it is first brought out of the Sepulchre; it being esteemed the most sacred and pure, as coming immediately from heaven. The two miracle-mongers had not been above a minute in the Holy Sepulchre, when the glimmering of the Holy fire was seen, or imagined to appear, through some chinks of the door; and certainly Bedlam itself never saw such an unruly transport as was produced in the mob at this sight.

" Immediately after, out came two priests with blazing torches in their hands, which they held up at the door of the Sepulchre; while the people thronged about with inexpressible ardour, every one striving to obtain a part of the first and purest flame. The Turks in the mean time, with huge clubs, laid on without mercy; but all this could not repel them, the excess of their fury making them insensible of pain. Those that got the fire applied it immediately to their beards, faces, and bosoms, pretending that it would not burn like an earthly flame. But I plainly saw none of them could endure this experiment long enough to make good that pretension. So many hands being employed, you may be sure it could not be long before innumerable tapers were lighted. The whole church, galleries, and every place, seemed instantly to be in a flame; and with this illumination the ceremony ended.

"It must be owned that those two within the Sepulchre performed their part with great quickness and dexterity; but the behaviour of the rabble without very much discredited the miracle. The Latins take a great deal of pains to expose this ceremony, as a most shameful imposture, and a scandal to the Christian religion; perhaps out of envy that others should be masters of so gainful a business. But the Greeks and Armenians pin their faith upon it: such is the deplorable unhappiness of their priests, that, having acted the cheat so long already, they are forced now to stand to it for fear of endangering the apostacy of their people. Going out of church after the rant was over, we saw several people gathered about the Stone of Unction, who, having got a good store of candles lighted with the holy fire, were employed in daubing pieces of linen with the wicks of them and the melting wax; which pieces of linen were designed for winding-sheets. And it is the opinion of these poor people, that if they can but have the happiness to be buried in a shroud smutted with this celestial fire, it will certainly secure them from the flames of hell."\*

---

\* Journey, p. 96. Mr Spence Hardy informs his readers, that when he witnessed this ceremony, "Pliny Fisk requested permission to enter (the Sepulchre) along with the bishop, stating that the conversion of an unbeliever would increase the celebrity of the fire, by confirming its truth; but he was told if he were present with the bishop when the fire appeared, his instant death would be the consequence. The people maintain that the fire will not burn those who believe in its powers; hence some of the men passed it quickly over their beards, and put it under their clothes, but in such a way that any other fire would be equally harmless. I have attended many descriptions of heathen festivals; I have seen the devil-dancers, apparently under Satanic influence, and the Mussulman devotees shout round their fires at the feast of Hussein Hassan; but I never witnessed any exhibition that excited in my mind feelings of deeper disgust, and this, too, in the name of Christ, and in a place probably not very far distant from the sacred spot where he bowed his head and died."—Notices of the Holy Land, pp. 159, 160.

Dr Richardson, who witnessed the same pitiful ceremony, is not inclined to give much honour to the performers with respect to skill or dexterous manipulation. On the contrary, he is of opinion that there is not a pyrotechnist in London who could not have improved the exhibition. From the station which he occupied in the church, being the organ-loft of the Roman Catholic division, he distinctly saw the flame issuing from a burning substance placed within the tomb, and which was raised and lowered according to circumstances. The priests meant to be very artful, but were in reality very ignorant. Like the Druids of old, no one, under the pain of excommunication, dared to light his torch at that of another; every individual was bound to derive his flame from the miraculous spark that descended from above, and which could only be conveyed by the hands of the chief priest.*

---

* " Je ne décrirai pas la suite de cérémonies réligieuses qui occupent le reste de la semaine sainte; c'est un récit qui peut bien édifier des âmes dévotes, mais non pas plaire à quelqu'un qui lit un voyage pour s'instruire et s'amuser.

" Il n'en est pas de même d'une pratique superstitieuse des Grecs schismatiques, dont la bizarrerie ne laissera pas de divertir un moment.

" Cette secte, abusée par ces prêtres, croit de bonne foi que Dieu fait annuellement un miracle pour lui envoyer le feu sacré.

" A en croire les prêtres Grecs, cette faveur divine, dont on ne peut pas douter, est une preuve insigne de l'excellence de leur communion. Mais ne pourrait-on pas objecter aux Grecs, que les Arméniens et les Cofes, qu'ils traitent d'hérétiques, participent à cette même grâce? Ennemis acharnés les uns des autres, les ministres de ces trois sectes se réunissent en apparence, pour la cérémonie du feu sacré. Cette réconciliation momentanée n'est due qu'à l'intérêt de tous; séparément ils seraient obligés de payer au gouverneur, pour la permission de faire le miracle, une somme aussi forte que celte qu'ils donnent ensemble.

" Ces prêtres portent la fourberie jusqu'à vouloir persuader au peuple que le feu sacré ne brûle pas ceux qui sont en état de grace. Ils se frottent les mains d'une certaine eau, qui les garantit de la brulure à la première approche, et par ce moyen ne se font aucun mal en touchant leurs cierges. Leurs prosélytes sont jaloux de les imiter; mais comme ils n'ont pas leur recette, bien souvent ils se brulent les doigts et le visage: il arrive delà que les prêtres, paraissant jouir exclusivement de la grâce de Dieu, en sont plus respectés et mieux payés."—Mariti, Voyages, &c. tome ii. p. 340.

Having seen the exhibition of this vile and infamous delusion, the traveller naturally inquires what credit he ought to give to the historical statements and local descriptions derived from the Christians who now occupy Jerusalem. Are the honoured spots within these walls really what the guardians of the metropolitan church declare them to be? Is the Mount Calvary shown at this day in the holy city the actual place where Christ expired upon the cross to redeem the human race? Is the sepulchre there exhibited really that of the just man Joseph of Arimathea, in which the body of the blessed Jesus was laid? Or are all these merely convenient spots fixed on at random, and consecrated to serve the interested views of a crafty priesthood?*

We agree in the conclusion, that it is of no consequence to the Christian faith in what way these questions shall be determined. The great facts on which the history of the gospel is founded are not so closely connected with particular spots of earth, or sacred buildings, as to be rendered doubtful by any mistake in the choice of a locality. Nor is there any material discrepancy between the opinions of Chateaubriand, which I am inclined to adopt, and those of Dr Clarke, who treats with contempt all the traditions respecting holy places; for the outline may be correct, although the minuter details are open to a just suspicion. For example, it is now extremely difficult to trace the boundaries of Calvary; the effects of time, and the operations of the destructive siege under the Roman prince, have obliterated some of the features by which that remarkable scene was distinguished. It has even ceased to present the appearance of a mount,—an appellation, by the way, which is nowhere given to it in Scripture. But it does not follow that the Christians, who returned from Pella to inhabit the ruins of the sacred metropolis, should have been equally ignorant of its extent and situation; nor is it at all probable that

---

* Richardson, vol. ii. p. 333.

places so interesting to the affections of the infant church would be allowed to fall into a speedy oblivion.*

The main error of the modern priests at Jerusalem arises from an anxiety to exhibit every thing to which any allusion is made by the evangelical historians; not remembering that the lapse of ages and the devastation of successive wars have destroyed much and disguised more, which the early disciples could most readily identify. The mere circumstance that almost all the events which attended the close of our Saviour's ministry are crowded into one scene, covered by the roof of a single church, might excite a very justifiable doubt as to the exactness of the topography maintained by the friars of Mount Moriah. " This edifice is less than one hundred paces long, and not more than sixty wide; and yet it is so contrived, that it is supposed to contain under its roof twelve or thirteen sanctuaries or places consecrated to a more than ordinary veneration, by being reputed to have some particular actions done in them relating to the death and resurrection of Christ."†

All that can now be affirmed, observes Dr Clarke, with any show of reason, is this, " that, if Helena had reason to believe she could identify the spot where the Sepulchre was, she took especial care to remove every trace of it, in order to introduce the fanciful and modern work which now remains. The place may be the same pointed out to her; but not a remnant of the original Sepulchre can now be ascertained. Yet, with our sceptical feelings thus awakened, it may prove how powerful the effect of sympathy is, if we confess, that when we entered into the supposed Sepulchre, and beheld, by the light of lamps there continually burning, the venerable figure of an aged monk, with streaming eyes and a long white beard, pointing to the ' place where the Lord lay,' and calling upon us to kneel and experience pardon for our sins,—we did kneel, and we participated

---

\* See above, p. 24, with the note from M. De Lamartine, p. 23.
† Maundrell's Journey, p. 69.

in the feelings of more credulous pilgrims. Captain Culverhouse, in whose mind the ideas of religion and of patriotism were inseparable, with firmer emotion, drew from its scabbard the sword he had so often wielded in the defence of his country and placed it upon the tomb. Humbler comers heaped the memorials of an accomplished pilgrimage; and, while their sighs alone interrupted the silence of the sanctuary, a solemn service was begun."*

It is observed by the author of the Itinéraire, that the ancient travellers were extremely fortunate in not being obliged to enter into all these critical disquisitions: in the first place, because they found in their readers that religion which never contends against truth; and, secondly, because every mind was convinced that the only way of seeing a country as it is, must be to see it with all its traditions and recollections. It is, in fact, with the Bible as his guide that a traveller ought to visit the Holy Land. If we are determined to carry with us a spirit of cavil and contradiction, Judea is not worth our going so far to examine it. What should we say to a man who, in traversing Greece and Italy, should think of nothing but contradicting Homer and Virgil? Such, however, is the course adopted by too many modern travellers; evidently the effect of our vanity, which would excite a high idea of our own abilities, and at the same time fill us with disdain for those of other people.†

A short time after M. Chateaubriand visited Jerusalem, the church of the Holy Sepulchre was destroyed by fire; and although it has been since repaired, it is admitted that both the architecture and the internal decorations are much inferior to those of the original edifice. The general plan of the whole building, however, as well as the arrangement of the holy stations, are so exactly preserved, that the descriptions of the earliest writers apply as correctly to its present as to its

---

* Travels, vol. iv. p. 315.　　† Vol. ii. p. 21.

former state. It is true, that the tombs of Godfrey de Bouillon and of Baldwin his brother, which called forth the enthusiastic admiration of the French author just named, have been annihilated by the malignant Greeks, so that not a vestige remains to mark the spot whereon they stood. The Corinthian columns of fine marble which formerly adorned the interior being rendered useless by the fire, the dome is now supported by tall slender pillars of masonry, plastered on the outside, and so closely grouped together as to produce the worst effect. We are told, indeed, that the meanness of every thing about the architecture of the central dome, and of the whole rotunda which surrounds the Sepulchre itself, can only be exceeded by the wretched taste of its painted decorations.*

It was of the older building that the Vicomte made the following remarks:—" The church of the Holy Sepulchre, composed of several churches erected upon an unequal surface, illumined by a multitude of lamps, is singularly mysterious; a sombre light pervades it, favourable to piety and profound devotion. Christian priests of various sects inhabit different parts of the edifice. From the arches above, where they nestle like pigeons, from the chapels below and subterraneous vaults, their songs are heard at all hours both of the day and night. The organ of the Latin monks, the cymbals of the Abyssinian priest, the voice of the Greek caloyer, the prayer of the solitary Armenian, the plaintive accents of the Coptic friar, alternately, or all at once, assail your ear. You know not whence these accents of praise proceed; you inhale the perfume of incense without perceiving the hand that burns it; you merely observe the pontiff, who is going to celebrate the most awful of mysteries on the very spot where they were accomplished, pass quickly by, glide behind the columns, and vanish in the gloom of the temple.

" Christian readers will perhaps inquire what were

---

\* Buckingham's Travels, vol. i. p. 384.

my feelings upon entering this sacred place. I really cannot tell. So many reflections rushed at once upon my mind, that I was unable to dwell upon any particular idea. I continued nearly half an hour upon my knees in the little chamber of the Holy Sepulchre, with my eyes riveted upon the stone, from which I had not the power to turn them. One of the two monks who accompanied me remained prostrate on the marble by my side, while the other, with the Testament in his hand, read to me by the light of the lamps the passages relating to the sacred tomb. All I can say is, that when I beheld this triumphant Sepulchre, I felt nothing but my own weakness; and that when my guide exclaimed with St Paul, O death, where is thy sting? O grave, where is thy victory? I listened, as if Death were about to reply that he was conquered and enchained in this monument. Where shall we look in antiquity for any thing so impressive, so wonderful, as the last scenes described by the Evangelists? These are not the absurd adventures of a deity foreign to human nature: it is a most pathetic history,—a history which not only extorts tears by its beauty, but whose consequences, applied to the universe, have changed the face of the earth. I had just beheld the monuments of Greece, and my mind was still profoundly impressed with their grandeur; but how far inferior were the sentiments which they excited to those I felt at the sight of the places commemorated in the gospel!"*

We must not presume to follow the ardent pilgrim along the *Via Dolorosa*, the name given to the way by which the Saviour passed from the house of Pilate to the Mount of Calvary. Nor can we stop to revere the arch, called *Ecce Homo*, where, we are told, the window may still be seen from which the Roman judge exclaimed to the vindictive Jews, "Behold the Man!" We cannot resign our belief to the minute description which recognises the house of Simon the Pharisee, where Mary

---

* Travels in Greece, Palestine, Egypt, &c. vol. ii. p. 22.

Magdalene confessed her sins; the prison of St Peter, and the dwelling of Mary the mother of Mark, in which the same apostle took refuge when he was set at liberty by the angel; and even the mansion of Dives, the rich man, at whose gate the mendicant Lazarus was laid, full of sores.

On crossing the small ravine which divides the modern city from Mount Sion, the attention of the traveller is drawn to three ancient monuments, or more properly ruins, covered with buildings comparatively modern,— the house of Caiaphas,—the place where Christ held his last Supper,—and the tomb or palace of David. The first of these is now a church, the duty of which is performed by the Armenians; the second, consecrated by the affecting solemnity with the memory of which it is still associated, presents a mosque and a Turkish hospital; while the third, a small vaulted apartment, contains only three sepulchres formed of dark-coloured stone. This holy hill is equally celebrated in the Old Testament and in the New. Here the successor of Saul built a city and a royal dwelling,—here he kept for three months the Ark of the Covenant,—here the Redeemer instituted the sacrament which commemorates his death,—here he appeared to his disciples on the day of his resurrection, —and here the Holy Ghost descended on the apostles. The place hallowed by the Last Supper, if we may believe the early Fathers, was transformed into the first Christian temple the world ever saw, where St James the Less was consecrated the first bishop of Jerusalem, and where he presided in the first council of the church. Finally, it was from this spot that the apostles, in compliance with the injunction to go and teach all nations, departed, without purse and without scrip, to seat their religion upon all the thrones of the earth.

Descending Mount Sion on the eastern side, the eye is attracted by the Fountain and Pool of Siloam, so celebrated in the history of our Saviour's miracles. The brook itself is ill supplied with water, and, compared with the ideas formed in the mind by the fine invocation of the poet, usually creates disappointment.* A few paces to the northward, is the source of the scanty rivulet, which is called by some the Fountain of the Virgin, from an opinion that she frequently went thither to drink. It appears in a recess about twenty feet lower than the surface, and under an arched vault of masonry tolerably well executed. The rock had been originally hewn down to reach this pool; and a small winding passage, of which only the beginning is seen, is said to convey the water out of the valley, and to supply the means of irrigating the little gardens still cultivated in that spot. Notwithstanding the dirty state of the water, and its harsh and brackish taste, it continues to be used by the devout for diseases of the eye.

It is said to have a kind of ebb and flow, sometimes discharging its current like the Fountain of Vaucluse, at others retaining and scarcely suffering it to run at all. The Levites, we are told, used to sprinkle the water of Siloam on the altar at the Feast of Tabernacles, saying, " Ye shall draw water with joy from the wells of salvation." The reader will find on the following page a representation of the Pool, as it appeared to the eye of an able traveller,—a considerable part of the arch having fallen down, or been destroyed by the barbarians who continue to hold the sacred capital in subjection.

The Valley of Jehoshaphat stretches between the eastern walls of the city and the Mount of Olives, containing a great variety of objects, to which allusion is made in the Sacred Writings. It was sometimes called

---

* The invocation alluded to must be familiar to the youngest reader:—

" Sing, heavenly muse, that on the secret top
Of Oreb or of Sinai didst inspire
That shepherd who first taught the chosen seed,
In the beginning, how the heavens and earth
Rose out of Chaos; or, if Zion Hill
Delight thee more, and Siloa's brook that flow'd
Fast by the oracle of God; I thence
Invoke thy aid to my advent'rous song."
*Paradise Lost*, book i.

Fountain of Siloam.

the King's Dale, from a reference to an event recorded in the history of Abraham, and was afterwards distinguished by the name of Jehoshaphat, because that sovereign erected in it a magnificent tomb. This narrow ravine seems to have always served as a burying-place for the inhabitants of the holy city: there are seen monuments of the most remote ages, as well as of modern times; thither the descendants of Jacob resort from the four quarters of the globe, to yield up their last breath; and a foreigner sells to them, for its weight in gold, a scanty spot of earth to cover their remains in the country of their ancestors. " Observing many Jews, whom I could easily recognise by their yellow turbans, quick dark eyes, black eyebrows, and bushy beards, walking about the place, and reposing along the Brook Kedron in a pensive mood, the pathetic language of the Psalmist occurred to me, as expressing the subject of their meditation—' By the rivers we sat down and wept when we remembered Zion.' Upon frequently inquiring the motive that prompted them in attempting to go to Jerusalem, the answer was, ' to die in the land of our fathers.' "*

This valley or dale still exhibits a very desolate appearance. The western side is a high chalk-cliff supporting the walls of the city, above which is seen Jerusalem itself; while the eastern acclivity is formed by the Mount of Olives and the Mount of Offence, so called from the idolatry which darkens the fame of Solomon. These two hills are nearly naked, and of a dull-red colour. On their slopes are observed a few bleak and parched vines, some groves of wild olive-trees, wastes covered with hyssop, chapels, oratories, and mosques in ruins. At the bottom of the valley is a bridge of a single arch, thrown across the channel of the Brook Kedron. The stones in the Jewish cemetery look like a heap of rubbish at the foot of the declivity, below the Arab village of Siloane, the paltry houses of which are scarcely to be distinguished from the surrounding sepulchres. From the stillness of the city, whence no smoke arises and no noise proceeds,—from the solitude of these hills, where no living creature is to be seen,—from the ruinous state of all these tombs, overthrown, broken, and half-open, one might imagine that the last trumpet had already sounded, and that the Valley of Jehoshaphat was about to render up its dead.

Amidst this scene of desolation three monuments arrest the eyes of the intelligent pilgrim,—the tombs of Zachariah, of Absalom, and of the king whose name still distinguishes the valley. The first mentioned of

---

* Travels by Rae Wilson, vol. i. p. 220.

these is a square mass of rock, hewn down into form, and isolated from the quarry out of which it is cut by a passage of twelve or fifteen feet wide on three of its sides ; the fourth or western front being open towards the valley and to Mount Moriah, the foot of which is only a few yards distant. This huge stone is eight paces in length on each side, and about twenty feet high in the front, and ten feet high at the back ; the hill on which it stands having a steep ascent. It has four semi-columns cut out of the same rock on each of its faces, with a pilaster at each angle, all of a mixed Ionic order, and ornamented in bad taste. The architraves, the full moulding, and the deep overhanging cornice which finishes the square, are all perfectly after the Egyptian manner; and the whole is surmounted by a pyramid, the sloping sides of which rise from the very edges of the square below, and terminate in a finished point.

The body of this monument, it has been already stated, is one solid mass of rock, as well as its semi-columns on each face, but the tapering ornament on the top appears to be of masonry ; its sides, however, are perfectly smooth, like the coated pyramids of Sahara and Dashour, and not graduated by stages like those of Djizeh in Lower Egypt.

Inconsiderable in size, and paltry in its decorations, this monument, nevertheless, is extremely curious. There is no appearance of an entrance into any part of it ; so that it seems, if a tomb, to have been as firmly closed as those of Egypt, and perhaps from the same respect for the repose of the dead. It is probable, indeed, that the original style and plan of the building are derived from the country of the Pharaohs, while the Grecian columns and pilasters may be the work of a much later period, when the Jews had learned to combine with the massy piles of their more ancient architecture the elegant lightness which distinguished the times of the Seleucidæ.*

---

* Buckingham's Travels in Palestine, vol. i. p. 297.

In the immediate vicinity is the Tomb of Jehoshaphat,—a cavern which is more commonly called the Grotto of the Disciples, from an idea that they went frequently thither to be taught by their Divine Master. The front of this excavation has two Doric pillars of small size, but of just proportions. In the interior are three chambers, all of them rude and irregular in their form, in one of which were several grave-stones, removed, we may suppose, from the open ground for greater security. Like all the rest, they were flat slabs of an oblong shape, from three to six inches in thickness, and evidently a portion of the limestone-rock which composes the adjoining hills.

Opposite to this, on the east, is the reputed Tomb of Absalom, resembling nearly, in the size, form, and decoration of its square base, that of Zachariah already described, except that it is sculptured with the metopes and triglyphs of the Doric order. This is surmounted by a sharp conical dome, having large mouldings running round its base, and on the top something like an imitation of flame. Here again there is so strange a mixture of style and ornament, that one knows not to what age to attribute the structure viewed as a whole. The square mass below is solid, and the Ionic columns, which are seen on each of its faces, are half-indented in the rock itself. The dome is of masonry, and on the eastern side of it there is a square aperture. Generally speaking, the sight of this mausoleum rather confirms the idea suggested by the Tomb of Zachariah, that the hewn mass of solid rock, the surmounting pyramid and dome of masonry, and the sculptured frieze and Ionic columns wrought on the faces of the square below, were works of different periods; being probably ancient sepulchres, the primitive character of which had been changed by the subsequent addition of foreign ornaments. There is, besides, every reason to believe that this monument really occupies the site of the one which was set up by him whose name it bears. " Now Absalom, in his lifetime, had reared up for himself a pillar,

Tomb of Absalom.

which is in the King's Dale: for he said, I have no son to keep my name in remembrance; and he called the pillar after his own name: and it is called unto this day, Absalom's Place."*

Chateaubriand is of opinion that, except the Pool of Bethesda at Jerusalem, we have no remains of the primitive architecture of its inhabitants. This reservoir, a hundred and fifty feet long and forty broad, is still to be seen near St Stephen's Gate, where it bounded the Temple on the north. The sides are walled by means of large stones, joined together by iron cramps, and covered with flints embedded in a substance resembling

---

* 2 Samuel, xviii. 18. Travels in Palestine, vol. i. p. 302.

plaster. Here the lambs destined for sacrifice were washed; and it was on the brink of this pool that Christ said to the paralytic man " Arise, take up thy bed and walk." It receives a melancholy interest from the fact, that it is probably the last remnant of Jerusalem as it appeared in the days of Solomon and of his immediate successors.

It cannot be denied that the tombs in the Valley of Jehoshaphat display an alliance of Egyptian and Grecian taste; and, in naturalizing in their capital the architecture of Memphis and of Athens, it is equally certain that the Jews mixed with it the forms of their own peculiar style. From this combination resulted a heterogeneous kind of structure, forming as it were the link between the Pyramids and the Parthenon,—monuments in which you discover a pensive yet bold and elevated genius, associated with a pleasing and cultivated imagination.

Our limits forbid us to follow the footsteps of the pilgrim in his minute survey of the " Sepulchres of the Kings," which, it is acknowledged, cannot be traced back to a remoter era than that of the Grecian dynasty at Antioch and Damascus. There are several other tombs and grottos to which tradition has attached venerable names, and even consecrated them as the scene of important events; but as they are not remarkable on any other account, we shall not extend to an undue length our description of the holy places under the walls of Jerusalem.

We shall simply remark, that a difference of opinion exists among modern travellers in regard to the extent of the ancient city; the ground it actually covered; the changes it has since undergone; and hence, also, with respect to the position of some of the more prominent objects which attract the attention of the inquisitive tourist in our own days. Dr Clarke, as may be gathered from statements already made, has distinguished himself by some bold speculations on this head, the effect of which is to derange all the received notions relative to the scene of the Crucifixion and the place of the Holy Sepulchre. It will, indeed, be readily granted, that it is a matter of very small importance to the faith of a Christian, to determine whether the decease which was accomplished at Jerusalem took place on the north-western or the south-eastern extremity of that metropolis. But as the history and tradition of many ages have fixed the spot where the cross was erected, and where the new tomb in the rock had its situation, it is requisite that the arguments of a writer who himself pays so little respect to authority should be examined with attention. In this case, it is obvious, an inspection of the ground, candidly and distinctly reported, is of much more weight than the most ingenious reasoning if destitute of facts; on which account we are happy to have it in our power to refer to the journal of a learned gentleman, hitherto unpublished, who a short time ago travelled in Syria and Palestine.

" We passed by the place of St Stephen's Martyrdom down into the Valley of Jehoshaphat. This valley, independently of associations, is highly picturesque. It is deep and narrow; the lower part is green with scattered olives. The slop up towards the city is also smooth and green, and crowned by the towers and battlements. On ascending the Mount of Olives, which we did towards the south, we had a splendid view of Jerusalem. The chief ornaments are the two domes of the Holy Sepulchre, the Mosque of Omar, and another large mosque, with a smaller dome; but the white houses make a good show, and the walls are picturesque. On looking at Jerusalem from this place, the great features seemed to me to agree entirely with the established maps, and Dr Clarke's theory appeared quite untenable. The only difficulty is, that there is no valley which *runs up all the way*, so as to divide entirely Mount Sion from Mount Moriah. A ravine does run far enough to cut off the Temple, but no more. The extent of this difficulty must depend on the description left us of the Tyropæum and Millo. Was there a deep valley such as time and change might not have obliterated? The people of the convent gave the name of the Mount of Offence to a low hill on the south of the Mount of Olives; but Clarke seems to think that the real Mount of Offence is that divided by Jehinnom from Sion, and called by our guide Monte de Mal Consiglio. We visited the Mohammedan chapel built over the place of the Ascension, and saw the alleged print of Christ's foot. We next went to the place called Viri Galilæi (ye men of Galilee), and after looking in vain for Dr Clarke's pagan remains, descended towards the Cave of the Prophets. We saw the well where Nehemiah found the fire of the altar, and then went up the Valley of Hinnom; first to the tomb called the Crypt of the Apostles, close to the Aceldama or Field of Blood. We saw many other grottos; one had της άγιας Σιων inscribed upon it, as had another much farther up. Near this last was that which Clarke maintained to be the Holy Sepulchre. We saw one which would do very well for it; but so would many others. This one was a cave, with a place for a body cut out in the back part of it; but raised like a stone trough, not sunk in the floor. There is, of course, not a shadow of reason for thinking Clarke's cave to be the real one, and very little, that I can see, for doubting that the nominal Holy Sepulchre is so in fact; or rather, that it is *on the site* of the real one, which must have been destroyed when Adrian erected his temple to Venus on the spot. From these caves we went by the pool of Bathsheba to the Bethlehem Gate, and so along the west side of the town to the Tombs of the Judges and Kings, which lie north or north-west of the city. I observed large foundations of ancient walls and heaps of rubbish west of the modern town, where Clarke seems to assume that there was anciently no part of the city. There, and on the north, I also observed wells opening into large covered reservoirs for water. We entered only one of the Tombs of the Judges, the rest being insignificant. That one was large, with a pediment which had dentiles and other Greek ornaments. Inside there were at least three chambers, surrounded by receptacles for bodies. In returning we went to the Tombs of the Kings, which, like the others, are cut out of the rock, and like them, too, have Grecian ornaments. There is one large cave; the front has a handsome entablature, the upper part ornamented with alternate circular garlands, bunches of grapes, and an ornament of acanthus leaves; the lower with a rich band of foliage disposed with much elegance."*

Hence it appears, that the weight of evidence preponderates decidedly in favour of the common opinions, as to the form of the ancient city and the places which are usually denominated holy. Why then should any one attempt to disturb the belief or acquiescence of the Christian world on a subject concerning which all nations have hitherto found reason to agree? The members of the primitive church had better means than we have of being fully informed respecting the scenes of the Evangelical history; and it is manifest that, amid all the changes which ensued in Jerusalem, either from conquest or superstition, nothing was more unlikely than that the faithful should forget the sacred spot where their redemption was completed, or that they should consent to transfer their veneration to any other.†

---

\* See Tour of the Holy Land, by the Rev. Robert Morehead, D. D.; in the Appendix to which are extracts from this anonymous manuscript.

† " Having so often mentioned Clarke, I must say that, although an animated and interesting writer, and not incorrect in his descriptions, he is more deficient in judgment than any traveller I am acquainted with; and I do not recollect an instance, either here or in Egypt, where he has attempted to speculate without falling into some very decided error. I mention this the more, as his enthusiasm and conviction of the truth of his own theories led me formerly to place great faith in his authority."—*Anonymous Journal*.

## CHAPTER VI.

*Description of the Country South and East of Jerusalem.*

Garden of Gethsemane—Tomb of Virgin Mary—Grottos on Mount of Olives—View of the City—Extent and Boundaries—View of Bethany and Dead Sea—Bethlehem—Convent Church of the Nativity described—Paintings—Music—Population of Bethlehem—Pools of Solomon—Dwelling of Simon the Leper—Of Mary Magdalene—Tower of Simeon—Tomb of Rachel—Convent of St John—Fine Church—Tekoa—Bethulia—Hebron—Sepulchre of Patriarchs—Al-baid—Kerek—Extremity of Dead Sea—Discoveries of Bankes, Legh, Irby, and Mangles—Convent of St Saba—Valley of Jordan—Mountains—Description of Lake Asphaltites—Remains of ancient Cities in its Basin—Quality of its Waters—Apples of Sodom—Tacitus, Seetzen, Hasselquist, Chateaubriand—Width of River Jordan—Jericho—Village of Rihhah—Balsam—Fountain of Elisha—Mount of Temptation—Place of Blood—Anecdote of Sir F. Henniker—Fountain of the Apostles—Return to Jerusalem—Markets—Costume—Science—Arts—Language—Jews—Present Condition of that People.

In proceeding from Jerusalem towards Bethany, the traveller skirts the Mount of Olives; or if he wishes to enjoy the magnificent view which it presents, both of the city and of the extensive tract watered by the Jordan, he ascends its heights, and at the same time inspects the remains of sacred architecture still to be seen on its summit. As he passes from the eastern gate, the Garden of Gethsemane meets his eyes, as well as the tomb which bears the name of the Blessed Virgin. This has a building over it with a pretty front, although the Grecian ornaments sculptured in relief are not quite in harmony with the pointed arch at the entrance. It is approached by a paved court, now a raised way, leading from the Mount of Olives over the Brook Kedron. The descent into it is formed by a handsome flight of steps composed of polished stone, being about fifty in number, and of a noble breadth. About midway down are two arched recesses in the sides, said to contain the ashes of St Anne the mother of Mary, as also those of Joseph her husband. Reaching the bottom of the stairs, the visiter is shown the tomb of the Holy Virgin herself, which is in the form of a simple bench coated with marble. Here the Greeks and Armenians say mass by turns, and near it is a humble altar for the Syrian Christians; whilst opposite to it is one for the Copts, consisting of earth, and entirely destitute of lamps, pictures, covering, and every other species of ornament. Chateaubriand observes that the Turks have a portion of this grotto: Buckingham asserts that they have no right to enter it, nor could he "learn from the keepers of the place that they ever had ;" whereas the author of the Anonymous Journal, from which I have already quoted, states distinctly that "there is a place reserved for the Mussulmans to pray, which at the Virgin's Tomb one would not expect to be much in request." So much for the clashing of authorities, even on the part of writers who could have no wish to deceive!

There are various other grottos on the acclivity of the hill, meant to keep alive the remembrance of certain occurrences which are either mentioned in the gospel, or have been transmitted to the present age by oral tradition. Among these is one, which is supposed to be the scene of the Agony and the Bloody Sweat; a second marks the place where St Peter and the two sons of Zebedee fell asleep when their Master retired to pray; and a third indicates the spot whereon Judas betrayed the Son of Man with a kiss. Here also is pointed out the rock from which our Saviour predicted the sack of Jerusalem and the destruction of the Temple,—that dreadful visitation of which the traces are still clearly visible both within and around the walls. The curious pilgrim is farther edified by the sight of a cavern where the Apostles were taught the Lord's Prayer; and of another where the same individuals at a later period are said to have met together to compose their creed. On the principal top of the Mount of Olives,—for the elevated ground presents three separate summits,—are a mosque and the remains of a church. The former is distinguished by a lofty minaret which commands an extensive prospect; but the latter is esteemed more remarkable, as containing a piece of rock imprinted with the mark of our Saviour's foot while in the act of ascension.

But the view of the venerable metropolis itself, which stretches out its lanes and sacred enclosures under the eye of the traveller, is still more interesting than the recapitulation of ambiguous relics. It occupies, as we have already seen, an irregular square of about two miles and a half in circumference. Eusebius gave a measurement of twenty-seven stadia, amounting to nearly a mile more than its present dimensions; a difference which can easily be explained, by adverting to the changes made on the line of fortifications by the Saracens and Turks, especially on the north-west and western extremities of the town. Its shortest side apparently is that which faces the east, and in this is the supposed gate of the ancient Temple—shut up by the Mussulmans from a superstitious motive—and the small projecting stone on which their Prophet is to sit when he shall judge the world assembled in the vale below. The southern side is exceedingly irregular, taking quite a zig-zag direction; the south-western entrance being terminated by a mosque built over what is esteemed the sepulchre of David, on the elevation of Mount Sion. The form and exact direction of the western and northern walls are not distinctly seen from the position now assumed; but every part of them appears to be a modern work, and executed nearly at the same time. They are flanked at certain distances by square towers, and have battlements all along their summits, with loopholes for arrows or musketry close to the top. Their height is about fifty feet, but they are not surrounded by a ditch. The northern wall runs over ground which declines slightly outward; the eastern wall passes straight along the brow of Mount Moriah, with the deep Valley of Jehoshaphat below; the southern wall crosses Mount Sion, with the Vale of Hinnom at its feet; and the western wall is carried over a more uniform level, near the summit of the bare hills which terminate at the Jaffa gate.*

---

* Buckingham, vol. i. p. 316.—The following words, put into the mouth of Titus by the eloquent author of the " Fall of Jerusalem," will be read with interest in connexion with the view just given. The son of Vespasian stands on the Mount of Olives:—

" It must be———
And yet it moves me, Romans! it confounds
The counsels of my firm philosophy,
That Ruin's merciless ploughshare must pass o'er
And barren salt be sown on yon proud city.
As on our olive-crowned hill we stand,
Where Kedron at our feet its scanty waters
Distils from stone to stone with gentle motion,
As through a valley sacred to sweet Peace,
How boldly doth it front us! how majestically!
Like a luxurious vineyard, the hill-side
Is hung with marble fabrics, line on line,
Terrace o'er terrace, nearer still, and nearer
To the blue heavens. Here bright and sumptuous palaces,
With cool and verdant gardens interspersed;
Here towers of war that frown in massy strength.
While over all hangs the rich purple eve,
As conscious of its being her last farewell
Of light and glory to that fated city.
And as our clouds of battle, dust, and smoke,
Are melted into air, behold the Temple,
In undisturb'd and lone serenity,
Finding itself a solemn sanctuary
In the profound of heaven! It stands before us
A mount of snow fretted with golden pinnacles!
The very sun, as though he worshipp'd there,
Lingers upon the gilded cedar roofs;
And down the long and branching porticos,
On every flowery sculptured capital
Glitters the homage of his parting beams.
By Hercules! the sight might almost win
The offended majesty of Rome to mercy."

Old Sandys, a simple and amusing writer, describes Jerusalem as follows:—" This citie once sacred and glorious, elected by God for his seate, and seated in the midst of nations; like a diadem crowning the head of the mountaines; the theatre of mysteries and

P-M

Village of Bethany, and Dead Sea.

Turning towards the east, the traveller sees at the foot of the hill the little village of Bethany, so often mentioned in the history of our Lord and his disciples; and at a greater distance, he beholds the magnificent scenery of the Jordan and the Dead Sea.

There are two roads from Jerusalem to Bethany; the one passing over the Mount of Olives; the other, the shorter and easier, winding round the eastern side of it. This village is now both small and poor, the cultivation of the soil around it being very much neglected by the indolent Arabs into whose hands it has fallen. Here are shown the ruins of a house, said to have belonged to Lazarus whom our Saviour raised from the dead; and, in the immediate neighbourhood, the faithful pilgrim is invited to devotion in a grotto, which is represented as the actual tomb wherein the miracle was performed. The dwellings of Simon the Leper, of Mary Magdalene, and of Martha, are pointed out by the inhabitants, who traffic on the credulity of ignorant Christians. Nay, they undertake to identify the spot where the barren fig-tree withered under the curse, and the place where Judas put an end to his life, oppressed by a more dreadful malediction.

There is no traveller of any nation, whatever may be his creed or his impressions with regard to the gospel, who does not make the usual journey from the Jewish capital to Bethlehem, the place of our Lord's Nativity. The road, as we find related, passes over ground extremely rocky and barren, diversified only by some cultivated patches bearing a scanty crop of grain, and by banks of wild-flowers which grow in great profusion. On the way the practised guide points out the ruined tower of Simeon,

---

miracles; was founded by Melchisedek (who is said to be the son of Noah, and that not unprobably) about the year of the world 2023, and called Salem (by the Gentiles Solyma) which signifieth Peace, who reigned here fifty years.—This citie is seated on a rocky mountaine; every way to be ascended (except a little on the north) with steep ascents and deep valleys naturally fortified; for the most part environed with other not far removed mountaines, as if placed in the midst of an amphitheater."—Lib. iii. p. 154.

who upon beholding the infant Messiah expressed his readiness to leave this world; the Monastery of Elias, now in possession of the Greeks; and the Tomb of Rachel, rising in a rounded top like the whitened sepulchre of an Arab sheik. "This," says the honest Maundrell, "may probably be the true place of her interment; but the present sepulchral monument can be none of that which Jacob erected, for it appears plainly to be a modern and Turkish structure." Farther on is the well of which David longed to drink, and from whence his mighty men, at the risk of their lives, procured him a supply of water; and here opens to view, in a great valley, that most interesting of all pastoral scenes, where the angel of the Omnipotent appeared by night to the shepherds, to announce the glad tidings that Christ was born in Bethlehem.*

As there was another town of the same name in the tribe of Zebulun, the one we now approach was usually distinguished by the addition of Ephrata, or by a reference to the district in which it was situated. The convent which marks the place of the Redeemer's birth was built by Helena, after removing the idolatrous structure said to have been erected by Adrian, from a feeling of contempt or jealousy towards the Christians. At present it is divided among the monks of the Greek, Roman, and Armenian sects, to whom are assigned separate portions, as well for lodging as for places of worship; though, on certain days, they may all celebrate the rites of their common faith on altars which

---

* "Bethlehem soon after came in sight,—a fine village, surrounded with gardens of fig-trees and olives. There is a deep valley below, and half-way down, on the top of a hill, is a green plain, the only one we have seen in Judea:—I could fancy Boaz's field forming part of it. The convent is a very remarkable building, and well worth seeing. Without, it is a perfect fortress, with heavy buttresses and small grated windows; on entering, we immediately came to a magnificent church, with a double row of ten Corinthian pillars of marble on each side,—forty pillars in all. On the arched roof are the remains of mosaic, of the Empress Helena's time. One part was very distinct: it represented a city with temples, &c., and over it was written in Greek characters, *Laodicea.*"—*Anonymous Journal.*

none of them have been hitherto allowed to appropriate exclusively. There are two churches, an upper and a lower, under the same roof. The former contains nothing remarkable, if we except a star inlaid in the floor immediately under the spot in the heavens where the supernatural sign became visible to the Wise Men, and, like it, directly over the place of the Nativity in the church below.

Subterranean Church of Bethlehem.

This last is an excavation in the rock, elegantly fitted up and floored with marble, and to which there is a descent by a flight of steps through a long narrow passage. Here are shown a great number of tombs, and among them one in which are said to have been buried all the babes murdered by the barbarous Herod. From hence the pilgrim is conducted into a handsome chapel, of which the floors and walls are composed of beautiful marble, having on each side five oratories, or recesses for prayer, corresponding to the ten stalls supposed to have been in the stable wherein our blessed Saviour was born. This sacred crypt is irregular in shape, because it occupies the site of the stable and the manger. It is thirty-seven feet six inches long, eleven feet three inches broad, and nine feet in height. As it receives no light from without, it is illumined by thirty-two lamps, sent thither by different princes of Christendom; the other embellishments are ascribed to the munificent Helena. At the farther extremity of this small church there is an altar placed in an arcade, and hollowed out below in the form of an arch, to embrace the sacred spot where Emmanuel, having laid aside his glory, first appeared in the garb of human nature. A circle in the floor, composed of marble and jasper, surrounded with silver, and having rays like those with which the sun is represented, is supposed to mark the very place wherein that stupendous event was realized. An inscription, denoting that "here Jesus Christ was born of the Virgin Mary," meets the eye of the faithful worshipper.

Hic de Virgine Maria Jesus Christus natus est.

Adjoining the Altar of the Nativity is the Manger in which the infant Messiah was laid. It is also formed of marble, and is raised about eighteen inches above the floor, bearing a resemblance to the humble bed which alone the furniture of a stable could supply. Before it is the Altar of the Wise Men,—a memorial of their adoration and praise at the moment when they saw the young child and Mary his mother.

This edifice is certainly of high antiquity, and, though often destroyed and as often repaired, it still retains marks of its Grecian origin. It is built in the form of a cross; the nave being adorned with forty-eight columns of the Corinthian order in four rows, which are at least two feet six inches in diameter at the base, and eighteen feet high including the base and capital. As the roof of the nave is wanting, these pillars support nothing but a frieze of wood, which occupies the place of the architrave and of the whole entablature. The windows, which are large, were formerly adorned with mosaic paintings, and passages from the Bible in Greek and Latin characters, the traces of which are still visible.

The top of the church affords a fine prospect into the surrounding country, extending to Tekoa on the south and En-gedi on the east. In the latter place is the grotto where David, a native of Bethlehem, cut off the skirt of Saul's garment. There is also the convent of Elias, in which is said to be a large stone still retaining an impression of his body. Between this point and Jerusalem, a recent traveller was struck with the appearance of several small detached towers of a square form built in the midst of vine-lands. These, he learned, were for the accommodation of watchmen appointed to guard the produce from thieves and wild beasts; hence, explaining a passage which occurs in the gospel according to St Mark,—" A certain man planted a vineyard, and set an hedge about it, and digged a place for the wine-fat, and built a *tower*, and let it out to husbandmen."\*

It is painful to find that the same animosity, which attends the claims of the several sects of Christians at Jerusalem for the possession of the Holy Sepulchre, disgraces their contentions at Bethlehem for the Grotto of the Nativity. A few years ago, during the celebration of the Christmas festival, at which Mr Bankes was present, a battle took place, in which some of the combatants were wounded and others severely beaten; and in the preceding season, the privilege of saying mass at the altar on that particular day had been disputed, at the door of the sanctuary itself, with drawn swords.

An author, whose scepticism with regard to the holy

---

\* Buckingham.

places in the capital has been already mentioned, grants, that the tradition respecting the Cave of the Nativity is so well authenticated as hardly to admit of dispute. Having been always held in veneration, the Oratory established there by the first Christians attracted the notice and indignation of the heathens so early as the time of Adrian, who, as is elsewhere stated, ordered it to be demolished, and the ground to be reserved for the rites of Adonis. This happened in the second century, and at a period in the emperor's life when the Grotto of the Nativity was as well known in Bethlehem as the circumstance to which it owed its fame. In the fourth age, accordingly, we find this fact appealed to by St Jerome, as an indisputable testimony by which the cave itself had been identified. Upon this subject there does not seem to be the slightest ground for scepticism; and the evidence afforded by such a writer respecting a locality where he himself resided, will be deemed sufficient for believing that the monastery erected over the sacred spot does at this day point out the exact place of our Saviour's birth.*

Nothing, it has been observed, can be more pleasing or better calculated to excite sentiments of devotion than this subterranean church. It is adorned with pictures of the Italian and Spanish schools, representing the mysteries peculiar to the place,—the Virgin and Child after Raphael; the Annunciation; the Adoration of the Wise Men; the Coming of the Shepherds; and all those miracles of mingled grandeur and innocence. The usual ornaments of the manger are of blue satin, embroidered with silver. Incense is continually smoking before the cradle of the Saviour. "I have heard," says an eloquent pilgrim, "an organ, touched by no ordinary hand, playing during mass the sweetest and most tender tunes of the

---

* " Bethleem nunc nostram, et augustissimum urbis locum de quo Psalmista canit (Ps. lxxxiv. 12). *Veritas de terra orta est*, lucus inumbrabat Thamus, id est, Adonidis; et in specu ubi quondam Christus parvulus vagiit, Veneris Amasius plangebatur."—*Epist. ad Paul.*

best Italian composers. These concerts charm the Christian Arab, who, leaving his camels to feed, repairs, like the shepherds of old, to Bethlehem to adore the King of kings in his manger. I have seen this inhabitant of the desert communicate at the altar of the Magi with a fervour, a piety, a devotion, unknown among the Christians of the West." No place in the world, indeed, excites more profound devotion. The continual arrival of large caravans from all the nations of Europe,—the public prayers,—the prostrations,—nay, even the richness of the presents sent thither by the most powerful princes, altogether produce feelings in the soul which it is much easier to conceive than to describe.*

It may be added, that the effect of all this splendour is heightened by an extraordinary contrast; for, on quitting the grotto where you have met with the riches, the arts, the religion of civilized nations, you find yourself in a profound solitude, amid wretched Arab huts, half-naked savages, and faithless Mussulmans. The place is nevertheless the same where so many miracles were displayed; but this sacred land, no longer daring to express its joy, is compelled to shut within its bosom the recollections of its glory.

---

* " Pour ce qui est des ornemens de ce saint Temple, il n'en reste que fort peu en comparison de ce qui y estoit. Car tous les murs estoient autrefois magnifiquement reuestus et couuertes de belles tables de marbre gris ondé, comme on en voit encore en quelques endroits que les Infidelles n'ont pû avoir. Comme ils ont emporté tout le reste pour en orner leurs Mosquées, c'est une chose pitoyable de voir que tous les murs sont remplis de gros clous et crampons de fer qui les tenoient attachez. Au-dessus des colomnes de la nef est un mur tout couvert, et peint de la plus belle et fine mosaïque qu'il est possible de voir, n'estant composée que de petites pierres fines et transparentes comme cristal de toutes les couleurs, qui représentent grandes figures et histoires de la Vie, Miracles, Mort, et Passion de Nostre Seigneur, si naïument faites des couleurs si vives et éclatantes, et le fonds d'un or si luysant, qu'il semble qu'elles sont faites depuis peu, encore qu'il y ait plus de treize cens ans. Entre ces figures sont treize fenestres de chacun costé, qui rendent un grand jour par toute l'Eglise: derrière la troisième et quatrième colomne de la main droite est un très-beau et riche base de marbre blanc de forme ronde à six pans de quelques trois pieds de diametre, qui sert de fonds baptismaux."—*Doubdan*, p. 133.

Bethlehem has usually shared the vicissitudes of Jerusalem, being, both from its situation and the nature of the relics it contains, exposed to the rage or cupidity of barbarian conquerors. It fell under the power of the Saracens when led by their victorious caliph; but for seven centuries it has been guarded by a succession of religious persons, who, it has been truly said, suffer a perpetual martyrdom. In the time of Volney, they reckoned about 600 men in this village capable of bearing arms, of whom about a hundred were Christians of the Latin church. The necessity of uniting for their common defence against the Bedouins, and the still more relentless agents of despotism, has in many instances prevailed over points of faith, and induced the monks to live on good terms with the Mohammedans. It is stated, that at present the town is equal to Nazareth in extent, and contains from 1000 to 1500 inhabitants, who are almost wholly believers. The number has also been given at 300,—an estimate, we should imagine, considerably below the actual population. The men are robust and well made, and the women, it is allowed, are among the fairest and most handsome in Palestine.

The neighbourhood of Bethlehem presents a variety of objects too important to be passed over without a slight notice. The Pools of Solomon, originating, it is probable, in a scheme for supplying Jerusalem with water, are usually visited by the more enlightened class of travellers, who combine in their researches a regard to the arts as well as to the religion of Judea. These reservoirs are four in number; being so disposed that the water of the uppermost may descend into the second, and that of the second into the third. Their figure is quadrangular; the breadth is the same in all, amounting to about ninety paces. In their length there is some difference; the first being one hundred and sixty paces long, the second two hundred, and the third two hundred and twenty. They are all lined with masonry, and plastered. The springs whence the pools are supplied seem to have been secured with great care; having, says the author of the Journey from Aleppo, "no avenue to them but by a little hole like to the mouth of a narrow well." Through this hole you descend directly about four yards, when you come to a chamber forty-five feet long and twenty-four broad, adjoining to which there is another apartment of the same kind, but not quite so large. Both these rooms are neatly arched, and have an air of great antiquity. The water, which rises from four separate sources, is partly conveyed by a subterranean passage into the ponds; the remainder being received into an aqueduct of brick pipes, and carried by many turnings and windings among the mountains to the walls of Jerusalem. The monks of Bethlehem are perfectly convinced that it was in allusion to this guarded treasure, so valuable in the East, that Solomon called his beloved spouse a "sealed fountain."

Of the aqueduct here mentioned some vestiges are still to be detected in the intermediate space, and denote an acquaintance with the principles of hydraulics, which we should not have expected among Hebrew architects. It was constructed all along upon the surface of the ground, and framed of perforated stones let into one another, with a fillet round the cavity so contrived as to prevent leakage, and united together with so firm a cement that they will sometimes sooner break than endure a separation. These pipes were covered with an arch or layer of flags, strengthened by the application of a peculiarly strong mortar; the whole "being endued with such absolute firmness as if it had been designed for eternity. But the Turks have demonstrated in this instance that nothing can be so well wrought but they are able to destroy it. For, of this strong aqueduct, which was carried formerly five or six leagues with so vast expense and labour, you see now only here and there a fragment remaining."*

In a valley contiguous to Bethlehem are the ruins of a church and convent, which were erected by the pious

---

* Maundrell, p. 90.

empress over the place where the angels appeared to the shepherds. No part of it has survived the desolation to which every edifice in Palestine has been repeatedly subjected, except a small grotto wherein the heavenly communication was vouchsafed to the simple keepers of the flock.

On the way back to Jerusalem the traveller is induced to leave the more direct route, that he may visit the convent of St John in the Desert. This monastery is built over the dwelling where the Baptist is supposed to have first seen the light; and accordingly, under the altar, the spot on which he was brought forth is marked by a star of marble, bearing this inscription,—

" Hic precursor Domini Christi natus est."
Here the forerunner of Christ the Lord was born.

The church belonging to this establishment has been described as one of the best in the Holy Land, having an elegant cupola, and a pavement of mosaic, with some paintings; but the appearance, nevertheless, is poor and deserted, as if its votaries were few, and but little concerned in preserving its ancient grandeur. The account given of it in the pages of the industrious Sandys will amuse the reader by the simplicity of the narrative, as well as by the deep interest the good man felt in the various scenes which passed before him:—" Having travelled about a mile and a halfe farther, we came to the cave where the Baptist is said to have lived from the age of seven until such time as he went into the Wilderness by Jordan; sequestred from the abode of men, and feeding on such wilde nourishment as these uninhabited places affoorded. This cave is seated on the northern side of a desart mountaine,—only beholden to the locust-tree,—hewne out of the precipitating rock, so as difficultly to be ascended or descended to; entered at the east corner, and receiving light from a window in the side. At the upper end there is a bench of the selfesame, whereon, they say, he accustomed to sleepe; of which whoso breaks a piece off stands forthwith excommunicate. Over this, on a little flat, stand the ruins of a monastery, on the south side naturally walled with the steepe of a mountain; from whence there gusheth a living spring, which entereth the rock, and again bursteth forth beneathe the mouth of the cave,—a place that would make solitarinesse delightful, and stand in comparison with the turbulent pompe of cities. This overlooketh a profound valley, on the far side hemmed with aspiring mountains; whereof some are cut (or naturally so) in degrees like alleys, which would be else unaccessibly fruitlesse; whose levels yet bear the stumps of decayed vines, shadowed not rarely with olives and locusts. And surely I think that all or most of those mountains have bin so husbanded, else could this little countrey have never sustained such a multitude of people. After we had fed of such provision as was brought us from the city by other of the Fraternitie that there met us, we turned towards Jerusalem, leaving the way of Bethlehem on the right hand, and that of Emmaus on the left. The first place of note that we met with was there where once stood the dwelling of Zachary, seated on the side of a fruitful hill, well stored with olives and vineyards. Hither came the Blessed Virgin to visit her cousin Elisabeth. Here died Elisabeth, and here in a grot on the side of a vault or chapell lies buried; over which a goodly church was erected, together with a monastery, whereof now little standeth but a part of the walls, which offer to the view some fragments of painting, which show that the rest have been exquisit. Beyond and lower is Our Lady's Fountaine (so called of the inhabitants), which maintaineth a little current thorow the neighbouring valley. Neer this, in the bottome and uttermost extent thereof, there standeth a temple, once sumptuous, now desolate; built by Helena, and dedicated to St John Baptist, in the place where Zachary had another house, possest as the rest by the beastly Arabians, who defile it with their cattell, and employ it to the basest of uses."*

---

* Relation of a Journey, p. 183.

It is a point still unsettled, whether the food of him who was sent to prepare the way consisted of fruit or of insects; the name locust being indiscriminately applied to either, and both being used by the inhabitants of Palestine. There is less doubt with regard to the opinions of the early Christians, who were unanimous in the belief that the Baptist lived on the produce of a particular tree which still abounds in the Desert. Nay, the friars at the present hour assert, that the very plants which yielded sustenance to the holy recluse continue to flourish in their ancient vigour; and the Popish pilgrims, says Mr Maundrell, who dare not be wiser than such blind guides, gather the fruit of them, and carry it away with much devotion.

But we must not permit the interesting associations of Bethlehem to detain us any longer in its vicinity. We proceed now towards the extremity of the Dead Sea; whence, after having visited the most remarkable scenes on its western shore,—the mouth of the Jordan and the position of Jericho,—we shall return to the capital by a different route.

After gratifying his curiosity in church and convent, the traveller turns his face southward to Tekoa and Hebron, those remoter villages of the Holy Land. The former, which was built by Rehoboam, and is distinguished as the birthplace of Amos the prophet, presents considerable ruins, and even some remains of architecture. It appears to have stood upon a hill, which Pococke describes as being about half a mile in length and a furlong broad. On the north-eastern corner there are fragments of an old building, supposed to have been a fortress, while about half-way up the ascent there are similar indications of a church, now in a state of complete dilapidation. There is preserved, however, a large font of an octagon form, composed of red and white marble; as also pieces of broken pillars consisting of the same material.

Farther towards the south, various manifestations present themselves of ancient civilisation, the tokens of which are most distinctly marked by places of worship and numerous strongholds. The traveller just named mentions a ruined castle called Creightoun, situated on the side of a steep hill, and a church dedicated to St Pantaleone. At a little distance there is an immense grotto, which is said on one occasion to have contained 30,000 men ; and therefore it is conjectured to be one of those retreats in the fastnesses of En-gedi to which David fled from the pursuit of Saul. About two miles farther, in a south-eastern direction, is the Mount of Bethulia, near a village of the same name,—a position which is thought to agree with that of Beth-haccerem, specified by Jeremiah as a proper place for a beacon, where the children of Benjamin were to sound the trumpet in Tekoa.*

There is a tradition that the knights of Jerusalem, during the Holy War, held this strong post forty years after the capital had fallen. It is a single hill, and very high ; and the top of it appears like a large mount formed by art, being defended by a double line of fortifications and several towers, which in a rude state of warfare might be pronounced impregnable. At the foot of an eminence towards the north there are the remains of a magnificent church as well as of other buildings. On a slope a little farther west there is a cistern connected with a pond, which appears to have had an island in it, and probably some structure suited to the supply of water. These works were also encompassed with a double wall ; and it is said that two aqueducts may still be perceived terminating in the basin, one from the Sealed Fountain of Solomon, and another from the hilly district which stretches between Bethlehem and Tekoa.

In reference to the tradition that the knights of Jerusalem held the garrison of Bethulia forty years, Captain Mangles remarks, that the place is too small to have

---

* " O ye children of Benjamin, gather yourselves to flee out of the midst of Jerusalem, and blow the trumpet in Tekoa, and set up a sign of fire in Beth-haccerem: for evil appeareth out of the north, and great destruction."—*Jer.* vi. 1.

contained even half the number of men which would have been requisite to make any stand in such a country; and the ruins, though they may be those of a place once defended by Franks, appear to have had an earlier origin, as the architecture seems to be decidedly Roman. There can be little doubt, indeed, that it is one of the works of Herod the Great; and its distance does not differ much from that of Herodium, which is described by Josephus as being about sixty furlongs from the metropolis. The delineation of the hill, too, by the same historian, corresponds with the Mount of the Franks; and, when he adds that water was conveyed to it at a great expense, we can no longer permit ourselves to question the identity of Herodium and the fortress of Bethulia.*

Hebron, Habroun, or, according to the Arabic orthography followed by the moderns, El Hhalil, is considerably removed from the usual track of pilgrims and tourists. An accident or quarrel once excited the indignation of the inhabitants against Europeans, who, during a long course of time, were dissuaded by the monks at Jerusalem from extending their researches beyond Bethlehem. Sandys could only report, apparently on the information of others, that Hebron was reduced to ruins; but he adds, there is a little village seated in the field of Machpelah, " where standeth a goodly temple, erected over the burying-cave of the Patriarchs by Helena, the mother of Constantine, converted now into a mosque." Without minutely analyzing the topography assigned by this author, we may repeat the assurance which he gives relative to the existence of the imperial monument, dedicated to the memory of Abraham and his immediate descendants. Burckhardt, who saw it in 1807, bears testimony to the fact that the sepulchre, once a Greek church, is now appropriated to the worship of Mohammed. The ascent

---

* Modern Traveller, vol. i. p. 183. Joseph. Antiq. lib. xiv. c. 13.

to it is by a large and fine staircase that leads to a long gallery, the entrance to which is by a small court. Towards the left is a portico resting upon square pillars. The vestibule of the temple contains two rooms; the one being the tomb of Abraham, the other that of Sarah. In the body of the church, between two large pillars on the right, is seen a small recess, in which is the sepulchre of Isaac, and in a similar one upon the left is that of his wife. On the opposite side of the court is another vestibule which has also two rooms, being respectively the dormitory of Jacob and of his spouse. At the extremity of the portico, upon the right hand, is a door which conducts to a sort of long gallery that still serves for a mosque; and passing from thence is observed another room containing the ashes of Joseph, which are said to have been carried thither by the children of Israel. All the sepulchres of the Patriarchs are covered with rich carpets of green silk, magnificently embroidered with gold; those of their wives are red, ornamented in like manner. The sultans of Constantinople furnish these carpets, which are renewed from time to time. Burckhardt counted nine, one over another, upon the Sepulchre of Abraham. The rooms also which contain the tombs are covered with rich carpets; the entrance to them is guarded by iron gates, and wooden doors plated with silver, having bolts and padlocks of the same metal. More than a hundred persons are employed in the service of this temple; affording, with the decorations lavished upon the structure, a remarkable contrast to the simple life of the venerable man to whose memory it is meant to do honour.

If the description given by Sandys in the seventeenth century was correct, we must conclude that Hebron has subsequently enjoyed a period of considerable improvement. According to the traveller whom we have just quoted, it contains about four hundred families, of which about a fourth part are Jews. It is situated on the slope of a mountain; has a strong castle; can boast abundance of provisions, a considerable number of shops, and some neat houses. The whole of the country between that town and Tekoa is finer and better cultivated than in the neighbourhood of Jerusalem ; while the sides of the hills, instead of being naked and dreary, are richly studded with the oak, the arbutus, the Scottish fir, and a variety of flowering shrubs.

Beyond this point the information of Europeans ceased until about twelve years ago, when the desert which stretches between the Sepulchre of Abraham and the Dead Sea was entered by Mr Bankes, Mr Legh, and Captains Irby and Mangles. After a journey of three days from Hebron towards the south, the travellers were informed of extensive ruins at Abdi in the Wilderness. On turning their faces to Kerek, the object of their search, the road led in the direction of the Lake Asphaltites, through a country which, although well cultivated, was extremely uninteresting. They observed a variety of ruins, with some subterranean tombs in the neighbourhood, denoting the existence of an ancient town ; when, after having advanced eight or nine miles farther, they found themselves on the borders of an extensive desert, entirely abandoned to the wandering Bedouins. Near the point at which this change of aspect begins, is a place called by the natives Al-baid, where there is a fountain in the rock and a pool of greenish water.

The travellers, at some distance from this halting-place, arrived at a camp of Jellaheen Arabs, who told them that in years of scarcity they were accustomed to retire into Egypt,—a practice which seems to have been observed from the days of the Patriarchs, or dictated by the same necessity that compelled the family of Jacob to adopt a similar expedient. At the distance of eight hours from Al-baid, in a deep barren valley, are the ruins of an old Turkish fort, standing on a solitary rock to the left of the track. Farther on, the cliff is excavated, at a considerable height, into loop-holes ; where it is probable a barrier was formerly established for levying a certain duty on goods and pilgrims.

The place is called El Zowar, or El Ghor. From hence a gravelly ravine, sprinkled with bushes of acacia and other shrubs, conducts to the great plain at the southern extremity of the Dead Sea;—bounded, at the distance of eight or nine miles, by a sandy cliff at least seventy feet high, which forms a barrier to the lake when at its greatest elevation. The existence of that long valley which extends from Asphaltites to the Ælanitic Gulf was first ascertained by Burckhardt; and the prolongation of it, as connected with the hollow of the Jordan, has been considered as a proof that the river at one time discharged its waters into the eastern branch of the Red Sea. The change is attributed to that great volcanic convulsion mentioned in the nineteenth chapter of Genesis, which, interrupting the course of the river, converted into a lake the fertile plain occupied by the cities of Adma, Zeboim, Sodom, and Gomorrah, and reduced all the valley southward to the condition of a sandy waste.*

But, having reached the shore of the Dead Sea by an unfrequented path, we have no guide to the examination of the wild country which rises on either side of it; we therefore prefer the more wonted route which leads to its northern extremity, near the mouth of the Jordan and the site of the ancient Jericho. Avoiding, at the same time, the track of the caravan from Jerusalem through the hilly district which intervenes, we shall return to Bethlehem, to accompany thence the eloquent Chateaubriand through the interesting valley of Santa Saba.

On leaving the Church of the Nativity the traveller pursues his course eastward, through a vale where Abraham is said to have fed his flocks. This pastoral tract, however, is soon succeeded by a range of hills, so extremely barren that not even a root of moss is to be seen upon them. Descending the farther side of this

---

* Burckhardt's Travels in Syria, Pref. vi. Modern Traveller, vol. i. p. 203. Doubdan, Voyage, pp. 322, 326.

meagre platform two lofty towers are perceived, rising from a deep valley, marking the site of the convent of Santa Saba. Nothing can be more dreary than the situation of that religious house. It is erected in a ravine, sunk to the depth of several hundred feet, where the Brook Kedron has formed a channel which is dry the greater part of the year. The church is on a little eminence at the bottom of the dell; whence the buildings of the monastery rise by an almost perpendicular flight of steps and passages hewn out of the rock, ascending thus to the top of the hill, where they terminate in the two square towers already mentioned. From this point you descry the steril summits of the mountains both towards the east and west; the course of the stream from Jerusalem; and the numerous grottos formerly occupied by Christian anchorites.

In advancing, the aspect of the country still continues the same, white and dusty, without tree, herbage, or even moss. At length the road seeks a lower level, and approaches the rocky border which bounds the valley of the Jordan; when, after a toilsome march of ten or twelve hours, the traveller sees stretching out before his eyes the Dead Sea and the line of the river. But the landscape, however grand, admits of no comparison to the scenery of Europe. No fields waving with corn,—no plains covered with rich pasture present themselves from the mountains of Lower Palestine. Figure to yourself two long chains of mountains, running in a parallel direction from north to south, without breaks and without undulations. The eastern, or Arabian chain, is the highest; and, when seen at the distance of eight or ten leagues, you would take it to be a prodigious perpendicular wall, resembling Mount Jura in its form and azure colour. Not one summit, not the smallest peak can be distinguished; you merely perceive slight inflections here and there, " as if the hand of the painter, who drew this horizontal line along the sky, had trembled in some places."

The mountains of Judea form the range on which the

observer stands as he looks down on the Lake Asphaltites. Less lofty, and more unequal than the eastern chain, it differs from it also in its nature and composition; exhibiting heaps of chalk and sand, whose form, it is said, bears some resemblance to piles of arms, waving standards, or the tents of a camp pitched on the border of a plain. The Arabian side, on the contrary, presents nothing but black precipitous rocks, which throw their lengthened shadow over the waters of the Dead Sea. The smallest bird of heaven would not find among these crags a single blade of grass for its sustenance; every thing announces the country of a reprobate people, and well fitted to perpetuate the punishment denounced against Ammon and Moab.

The valley confined by these two chains of mountains displays a soil resembling the bottom of a sea which has long retired from its bed,—a beach covered with salt, dry mud, and moving sands, furrowed as it were by the waves. Here and there stunted shrubs vegetate with difficulty upon this inanimate tract; their leaves are covered with salt, and their bark has a smoky smell and taste. Instead of villages you perceive the ruins of a few towers. In the middle of the plain flows a discoloured river, which reluctantly throws itself into the pestilential lake by which it is engulfed. Its course amid the sands can be distinguished only by the willows and the reeds that border it; among which the Arab lies in ambush to attack the traveller and to murder the pilgrim.*

The same author remarks, that when you travel in Judea the heart is at first filled with profound melancholy. But when, passing from solitude to solitude, boundless space opens before you, this feeling wears off by degrees, and you experience a secret awe, which, so far from depressing the soul, imparts life and elevates the genius. Extraordinary appearances every where proclaim a land teeming with miracles. The burning

---

* Chateaubriand, tom. i. p. 408.

sun, the towering eagle, the barren fig-tree, all the poetry, all the pictures of Scripture are here. Every name commemorates a mystery,—every grotto announces a prediction,—every hill re-echoes the accents of a prophet. God himself has spoken in these regions, dried up rivers, rent the rocks, and opened the grave. " The Desert still appears mute with terror; and you would imagine that it had never presumed to interrupt the silence since it heard the awful voice of the Eternal."

The celebrated lake which occupies the site of Sodom and Gomorrah is called in Scripture the Dead Sea. Among the Greeks and Latins it is known by the name of Asphaltites; the Arabs denominate it Bahar Loth, or Sea of Lot. Chateaubriand does not agree with those who conclude it to be the crater of a volcano; for, having seen Vesuvius, Solfatara, the Peak of the Azores, and the extinguished volcanoes of Auvergne, he remarked in all of them the same characters; that is to say, mountains excavated in the form of a tunnel, lava, and ashes, which exhibited incontestable proof of the agency of fire. The Salt Sea, on the contrary, is a lake of great length, curved like a bow, placed between two ranges of mountains, which have no mutual coherence of form, no similarity of composition. They do not meet at the two extremities of the lake; but while the one continues to bound the Valley of Jordan, and to run northward as far as Tiberias, the other stretches away to the south till it loses itself in the sands of Yemen. There are, it is true, hot springs, quantities of bitumen, sulphur, and asphaltos; but these of themselves are not sufficient to attest the previous existence of a volcano. With respect, indeed, to the engulfed cities, if we adopt the idea of Michaelis and of Büsching, physics may be admitted to explain the catastrophe without offence to religion. According to their views Sodom was built upon a mine of bitumen,—a fact which is ascertained by the testimony of Moses and Josephus, who speak of wells of naphtha in the Valley of Siddim.

Lightning kindled the combustible mass, and the guilty cities sank in the subterranean conflagration. Malte-Brun ingeniously suggests that Sodom and Gomorrah themselves may have been built of bituminous stones, and thus have been set in flames by fire from heaven.

According to Strabo there were thirteen towns swallowed up in the lake; Stephen of Byzantium reckons eight; the book of Genesis, while it names five as situated in the Vale of Siddim, relates the destruction of two only; four are mentioned in Deuteronomy, and five are noticed by the author of Ecclesiasticus. Several travellers, and among others Troilo and D'Arvieux, assure us, that they observed fragments of walls and palaces in the Dead Sea. Maundrell himself was not so fortunate; owing, he supposes, to the height of the water; but he relates that the Father Guardian and Procurator of Jerusalem, both men of sense and probity, declared that they had once actually seen one of these ruins; that it was so near the shore, and the lake so shallow, that they, together with some Frenchmen, went to it, and found there several pillars and other fragments of buildings. The ancients speak more positively on this subject. Josephus, who employs a poetical expression, says, that he perceived on the shores of the Dead Sea " the shades of the overwhelmed cities." Strabo gives a circumference of sixty stadia to the ruins of Sodom, which are also mentioned by Tacitus.*

It is surprising that no pains have been taken by recent travellers to throw light upon this interesting point, or even to learn whether the periodical rise and fall of the lake affords any means for determining the accuracy of the ancient historians and geographers. Should the Turks ever give permission, and should it be found practicable to convey a vessel from Jaffa to this inland sea, some curious discoveries would certainly be made.

---

* " Haud procul inde campi, quos ferunt olim uberes, magnisque urbibus habitatos, fulminum jactu, arsisse; et manere vestigia, terramque ipsam, specie torridam, vim frugiferam perdidisse."—*Tacit. Hist.* lib. v. cap. 7.

Is it not amazing that, notwithstanding the enterprise of modern science, the ancients were better acquainted with the properties, and even the dimensions of the Lake Asphaltites, than the most learned nations of Europe in our own times? It is described by Aristotle, Strabo, Diodorus Siculus, Pliny, Tacitus, Solinus, Josephus, Galen, and Dioscorides. The Abbot of Santa Saba is the only person for many centuries who has made the tour of it. From his account we learn, through the medium of Father Nau, that at its extremity it is separated as it were into two parts, and that there is a way by which you may walk across it, being only mid-leg deep, at least in summer; that there the land rises, and bounds another small lake of a circular or rather an oval figure, surrounded with plains and hills of salt; and that the neighbouring country is peopled by innumerable Arabs.*

It is known that seven considerable streams fall into this basin, and hence it was long supposed that it must discharge its superfluous stores by hidden channels into the Mediterranean or the Red Sea. This opinion is now

---

\* The Abbé Mariti, who himself saw little, is not willing to allow to others the advantage of having been more fortunate. " Quelques voyageurs ont avancé qu'on distinguoit encore les débris de ces villes infortunées, lorsque les eaux de la mer etoient basses et limpides. Il en est même qui disent avoir apperçu des restes de colonnes avec leurs chapitaux. Mais il faut que l'imagination les ait trompés, ou que depuis leur retour cette mer ait éprouvé de nouvelles secousses ; car je n'y peux rien voir de semblable, malgré toute ma bonne volonté. Un père capucin crut aussi reconnoître sur ces bords les effets frappans de la malédiction céleste. Ici, ce sont des traces de feu, là, une surface de cendres, partout des champs arides et maudits. Il croit même respirer encore une odeur de soufre. Pour moi, je suis affecté en sens contraire : rien dans ce lieu ne me rappelle la désolation dont parle la bible. L'air y est pure, le gazon d'un beau vert : en plus d'un endroit mon œil se rafraîchit aux eaux argentines qui jaillissent en gerbes du sommet des monts ; la sterilité dont une partie de ces campagnes fut frappée des la naissance du monde, rend plus douce par le contraste l'apparence de fertilité que je remarquai dans le sol d'Alvona. Mais d'où vient donc que deux voyageurs peuvent être si opposés ? C'est qu'un capucin porte partout les cinq sens de la foi, et que moi je ne suis doué que de ceux de la nature."—Tom. ii. p. 334.

every where relinquished, in consequence of the learned remarks on the effect of evaporation in a hot climate, published by Dr Halley many years ago; the justness of which were admitted by Dr Shaw, though he calculated that the Jordan alone threw into the lake every day more than six million tuns of water. It is deserving of notice, that the Arabian philosophers, if we may believe Mariti, had anticipated Halley in his conclusions with regard to the absorbent power of a dry atmosphere.*

The marvellous properties usually assigned to the Dead Sea by the earlier travellers have vanished upon a more rigid investigation. It is now known that bodies sink, or float upon it in proportion to their specific gravity; and that, although the water is so dense as to be favourable to swimmers, no security is found against the common accident of drowning. Josephus indeed asserts that Vespasian, in order to ascertain the fact now mentioned, commanded a number of his slaves to be bound hand and foot and thrown into the deepest part of the lake; and that, so far from any of them sinking, they all maintained their place on the surface until it pleased the emperor to have them taken out. But this anecdote, although perfectly consistent with truth, does not justify all the inferences which have been drawn from it. "Being willing to make an experiment," says Maundrell, "I went into it, and found that it bore up my body in swimming with an uncommon force; but as for that relation of some authors, that men wading into it were buoyed up to the top as soon as they got as deep as the middle, I found it, upon trial, not true."†

The water of this sea has been frequently analyzed both in France and England. The specific gravity of it, according to Malte-Brun, is 1·211, that of fresh water being 1·000. It is perfectly transparent. The applica-

---

\* " Ou plutôt doit on admettre l'opinion des physiciens Arabes, qui établissent, non sans quelque fondement, qu'elles se dissipent en évaporation ?"—Tom. ii. p. 334.

† Mr Gordon, however, maintains, that persons who have never learned to swim will float on its surface. Chateaubriand, i. p. 412.

tion of tests, or re-agents, prove that it contains the muriatic and sulphuric acids. There is no alumina in it, nor does it appear that it is saturated with marine salt or muriate of soda. It holds in solution the following substances, and in the proportions here stated:—

    Muriate of lime .................................. 3·920
    Magnesia, ......................................... 10·246
    Soda, ................................................ 10·360
    Sulphate of lime .............................. ·054

We need not add that such a liquid must be equally salt and bitter. As might be expected, too, it is found to deposite its salts in copious incrustations, and to prove a ready agent in all processes of petrifaction. Clothes, boots, and hats, if dipped in the lake, or accidentally wetted with its water, are found, when dried, to be covered with a thick coating of these minerals. Hence we cannot be surprised to hear that the lake does not present a great variety of fish. Mariti roundly asserts that it produces none, and even that those which are carried into it by the rapidity of the Jordan, perish almost immediately upon being immerged in its acrid waves. A few shell-snails constitute the sole tenants of its dreary shores, unmixed either with the helix or the muscle.

It was formerly believed that the approach to the Asphaltites was fatal to birds, and that, like another lake of antiquity, it had the power of drawing them down from the wing into its poisonous waters. This dream, propagated by certain visionary travellers, is now completely discredited. Flocks of swallows may be seen skimming along its surface with perfect impunity, while the absence of every other species is easily explained by a glance at the naked hills and barren plains, which supply no vegetable food to bird or beast.

Josephus, who measured the Dead Sea, found that in length it extended about five hundred and eighty stadia, and in breadth one hundred and fifty; that is, according to our standard, somewhat more than seventy miles by nineteen. A recent traveller, to whose unpublished journal I have repeatedly alluded, remarks that the lake, when he visited it, was sunk or hollow, and that the banks had been recently under water, being still very miry and difficult to pass. The shores were covered with dry wood, some of it good timber, which they say is brought by the Jordan from the country of the Druses. " The water is pungently salt, like oxymuriate of soda. It is incredibly buoyant. G—— bathed in it, and when he lay still on his back or belly, he floated with one-fourth at least of his whole body above the water. He described the sensation as extraordinary, and more like lying on a feather-bed than floating on water. On the other hand, he found the greatest resistance in attempting to move through it: it smarted his eyes excessively. I put a piece of stick in; it required a good deal of pressure to make it sink, and when let go it bounded out again like a blown bladder. The water was clear, and of a yellowish tinge, which might be from the colour of the stones at bottom, or from the hazy atmosphere. There were green shrubs down to the water's edge in one place, and nothing to give an idea of any thing blasting in the neighbourhood of the sea; the desert character of the soil extending far beyond the possibility of being affected by its influence."*

The bitumen supplied by this singular basin affords the means of a comfortable livelihood to a considerable number of Arabs who frequent its shores. The Pasha of Damascus, who finds it a valuable article of commerce, purchases at a small price the fruit of their labours, or supplies them with food, clothing, and a few ornaments,

---

* " Le Cardinal de Vitry la nomme la Mer du Diable, et Marinus Sanutus dit qu'elle est tousjours couuerte d'une fumée epaisse et de vapeurs noires, comme quelque soûpirail ou cheminée d Enfer. D'autres disent que son eau est noire, gluante, epaisse, grasse, fangueuse, et de très-mauvaise odeur ; et toutefois j ay parlé a des Religieux qui m'ont asseuré y avoir été, et que cette eau est claire, nette, et liquide : mais très-amère et salée. Et comme j'ay dit, je n'y ay veu ny fumée ny brouillards."—*Doubdan, Voyage de la Terre Sainte,* p. 317.

in return for it. In ancient times it found a ready market in Egypt, where it was used in large quantities for embalming the dead: it was also occasionally employed as a substitute for stone, and appeared in the walls of houses and even of temples.

Associated with the Dead Sea, every reader has heard of the apples of Sodom,—a species of fruit which, extremely beautiful to the eye, is bitter to the taste, and full of dust. Tacitus, in the fifth book of his history, alludes to this singular fact, but, as usual, in language so brief and ambiguous, that no light can be derived from his description, *atra et inania velut in cinerem vanescunt.* Some travellers, unable to discover this singular production, have considered it merely as a figure of speech, depicting the deceitful nature of all vicious enjoyments. Hasselquist regards it as the production of a small plant called *Solanum melongena*—a species of nightshade which is to be found abundantly in the neighbourhood of Jericho. He admits that the apples are sometimes full of dust; but this, he maintains, appears only when the fruit is attacked by a certain insect, which converts the whole of the inside into a kind of powder, leaving the rind wholly entire, and in possession of its beautiful colour.

M. Seetzen, again, holds the novel opinion, that this mysterious apple contains a sort of cotton resembling silk; and, having no pulp or flesh in the inside, might naturally enough, when sought for as food, be denounced by the hungry Bedouin as pleasing to the eye and deceitful to the palate. Chateaubriand has fixed on a shrub different from all the others. It grows two or three leagues from the mouth of the Jordan, and is of a thorny appearance with small tapering leaves. Its fruit is exactly like the Egyptian lemon, both in size and colour. Before it is ripe it is filled with a corrosive and saline juice; when dried, it yields a blackish seed that may be compared to ashes, and which in taste resembles bitter pepper. There can be little doubt that this is the true apple of Sodom, which flatters the sight while it mocks the appetite.*

In ascending the western shore, the traveller at length reaches the point where the Jordan mixes its muddy waters with those of the lake. Hasselquist, the only modern author who describes the mouth of that celebrated river, tells us that the plain which extends from thence to Jericho, a distance of more than three leagues, is, generally speaking, level, but uncultivated and barren. The soil is a grayish sandy clay, so loose that his horses often sank up to the knees in it. The whole surface of the earth is covered with salt in the same manner as on the banks of the Nile, and would, it is probable, prove no less fruitful were it irrigated with equal care. The stones on the beach, it is added, were all quartz, but of various colours; some specimens of which, having a slaty structure, emitted, when exposed to fire, a strong smell of bitumen, thereby denoting, perhaps, a volcanic origin.

There is a great want of unanimity among authors with respect to the width of the Jordan. The Swede whom I have just quoted relates, that opposite to Jericho it was eight paces over, the banks perpendicular, six feet in height, the water deep, muddy, warm rather than cold, and much inferior in quality to that of the Nile. Chateaubriand, again, who measured it in several places, reports that it was about fifty feet in breadth, and six feet deep close to the shore,—a discrepancy which must arise from the different periods of the year when it was seen by these distinguished writers.†

---

* "As for the apples of Sodom, so much talked of, I neither saw nor heard of any hereabouts; nor was there any tree to be seen near the lake from which one might expect such a fruit. Which induces me to believe that there may be a greater deceit in this fruit than that which is usually reported of it; and that its very being, as well as its beauty, is a fiction, only kept up, as my Lord Bacon observes other false notions are, because it serves for a good allusion, and helps the poet to a similitude."—*Maundrell*, p. 85.

† The reading in Hasselquist must be *eighteen* instead of eight, or eight fathoms, instead of paces; for Mr Maundrell remarks that the breadth of the river "might be about twenty yards over, and in depth it far exceeded my height."—*Journey*, p. 83.

The Old Testament abounds with allusions to the swellings of Jordan; but at present, whether the current has deepened its channel, or whether the climate is less moist than in former days, this occurrence is seldom witnessed,—the river has forgotten its ancient greatness. Maundrell could discern no sign or probability of such overflowings; for although he was there on the 30th of March,—the proper season of the inundation,—the river was running two yards at least under the level of its banks. The margin of the stream, however, continues as of old to be closely covered with a natural forest of tamarisk, willows, oleanders, and similar trees, and to afford a retreat to several species of wild beasts. Hence the fine metaphor of the prophet Jeremiah, who assimilates an enraged enemy to a lion coming up "from the swellings of Jordan," driven from his lair by the annual flood, and compelled to seek shelter in the surrounding desert.

Jericho, which is at present a miserable village inhabited by half-naked Arabs, derives all its importance from history. It was the first city which the Israelites reduced upon entering the Holy Land. Five hundred and thirty years afterwards it was rebuilt by Heliel of Bethel, who succeeded in restoring its population, its splendour, and its commerce; in which flourishing condition it appears to have continued during several centuries. Mark Antony, in the pride of power, presented to Cleopatra the whole territory of Jericho. Vespasian, in the course of the sanguinary war which he prosecuted in Judea, sacked its walls, and put its inhabitants to the sword. Re-established by Adrian in the 138th year of our faith, it was doomed at no distant era to experience new disasters. It was again repaired by the Christians, who made it the seat of a bishop; but in the twelfth century it was overthrown by the infidels, and has not since emerged from its ruins. Of all its magnificent buildings there remain only the part of one tower, supposed to be the dwelling of Zaccheus the publican, and a quantity of rubbish, which is understood to mark the line of its ancient walls.

Mr Buckingham saw reason to believe that the true site of Jericho, as described by Josephus, was at a greater distance from the river than the village of Rahhah, now commonly supposed to represent the City of Palms. Descending from the mountains, which bound the valley on the western side, he observed the ruins of a large settlement, covering at least a square mile, whence, as well as from the remains of aqueducts and fountains, he was led to conclude that it must have been a place of considerable consequence. Some of the more striking objects among the wrecks of this ancient town were large tumuli, evidently the work of art, and resembling those of the Greek and Trojan heroes on the Plains of Ilium. There were, besides, portions of ruined buildings, shafts of columns, and a capital of the Corinthian order; tokens not at all ambiguous of former grandeur and of civilized life.

Josephus fixes the position of Jericho at the distance of one hundred and fifty furlongs from Jerusalem, and sixty from the river Jordan; stating that the country, as far as the capital, is desert and hilly, while to the shores of the Lake Asphaltites it is low, though equally waste and unfruitful. Nothing can apply more accurately, in all its particulars, than this description does to the ruins just mentioned. The spot lies at the very foot of the steril mountains of Judea, which may be said literally to overhang it on the west; and these ridges are still as barren, as rugged, and as destitute of inhabitants as formerly, throughout their whole extent, from the Lake of Tiberias to the Dead Sea. The distance, by the computation in time, amounted to six hours, or nearly twenty miles, from Jerusalem; the space between the supposed city and the river being little more than one-third of that amount, the precise proportion indicated by the Jewish historian.

The soil round Jericho was long celebrated for a precious balsam, which used to be sold for double its weight of silver. The historian Justin relates, that the trees from which it exudes bear a resemblance to firs, though they are shorter, and cultivated after the manner of vines. He adds, that the wealth of the Jewish nation arises from their produce, as they grow in no other part of Syria. At present, however, there is not a tree of any description, either palm or balsam, to be seen near the site of this deserted town; but it is admitted, that the complete desolation with which its ruins are invested ought to be attributed to the cessation of industry, rather than to any perceptible change either in the climate or the soil.

Rahhah stands about four miles nearer the river, or about half-way between the assumed position of Jericho and the bank of the current. It consists of about fifty dwellings, all very mean in their appearance, and every one fenced in front with thorny bushes; one of the most effectual defences that could be raised against the incursions of the Bedouins, whose horses will not approach these formidable thickets. The inhabitants, without exception, are professed believers in the creed of Islamism. Their habits are those of shepherds rather than of cultivators of the soil; this last duty, indeed, when performed at all, being done chiefly by the women and children, as the men roam the plain on horseback, and derive their principal means of subsistence from robbery and plunder. They are governed by a sheik, whose influence among them is more like the authority of a father over his children than that of a magistrate; and who is, moreover, checked in the exercise of his power by the knowledge that he would instantly be deprived of life and station were he to exceed the bounds which, in all rude countries, are opposed even to the caprices of despotism. It is remarkable that the name of this village corresponds to Rahab, the name of the hostess who received into her house the Hebrew spies, and signifies odour or perfume; the slight change on the form of the Arabic term implying no difference in the import of the root whence they are both originally derived.

The mountains on the eastern side of the Jordan are

more lofty than those which skirt the Vale of Jericho, being not less than 2000 feet in height. From the summit of a towering peak, which the traveller still delights to recognise, Moses was permitted to behold the promised inheritance, stretching towards the west, the south, and the north,—" All the land of Gilead unto Dan, and all Naphtali, and the land of Ephraim, and Manasseh, and all the land of Judah unto the utmost sea, and the south, and the plain of the Valley of Jericho, the city of palm-trees, unto Zoar. And the Lord said unto him, This is the land which I sware unto Abraham, unto Isaac, and unto Jacob, saying, I will give it unto thy seed: I have caused thee to see it with thine eyes, but thou shalt not go over thither. So Moses, the servant of the Lord, died there, in the land of Moab, according to the word of the Lord. And he buried him in a valley in the land of Moab, over against Beth-peor; but no man knoweth of his sepulchre unto this day."*

The road from Jericho to Jerusalem presents some historical reminiscences of the most interesting nature. When entering the mountains which protect the western side of the plain, the attention of the traveller is invited to the Fountain of Elisha, the waters of which were sweetened by the power of the prophet. The men of Jericho represented to him that though the situation of the town was pleasant, " the water was naught, and the ground barren. And he said, Bring me a new cruse, and put salt therein; and they brought it to him. And he went forth unto the spring of the waters, and cast the salt in there, and said, Thus saith the Lord, I have healed these waters; there shall not be from thence any more death or barren land. So the waters were healed unto this day, according to the saying of Elisha which he spake."†

Its waters are at present received in a basin about nine or ten paces long, and five or six broad; and from

---

\* Deuter. xxxiv. 1-7.       † 2 Kings, ii. 19-23.

thence, issuing out in a copious stream, divide themselves into several small rills, dispersing their refreshment to all the contiguous land, and rendering it exceedingly fruitful.

Advancing into the savage country, through which the usual road to the capital is formed, the tourist soon finds himself at the foot of the mountain called Quarantina, from being the supposed scene of the Temptation and fast of forty days endured by our Saviour, who,

> ———" Looking round on every side, beheld
> A pathless desert dusk with horrid shades:
> The way he came not having mark'd, return
> Was difficult, by human steps untrod;
> And he still on was led, but with such thoughts
> Accompanied of things past and to come
> Lodged in his breast, as well might recommend
> Such solitude before choicest society."*

The neighbourhood of this lofty eminence is, according to Mr Maundrell, a dry, miserable, barren place; consisting of high rocky mountains, so torn and disordered, " as if the earth had here suffered some great convulsion, in which its very bowels had been turned outward." In a deep valley are seen the ruins of small cells and cottages, thought to be the remains of those sequestered habitations to which hermits were wont to retire for penance and mortification; and it is remarked that, in the whole earth, a more comfortless and desert place could not have been selected for so pious a purpose. From these hills of desolation, however, there is obtained a magnificent prospect of the Plain of Jericho, the Dead Sea, and of the distant summits of Arabia; for which reason the highest of the group has been assigned by tradition as the very spot whence all the kingdoms of the world were seen in a moment of time. It is, as St Matthew styles it, an exceeding high mountain, and in its ascent not only difficult but dangerous. It has a small chapel at the top, and another about half-way down, founded upon a projecting part of the rock. Near

---

* Paradise Regained, book i. v. 295, &c.

the latter are observed several caves and holes, excavated by the solitaries, who thought it the most suitable place for undergoing the austerities of Lent,—a practice which has not even at the present day fallen altogether into disuse. Hasselquist describes the path as " dangerous beyond imagination. I went as far up on this terrible mountain of Temptation as prudence would admit, but ventured not to go to the top ; whither I sent my servant, to bring what natural curiosities he could find, whilst I gathered what plants and insects I could find below."*

Mariti, whose religious zeal was fanned into a temporary flame, ascended the formidable steep as far as the grottos, which he delineates with much minuteness. He pronounces the chapel inaccessible from the side on which he stood, and is very doubtful whether it could now be approached on any quarter, the ancient road being so much neglected. But it should seem that most travellers are smitten with the feeling which seized the breast of Maundrell, although all of them have not the candour to acknowledge it. Alluding to the Arabs, who demanded a sum of money for liberty to ascend, he says, " we departed without farther trouble, not a little glad to have so good an excuse for not climbing so dangerous a precipice."†

The imagination of Milton has thrown a captivating splendour around this scene, which, at the same time, he appears to have transferred to the mountain-range beyond the Jordan, in the country of the Moabites.

> " Thus wore out night; and now the herald lark
> Left his ground nest, high towering to descry
> The morn's approach, and greet her with his song:
> As lightly from his grassy couch up rose
> Our Saviour, and found all was but a dream ;
> Fasting he went to sleep, and fasting waked.
> Up to a hill anon his steps he rear'd,
> From whose high top to ken the prospect round,
> If cottage were in view, sheep-cote or herd;
> But cottage, herd, or sheep-cote, none he saw ;

---

* Amongst these he found, with great delight, a very curious new cimex or *bug*, p. 129.
† Journey, p. 80.

> Only in a bottom saw a pleasant grove,
> With chant of tuneful birds resounding loud:
> Thither he bent his way; determined there
> To rest at noon, and enter'd soon the shade,
> High roof'd, and walks beneath, and alleys brown,
> That open'd in the midst a woody scene."*

Leaving the Quarantina, with its dreary shades and solemn recollections, the pilgrim, returning from the Jordan, finds himself on a beaten path which, since the days of Moses, it is probable has connected the rocks of Salem with the banks of the sacred river. Chateaubriand informs us that it is broad, and in some parts paved; having undergone, as he conjectures, several improvements while the country was in possession of the Romans. On the top of a mountain there is the appearance of a castle, which, we may conclude, was meant to protect and command the road; and at a little distance, in the bottom of a deep gloomy valley, is the Place of Blood, called in the Hebrew tongue Abdomim, where once stood a small town belonging to the tribe of Judah, and where the good Samaritan is imagined to have succoured the wounded traveller who had fallen into the hands of thieves. That sombre dell is still entitled to its horrible distinction; it is still the place of blood, of robbery, and of murder; the most dangerous pass for him who undertakes to " go down from Jerusalem to Jericho."

As a proof of this, we may shortly mention an assault which was made upon Sir F. Henniker, who a few years ago resolved to accomplish that perilous journey. "The route is over hills, rocky, barren, and uninteresting. We arrived at a fountain, and here my two attendants paused to refresh themselves; the day was so hot that I was anxious to finish the journey, and hastened forwards. A ruined building, situated on the summit of a hill, was now within sight, and I urged my horse towards it; the janizary galloped by me, and, making signs for me not to precede him, he himself rode into and round the building, and then motioned me to advance. We next came

---

* Paradise Regained, book ii. v. 281.

to a hill, through the very apex of which has been cut a passage, the rocks overhanging it on either side. I was in the act of passing through this ditch when a bullet whizzed by close to my head. I saw no one, and had scarcely time to think when another was fired some short distance in advance. I could yet see no one; the janizary was beneath the brow of the hill in his descent. I looked back, but my servant was not yet within sight. I looked up, and within a few inches of my head were three muskets, and three men taking aim at me. Escape or resistance was alike impossible. I got off my horse. Eight men jumped down from the rocks, and commenced a scramble for me.—As he (the janizary) passed, I caught at a rope hanging from his saddle; I had hoped to leap upon his horse, but found myself unable; my feet were dreadfully lacerated by the honey-combed rocks; nature would support me no longer; I fell, but still clung to the rope; in this manner I was drawn some few yards, till, bleeding from my ancle to my shoulder, I resigned myself to my fate. As soon as I stood up one of my pursuers took aim at me; but the other, casually advancing between us, prevented his firing. He then ran up, and with his sword aimed such a blow as would not have required a second: his companion prevented its full effect, so that it merely cut my ear in halves, and laid open one side of my face: they then stripped me naked."[*]

It is impossible not to suspect that the depraved government at Jerusalem connived at such instances of violence, in order to give some value to the protection which they sold at a very dear rate to Christian travellers. The administration of Mohammed Ali, if fully established, would be a blessing to Palestine, inasmuch as it would soon render the intercourse between the capital and the Dead Sea as safe as that between Alexandria and Grand Cairo.

Refreshing himself at the fountain where our Lord and his Apostles, according to a venerable tradition, were wont to rest on their journey to the holy city, the tourist

---

[*] A Visit to Egypt, &c. p. 285.

sets his heart on revisiting the sacred remains of that decayed metropolis. When at the summit of the Mount of Olives, he is again struck with the mixture of magnificence and ruin which marks the queen of nations in her widowed estate. Owing to the clear atmosphere and the absence of smoke, the view is so distinct that one might count the separate houses. The streets are tolerably regular, straight, and well paved; but they are narrow and dull, and almost all on a declivity. The fronts of the houses, which are generally two or three stories high, are quite plain, simply constructed of stone without the least ornament; so that in walking past them a stranger might fancy himself in the galleries of a vast prison. The windows are very few, and extremely small; and, by a singular whim, the doors are so low that it is commonly requisite to bend the body nearly double in order to enter them. Some families have gardens of moderate dimensions; but, upon the whole, the ground within the walls is fully occupied with buildings, if we except the vast enclosures in which are placed the mosques and churches.

There is not observed at Jerusalem any square, properly so called; the shops and markets are universally opened in the public streets. Provisions are said to be abundant and cheap, including excellent meat, vegetables, and fruit. Water is supplied by the atmosphere, and preserved in capacious cisterns; nor is it necessary, except when a long drought has exhausted the usual stock, that the inhabitants should have recourse to the spring near the Brook Kedron. Rice is much used for food; but as the country is quite unsuited to the production of that aquatic grain, it is imported from Egypt in return for oil, the staple of Palestine.

There is a great diversity of costume in the holy city, as every body adopts that which he likes best, whether Arab, Syrian, or Turk; but the lower order of people generally wear a shirt, fastened round the waist with a girdle, after the example of their neighbours in the Desert. Ali Bey remarks that he saw very few handsome females in the metropolis; on the contrary, they had in general that bilious appearance so common in the

East,—a pale citron colour, or a dead yellow like paper or plaster,—and, wearing a white fillet round the circumference of their faces, they have not unfrequently the appearance of a walking corpse. The children, however, are much healthier and prettier than those of Arabia and Egypt.

The Christians and Jews wear as a mark of distinction a blue turban. The villagers and shepherds use white ones, or striped like those of the Moslem. The Christian women appear in public with their faces uncovered as they do in Europe.

The arts are cultivated to a certain extent; but the sciences have entirely disappeared. There existed formerly large schools belonging to the Haram; but there are hardly any traces of them left, if their place be not supplied by a few small seminaries, where children of every form of worship learn to read and write the code of their respective religion. The grossest ignorance prevails even among persons of high rank, who on the first interview appear to have received a liberal education.*

The Arabic language is generally spoken at Jerusalem, though the Turkish is much used among the better class. The inhabitants are composed of people of different nations and different creeds, who inwardly despise one another on account of their varying opinions; but, as the Christians are very numerous, there reigns among the whole no small degree of complaisance, as well as an unrestrained intercourse in matters of business, amusement, and even of religion.†

It is well remarked by Chateaubriand, who had tra-

---

\* Travels of Ali Bey, vol. ii. p. 251.

† "The Mussulmans say prayers in all the holy places consecrated to the memory of Jesus Christ and the Virgin, except the Tomb of the Holy Sepulchre, which they do not acknowledge. They believe that Jesus Christ did not die, but that he ascended alive into heaven, leaving the likeness of his face to Judas, who was condemned to die for him; and that, in consequence, Judas having been crucified, his body might have been contained in this sepulchre, but not that of Jesus Christ. It is for this reason that the Mussulmans do not perform any act of devotion at this monument, and that they ridicule the Christians who go to revere it."—*Ali Bey*, vol. ii. p. 237.

velled among the native tribes of North America as extensively as among the Arabs of the Syrian wilderness, that amidst the rudeness of the latter you still perceive a certain degree of delicacy in their manners; you see that they are natives of that East which is the cradle of all the arts, all the sciences, and all the religions. Buried at the extremity of the West, the Canadian inhabits valleys shaded by eternal forests and watered by immense rivers; the Arab, cast as it were upon the high-road of the world between Africa and Asia, roves in more brilliant regions over a soil without trees and without water.

The Jews,—the children of the kingdom,—have been cast out; and many have come from the east and the west to occupy their place in the desolate land promised to their fathers. They usually take up their abode in the narrow space between the Temple and the foot of Mount Sion, defended from the tyranny of their Turkish masters by their indigence and misery. Here they appear covered with rags, and sitting in the dust with their eyes fixed on the ruins of their ancient sanctuary. It has been observed that those descendants of Abraham, who come from foreign countries to fix their residence at Jerusalem, live but a short time; while such as are natives of Palestine are so wretchedly poor, as to be obliged to send every year to raise contributions among their brethren of Egypt and Barbary.\*

The picture given by Dr Richardson is much more flattering. He assures his readers that many of the Jews are rich and in comfortable circumstances; but that they are careful to conceal their wealth from the jealousy of their rulers, lest, by awakening their cupidity, some plot of robbery or murder should be devised. The whole population has been estimated by different travellers as amounting from fifteen to thirty thousand, consisting of Mohammedans, Jews, and the various sects of Christians.

---

\* Chateaubriand, Itinéraire, tome ii. p. 169.

## CHAPTER VII.

*Description of the Country Northward of Jerusalem.*

Grotto of Jeremiah—Sepulchres of the Kings—Singular Doors—Village of Leban—Jacob's Well—Valley of Shechem—Nablous—Samaritans—Sebaste—Jennin—Gilead—Geraza or Djerash—Description of Ruins—Gergasha of the Hebrews—Rich Scenery of Gilead—River Jabbok—Souf—Ruins of Gamala—Magnificent Theatre—Gadara—Capernaum or Talhewm—Sea of Galilee—Bethsaida and Chorazin—Tarachea—Sumuk—Tiberias—Description of modern Town—House of St Peter—Baths—University—Mount Tor or Tabor—Description by Pococke, Maundrell, Burckhardt, and Doubdan—View from the Top—Great Plain—Nazareth—Church of Annunciation—Workshop of Joseph—Mount of Precipitation—Table of Christ—Cana or Kefer Kenna—Water-pots of Stone—Saphet or Szaffad—University—French—Sidney Smith—Dan—Sepphoris—Church of St Anne—Description by Dr Clarke—Baalbec—Temple of Aphaca—Vale of Zabulon—Vicinity of Acre.

Upon leaving the northern gate of Jerusalem, on the road which leads to Damascus, there is seen a large grotto much venerated by Christians, Turks, and Jews, said to have been for some time the residence, or rather the prison, of the prophet Jeremiah. The bed of this holy man is shown, in the form of a rocky shelve about eight feet from the ground; and the spot is likewise pointed out, on which he is understood to have written his book of Lamentations. In the days of Maundrell this excavation was occupied by a college of dervises.

I have already alluded to the Sepulchres of the

Kings, as very singular remains of ancient architecture, and standing at a little distance from the city. There still prevails some obscurity with regard to the origin and intention of these places of burial, occasioned chiefly by the fact recorded in holy Scripture, that the tombs of the kings of Judah were on Mount Sion. Pococke held the opinion that they derived their name from Helena, the queen of Adiabene, whose body was deposited in a cave outside the northern wall of Jerusalem,— a conclusion which, as it derives some countenance from the language of Josephus, has been adopted by Dr Clarke. M. de Chateaubriand, on the contrary, supposes these grottos to have been appropriated to the family of Herod; and in support of his views quotes a passage from the Jewish historian, who, speaking of the wall which Titus erected to press the city still more closely, says, "this wall, returning towards the north, enclosed the Sepulchre of Herod." Now this, adds the Frenchman, is the situation of the royal caverns.

But whoever was buried here, this is certain, to use the words of the accurate Maundrell, that the place itself discovers so great an expense both of labour and treasure, that we may well suppose it to have been the work of kings. You approach it on the east side through an entrance cut out of the rock, which admits you into an open court of about forty paces square. On the south side is a portico nine paces long and four broad, likewise hewn out of the natural rock, and having an architrave running along its front adorned with sculpture of fruits and flowers. The passage into the sepulchre is now so greatly obstructed with stones and rubbish that it is no easy matter to creep through; but having overcome this difficulty you arrive at a large room, seven or eight yards square, excavated in the solid body of the hill. Its sides and ceiling are so exactly square, and its angles so just, that no architect could form a more regular apartment; while the whole is so firm and entire, that it resembles a chamber hollowed out of one piece of marble. From this room you pass into six others, all of the same construction; the two innermost being somewhat deeper than the rest, and are descended to by a certain number of steps.

In every one of these, except the first, were coffins of stone placed in niches formed in the sides of the chamber. They had at first been covered with handsome lids; but the most of them have been long broken to pieces, and either scattered about the apartment, or entirely removed. One composed of white marble was observed by Dr Clarke, adorned with the richest and most beautiful carving; though, like all the other sculptured work in the tombs, it represented nothing of the human figure, nor of any living thing, but consisted entirely of foliage and flowers, and principally of the leaves and branches of the vine. The receptacles for the dead bodies are not much larger than European coffins; but, having the more regular form of parallelograms, they thereby differ from the usual appearance presented in the sepulchral crypts of the country, where the soros is of considerable size, and generally resembles a cistern. The taste manifested in the interior of these chambers seems also to denote a later period in the history of the arts; the skill and neatness visible in the carving is admirable, and there is much of ornament displayed in several parts of the work.

But the most surprising thing belonging to these subterranean chambers is their doors; of which, when Mr Maundrell visited Jerusalem, there was still one remaining. " It consisted of a plank of stone of about six inches in thickness, and in its other dimensions equalling the size of an ordinary door, or somewhat less. It was carved in such a manner as to resemble a piece of wainscot: the stone of which it was made was visibly of the same kind with the whole rock; and it turned upon two hinges in the nature of axles. These hinges were of the same entire piece of stone with the door, and were contained in two holes of the immovable rock, one at the top and another at the bottom."[*]

---

[*] Journey, p. 76.

We are informed by Dr Clarke, that the same sort of contrivance is to be found among the sepulchres at Telmessus; and, moreover, that the ancients had the art of being able to close these doors in such a manner that no one could have access to the tomb who was not acquainted with the secret method of opening them, unless by forcing a passage through the stone, and thereby violating the abode of the dead. This has been done in several instances at the place just named; but the doors, though broken, still remain closed with their hinges unimpaired.*

In pursuing the road to Nablous, the ancient Shechem, the first village which meets the eye of the traveller is Beer, so named from the well or spring where the wayfaring man stops to quench his thirst.† The inhabitants, who appear to be chiefly Arabs, are in the greatest poverty, oppressed and alarmed by the incessant demands of their Turkish rulers. It is the Michmash of Scripture, celebrated as the place whither Jotham fled from the anger of his brother Abimelech. It presents, too, the remains of an old church, erected, as tradition reports, by the pious Helena, on the spot where the Virgin sat down to bewail the absence of her son, who had tarried behind in Jerusalem to commune with the doctors in the Temple.

Beyond this interesting hamlet, at the distance of about four hours, is Leban, called Lebonah in the Bible, a village situated on the eastern side of a delicious vale. The road between these two places is carried through a

---

* Pausanias, describing the Sepulchre of Helena at Jerusalem, mentions this device: It was so contrived that the door, which was of stone, and similar in all respects to the sepulchre itself, could never be opened except upon the return of the same day and hour in each succeeding year. It then opened of itself by means of the mechanism alone, and after a short interval closed again. Such was the case at the time stated; had you tried to open it any other time, you would not have succeeded, but broken it first in the attempt. Paus. in Arcad. cap. xvi.—*Clarke's Travels*, vol. iv. p. 383.

† Nablous or Nabloos is a corruption of Neapolis, the "new city," a name bestowed by the Grecian rulers of the Holy Land. Naples, in Italy, presents a similar change in popular pronunciation.

wild and very hilly country, destitute of trees or other marks of cultivation, and rendered almost totally unproductive by the barbarism of the government. In a narrow dell, formed by two lofty precipices, are the ruins of a monastery, being in the neighbourhood of that mystic Bethel where Jacob enjoyed his vision of heavenly things, and had his stony couch made easy by the beautiful picture of ministering angels ascending and descending from the presence of the Eternal.

The next object of interest is connected with the name of the same patriarch. It is Jacob's Well,—the scene of the memorable conference between our Saviour and the woman of Samaria. Such a locality was too important to be omitted by Helena while selecting sites for Christian churches. Over it, accordingly, was erected a large edifice ; of which, however, the " voracity of time, aided by the Turks," has left nothing remaining but a few marks of the foundation. Maundrell tells us that " the well is covered at present with an old stone vault, into which you are let down through a very strait hole ; and then removing a broad flat stone you discover the mouth of the well itself. It is dug in a firm rock, and extends about three yards in diameter and thirty-five in depth ; five of which we found full of water. This confutes a story, commonly told to travellers who do not take the pains to examine the well, namely, that it is dry all the year round except on the anniversary of that day on which our Blessed Lord sat upon it ; but then bubbles up with abundance of water."\*

At this point the traveller enters the narrow Valley of Shechem, or Sychar as it is termed in the New Testament, overhung on either side by the two mountains Gerizim and Ebal. These eminences, it is well known, have obtained much celebrity as the theatre on which was pronounced the sanction of the Divine law—the blessings which attend obedience, and the curses which follow the violation of the heavenly statutes. " And it

---

\* Journey, p. 63.

shall come to pass, when the Lord thy God hath brought thee in unto the land whither thou goest to possess it, that thou shalt put the blessing upon Mount Gerizim, and the curse upon Mount Ebal. Are they not on the other side Jordan, by the way where the sun goeth down, in the land of the Canaanites, which dwell in the champaign over against Gilgal, beside the plains of Moreh?"*

Every reader is aware that the Samaritans, whose principal residence since the captivity has been at Shechem, have a place of worship on Mount Gerizim, to which they repair at certain seasons to perform the rites of their religion. It was upon the same hill, according to the reading in their version of the Pentateuch, that the Almighty commanded the children of Israel to set up great stones covered with plaster, on which to inscribe the body of their law; to erect an altar; to offer peace-offerings; and to rejoice before the Lord their God. In the Hebrew edition of the same inspired books, Mount Ebal is selected as the scene of these pious services,—a variation which the Samaritans openly ascribe to the hatred and malignity of the Jews, who, they assert, have in this passage corrupted the sacred oracles.† In the immediate vicinity of the town is seen a small mosque, which is said to cover the Sepulchre of Joseph, and to be situated in the field bought by Jacob from Hamor, the father of Shechem, as is related in the book of Genesis,

---

* Deut. xi. 29, 30. Alluding to an occurrence mentioned by the sacred historian, Mr S. Hardy remarks, "a better situation could not be conceived for this purpose, as the hills are at such a distance from each other, that the hosts of Israel might stand between, and the voice from either side be heard distinctly on a calm day throughout the whole assembly. The hills are of equal height, about 600 feet, and are neither of them cultivated, but Gerizim has the more pleasing appearance. From the top of this mountain Jotham addressed his fable of the trees to the men of Shechem, when they made Abimelech king. According to Josephus, the first temple erected here was by Manasseh, after the captivity; it was dedicated to the worship of Jehovah in association with the worship of idols."—Pp. 217, 218.

† Kennicot defends the reading of the Samaritan copies.

and alluded to by St John in the fourth chapter of his gospel.*

The road from Leban to Nablous is described as being extremely mountainous, rocky, and full of loose stones. Yet, it is added, the cultivation is every where marvellous; affording one of the most striking pictures of human industry that it is possible to behold. The limestone rocks and shingly valleys of Judea are entirely covered with plantations of figs, vines, and olive-trees; not a single spot seemed to be neglected. The hills, from their bases to their utmost summits, are overspread with gardens; all of them free from weeds, and in the highest state of improvement. Even the sides of the most barren mountains have been rendered fertile, by being divided into terraces, like steps rising one above another, upon which soil has been accumulated with astonishing labour. A sight of this territory can alone convey any adequate idea of its surprising produce; it is truly the Eden of the East, rejoicing in the abundance of its wealth. The effect of this upon the people was strikingly portrayed in their countenances. Instead of the depressed and gloomy looks seen on the desolated plains belonging to the Pasha of Damascus, health and hilarity every where prevailed. Under a wise and beneficent government, the produce of the Holy Land, it is asserted, would exceed all calculation. Its perennial harvests, the salubrity of its air, its limpid springs, its rivers, lakes, plains, hills, and vales, added to the serenity of its climate, prove this land to be indeed a " field which the Lord hath blessed."†

The ancient Shechem is one of the most prosperous towns in the Holy Land, being still the metropolis of a rich and extensive country, and abounding in agricultural wealth. Nor is there any thing finer than its appearance when viewed from the heights by which it is surrounded.

---

* " Then cometh he to a city of Samaria, which is called Sychar, near to the parcel of ground that Jacob gave to his son Joseph. Now Jacob's well was there."—*St John*, iv. 5, 6.

† Clarke's Travels, vol. iv. p. 284.

It strikes the eye of the traveller who advances from the north, as being embosomed in the most delightful and fragrant bowers, half concealed by rich gardens and stately trees, collected into groves all round the beautiful valley in which it stands. There is a considerable trade, as well as a flourishing manufacture of soap; and the population has been reckoned as high as ten thousand,—an estimate, however, which Mr Buckingham thinks somewhat overrated. Within the town are six mosques, five baths, one Christian church, an excellent covered bazaar for fine goods, and an open one for provisions, besides numerous cotton-cloth manufactories, and shops of every description. The inhabitants are chiefly Mohammedans. The Jews, inheriting their ancient enmity towards the Samaritans, avoid the country which the latter formerly possessed; while the Christians, alienated by the suspicion of heresy among their brethren at Nablous, prefer the more orthodox assemblies at Jerusalem and Nazareth.*

The Samaritans themselves do not exceed forty in number. They have a synagogue in the town where they perform Divine Service every Saturday. Four times a-year they go in solemn procession to the old temple on Mount Gerizim; on which occasion they meet before sunrise, and continue reading the Law till noon. On one of these days they kill six or seven rams. They have but one school in Nablous where their language is taught, though they take much pride in preserving ancient manuscripts of their Pentateuch in the original character. Mr Connor saw a copy which is reported to be three thousand five hundred years old, but was not allowed to examine nor even to touch it.

If any thing connected with the memory of past ages be calculated to awaken local enthusiasm, the land around this city is eminently entitled to that distinction.

* Mr Hardy is of opinion that this town may contain about six thousand inhabitants; and he adds, that the gardens by which it is surrounded have a richer appearance than any he had seen since leaving the valley of the Nile.—P. 229.

The sacred record of events transacted in the fields of Shechem is from our earliest years remembered with delight. " Along the valley," observes a late traveller, " we beheld a company of Ishmaelites coming from Gilead, as in the days of Reuben and Judah, with their camels, bearing spicery, and balm, and myrrh; who would gladly have purchased another Joseph of his brethren, and conveyed him as a slave to some Potiphar in Egypt. Upon the hills around flocks and herds were feeding as of old; nor in the simple garb of the shepherds of Samaria was there any thing to contradict the notions we may entertain of the appearance formerly exhibited by the sons of Jacob."\*

It has been remarked in reference to Jacob's Well, where our Lord held his conversation with the woman of Samaria, that no Christian scholar ever read the fourth chapter of St John's Gospel without being struck with the numerous internal evidences of truth which crowd upon the mind in its perusal. Within so small a compass it is impossible to find, in other writings, so many sources of reflection and of interest. Independently of its importance as a theological document, it concentrates so much information that a volume might be filled with its singular illustrations of the history of the Jews and the geography of the country. All that can be collected upon these subjects from Josephus, seems to be but a comment on this chapter. The journey of our Lord from Judea into Galilee,—the cause of it,—his passage through Samaria,—his approach to the metropolis of that country,—its name,—his arrival at the Amorite field which terminates the narrow Valley of Shechem,—the ancient custom of stopping at a well,—the female employment of drawing water,—the disciples sent into the city for food, by which the situation of the well and of the town is so obviously implied,—the question of the woman referring to existing prejudices which separated the Jews from the Samaritans,—the depth of the

---

\* Clarke, vol. iv. p. 275.

well,—the oriental allusion contained in the expression, "living water,"—the history of the well itself, and the customs thereby illustrated,—the worship upon Mount Gerizim,—all these occur within a few verses, and supply a species of evidence for the truth of the narrative in which they are embodied, that no candid mind has ever been able to resist.*

The ancient Samaria presents itself to the traveller in these days under the name of Sebaste or the Venerable,—an appellation conferred upon it by Herod in honour of his patron Augustus. The Jewish historian describes at length the buildings erected by the Idumean prince, especially a citadel, and a noble temple which he intended to exhibit to future generations as a specimen of his taste and munificence. He adds, that the town was twenty furlongs in circumference, and distant one day's journey from Jerusalem,—a computation which, by modern tourists, is extended to more than forty miles. The situation is extremely beautiful, as well as naturally strong, occupying the summit of a hill encompassed all round by a deep valley, and therefore capable of an easy and complete fortification. But the splendid city of Herod is now reduced to a village, small and poor, exhibiting only the remains of its former greatness. In one place, according to Dr Richardson, there are sixty columns of the Ionic order extended in a single row, marking the site of some gorgeous structure erected by the imperial vassal. Mr Buckingham counted eighty-three of these pillars, and alludes to a tradition current among the natives, that they formed part of Herod's own palace. This may indeed be the edifice mentioned by Josephus, who says that the king just named built a sacred place a furlong and a half in circuit, and adorned it with all sorts of decorations; and therein constructed a temple remarkable both for its largeness and its beauty.

Mr Maundrell relates that in his time the ground

---

* Clarke, vol. iv. p. 280.

where the city had stood was entirely converted into gardens; and all the tokens which remain to testify that there ever was such a metropolis are only a large square piazza surrounded with pillars, and some poor ruins of a church, said to have been built by the Empress Helena over the place where St John the Baptist was beheaded. In the body of this temple you go down a staircase into the very dungeon where that holy blood was shed. The Turks hold the prison in great veneration, and over it have erected a small mosque; but for a piece of money they suffer you to go in and satisfy your curiosity at pleasure.

A hundred and thirty years, aided by the destructive habits of Mohammedans, seem to have made a deep impression upon the remains of Sebaste; for when Dr Clarke passed through it, he could not discover even the relics of a great city, and was therefore disposed to question the existence of the splendid ruins mentioned by Maundrell, and more minutely described by Richardson and Buckingham. He is inclined to identify the site of the ancient Samaria with the high ground on which stands the castle of Santorri; but his reasoning on this subject is not sufficiently conclusive to satisfy the mind even of the least reflecting among his readers.*

At this point we leave the territory of Ephraim, and pass into that of the half-tribe of Manasseh. Pursuing his course northwards, the traveller reaches a small hamlet called Beth-amareen; and afterwards, at the distance of three or four miles, he finds himself at Gibba, a village surrounded with trees bearing olives and pome-

---

* A recent pilgrim describes Sebaste as standing on a rounded hill, of moderate and gentle ascent, in the centre of a valley, surrounded at a few miles' distance by mountains of considerable elevation. The town is situated on the eastern slope of the hill, and has an interesting appearance, from the remains of an old convent that rise among the meaner buildings. Higher up the hill, stone columns are seen in every direction, but without capitals. "We counted eighty in an upright position, besides many that are prostrate. The summit of the hill appears to have been scarped, as there is a steep ascent nearly all round, and in this place may have been the citadel."—*Notices of the Holy Land*, p. 222.

granates, and occupying a lofty station over a narrow valley. This place is succeeded by Sannour, which appears to be nothing more than a castle erected on an insular hill, and is more commonly known by the name of Fort Giurali. Another village, called Abati, presents itself on the right hand, embosomed in a grove of fruit-trees; but the stranger, desirous to proceed, advances along the valley until, after having ascended a rising ground, he beholds stretched out at his feet the fine Plain of Esdraëlon covered with the richest pasture.*

On the slope of the hill, which bounds the southern extremity of this fertile valley, stands the town of Jennin, a place, like most of the cities of Palestine, more remarkable for decayed grandeur than for actual wealth, beauty, or power. Its ancient name was Ginoa, and it is found described in the works of some of the older writers as a frontier-place between Samaria and Galilee. The population at present is said to amount to about eight hundred; but the ruins of a palace and a mosque prove that it once possessed a greater importance than now belongs to it. Marble pillars, fountains, and even piazzas, still remain in a very perfect state; and an Arabic inscription over one of which, induces the reader to believe that it was erected by a commander named Selim.

Instead of pursuing our course towards Nazareth and the Lake of Tiberias, we shall now cross the Jordan into the Land of Gilead, and lay before our readers a brief outline of the discoveries which have been recently made

---

* Richardson, vol. ii. p. 415. This fine vale, the most extensive in Palestine, is, says Mr Hardy, about fifty miles long and twenty broad, and is sometimes called the Great Plain and the Valley of Jezreel. From Mr Maddox we learn that there is considerable inequality in the ground; and in the wet season, when he passed through it, on his journey from Damascus to Jerusalem, he found " many places very swampy." Mr Madden states, that the " plain extends about twenty-four miles in length, and that its breadth is from ten to twelve,"—a discrepancy which can only be explained by reference to the fact, that the expanse is divided by hilly ground. —Excursions in the Holy Land, Egypt, Nubia, Syria, &c. vol. ii. p. 206. Travels, vol. ii. p. 305.

in that section of Palestine, the inheritance of Reuben and of Gad. We have already remarked, that to the indefatigable exertions of Dr Seetzen the world are indebted for much of the knowledge they possess relative to the ancient city of Geraza, the ruins of which are pointed out by the Arabs under the name of Djerash.

Approaching it from the south, the traveller first observes a triumphal gateway, nearly entire, bearing a striking resemblance in point of workmanship to the remains of Antinoë in Upper Egypt. The front presents four columns of a small diameter, and constructed of many separate pieces of stone: their pedestals are of a square form, but tall and slender. On each of these is placed a design of leaves, very like a Corinthian capital without the volutes; and on this again rises the shaft, which is plain, and composed of many small portions. As all the columns were broken near the top, the crowning capitals are not seen. The pediment and frieze are also destroyed; but enough remains to give an accurate idea of the original design, and to prove that the order of the architecture was Corinthian. The building appears to have been a detached triumphal arch, erected for the entrance of some victorious hero passing into the city.

Just within this gateway is perceived an extensive naumachia, or theatre for the exhibition of sea-fights, constructed of fine masonry, and finished on the top with a large moulding wrought in the stone. The channels for filling it with water are still visible. Passing onward there is seen a second gateway, exactly similar in design to the one already mentioned, but connected here on both sides with the walls of the city, to which it seems to have formed the proper entrance. Turning to the left the stranger advances into a large and beautiful colonnade arranged in a circular form, all of the Ionic order, and surmounted by an architrave. He next perceives beyond this point a long avenue of columns in a straight line, supposed to mark the direction of some principal street that must have extended the whole length of the town. These columns are all of the Corinthian order, and the ascent to the range on each side is accomplished by a flight of steps.

Making his way along this imaginary street over masses of ruins, the traveller is attracted by four magnificent pillars, of greater height and larger diameter than the rest; but, like all the others, supporting only an entablature, and probably standing before the front of some principal edifice now destroyed. He next arrives at a square formed by the first intersection of the main street by one crossing it at right angles, and like it also, apparently, once lined on both sides by an avenue of columns. At the point of intersection are four masses of building resembling pedestals; on the top of which there probably stood small Corinthian columns, as shafts and capitals of that order are now scattered below. Passing the fragments of a solid wall on the left, which appears to have constituted the front of a large edifice, the tourist next comes to the ruins of a temple of a semicircular form, with four columns in front, and facing the principal street in a right line. The spring of its half-dome is still remaining, as well as several columns of yellow marble and of red granite. The whole seems to have been executed with peculiar care, especially the sculpture of the friezes, cornices, pediments, and capitals, which are all of the Corinthian order, and considered not less rich and chaste than the works of the best ages. On a broken altar near this ruin is observed an inscription, containing the name of Marcus Aurelius. "Beyond this again," says Mr Buckingham, " we had temples, colonnades, theatres, arched buildings with domes, detached groups of Ionic and Corinthian columns, bridges, aqueducts, and portions of large buildings scattered here and there in our way; none of which we could examine with any degree of attention, from the restraint under which our guides had placed us."*

---

* Travels in Palestine, &c., vol. ii. p. 144.

The author of the unpublished journal, from which I have already drawn some rich materials, inspected the remains of Geraza a few years ago. " We set out for the ruins, and reached them before sunrise. Having seen them only partially, by a faint light and from a distance, the previous evening, I had not formed a high opinion of them, and wondered that they should ever have been brought into comparison with Palmyra. A full examination now altered my decision, and left me and all the party full of admiration at the grandeur and the elegance of the ruins. We were struck with the view down the main street of the city. Close to us was a temple, a fine mass of building, surrounded by innumerable fallen columns and ruined cornices. Beneath was the great street, commencing in an elegant circular or rather oval colonnade of fifty-seven pillars, and containing a succession of straight colonnades on each side, crossed at right angles by another line of columns with an entablature. On one side was a splendid temple, with columns, on a height; and on the other a bridge crossing the stream on which the ruins stand. Close to this temple is a theatre in remarkably high repair; almost all the seats are quite entire. The proscenium is still sufficiently so to give a complete idea of the plan; and it is easy to sit on one of the benches and fancy a Greek play performing to a Gerazan audience as it was seventeen hundred years ago. Proceeding northward along the great street, we soon came to a building which seemed to me one of the finest things in Djerash. It was a sort of semicircular temple, in front of which had been a portico of Corinthian columns, composing part of the grand colonnade. I do not think they can be under fifty feet in height, and their form is very elegant. The semicircular building itself is covered with a half-dome, and ornamented with particular richness and beauty. It is remarkable throughout these ruins, how admirably the columns and buildings are disposed for producing effect in combination.— Of two bridges, a good deal of the one to the east remains, and the arches reach across the river, though it is not passable, owing to the destruction of the upper part. There is a paved road between the colonnades leading from the bridge."

The ground occupied by this city, which was nearly in the form of a square, might have been enclosed by a line four English miles in length; the distance from the ruined gateway on the south to the small temple on the north being about five thousand feet. It stood on the corresponding slopes of two opposite hills, with a narrow but not a deep valley between them, through which ran a clear stream of water springing from fountains near the centre of the town, and bending its way thence to the southward. But so complete is the desolation of this once magnificent place, that Bedouin Arabs now encamp among its ruins for the sake of the rivulet by which they are washed, as they would collect near a well in the midst of their native desert. Such portions of the soil as are still cultivated, are ploughed by men who claim no property in it; and the same spot accordingly is occupied by different persons every succeeding year, as time and chance may happen to direct.

Mr Buckingham thinks that the similarity of situation, as well as of name, would lead to the conclusion that this Djerash of the Arabs is the same with the Gergasha of the Hebrews. Reland gives a variety of derivations, quoted from Pliny, Jamblichus, Epiphanius, and Origen; all of which are much more satisfactory, as they regard the position of a certain town in the Land of Gilead, than as they convey any precise ideas as to its etymological import. After the Romans conquered Judea, the country beyond the Jordan became one of their favourite colonies; to which, from the circumstance of its containing ten cities, they gave the name of Decapolis, —an appellation recognised by St Mark in the seventh chapter of his gospel. Geraza, it is presumed, was one of those cities; and, although its history is darkened with more than the usual doubt which attaches to the Jewish annals after the fall of Jerusalem, there is reason to believe that in the time of Vespasian it suffered the penalty of rebellion, and was finally destroyed by the Saracens when they attacked the eastern boundaries of the empire.

We must satisfy ourselves with a mere glance at the hills of Gilead—the rich pasture-grounds of the tribe of Reuben, and formerly the kingdom of the gigantic Og, the monarch of Bashan. It is well known that the Valley of the Jordan is bounded on the east by a range of mountains still more lofty than those which skirt its western limits; but it was not suspected, till lately, that the former concealed in their recesses some of the richest scenery and most valuable lands any where to be found in Palestine. Rising gradually from the bed of the river, the traveller soon finds himself on a platform seven or eight hundred feet above its level; forming a district of extraordinary fertility, abounding with the most beautiful prospects, clothed with thick forests, diversified with verdant slopes, and possessing extensive plains of fine soil, yielding in nothing to the most prolific parts of Galilee and Samaria. "We continued our way," says Mr Buckingham, "to the north-east, through a country the beauty of which so surprised us, that we often asked each other what were our sensations; as if to ascertain the reality of what we saw, and persuade each other, by mutual confessions of our delight, that the picture before us was not an optical illusion. The landscape alone, which varied at every turn, and gave us new beauties from any point of view, was of itself worth all the pains of an excursion to the eastward of the Jordan; and the park-like scenes that sometimes softened the romantic wildness of the general character as a whole, reminded us of similar spots in less neglected lands."*

The scenery continues of the same fascinating description till the traveller reaches the Nahr el Zerkah, or River Jabbok, the ancient boundary between the Amorites and the Children of Ammon. The banks are thickly clothed with the oleander and plane-tree, the wild olive and almond, and many flowering shrubs of

---

* Travels in Palestine, vol. ii. p. 104.

great variety and elegance. The stream is about thirty feet broad, deeper than the Jordan, and nearly as rapid, rushing downwards over a rocky channel. On the northern side begins the kingdom of Bashan, celebrated for its oaks, its cattle, and the bodily strength of its inhabitants. The opposite plate exhibits a view of the Jabbok, and of the bold Alpine range which fenced the territory of one of the most formidable enemies of Israel; verifying in its fullest extent the description of Moses, who says, "The border of the children of Ammon was strong."*

The curious reader will find in the Travels of Mr Buckingham some ingenious reasoning employed by him to fix the locality of Bezer, Ramoth, Jabesh, and other towns situated in Gilead; places which were rendered important by the various events recorded in the sacred volume.

About six miles from Djerash towards the north stands the village of Souf, on the brow of a lofty hill, and flanked by a deep ravine. It retains several marks of having been the site of some more ancient and considerable town, presenting large blocks of stone, with mouldings and sculpture, wrought into the modern buildings. In the neighbourhood are seen the walls of an edifice apparently Roman, as also the ruins of two small towers which may with equal certainty be traced to the age of Saracenic domination. Souf can boast of nearly five hundred inhabitants, all rigid Mohammedans, and remarkable for a surly and suspicious character.

Leaving this rather inhospitable village, the traveller who wishes to visit the remains of Gamala proceeds in a north-westerly direction, descending into a fine valley, and again rising on a gentle ascent, the whole being profusely wooded with evergreen oaks below, and pines upon the ridge of the hill above. Mr Banks, who had seen the whole of England, the greater part of Italy and France, and almost every province of Spain and Portugal, has remarked, that in all his travels he met with

---

* Numbers, xxi. 24. Deut. ii. 37.

River Jabbok, and Hills of Bashan.

nothing equal to it, excepting only in some parts of the latter country,—Entre Minho-and-Douro,—to which alone he could compare it."*

Several hamlets, and some obscure indications of ancient buildings, meet the eye in course of the journey to Om Keis. But before reaching this town, the road emerges into a hilly district, bleak, rocky, and ill cultivated; whence the view is as monotonous as that from Jerusalem, forming a striking contrast to the rich, verdant, and beautiful scenery which distinguishes Bashan and Gilead.

Gamala, for under that name the ruins of the Roman station are most familiarly known, must have covered a site nearly square; its greatest length, from east to west, being seventeen hundred short paces, and its breadth about one-fourth less. A considerable portion of it seems to have stood on the summit of a hill, well fortified all round; the traces of towers and other works of defence being still visible even on its steepest parts. The portals of the eastern gate remain, from which point a noble street appears to have run through the whole length of the city, lined by a handsome colonnade of Ionic and Corinthian pillars. The pavement is formed of square blocks of volcanic stone, and is still so perfect, that the ruts of carriage-wheels are to be seen in it, of different breadths, and about an inch in depth, as at the ruins of Pompeii and Herculaneum in Italy.†

The first edifice which presents itself on entering the eastern gate is a theatre, the scene and front of which are entirely destroyed, but the benches are preserved. Still farther on are appearances of an Ionic temple, the colonnade of the street being continued; and about half-way along is a range of Corinthian pillars on pedestals, marking the position of some grand edifice. Not a column, indeed, continues erect; but the plan can still be distinctly traced. This supposed temple must have been a hundred paces in depth from north to south; and its

---

* Buckingham, vol. ii. p. 244.  † Travels in Palestine, p. 259.

façade, which fronted the street and came in a line with the grand colonnade already mentioned, cannot have been less than a hundred and eighty feet in breadth. The chief peculiarity of this structure, however, consists in its having been built on a range of fine arches, so that its foundations were higher than the general level of the town ; and hence, as the pedestals of the columns were elevated considerably above the street, it must have presented a very striking object.

There are the remains of numerous other edifices, theatres, and temples ; but they are all too indistinct to enable even a professional eye to pronounce with confidence on their plan. The prevailing orders of architecture are Ionic and Corinthian, though some few capitals decidedly Doric are discovered among the ruins. The stone generally used throughout the city is that of the neighbouring mountains,—a species of gray rock approaching to a carbonate of lime ; but the shafts of some of the pillars are formed of a black substance, supposed to have a volcanic origin, and most commonly preferred for the internal decorations of funereal vaults and sarcophagi.*

As the ruins here described are not precisely in the position usually assigned to Gamala on the maps, and as Dr Seetzen, the only person besides Mr Buckingham who has published any account of them, thinks that they are those of Gadara, the latter traveller enters into a lengthened discussion in support of his own views, employing the statements of several ancient writers to establish his position. But the reader will soon discover that much of the ambiguity which prevails on this point arises from the fact of there being in different parts of Canaan several towns of the same name. For example there was unquestionably a place called Gadara on the eastern shore of the Lake of Tiberias ; while, from the testimony of Josephus, it is equally certain that the same appellation was given to the capital of Perea. In the

---

* Buckingham, vol. ii. p. 261.

New Testament, the country of the Gadarenes is described as being on the other side of the sea, over against Galilee,—a notice which removes all doubt with respect to the opinion of those who maintain the existence of a town or village, named Gadara, situated to the northward of the site generally claimed for Gamala, and nearer the body of the lake.

The same author tells us, that the account given in the Gospel of the habitation of the demoniac, out of whom the legion of devils was cast, struck him very forcibly while wandering among savage mountains and surrounded by tombs, still used as houses by individuals and even by whole families. A finer occasion for expressing the passions of madness in all their violence, contrasted with the serene virtue and benevolence of Him who went about continually doing good, could hardly be chosen for the pencil of an artist; and a faithful delineation of the rugged and wild majesty of the mountain-scenery on the one hand, with the still calm of the lake on the other, would give an additional charm to the picture.*

Amid the interesting ruins of Gamala, situated in a barren district, alike unfavourable for agriculture, manufactures, and commerce, it is impossible not to be surprised at the indications of wealth and luxury which must have centred within its walls. The opulence cannot but have been considerable, which raised such splendid temples and colonnades, and supported two large theatres; erecting, at the same time, such massive tombs and splendid sarcophagi for all classes of the people. Its desolation may be traced to the rebellious spirit of the inhabitants, and the sanguinary wars to which it led under successive emperors. Vespasian, whose name is so closely associated with the history of Palestine not less for evil than for good, directed against it on more than one occasion the fury of the Roman legions, and finally levelled its walls, that they might not again be defended by such

---

* Travels in Palestine, vol. ii. p. 261.

desperate insurgents. At a later period, its remote situation withdrew it from the attention of Europeans; and, in truth, its very existence had ceased to be remembered, until its ruins were once more visited by travellers in the course of the present century.

Passing along the eastern border of the lake, and advancing towards its northern extremity, the traveller easily recognises that desert place where the multitude was fed upon the miraculous loaves and fishes. Here, too, was the scene of the remarkable punishment inflicted upon the Gadarenes for their insensibility to Divine instruction, as also, perhaps, for the unhallowed occupation of feeding animals the use of which was forbidden by the law of Moses. The brink of the water presents many steep places where such a catastrophe might be easily realized.

At the upper end of the lake are the remains of Capernaum, now called Talhewm, or Tel Hoom, situated about ten miles from Tiberias, in a north-easterly direction. This village, although at present nothing more than a station of Bedouins, appears to have been occupied in former times by a settlement of some importance, as the ruins of stately buildings are found scattered over a wide space in the neighbourhood. The foundations also of a magnificent edifice can still be traced; but the structure itself is so much dilapidated that it is no longer possible to determine whether it was a temple or a palace. The northern end is sixty-five paces in length, and, as the eastern wall seems to have extended to the very edge of the water, its length could not be less than five hundred feet. Within this space are seen large blocks of sculptured stone, in friezes, cornices, and mouldings.

The appearance of the Sea of Galilee, as seen from this point of view at Capernaum, is very grand. Its greatest length runs nearly north and south from fifteen to eighteen miles, while its breadth averages from five to six. The barren aspect of the mountains on each side, and the total absence of wood, give, however, a cast of dulness to the picture; and this is increased even to a feeling of melancholy by the dead calm of its surface, and the silence which reigns throughout its whole extent, where not a boat or vessel of any kind is to be found. No fisherman any longer plies his laborious craft on the bosom of the lake, nor seeks to vary his scanty meal by letting down his net for a draught. Mr Buckingham observed, from the heights above, shoals of fish darting through the water, and the shore in some places covered with storks and diving-birds, which repair thither in search of food; but when, on one occasion, he suggested that a supper might be procured for his party by exercising a little skill with the rod or net, he discovered that the ignorant barbarians whom he addressed had not yet taken a lesson from the fowls of the air.

A circumstance deserving of notice is mentioned by Hasselquist, in regard to the tenants of this lake. He thought it remarkable that the same kind of fishes which frequent the Nile should be met with here,—charmuth, silurus, bænni, mulsil, and sparus Galilœus. This explains the observations of certain travellers, who speak of the Sea of Tiberias as presenting fish peculiar to itself; not being acquainted perhaps with the produce of the Egyptian river. Josephus was of the same opinion; and yet it is worthy of remark that, in describing the Fountain of Capernaum, his conjectures tend to confirm the conclusions of the Swedish naturalist:—"Some consider it," says the Jewish historian, "as a vein of the Nile, because it brings forth fishes resembling the coracinus of the Alexandrian lake."*

That Capernaum was a place of some wealth and consequence in the time of our Saviour, may be inferred from the expostulation addressed to it, when he upbraided the other cities wherein most of his mighty works were done:—" Woe unto thee, Chorazin! Woe unto thee, Bethsaida! And thou, Capernaum, which art exalted unto heaven, shalt be brought down to hell." But the

---

* Joseph. lib. iii. De Bell. Jud. Hasselquist, p. 157. Clarke, vol. iv. p. 227.

history of all the towns on the Lake of Gennesareth has been covered with a cloud which it is now impossible to dispel; and nothing, accordingly, is more difficult than to determine the situations occupied, even during the latter period of Roman ascendency, by some of the principal places on which the emperors lavished their wealth and taste. Bethsaida was converted by Herod from an insignificant village into the dignity and grandeur of a city, named Julias, in compliment to the daughter of Augustus. At the present moment, however, no traces remain to point out the line of its walls or the foundations of its palaces. Gennesareth has in like manner disappeared; or if there be any relics of the town, which once gave its name to the inland sea whose shore it adorned, they are so indistinct and ambiguous as hardly to merit the notice of the traveller. Tarachea is represented by the hamlet of Sumuk, and the ruins of Chorazin are imagined to meet the eye somewhere on the opposite coast; but, upon the whole, the denunciation uttered against the unbelieving cities of Galilee has been literally fulfilled, as they are now brought down to the lowest pitch of obscurity and oblivion.*

Tiberias is the only place on that venerated Sea which retains any marks of its ancient importance. It is understood to cover the ground formerly occupied by a town of a much remoter age, and of which some traces can still be distinguished on the beach, a little to the southward of the present walls. History relates that it was built by Herod Antipas, and dedicated to Tiberius, his patron; although there also prevails an obscure tradition, that the new city owed its foundation entirely to the imperial pleasure, and was named by him who commanded it to be erected. Josephus notices

---

* Travels in Palestine, vol. ii. p. 359. " Quæ urbes, quod ipse Servator iis prædixerat, hodie in ruinis jacent."—*Cluverius*, lib. 5. cap. 20. " Capernaum was visited in the sixth century by Antoninus the Martyr, an extract from whose Itinerary is preserved by Reland, who speaks of a church erected upon the spot where St Peter's dwelling once stood."—*Clarke's Travels*, vol. iv. p. 211.

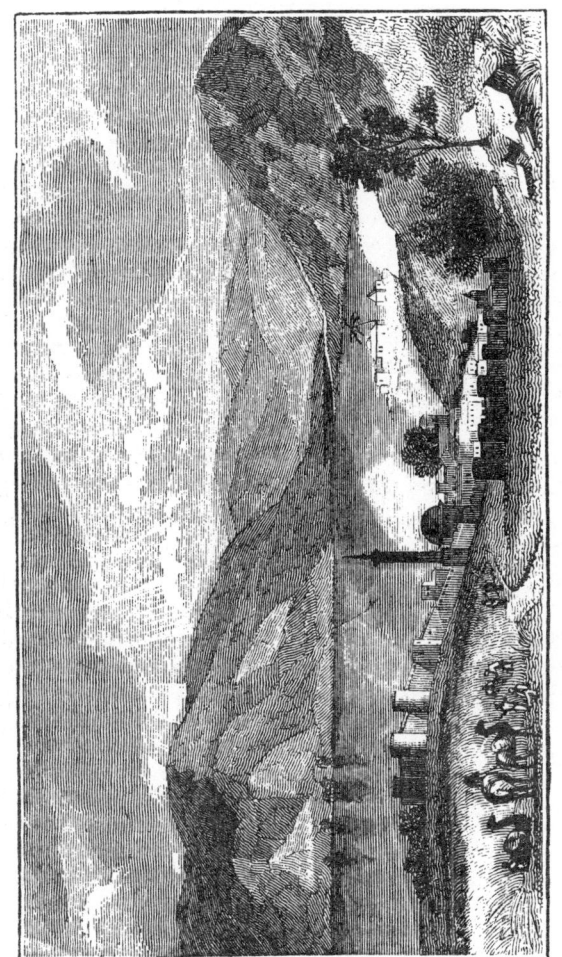

Sea of Galilee, Town of Tiberias, and Baths of Emmaus.

the additional circumstance—which of itself gives great probability to the opinion of its being established on the ruins of an older one—that, as many sepulchres were removed in order to make room for the Roman edifices, the Jews could hardly be induced to take possession of the houses, which, according to their notions, were legally impure. Adrichomius considers this place to be the Chinneroth of the Hebrews, and says, that it was captured by Benhadad, king of Syria, who destroyed it, and was at a later age restored by Herod, who surrounded it with walls, and adorned it with magnificent buildings. The old Jewish town, whatever was its name, probably owed its existence to the reputation of its hot-baths,—an origin to which many temples and even cities may be distinctly traced.

Tabaria, as it is now commonly denominated, has the form of an irregular crescent, and is enclosed towards the land by a wall flanked with circular towers. It lies nearly north and south along the edge of the lake, and has its eastern front so close to the water, on the brink of which it stands, that some of the houses are washed by the sea. The whole does not appear more than a mile in circuit, and cannot, from the manner in which they are placed, contain above 500 separate dwellings. There are two gates visible from without, one near the southern and the other in the western wall; there are appearances also of the town having been surrounded by a ditch, but this is now filled up and used for gardens.

The interior presents but few interesting objects; among which are a mosque with a dome and minaret, and two Jewish synagogues. There is a place of Christian worship called the House of St Peter, which is thought by some to be the oldest building used for that purpose in any part of Palestine. It is a vaulted room, thirty feet long by fifteen broad, and perhaps fifteen in height, standing nearly east and west, with its door of entrance at the western front, and its altar immediately opposite in a shallow recess. Over this door is one small window, and on each side four others, all arched and open. The structure is of a very ordinary kind, both in workmanship and material; the pavement within is similar to that used for streets in this country ; and the walls are entirely devoid of sculpture or any other architectural ornament. But it derives no small interest from the popular belief that it is the very house which Peter inhabited at the time of his being called from his boat to follow the Messias. It is manifest, notwithstanding, that it must have been originally constructed for Divine worship, and probably at a period much later than the days of the apostle whose name it bears; although there is no good ground for questioning the tradition which places it on the very spot that has been long venerated as the site of his more humble habitation. Here too it was, say the dwellers in Tiberias, that he pushed off his boat into the lake when about to have his faith rewarded by the miraculous draught of fishes.\*

Besides the public buildings already specified, are the house of the aga, on the rising ground near the northern quarter of the town, a small bazaar, and two or three coffee-sheds. The ordinary dwellings of the inhabitants are such as are commonly seen in Eastern villages, but marked by a peculiarity which Mr Buckingham witnessed there for the first time. On the terrace of almost every house stands a small square enclosure of reeds, loosely covered with leaves ; to which, he learned, heads of families are wont to resort during the summer months, when, from the low situation of the town, and the absence of cooling breezes, the heat of the nights is literally intolerable.†

---

\* Buckingham, vol. ii. p. 366. Speaking of this house of prayer, the author of Notices of the Holy Land informs us, that " there are several pictures at the eastern end, all, except one, very rude ; but what is somewhat remarkable in a Latin church, there is not a single image. The service-books are all in Arabic. I counted fifty people at matins, which speaks well for them, and may give some idea of the number of Christians in the place. We had a long conversation with the priest, and there appeared to be something good about him, though alloyed with much ignorance."—P. 235.

† " Within two hours and a half of Tiberias, we looked down on a fine cultivated plain, quite bare of trees ; beyond which, at a

According to the opinion of the best informed among the inhabitants, the population of Tiberias, or Tabareeah as they pronounce it, does not exceed two thousand. Of these about one-half are Jews, many of whom are from Europe, particularly from Germany, Russia, and Poland ; the rest are Mohammedans, with the exception of twenty or thirty Christian families, who profess the tenets of the Latin Church.

The warm baths, which have given celebrity to that neighbourhood, are still found at the distance of between two and three miles southward from the town. The building erected on the spring is small and mean, and altogether the work of the present rulers of Palestine. The bath itself is a square room of eighteen or twenty feet, covered with a low dome, and having seats or benches on each side. The cistern for containing the hot water is in the centre of this room, and sunk below the pavement. It is a square of eight or nine feet only, and the spring rises to supply it through a small head of some animal ; but this is so badly executed that it is

---

much lower level, lay the narrow Valley of the Jordan. This plain was pastured over by horses from the town, for the keepers of which white tents were scattered about in all directions. We now came in sight of the Sea of Galilee—we only saw the northern half, and its size disappointed us ; but the dark-blue still water, the green hills around covered with bushes, and the high snowy ridge of Djibbel el Sheik, made a very delightful landscape. Tiberias, with its high feudal citadel, its walls and towers, now forms a remarkable feature in the view ; and the steep hills, which descend at once to the lake on the east, attract attention from their strangely-channelled sides, diversified with dark-green bushes and white chalky soil. The lake at the town may be six or eight miles broad. We could see no stream formed by the Jordan through it. Before it was dark we had a very fine view of the lake ; at the southern part it is narrow and the sides bold. The sun threw a deep shade on this side and on the water, while it marked the hills and valleys on the opposite side with strong light and shade. The northern part is much wider and tamer ; but the hills are still high and green, and the lofty snowy mountain of Djibbel el Sheik, rising over them, gives great dignity to the landscape. This mountain was very striking, late in the evening, as retaining the sun's rays after every thing around us was in darkness. In all respects, it is the greatest ornament of the lake, and I am surprised that travellers have not mentioned it more."—*Anonymous Journal.*

difficult to know for what it is intended. One traveller states that his thermometer, when immersed in the water, instantly rose to 130°, which was the utmost limit of the instrument. He is satisfied, however, that the heat was much greater, because as it issued from the spout it was painful to the hand, and could only be borne by those who had bathed in the cistern.*

This town makes a conspicuous figure in the Jewish annals, and was the scene of some of the most remarkable events which are recorded by Josephus. After the downfal of Jerusalem, it continued until the fifth century to be the residence of Jewish patriarchs, rabbis, and learned men. A university was established within its boundaries; and, as the patriarchate was allowed to be hereditary, the remnant of the Hebrew people enjoyed a certain degree of weight and consequence during the greater part of four centuries. In the sixth age, if we may confide in the accuracy of Procopius, the Emperor Justinian rebuilt the walls; but in the following century, the seventh of the Christian era, the city was taken by the Saracens under Caliph Omar, who stripped it of its privileges, and demolished some of its finest edifices. It must not be concealed, however, that in the Itinerary of Willibald, who performed his journey into the Holy Land towards the close of the eighth century, mention is made of many churches and synagogues which the conquerors had either not destroyed or allowed to be repaired.†

---

* Buckingham, vol. ii. p. 368. Mr Hardy mentions that "the baths are in ruins, especially the division allotted to the females. Several Jews and Jewesses were bathing, as is their custom every Friday, to prepare themselves for the Sabbath. There is a magnificent bath in the course of erection for Ibrahim Pasha, at a little distance from the former building, surmounted by an open colonnade, which is supported by marble pillars taken from ancient ruins."

† Dr Clarke relates that " the French, during the time their army remained under Bonaparte in the Holy Land, constructed two very large ovens in the earth at Tiberias. Two years had elapsed at the time of our arrival since they had set fire to their granary; and it was considered as a miracle by the inhabitants that the combustion was not yet extinguished. We visited the place, and per-

From Tiberias to Nazareth the traveller has to encounter an almost uninterrupted ascent. The village of Caber Sabet first attracts his attention by its architectural remains, indicating the existence of an ancient building, which must have had marble columns and a magnificent portico. He soon afterwards reaches Soak el Khan,—a place chiefly celebrated for a weekly market, where every description of commodity in use among the people is collected for sale. It also presents the ruins of a Saracenic fort of a square shape, with circular towers at the angles and in the centre of each wall.

In pursuing this route we have Mount Tor, or Tabor, on the left hand, rising in solitary majesty from the Plain of Esdraëlon. Its appearance has been described by some authors as that of a half-sphere, while to others it suggests the idea of a cone with its point struck off. According to Mr Maundrell, the height is such as to require the labour of an hour to reach the summit; where is seen a level area of an oval figure, extending about two furlongs in length and one in breadth. It is enclosed with trees on all sides except the south, and is most fertile and delicious. Having been anciently surrounded with walls and trenches, there are remains of considerable fortifications at the present day. Burckhardt says, a thick wall, constructed of large stones, may be traced quite round the summit, close to the edge of the precipice; on several parts of which are relics of bastions. The area too is overspread with the ruins of private dwellings, built of stone with great solidity.

Pocockc assures us that it is one of the finest hills he ever beheld, being a rich soil that produces excellent herbage, and most beautifully adorned with groves and clumps of trees. The height he calculates to be about two miles, making allowance for the winding ascent; but he adds, that others have imagined the same path

---

ceived that, whenever the ashes of the burnt corn were stirred by thrusting a stick among them, sparks were even seen glowing throughout the heap; and a piece of wood left there became charred."

to be not less than four miles. Hasselquist conjectures that it is a league to the top, the whole of which may be accomplished without dismounting,—a statement amply confirmed by the experience of Van Egmont and Heyman. These travellers relate that "this mountain, though somewhat rugged and difficult, we ascended on horseback, making several circuits round it, which took up about three quarters of an hour. It is one of the highest in the whole country, being thirty stadia, or about four English miles. And it is the most beautiful we ever saw with regard to verdure, being every where decorated with small oak-trees, and the ground universally enamelled with a variety of plants and flowers. There are great numbers of red partridges, and some wild-boars; and we were so fortunate as to see the Arabs hunting them. We left, but not without reluctance, this delightful place, and found at the bottom of it a mean village, called Deboura, or Tabour, a name said to be derived from the celebrated Deborah mentioned in the book of Judges."

But this mountain derives the largest share of its celebrity from the opinion entertained among Christians since the days of Jerome, that it was the scene of a memorable event in the history of our Lord. On the eastern part of the hill are the remains of a strong castle; and within the precincts of it is the grotto, in which are three altars in memory of the three tabernacles that St Peter proposed to build, and where the Latin friars always perform mass on the anniversary of the Transfiguration. It is said there was a magnificent church built here by Helena, which was the cathedral when this town was made a bishop's see. On the side of the hill they show a church in a grot, where they say Christ charged his disciples not to tell what things they had seen till he should be glorified.

It is very doubtful, however, whether this tradition be well founded, or whether it has not, as Mr Maundrell and other writers suspect, originated in the misinterpretation of a very common Greek phrase. Our Saviour is

Mount Tabor.

said to have taken with him Peter, James, and John, and brought them into a high mountain " apart;" from which it has been rather hastily inferred that the description must apply to Tabor, the only insulated and solitary hill in the neighbourhood. We may remark with the traveller just named, that the conclusion may possibly be true, but that the argument used to prove it seems incompetent; because the term " apart" most likely relates to the withdrawing and retirement of the persons here spoken of, and not to the situation of the mountain. In fact, it means nothing more than that our Lord and his three disciples betook themselves to a private place for the purpose of devotion.

The view from Mount Tabor is extolled by every traveller. " It is impossible," says one, " for man's eyes to behold a higher gratification of this nature." On the north-west you discern in the distance the noble expanse of the Mediterranean, while, all around, you see the spacious and beautiful plains of Esdraëlon and Galilee. Turning a little southward, you have in view the high mountains of Gilboa, so fatal to Saul and his sons. Due east you discover the sea of Tiberias, distant about one day's journey. A few points to the north appears the mount of Beatitudes, the place where Christ delivered his sermon to his disciples and the multitude. Not far from this little hill is the city of Saphet, or Szaffad, standing upon elevated and very conspicuous ground. Still farther, in the same direction, is seen a lofty peak covered with snow, a part of the chain of Anti-Libanus. To the south-west is Carmel, and in the south the hills of Samaria.*

---

* The following extract, from the unpublished journal already so often referred to, will amuse the reader :—" We arrived at the foot of Mount Tabor. It is, in its general outline, a round regular-shaped hill, but is rocky and rough enough when it is to be ascended. It has many trees, mostly Valonia oaks. It stands on the east of the great Plain of Esdraëlon, up a recess formed by Mount Hermon on the one side, and the hills towards Nazareth on the other. Its height from the plain I should guess at 1000 feet. We ascended the greater part of the way on mules. On the top of the hill is one

The plain around, the most fertile part of the Land of Canaan, being one vast meadow covered with the richest pasture, is the inheritance where the tribe of Issachar " rejoiced in their tents." Here it was that Barak, descending with his ten thousand men from Tabor, discomfited Sisera and all his chariots. In the same neighbourhood Josiah, king of Judah, fought in disguise against Necho, king of Egypt, and fell by the arrows of his antagonist, deeply lamented. The great mourning in Jerusalem, foretold by Zechariah, is said to be as the lamentations in the plain of Esdraëlon, as the mourning of Hadadrimmon in the Valley of Megiddon. Vespasian reviewed his army in the same great plain. It has been a chosen place for encampments in every contest carried on in this country, from the days of Nebuchadnezzar, king of the Assyrians, down to the disastrous invasion of the Emperor Napoleon. Jews, Gentiles, Saracens, Egyptians, Persians, Druses, Turks, Arabs, Christian Crusaders, and Anti-christian Frenchmen,—warriors out of every nation under heaven,—have pitched their tents upon the plain of Esdraëlon, and have beheld their various banners wet with the dews of Tabor and of Hermon. And shall we not add that here too is to be fought the great battle of Armageddon, so well known to all interpreters of prophecy, which is expected to change the aspect of the eastern world? When the French entered Syria in 1799, General Kleber was attacked near a village called Fouleh, in the Great Plain, by an army of 25,000 Turks. At the head of twelve or fifteen hundred men, whom he formed into a square, he continued fighting from sunrise till mid-day, when he had expended all his ammunition. Bonaparte, at length,

---

of those large cisterns, or granaries, so often alluded to before. There was one also near Jennin, which we observed in coming in. I have since seen them in numerous other places, which puts an end to Dr Clarke's Pagan Remains. The whole of the Great Plain is fully cultivated, yet we could hardly see a single village, which adds to the peculiarity of its appearance,—one sheet of cultivation without a rock or tree."

informed of his perilous situation, advanced to his support with six hundred soldiers; at the sight of whom the enemy, after having lost several thousands in killed and wounded, commenced a hurried retreat, in the course of which many of them were drowned in the river Daboury, at that time, like another Kishon, overflowing its banks. In a word, the champaign country which stretches northwest from Tabor has been the theatre of real or of mimic warfare in all ages. "We had the pleasure," says Doubdan, " to view from the top of that mountain Arabs encamped by thousands; tents and pavilions of all colours, green, red, and yellow; with so great a number of horses and camels, that it seemed like a vast army, or a city besieged."*

But we now proceed towards Nazareth, the modern Naszera or Nassera, a journey of about two hours from the foot of the mountain which we have just examined. It seems, says one writer, as if fifteen mountains met to form an enclosure for this delightful spot; they rise round it like the edge of a shell to guard it from intrusion. It is a rich and beautiful field in the midst of barren hills. The church stands in a cave supposed to be the place where the Blessed Virgin received the joyful message of the angel, recorded in the first chapter of St Luke's Gospel. It resembles the figure of a cross. That part of it which stands for the tree of the cross is fourteen paces long and six broad, and runs directly into the grot, having no other arch over it at top but that of the natural rock. The transverse part is nine paces in length and four in width, and is built athwart the mouth of the cave. Just at the section of these divisions are erected two granite pillars, two feet in diameter, and about three feet distant from each other. They are supposed by the faithful to stand on the very places where the angel and

---

* Clarke, iv. p. 260. Doubdan, Voyage de la Terre Sainte, p. 507. Paris, 1661.—It is remarkable that all the descriptions of the view from Mount Tabor appear to be borrowed from this sedulous Frenchman, whose work, in point of topography, is still unequalled.

the Blessed Virgin respectively stood at the time of the Annunciation.*

When Dr Clarke visited this sanctuary, the friars pointed out the kitchen and the fireplace of the Virgin Mary; and as all consecrated spots in the Holy Land contain some supposed miracle for exhibition, the monks, he informs us, have taken care not to be altogether deficient in supernatural rarities. Accordingly, the first things they show to strangers who descend into the cave are two stone pillars in the front of it; one of which, separated from its base, is said to sustain its capital and a part of its shaft miraculously in the air. The fact is, that the capital and a piece of the shaft of a pillar of gray granite have been fastened to the roof of the grotto; and " so clumsily is the rest of the *hocus pocus* contrived, that what is showed for the lower fragment of the same pillar resting upon the earth, is not of the same substance, but of Cipolino marble."†

A variety of stories are circulated about the fracture of this miraculous pillar. The more ancient travellers were told that it was broken by a pasha in search of hidden treasure, who, for his impiety, was struck with blindness; at present it is said that it separated into two parts, in the manner in which it still appears, when the angel announced to Mary the glad tidings with which he was commissioned. Maundrell was not less observant than the author just quoted, although he does not so openly expose the deception. " It touches the roof above, and is probably hanged upon that; unless you had rather take the friars' account of it, namely, that it is supported by a miracle."

Pococke has proved that the tradition concerning the dwelling-place of the parents of Jesus Christ existed at a very early period; because the church built over it is mentioned by writers of the seventh century. Nor is there in the circumstance, that their abode was fixed in a grotto or natural cave, any thing repugnant to the

---

\* Journey, p. 112.  † Travels, vol. iv. p. 170.

notions usually entertained either of the ancient customs of the country or of the class of society to which Joseph and his espoused wife belonged. But when we are called upon to surrender our belief to the legends invented by men, whose ignorance is the best apology we can urge for their superstition, a certain degree of disgust and indignation is perfectly justifiable.

In such a case we are disposed to question the good effects ascribed by some authors to the pious zeal of the Empress Helena, who, although she did not in fact erect one-half of the buildings ascribed to her munificence, most undoubtedly laboured, by her architectural designs, to obliterate every trace of those simple scenes which might have been regarded with reasonable veneration in all ages of the church. Dr Clarke, in a fit of spleen with which we cannot altogether refuse to sympathize, remarks, that had the Sea of Tiberias been capable of annihilation by her means, it would have been dried up, paved, covered with churches and altars, or converted into monasteries and markets of indulgences, until every feature of the original had disappeared; and all this by way of rendering it more particularly holy.*

Of the original edifice, said to have been erected by the mother of Constantine, some remains may still be observed in the form of subverted columns, which, with the fragments of their capitals and bases, lie near the modern building. The present church and convent are of a comparatively recent date, at least so far as the outward structure and internal decorations are concerned; the former being filled with pictures supplied by the modern school, all of which are described as being below mediocrity.

Besides the antiquities already mentioned, as having

---

* Vol. iv. p. 174. "Up stairs, above the Chapel of the Incarnation," says Dr Richardson, "we were shown another grotto, which was called the Virgin Mary's Kitchen, and a black smoked place in the corner, which was called the Virgin Mary's Chimney. I believe none of the cinders, fire-irons, or culinary instruments have been preserved; these probably fled with the Santa Casa, or Holy House, to Loretto; and our only astonishment is, that the house should have taken flight and left the chimney and kitchen behind."—Vol. ii. p. 440.

a reference to the early history of our Lord, the traveller is conducted to the "workshop of Joseph," which is near the convent, and was formerly included within its walls. It is now a small chapel, perfectly modern, and whitewashed like a Turkish sepulchre. After this is shown the synagogue where the Redeemer is said to have read the Scriptures to the Jews; and also the precipice from which the monks aver he leaped down to escape the rage of his townsmen, who were offended at his application of the sacred text. " And all they in the synagogue, when they heard these things, were filled with wrath, and rose up, and thrust him out of the city, and led him unto the brow of the hill whereon their city was built, that they might cast him down headlong. But he, passing through the midst of them, went his way."*

The Mount of Precipitation, as it is now called, is, according to Mr Buckingham, about two miles distant from Nazareth; is almost inaccessible, from the steep and rocky nature of the road; and is decidedly not upon the hill where the town could ever have been built. Dr Clarke, on the other hand, maintains that the words of the evangelist are most explicit, and prove the situation of the ancient city to have been precisely that which is occupied by the modern town. In a recess there is an altar hewn out of the rock, said to be the very spot where Christ dined with his disciples. Close by are two large cisterns for preserving rain-water, and several portions of buildings, all described as the remains of a religious establishment founded by the pious and indefatigable Helena. Immediately over this scene, and on the edge of a precipice about thirty feet in height, are two flat stones set up on their edges. In the centre, and scattered over different parts of one of them, are several round marks like the deep imprint of fingers on wax; and it is insisted that these are the impression of our Saviour's hand when he clung to the stone, and thereby escaped being thrown headlong down.†

---

* Luke, iv. 28, 29, 30. † Travels in Palestine, vol. ii. p. 315.

One celebrated relic still remains to be noticed, which, although it is not alluded to in the New Testament, is regularly authenticated by the Pope; who, besides, grants a plenary indulgence to every pilgrim who has visited the place where it is exhibited. This is nothing more than a large stone, on which it is affirmed that Christ did eat with his disciples both before and after his resurrection from the dead. A chapel has been built over it, on the walls of which are several copies of a printed certificate, stating the grounds of its claim to veneration. Dr Clarke transcribed this curious document, which is given in a note below, accompanied with a translation, for the use of such readers as have not formed an acquaintance with the Latin tongue.*

There is not an object in all Nazareth so much the resort of pilgrims,—Greeks, Catholics, Arabs, and even Turks,—as this stone : the former classes on account of the seven years' indulgence granted to those who visit it; the two latter, because they believe some virtue must reside in a slab before which all comers are so eager to prostrate themselves.

In a valley near the town is a fountain which bears the name of the Virgin, and where the women are seen passing to and fro with pitchers on their heads, as in the days of old. It is justly remarked, that, if there be a spot throughout the Holy Land which was more parti-

---

* " Traditio continua est, et nunquam interrupta, apud omnes nationes Orientales, hanc petram, dictam ' Mensa Christi.' illam ipsam esse supra quam Dominus noster Jesus Christus cum suis comedit Discipulis ante et post suam resurrectionem a mortuis.

" Et sancta Romana Ecclesia INDULGENTIAM concessit septem annorum et totidem quadragenarum omnibus Christi fidelibus hunc sanctum locum visitantibus, recitando saltem ibi unum Pater, et Ave, dummodo sint in statu gratiæ."

" It is a continued and uninterrupted tradition among all the Eastern churches, that this stone, called the ' Table of Christ,' is that very one upon which our Lord Jesus Christ ate with his Disciples both before and after his resurrection from the dead.

" And the holy Roman Church hath granted an INDULGENCE of seven years, and as many lents, to all the faithful in Christ visiting this sacred place, upon reciting at least one Pater Noster and an Ave, provided they be in a state of grace."

cularly honoured by the presence of Mary, we may
consider this to be the place ; because the situation of a
copious spring is not liable to change, and because the
custom of repairing thither to draw water has been
continued among the female inhabitants of Nazareth
from the earliest period of its history.

As another memorial of primitive times, we may
mention that it is still common there to see " two women grinding at the mill ;" illustrating the remarkable
saying of our Lord in reference to the destruction of
Jerusalem. The two females, seated on the ground
opposite to each other, hold between them two round
flat stones, such as are seen in Lapland, and which in
Scotland are usually called querns. In the centre of
the upper stone is a cavity for pouring in the corn ; and
by the side of this an upright wooden handle for moving
it. To begin the operation, one of the women with her
right hand pushes this handle to her companion, who in
her turn sends it back to the first,—thus communicating
a rotatory and very rapid motion to the upper stone ;
their left hands being all the while employed in supplying fresh corn, as fast as the bran and flour escape
from the sides of the machine.\*

It is not without pleasure that the traveller contemplates these unaltered tokens of the simple life which
prevailed in Palestine at the time when our Saviour
abode in the house of Mary his mother ; and more especially, as he cannot fail to contrast them with the pernicious mummery which now disgraces the more artificial
monuments of Christian zeal. From the extravagances
chargeable upon the priesthood at all the holy places in
Canaan, there has resulted this most melancholy fact,
that devout but weak men, unable to distinguish between
monkish fraud and simple truth, have considered the
whole series of topographical evidence as one tissue of
imposture, and have left the Holy Land worse Christians than when they entered it. Credulity and scepti-

---

\* Clarke, vol. iv. p. 167.

cism are extremes too often found to approximate; and the man, accordingly, who suddenly relinquishes the one, is almost sure to adopt the other.

Burckhardt remarks that the Church of Nazareth, next to the one over the Holy Sepulchre, is the finest in Syria, and possesses two tolerably good organs. Within the walls of the convent are several gardens and a small burying-ground; the building is very strong, and serves occasionally as a fortress to all the Christians in the town. There are eleven friars on the establishment, the yearly expenses of which, amounting to about £900, are defrayed by the rent of a few houses and the produce of a small portion of land, the property of the good fathers.

Before quitting this interesting place,—the scene where our Lord passed the days of his childhood and youth,— we may observe, that there is a great variation in the accounts given by different travellers as to the number of its inhabitants. Dr Richardson restricts it to six or seven hundred; Mr Buckingham raises it to two thousand; while others assert that it does not fall short of half as many more. There are five hundred Turks, and the remainder are Christians,—the latter described as a civil and very industrious class of people.*

At about an hour and a half towards the north-east, situated on the slope of a hill, stands Kefer Kenna, or Cana of Galilee, the village where the Redeemer performed his first miracle. Here, in a small church belonging to the Greek communion, is shown an old stone pot made of the common rock of the country, and which is said to be one of the original vessels that contained the water afterwards converted into wine. It is worthy of note, says Dr Clarke, that in walking among the ruins of Cana one sees large massy pots of stone answering to the description given by the evangelist; not pre-

---

* " Nazareth may at present contain 3000 inhabitants, a great number of whom are Christians of the Greek Church."—*Notices of the Holy Land*, p. 228.

served nor exhibited as relics; but lying about disregarded by the present inhabitants, as antiquities with the original use of which they are altogether unacquainted. From their appearance, and the number of them, it is quite evident that the practice of keeping water in large stone pots, each holding from eighteen to twenty-seven gallons, was once common in the country.

The remains of the house in which the marriage was celebrated are likewise pointed out to the traveller, who, at the present day, is permitted to examine curiosities with greater deliberation than was allowed to honest Doubdan.\* This pious confessor, whose zeal prompted him to leave nothing unexplored, found an old church in the village, ascribed as usual to the inexhaustible beneficence of St Helena; but his attention was more pleasantly engaged in tracing the course of the stream which issues from the sacred fountain whence the water was drawn for the marriage-feast. There is still a limpid rill near the village, which affords to the inhabitants their daily supply of a delicious beverage. Pilgrims repair to it moved by feelings of piety, or, as he expresses it, to satisfy at once their devotion and their thirst. A few olive-trees being near the spot, travellers alight, spread their carpets, and, having filled their pipes, generally smoke tobacco and take some coffee; always preferring repose in these places to any accommodation which can be obtained in the village. Such has been the custom of the country from time immemorial; extending not only to the wayfaring man, but also to the shepherds on the surrounding hills, and to the companies of merchantmen whose trade carries them through the neighbouring deserts.†

---

\* " De là nous retournasmes sur nos pas, à l'entrée du village par où nous avions passé, pour aller voir la Fontaine où on alla puiser l'eau qui servit a ce miracle; mais en allant ces femmes et enfans nous penserent accabler de pierres et d'injures, tant ils sont inhumains et ennemies des Chrestiens."—*Le Voyage*, &c. p. 512.

† Clarke, iv. p. 187. " We were afterwards conducted into the chapel, in order to see the relics and sacred vestments there preserved. When the poor priest exhibited these, he wept over them

The distant view of the landscape which stretches from the Lake of Tiberias to the sources of the Jordan, is at once grand and beautiful; the mountains that terminate the prospect being extremely magnificent, and some of them covered with perpetual snow. The intervening country, too, is in many parts uncommonly fine, presenting luxuriant crops, thriving villages, and other tokens of security and comfort. The Jordan issues from Lake Hoole, or Julias, which in its turn is fed by so many streams, that it becomes very difficult to determine the true fountain of the sacred river.

The only town of consequence, between the ruins of Capernaum and the alpine range of Hermon, is Saphet, already mentioned, being one of the four cities consecrated by the religious veneration of the Hebrews. According to recent travellers, it stands upon several low hills that divide it into quarters, the largest of which is occupied by Jews. The whole may contain six hundred houses, whereof one hundred and fifty belong to the people just named, and nearly as many to the Christians. The summit of the principal eminence is crowned with an ancient castle, part of which is regarded by the descendants of Israel as being contemporary with their earliest kings.

Saphet is still a sort of university for the education of the Jewish rabbis, of whom there are usually twenty or thirty resident, collected from different countries of Europe, Africa, and Asia. They have no fewer than seven synagogues. Their attachment to this place arises from various motives, and especially from the traditionary belief that the Messias is to reign here forty years before he assumes the government at Jerusalem. Northward of the hill on which the castle stands there are several wells, which, it is maintained by some

---

with so much sincerity, and lamented the indignities to which the holy places were exposed in terms so affecting, that all our pilgrims wept also. Such were the tears which formerly excited the sympathy and roused the valour of the Crusaders. The sailors of our party caught the kindling zeal, and nothing more was necessary to incite in them a hostile disposition towards every Saracen they might afterwards encounter."

authors, were dug by the patriarch Isaac, and became the cause of contention between his herdsmen and those of Gerar; but, says Pococke, such writers have much mistaken the place, the Valley of Gerar being at a great distance on the other side of Jerusalem. This town, which is only mentioned in the book of Tobit as belonging to the tribe of Naphtali, became famous during the Crusades; it was occupied also by a detachment of French troops during the invasion of the country by Bonaparte.

It is worthy of notice, that when the celebrated chief now named retreated from before Acre, the tyrant Djezzar Pasha, to avenge himself on the Franks, inflicted a severe punishment on the Jewish and Christian inhabitants of Saphet. It is said that he had resolved to massacre all the believers in Moses and Jesus Christ who might be found in any part of his dominions, and had actually sent orders to Nazareth and Jerusalem to accomplish his barbarous design. But Sir Sidney Smith, on being apprized of his intention, conveyed to him the assurance, that if a single Christian head should fall, he would bombard Acre, and set it on fire. The interposition of the British admiral is still remembered with heartfelt gratitude by all the inhabitants, who looked upon him as their deliverer. " His word," says Burckhardt, " I have often heard both Turks and Christians exclaim, was like God's word,—it never failed."

It were in vain that we should endeavour to ascertain the position of Dan, the extreme point of the proper territory originally assigned to the Hebrews. Its proximity to the Fountains of Jordan might be supposed to prove a sufficient guide to the geographer in his local researches; but, as has been already mentioned, the rivulets which contribute to form the main stream of this celebrated river are so numerous, and apparently so equally entitled to the honour of being accounted the principal source, that the precise situation of the temple where Jeroboam set up one of his golden calves is still open to conjecture.*

---

* " At noon I and my servant began to ascend the hill to the north-east of Saphet, and in little more than an hour we found our-

The position occupied by the town which bore the name of Dan is usually conceived to have marked the limits of the Israelitish kingdoms towards the north. But we find in the inspired history, that the successor of Moses " took all that land, from the mount Halak which goeth up to Seir, even unto Baal-gad in the valley of Lebanon, under Mount Hermon." Among the cities, too, mentioned in the second book of Chronicles, as built by Solomon, is Balaath in Lebanon, which may perhaps be identified with that ancient town where the conquests of Joshua are said to have terminated. Allusion is likewise made to a splendid structure erected by the same magnificent king, called the house of the forest of Lebanon; the length whereof was a hundred cubits, and the breadth fifty cubits, and the height thirty cubits.—And he made a porch of pillars, the length whereof was fifty cubits.\*

These statements make manifest that the dominion of the Jewish sovereigns extended at one period into Cælesyria, and even give some probability to the opinion that a portion of the ruins at Baalbec still represent the grandeur of one of the most prosperous and brilliant of their reigns. The house of the forest was composed of " costly stones, according to the measure of hewed stones, sawed with saws within and without, even from the foundation to the coping, and so on the outside towards the great court, and the foundation was of costly

---

selves in the plain of the sea of Galilee. There were no houses in sight from the hills, but in different places we could see the shepherds keeping watch over their flocks. In two hours, from the foot of the hill, we arrived at a bridge over the Jordan, called the Bridge of the Sons of Jacob. Between the bridge and the sea of Galilee, which may be about four miles distant, there is an old fortress, for what purpose built I cannot tell, unless the Jordan be sometimes fordable at that place. About two miles to the northward is Bahr el Houl, or " Waters of Merom," four miles broad, and six long. The banks are low, and the whole presents the appearance of a marsh. A few miles from this lake stands Cæsarea Philippi, now called Baneas, and long supposed to be the source of the Jordan. It is the Dan of the Old Testament."—*Notices of the Holy Land,* p. 248.

\* Joshua, xi. 16-17. 2 Chronicles, viii. 6. 1 Kings, vii. 2-7.

stones, even great stones, stones of ten cubits, and stones of eight cubits." Josephus further informs us, that Baalath was one of the places built by Solomon within the Syrian border, on account of the temperate climate, the delicacy of the fruits, and the excellence of the air and water.

By Gesenius and other biblical critics, Baalbec is supposed to be either Baal-gad, a town at the foot of Lebanon, or Baal-hamon, which is mentioned in the eighth chapter of the Song of Solomon. Baalbec appears to have been the original name, which the Greeks, using their wonted license, changed into Heliopolis, a term of similar import, and denoting the City of the Sun. The Romans, adopting this translation, have not preserved the ancient phrase in any of their writings; but the language of the country, notwithstanding, has perpetuated the primitive appellation, while the tongue of the conquerors has perished with their dominions. It stands in a delightful situation on the eastern side, and near the head of the valley of Beka, which leads down in a south-western direction to Tyre, and opens by a narrow defile upon the Orontes towards the east, communicating with Tadmor, Hamath, and Mesopotamia; and it must therefore have been a great commercial depot when Babylon and Nineveh, Tyre and Sidon, possessed the trade of nearly all the world. The magnificence of its ruins, indeed, sufficiently testify its ancient splendour and opulence.

Since the Viceroy of Egypt succeeded in establishing his authority over that interesting section of the Turkish empire, the fine valley which stretches between Libanus and Anti-Libanus has been frequently visited by European travellers. The noble ruins which have given celebrity to it are seen from a considerable distance, rising above the thicket of walnut and fruit trees by which they are surrounded. The last rays of the setting sun ere he sank in a flood of glory behind Lebanon, were, says a late writer, gilding the upper portion of the temples and columns, while the gradually encroaching shadows of the mountains had thrown the gigantic platform on which they stood into obscurity. The colossal magnitude of this enormous mass, the effect of which was heightened to sublimity by the uncertain light, filled the breast with the deepest impressions of awe. It appeared the work of some mightier being than man. The cyclopean remains in Italy dwindle to nothing in comparison; while above, shooting up into the twilight, rose the columns of a later age, so light, so beautiful, so exquisitely proportioned!*

The enclosure in which the principal ruins stand, having been used by the Turks as a fortification, exhibits in some parts the strangest mixture of ancient and modern building; walls consisting of broken cornices, architraves, and pillars, massed together in the utmost disorder. The chief entrance is through a screen leading into an hexagonal court, every portion of which is in a state of entire dilapidation. From thence there is an approach into a quadrangle of considerable size, round which formerly ran a series of arcades, no longer in existence, but the walls whereon they rested still remain, having two alcoves, or semicircular recesses on each side. This square affords a passage into the court containing the great temple, which stands on the left, while on the right are six tall columns, the relics of a similar sanctuary.

"This temple," observes an intelligent author who recently explored the antiquities of Lebanon, "is wonderfully perfect; the architecture is of the Corinthian order, and belongs to the most classical age of Roman art. I have seen nothing in Italy that surpasses, indeed I may say nothing that equals it. It is built of a compact primitive limestone; the pillars, of which there are fourteen on each side, and eight at the extremities, I computed to be rather above sixty feet in height, composed of three pieces joined together by a square piece of iron fitted in sockets in the centre. One or two of

---

* Three Weeks in Palestine, p. 122.

these had slipped from their pedestals, and reclined unbroken against the wall of the temple. They were crowned by a noble architrave and beautifully carved cornice. The peristyle was covered by an arched roof of stone, cut in patterns, with medallions in high relief of mythological subjects admirably executed. The portico, which once displayed a double row of columns, is destroyed; the pronaos is also much dilapidated, and the pillars that supported the roof are gone. The doorway leading from thence into the body of the temple is twenty-one feet in width; the moulding and other ornaments are the richest I ever beheld. The lintel is composed of three huge blocks, two on either side entering far into the wall, the third the form of a wedge. Upon this is carved a splendid relief of an eagle grasping a caduceus in his talons, and surrounded by a wreath, the two ends of which he holds in his beak. On each side a spiral staircase ascended to the top; the roof however has fallen in. The interior walls of the temple are surrounded by a double row of pilasters, having niches for statues between them, and at the upper end is the recess that once contained the image of the deity to which it was dedicated. The dimensions are 192 feet in length by 96 in breadth. The interior is much encumbered by fragments and rubbish; and without are seen lying in every direction broken shafts, capitals, and other architectural remains which would supply a rich treat both to the architect and the painter."*

But beautiful as are those buildings, and replete with interest and delight to every person of taste, they yield as objects of wonder to the wall which encircles them. Maundrell, writing in an age when these were little known, seems almost afraid to hazard the delineation. " Here," says he, " is another curiosity of this place, which a man had need to be well assured of his credit before he ventures to relate, lest he should be thought to strain the privilege of a traveller too far; that which

---

* Three Weeks in Palestine and Lebanon, p. 129.

I mean is a large piece of old wall which encompassed these structures last described." The whole is composed of blocks of stone of such magnitude that the smallest of them would excite astonishment, if seen elsewhere; but here, being eclipsed by three enormous masses, placed contiguously in the same course of the building, about twenty-five feet from the ground, they are overlooked as comparatively insignificant. They are at too great a height to admit of being accurately measured; but in the quarry whence they were hewn, about a mile distant, at the foot of Anti-Libanus, there yet remains a similar block, apparently of the same dimensions, and which was found to be sixty-eight feet in length, fourteen in height, and sixteen and a half in breadth. If, then, as there seemed the best reason to conclude, the three stones in the wall be of the same size, they must occupy a space of sixty-eight yards in length: and by what mechanical powers they were conveyed to the distance of a mile, and then raised to their present position, no one can now conjecture. It cannot therefore be surprising that such an achievement should be referred by the people of the country to diabolical agency. The height of the wall is in proportion to the bulky nature of its materials, and is evidently not the work of those who erected the temples, but belongs to some remoter age.*

---

* Three Weeks in Palestine and Lebanon, p. 132. Mr Madox informs his readers that he measured some of these immense stones, of which those in the fosse are the largest. The stone at the corner forms two sides of it, one of which sides measures sixty-seven feet, and the other twenty feet six inches. Eight stones in the north wall or screen, each measured thirty feet in length, nine feet nine inches in breadth, and twelve feet six inches in depth.—*Excursions*, vol. ii. p. 62.

Dr Richardson observes that the "soil of age with which the stones are covered, compared with other parts of the building which are decidedly Roman, would warrant our referring them to the remote period of eight and twenty hundred years; the era of Solomon, king of Israel, who built Hamath and Tadmor in the desert. The second builders of this pile have built upon the foundations of the former building; and in order that the appearance of the whole might seem

In the latest work containing any reference to these remains of Syrian grandeur, the author states that while, with regard to their magnitude, his expectations were more than realized, he was disappointed in the effect. " It was," says he, " the first ruin of Grecian architecture I had ever visited ; and having been accustomed from my earliest days to associate with this style all that is chaste and beautiful, I do confess that I expected the temple of Baalbec would have excited in me greater enthusiasm. I saw it in different lights, and from different situations, but the voice with which it spoke to me was always the same. The moss and ivy of the ruins in England give them an inexpressible charm ; the massiness of the Egyptian structures strikes the mind with awe ; and even the caves and temples of India have something about them that attracts and fixes the attention. But in looking at these immense stones and columns, the feeling was one of melancholy alone, that time should have been so merciless in his devastations, without adding any of those telling touches that in other places make us almost forgive him for his deed. The simplicity of the Grecian architecture appears to me to be lost when exhibited in proportions so colossal."*

In crossing Libanus towards the coast of the Mediterranean some interesting objects present themselves, connected as well with the ancient idolatry as with the purer recollections suggested by sacred history. Eusebius relates that between Heliopolis—the modern Baalbec—and the sea, at a place named Aphaca, among the heights of Lebanon near a small lake, was a temple dedicated to the foul fiend Venus ; and hence it is conjectured that a village called Afka was the seat of this celebrated fane. Burckhardt failed in his endeavours to discover it,

---

to be of one date, they have cut a new surface upon the old stones. This operation has not been completely finished, and some of the stones remain half cut, exhibiting part of the old surface and part of the new ; so that the different eras of the building are exemplified in the same stone.

* Notices of Holy Land, p. 266.

owing to the circumstance that the main line of road no longer passes the lake on the margin of which it was erected. A subsequent traveller was more fortunate, who, being compelled to deviate from the beaten path, discovered at Liamoony a ruined structure which, both from its position and architectural properties, seems to identify itself with the building mentioned by the ecclesiastical historian. The remains are scattered in the centre of an area, forming a square of at least eighty paces across, bounded by a massive wall of hewn stones ingeniously put together without mortar. From this external boundary, to which a large gateway gave access, the ground everywhere rose by a regular ascent to a mass of fallen materials, resting on a basement elevated by three steps above the adjacent soil. This mass exhibited fragments of Doric columns, pieces of entablature, and many other ponderous stones thrown together in a confused heap, apparently by some sudden and violent shock. Here there were evidently the wrecks of an ancient temple; the gateway can still be traced, as well as traces of a portico; and a wide flight of steps connecting the entrance with the main, are seen half-buried beneath the shattered architrave and broken columns. Every part had been massive, but rather coarsely executed; the cella had consisted of five or six columns on each side, of large diameter, now completely overthrown; and such is the degree of dilapidation that considerable pains would be necessary to ascertain the precise plan of the edifice. The adjoining lake is shallow, and of no great extent; but a wide gravelly strand proves that, at some seasons, its dimensions are greatly increased.*

The cedars of Libanus are associated in the mind of every reader with the magnificence of the most opulent of Hebrew kings, and also with the sublimest descriptions of mountain scenery. Upon leaving Baalbec, and

---

* Hogg's Visit to Alexandria, Damascus, and Jerusalem, vol. i. p. 243.

approaching the high grounds, towering walnut trees, either singly or in groups, and a rich carpet of verdure, the offspring of numerous springs, give a charm to this romantic district, so majestically bounded with snowy cliffs. At Dier el Akmar the ascent begins, winding among dwarf oaks, hawthorns, and a great variety of shrubs and flowers. After passing the summit of the first ridge the traveller obtains a view of the celebrated cedars. Seven of the most ancient still remain; which, being considered coeval with Solomon, are held most sacred. Rude altars have been erected near them, and an annual Christian festival is held, when worship is performed beneath their venerable branches. Other cedars, varying in age and size, form around them a protecting grove. Many indeed have sprung up from ancient roots; but enumerating all that present independent trunks, including the patriarchal trees, they amount to 343. It is observed with surprise by every traveller, that, with the exception of the shoots just mentioned, there is no succession of young ones springing up; but whether this arises from their being destroyed in their tender state by the flocks of goats which cover the mountains, or whether the seeds are swept away by the tempests and torrents of winter, is a question which none of them have been able to determine.*

Instead of penetrating the ravines of Libanus, with the view of making our way to the country of the ancient Phenicians on the shores of the Mediterranean,

---

* According to Berggren, a Swedish traveller, there are still 800 or 900 cedars on Mount Lebanon; but few of them put forth new shoots. The gazelles and other game hurt the young plants. The oldest cedars are thirty-six to forty feet in circumference. Ferugiac Bulletin, xiv. 357. Ehrenberg and Hemprich in two months collected 1140 plants on Mount Lebanon. Ibid. tome xiv. p. 228. For farther information concerning the remains of Baalbec and the peculiar beauties of the surrounding scenery, the reader is referred to the works already quoted, and also to Dr Richardson's Travels, vol. ii. p. 502; Irby and Mangles' Travels, p. 215; Rae Wilson's Travels, vol. ii. p. 147; and more especially to the " Ruins of Baalbec," by Mr Wood, in which the most copious details are illustrated by numerous engravings.

we shall descend the course of the Jordan till we reach Nazareth, and from thence proceed to the renowned city of Tyre, the modern Tsour. The road for some time goes over a barren rocky tract, which Hasselquist informs us is a continuation of a species of territory peculiar to the same meridian, and stretching through several parallels of latitude. At length the traveller reaches Sephouri, or Sepphoris, the Zippor of the Hebrews, and the Diocesarea of the Romans, once the chief town and bulwark of Galilee. The relics of its fortifications exhibit one of the works of Herod, who, after its destruction by Varus, not only rebuilt and strengthened it, but made it the principal city of his tetrarchy. Its inhabitants often revolted against the Romans, relying on the advantages for defence supplied by its natural position. It is mentioned in the Talmud as the seat of a Jewish university, and was long famous for the learning of its rabbis. Here also was held one of the five sanhedrims, authorized by the spiritual governors of Palestine; the others being established at Jerusalem, Jericho, Gadara, and Amathus. But its chief celebrity is connected with the tradition, that it was the residence of Joachim and Anna, the parents of the Virgin Mary. The house of St Anne, it has been said, is the " commencement of that superstitious trumpery which for a long time has constituted the chief object of devotion and of pilgrimage in the Holy Land." No sooner was the spot discovered where the pious couple had lived, than Constantine issued instructions to build upon it a magnificent church, the remains of which have been minutely described by the enterprising traveller to whom we have just alluded.

" We were conducted to the ruins of a stately Gothic edifice, which seems to have been one of the finest structures in the Holy Land. Here we entered beneath lofty massive arches of stone. The roof of the building was of the same materials. The arches are placed at the intersection of a Greek cross, and originally supported a dome or a tower; their appearance is highly picturesque, and they exhibit the grandeur of a noble style of architecture. Broken columns of granite and marble lie scattered among the walls, and these prove how richly it was decorated. We measured the capital of a pillar of the order commonly called Tuscan, which we found lying against one of granite. The top of this formed a square of three feet. One aisle of this building is still entire; at the eastern extremity a small temporary altar had been recently constructed by the piety of pilgrims; it consisted of loose materials, and was of very modern date. Some fragments of the original decorations of the church had been gathered from the ruins and laid upon this altar; and although they had remained open to every approach, even the Moslems had respected the votive offerings."*

The date of this building is incidentally mentioned by Epiphanius, who relates that one Joseph, a native of Tiberias, was authorized by Constantine to erect a number of such edifices in the Holy Land, and that he fulfilled the intention of his sovereign at Tiberias, Capernaum, and Diocesarea. Reland, following Theophanes, places its destruction in the year 339 of the Christian era, when the town was demolished on account of the seditious conduct of its inhabitants.

It is perhaps worthy of notice, that Dr Clarke examined some pictures which had been recently discovered among these ruins. One appears to represent the interview between our Saviour and the two disciples at Emmaus, when in the act of making himself known to them by the breaking of bread. Another exhibits the Virgin bearing in swaddling-clothes the infant Jesus; and a third seems to illustrate the same subject in circumstances somewhat different. They are said to bear a great resemblance to those used in the churches of Russia, being executed upon a square piece of wood about half an inch in thickness. As they were not valued highly by the person into whose hands they had accidentally

---

* Clarke's Travels, iv. p. 141.

fallen, our countryman bestowed a trifle on the ignorant Mohammedan, and took them into safer custody.

The Vale of Zabulon divides the village just described from the ridge of hills which look down on Acre and the shores of the Great Sea. This delightful plain appears every where covered with spontaneous vegetation, flourishing in the wildest exuberance. The scenery is described as not less beautiful than that of the rich valleys upon the south of the Crimea; reminding an Englishman of the finest parts of Kent and Surrey. The prickly pear, which grows to a prodigious size in the Holy Land, sprouts luxuriantly among the rocks, displaying its gaudy blossoms, and promising abundance of a delicious fruit. On either side of the road the ruins of fortified places exercise the ingenuity of the antiquary, who endeavours, through the mist of tradition and the perplexing obscurity of modern names, to identify towns which make a figure in Jewish and Roman history. All remains of the strong city of Zabulon, called by Josephus the " city of men," have disappeared; and its " admirable beauty," rivalling that of Tyre, Sidon, and Berytus, is now sought for in vain among Arab huts and scattered stones.

The plain, which skirts the Mediterranean from Jaffa to Cape Blanco, presents many interesting memorials of Hebrew antiquity and of European warfare. Every town along the coast has been the scene of contention between the armies of Christendom and those of Islamism; on which account I have thought proper to reserve the history of these cities, so as to incorporate it, in a subsequent chapter, with the narrative of the exploits whereon their fortunes have chiefly depended. Suffice it to mention as we go along, that the vicinity of Acre invites the attention of the naturalist, on account of certain facts recorded by Pliny, and repeated by subsequent historians. It is said by this writer, that it was at the mouth of the river Belus the art of making glass was first discovered. A party of sailors, who had occasion to visit the shore in that neighbourhood, propped up the kettle in which they were about to cook their provisions with sand and pieces of nitre ; when to their surprise they found produced by the action of the fire on these ingredients a new substance, which has added immensely to the comforts of life and to the progress of science. The sand of this remarkable stream continued for ages to supply not only the manufactories of Sidon, but all other places, with materials for that beautiful production. Vessels from Italy were employed to remove it for the glass-houses of Venice and Genoa so late as the middle of the seventeenth century.

There is another circumstance connected with the same river, which, in the mythological writings of antiquity, makes a still greater figure than the discovery just described. Lucian relates that the Belus, at certain seasons of the year, especially about the feast of Adonis, is of a bloody colour,—a fact which the heathens looked upon as proceeding from a kind of sympathy in the death of this favourite of Venus, who was killed by a wild boar in the mountains whence the stream takes its rise. " Something like this," says Maundrell, " we saw actually come to pass ; for the water was stained to a surprising redness, and, as we had observed in travelling, had discoloured the sea a great way into a reddish hue, occasioned doubtless by a sort of minium, or red earth, washed into the river by the violence of the rain, and not by any stain from Adonis' blood."*

The excellency of Carmel, which here rises into view, has in a great measure passed away. The curse denounced by Amos,—" the top of Carmel shall wither," —has fallen upon it; for it is now chiefly remarkable as a mass of barren and desolate rocks. Its sides are indeed graced by some native cedars, and even the brambles are still intermingled with wild vines and olives, denoting its ancient fertility or more careful cultivation ; but there are no longer any rich pastures to render it the " habitation of shepherds," or to recall to

---

* Journey from Aleppo to Jerusalem, p. 35.

the fancy the beauty of Carmel and of Sharon, and to justify the comparison of it to the glory of Libanus. It owes to its name and to its prominent situation on the coast, as a sentinel of the Holy Land, all the interest that can now be claimed for the mountain on which Elias vindicated the worship of Jehovah, and where thousands of holy Christians have spent their lives in meditation and prayer.

The monastery which stands on the summit of the hill, near the spot where the prophet offered up his sacrifice, was long the principal residence of the Carmelite friars. It appears not to have ever been a fine building, and is now entirely abandoned. During the campaign of the French in Syria, it was made an hospital for their sick, for which it was well adapted by its healthy and retired situation. It has been since ravaged by the Turks, who have stripped its shrines and destroyed its roof; though there still remains, for the solace of devout visiters, a small stone altar in a grotto dedicated to Saint Elias, over which is a coarse painting representing the holy man leaning on a wheel, with fire and other instruments of sacrifice at his side.[*]

---

[*] Buckingham, vol. i. p. 181.

## CHAPTER VIII.

*The History of Palestine from the Fall of Jerusalem to the Present Time.*

State of Judea after Fall of Jerusalem—Revolt under Trajan—Barcochab—Adrian repairs Jerusalem—Schools at Babylon and Tiberias—The attempt of Julian to rebuild the Temple—Invasion of Chosroes—Sack of Jerusalem—Rise of Islamism—Wars of the Caliphs—First Crusade—Jerusalem delivered—Policy of Crusades—Victory at Ascalon—Baldwin King—Second Crusade—Saladin—His success at Tiberias—He recovers Jerusalem—The Third Crusade—Richard Cœur de Lion—Siege and Capture of Acre—Plans of Richard—His Return to Europe—Death of Saladin—Fourth Crusade—Battle of Jaffa—Fifth Crusade—Fall of Constantinople—Sixth Crusade—Damietta taken—Reverses—Frederick the Second made King of Jerusalem—Seventh Crusade—Christians admitted into the Holy City—Inroad of Karismians—Eighth Crusade under Louis IX.—He takes Damietta—His Losses and Return to Europe—Ninth Crusade—Louis IX. and Edward I.—Death of Louis—Successes of Edward—Treaty with Sultan—Final Discomfiture of the Franks in Palestine, and Loss of Acre—State of Palestine under the Turks—Increased Toleration—Bonaparte invades Syria—Siege of Acre and Defeat of French—Rupture between the Porte and the Viceroy of Egypt—Successes of Ibrahim—Crosses Mount Taurus—His Victory at Koniah—Actual State of the Holy Land—Number, Condition, and Character of the Jews.

The destruction of Jerusalem, though it put an end to the polity of the Hebrew nation as an independent people, did not entirely disperse the remains of their miserable tribes, nor denude the Holy Land of its proper inhabitants. The number of the slain was indeed immense, and the multitude of captives carried away by Titus glutted the slave-markets of the Roman empire; but it is true, nevertheless, that many fair portions of

Palestine were uninjured by the war, and continued to enjoy an enviable degree of prosperity under the government of their conquerors. The towns on the coast generally submitted to the legions without incurring the chance of a battle or the horrors of a siege; while the provinces beyond the Jordan, which formed the kingdom of Agrippa, maintained their allegiance to Rome throughout the whole period of the insurrection, elsewhere so fatal, and especially to the inheritance of Judah and of Benjamin.

It has been already suggested that soon after the Roman army was withdrawn, many of the Jewish families, Christians as well as followers of the Mosaical Law, returned to their sacred capital, and sought a precarious dwelling among its ruins. To prevent the rebuilding of the city, Vespasian found it necessary to establish on Mount Sion a garrison of eight hundred men. The same emperor, it is related, commanded strict search to be made for every one who claimed descent from the house of David, in order to cut off, if possible, all hope of the restoration of that royal race, and more especially of the advent of the Messiah, the confidence in whose speedy coming still burned with feverish excitement in the heart of every faithful Israelite. A similar jealousy, which dictated a similar inquisition, was continued in the subsequent reign,—a fact strongly illustrative of the spirit which prevailed at that period among the descendants of Abraham, and explanatory also of their successive revolts against the Roman power.

Under the mild sway of Trajan, the Jews in Egypt, Cyprus, and even in Mesopotamia, flew to arms, to avenge the insults to which they had been subjected, or to realize the hopes that they have never ceased to cherish. After a war, remarkable for the waste of blood with which it was accompanied, the unhappy insurgents were every where suppressed; having lost, according to their own confession, more than half a million of men in the field of battle, or the sack of towns. The skill and fortune of Adrian, who soon afterwards occupied the imperial throne, were displayed in the island of Cyprus, from which the Jews were expelled with tremendous slaughter, and prohibited from ever again touching its shores.

To check the mutinous disposition, or to weaken the influence of the vanquished tribes, an edict was promulgated by their Roman masters, forbidding circumcision, the reading of the Law, and the observance of the weekly Sabbath. Still farther to defeat their favourite schemes, and to blast all hopes of a restoration to civil power in Jerusalem under their Messiah, it was resolved by the government at Rome to repair to a certain extent the city of the Jews, and to establish in it a regular colony of Greeks and Latins. At this crisis appeared the notorious Barcochab, whose name, denoting the "son of a star," made him be instantly hailed by a large majority of the nation as that predicted light which was to arise out of Jacob in the latter days. Recommended by Akiba, one of the most popular of the Rabbim, to the confidence of Israel, this impostor soon saw himself at the head of a powerful army ; amounting, say the Jewish annalists, to more than two hundred thousand men. In the absence of the legions, now called to other parts of the East, he found little difficulty in taking possession of the capital ; and before a competent force, under the renowned Julius Severus, could arrive in Palestine, the false Messias had seized fifty of the strongest castles, and a great number of open towns.

The details of the sanguinary campaigns which followed are given by the vanquished Jews with more minuteness than probability. Severus, who had learned all the arts of desultory warfare when employed against the barbarians of Britain, used a similar policy on the banks of the Jordan ; choosing to cut off the supplies of the enemy, and attack their posts with overwhelming numbers, rather than encounter their furious fanaticism in a general engagement. Bither, a strong city, and defended by Barcochab in person, was the last to yield to the Romans. At length it was taken by storm, at the expense of much human life on either side; but as the leader of the rebellion was among the slain, the victors did not consider their success too dearly bought, for, with the star whose light was extinguished in the carnage of Bither, the hope of Israel sank to the earth. Dio Cassius relates, that during this war no fewer than 580,000 fell by the sword, besides those who perished by famine and disease. The whole of Judea was converted into a desert,—wolves and hyenas howled in the streets of the desolate cities, and all the villages were consumed with fire.

It was after these events that Adrian, to annihilate for ever all hopes of the restoration of the Jewish kingdom, accomplished his plan of founding a new city on the waste places of Jerusalem, to be peopled by a colony of foreigners. This town, as we have elsewhere observed, was called Ælia Capitolina; the former of these epithets alluding to Ælius, the prænomen of the emperor,—the latter denoting that it was dedicated to Jupiter Capitolinus, the tutelar deity of Rome. An edict was issued, interdicting every Jew from entering the new city on pain of death, or even approaching so near it as to be able to contemplate its towers, and the venerable heights on which it stood. The more effectually to keep them away, the image of a sow was placed over the gate which leads to Bethlehem. But the more peaceful Christians, meanwhile, were permitted to establish themselves within the walls; and Ælia, it is well known, soon became the seat of a flourishing church and of a bishopric.*

From this period, the history of the Holy Land is less connected with the Jews than with the policy of the different governments by which their country has been occupied. More attached to their ancient faith than when it was established at Jerusalem, we find them both in the East and in the West labouring with the most indefatigable zeal to revive its principles and

---

* History of the Jews, vol. iii. p. 124.

extend its authority. In pursuance of these important objects, they founded their celebrated schools at Babylon and Tiberias,—the source of all legislation, and the seat of judgment in all cases of doubtful opinion. Hence, too, those mixed titles, so long recognised in their tribes, the Patriarch of Tiberias and the Prince of the Captivity,—appointments which, during a long period, constituted a bond of union, partly spiritual and partly political, among all the descendants of Jacob. The numerous remains of that people, though still excluded from the precincts of Jerusalem, were nevertheless permitted to form and to maintain considerable establishments both in Italy and in the provinces ; to acquire the freedom of Rome ; to enjoy municipal honours ; and to obtain, at the same time, an exemption from the burdensome and expensive offices of society. The moderation or the contempt of the Romans gave a legal sanction to the form of ecclesiastical police which was instituted by the vanquished sect. The Patriarch was empowered to appoint his subordinate ministers, to exercise a domestic jurisdiction, and to receive from his brethren an annual tribute. New synagogues were erected in some of the principal cities of the empire ; and the sabbaths, the fasts, and the festivals, which were either commanded by the Mosaic Law or enjoined by the traditions of the Rabbim, were celebrated in the most solemn and public manner. They were likewise restored to the privilege of circumcising their children, on the easy condition that they should never confer on any foreign proselyte the distinguishing mark of the Hebrew race. Such gentle treatment insensibly assuaged the stern temper of the Jews. Awakened from their dream of prophecy and conquest, they assumed the behaviour of peaceable and industrious subjects. Their hatred of mankind, instead of flaming out in acts of blood and violence, evaporated in less dangerous gratifications. They embraced every opportunity of overreaching the idolaters in trade ; and they pronounced secret and ambiguous imprecations against the haughty kingdom of Edom,—the name under which they were now pleased to denounce the Roman empire.*

The glories which were shed upon Palestine by the munificent zeal of Constantine and his mother have already been repeatedly mentioned. The splendid buildings which arose in every part of the Holy Land announced the triumph of the new faith in the country where it had its origin; exciting at once the pride of the Christian, and the jealousy, resentment, and despair of the Jew. The government of Constantius was not more favourable to the despised children of Israel; nor was it till the accession of Julian that they were encouraged to look for revenge upon their enemies, if not for protection to their despised countrymen. The edict to rebuild the Temple on Mount Moriah, and to establish once more at Jerusalem the worship enjoined by Moses, called forth their utmost exertions in behalf of a prince who had openly abjured the rival religion, destined, as they now apprehended, to supplant their own more ancient ritual.

The issue of this attempt to reinstate the ceremonies of the Jewish Law in the capital of Palestine, is known to every reader. The workmen employed in digging the foundation of the new Temple were terrified by flames of fire darting forth from the ground, and accompanied with the most frightful explosions. No inducement could prevail on them to persevere in labours which appeared to excite the anger of Heaven. The enterprise was relinquished, as at once hopeless and impious; and there is no doubt that, whatever additions may have been made to the circumstances by ignorance and a too easy belief, the views of Julian were frustrated by the occurrence of some very extraordinary event, which still finds a place even in Roman history. The sceptic may smile when he reads in the pages of a Christian Father, that flakes of fire which assumed the form of a cross settled on the dresses of the artisans and spectators; that a horseman was seen careering

---

* Decline and Fall, vol. ii. p. 385.

amid the flames; and that, when the affrighted labourers fled to a neighbouring church, its doors, fastened by some preternatural force within, refused to admit them into the sacred building. In such details the imagination is consulted more than the reason; and it cannot be denied that certain authors, who wrote long after the reign of Julian, have admitted traditionary anecdotes into the narrative of a grave event. But it is deserving of notice, that the mark of the Cross, said to have been impressed upon the bystanders, is not the most incredible of the circumstances recorded. Many instances have been known of persons touched by the electric fluid, whose bodies exhibited similar traces of its operation,— straight lines cutting one another at right angles,—and hence that part of the description which appears the least entitled to belief, will be found, upon due investigation, strictly within the limits of nature.*

The policy of the emperors continued to depress the Jews in Palestine, while it granted to them the enjoyment of considerable privileges in all the other provinces, where their presence and peculiar views were less hazardous to the public peace. During the same period the Christian church possessed the countenance of the civil power, and gradually extended its doctrines into Armenia, as well as into the more important region of the Lower Mesopotamia. Nor was it till the beginning of the seventh century that the course of events was materially disturbed by an invasion of the Persians under Chosroes, who had resolved to humble the government of Constantinople, and to check its pretensions in the East. The part of the army appointed to serve against Palestine was intrusted to Carnsia, an experienced general, who invited the Jews to join his standard. This people, ever ready to aid the cause of revolt, assembled, it is said, to the number of 24,000 men, and

---

* The reader who wishes to examine the evidence for the miraculous nature of the interruption sustained by the agents of Julian, will find an ample discussion in the pages of Basnage, Lardner, Warburton, Gibbon, and in the History of the Jews.

made preparations for an attack on Jerusalem. A sanguinary warfare had ensued even before the arrival of their allies from beyond the Euphrates; and both sides accordingly had been for some time exasperated to the highest degree of fury, and were importuning Heaven to hasten the moment of revenge. The Christians within the walls massacred their enemies in cold blood; while the assailants without carried destruction to every point which their arms could reach. At length the advance of the Persians secured to the Jews the hour of triumph and retaliation, when they fully quenched their thirst for vengeance in the blood of the Nazarenes. The victors are accused of having sold the miserable captives for money. Still the rage of the Jews was stronger than their avarice; for not only did they not scruple to sacrifice their treasures in the purchase of these devoted bondsmen at a lavish price, but they put to death without remorse all whom they bought. It was rumoured that the number of believers who perished was not less than ninety thousand. Every church was demolished, including that of the Holy Sepulchre,—the greatest object of Jewish hatred. The stately building of Helena and Constantine was abandoned to the flames, and the devout offerings of three hundred years were rifled in one sacrilegious day.

But the arms of Persia did not long support the persecuting spirit of the Jews. The Emperor Heraclius, who had spent some inglorious years on the throne, was alarmed into activity by the progress of the invaders, who had threatened even the walls of Constantinople itself. The discipline of ancient Rome, which was not yet quite extinct among the legionary soldiers, maintained its wonted superiority over the less martial troops of Chosroes, and recovered in the course of a few campaigns all the provinces that they had overrun. Heraclius visited Jerusalem as a pilgrim, when the wood of the true cross, which it was rumoured had been carried away to Persia, was reinstated with due solemnity. Several churches, too, were restored to their former magnificence;

and the law of Adrian was again put in force, which prohibited the Jews from approaching within three miles of the holy city.*

Palestine continued to acknowledge the power of the emperor until the rise of Islamism changed the face of Western Asia. The armies of the caliphs, which wrested from Persia the dominion of the surrounding nations, conquered in succession the provinces of Arabia, Syria, and Egypt, and at length planted the Crescent on the walls of Jerusalem. The victories of Omar, in 636, decided the fate of the venerable city, and laid the foundations of a mosque on the sacred hill where the Temple of Solomon had stood. This conqueror was assassinated at Jerusalem in 643; after which the establishment of several caliphates in Arabia and Syria, the fall of the Ommiades, and the elevation of the Abassides, involved the country in trouble for more than two hundred years. In 868, Achmet, a Turk, who from being governor had made himself sovereign of Egypt, seized the metropolis of Palestine; but his son having been defeated by the caliphs of Bagdad, the holy city again returned under their dominion in the year 905 of our era. Mohammed Ikschid, another Turk, about thirty years after, having in his turn usurped the throne of the Pharaohs, carried his arms into Judea and reduced the capital. The Fatimites, again, issuing from the sands of Cyrene, expelled the Ikschidites from Egypt in 968, and conquered several towns in the ancient kingdom of David. Ortok, towards the end of the tenth century, made himself master of the sacred town, whence his children were for a time driven out by Mostali, caliph of Egypt. In 1076, Meleschah, the third of the Turkish race, took it again, and ravaged the whole country. The Ortokides, who, as we have just related, were dispossessed by Mostali, returned thither, and maintained themselves in it against Redouan, prince of Aleppo. They were expelled once more by the Fatimites, who

---

* History of the Jews, vol. iii. p. 239.

continued to occupy the place until the date when the Crusaders first appeared on the confines of Syria.

Several generations passed away, during which the affairs of the Holy Land created no interest in Europe; while the native Christians and Jews, who could hardly obtain the most limited toleration from their Mohammedan masters, sought an asylum among the different states of Europe. In the Travels of Benjamin of Tudela are to be found some incidental notices, which leave no doubt as to the fact that his countrymen, unable to bear the persecution directed against them, had gradually abandoned the birthplace of their fathers. Jerusalem, in the twelfth century, did not contain more than two hundred descendants of Abraham, poor, depressed, and calumniated; whilst at Tiberias, the seat of learning and of their sovereign Patriarch, the number did not exceed fifty,—the victims of supicion and jealousy, not less on the part of the Christians than of the Moslem, who had already begun to contend with each other for the possession of the holy Sepulchre.

It has often been observed, that pilgrimage to the holy places of Palestine was from a very early period regarded as at once a wholesome discipline and an acceptable reverence in all faithful worshippers. The Arabian caliphs were, on various accounts, inclined to favour the resort of Europeans to these consecrated shrines. They saw in it a fruitful source of revenue; while influenced by the recollection that they themselves were the progeny of Abraham, they were not disposed to take offence at the veneration lavished upon the prophetic son of David, whose tomb the fortune of war had placed in their hands. But the Seljukian Turks, those irreclaimable barbarians, who had no sympathy with the believers in Christ, laid on them such burdens and vexatious restraints as were altogether intolerable. The cries of the unhappy pilgrims had long resounded throughout Christendom; and the indignation which was universally felt against the bigoted Mussulmans was inflamed in no slight degree by the eloquence of Peter the Hermit, who had witnessed in foreign lands the afflictions of his brethren. Yielding to the impulse of the age, Pope Urban the Second convoked a general council at Clermont in Auvergne, to whom he addressed an oration well fitted to confirm the enthusiasm which he found already kindled. He encouraged them to attack the enemies of God, and in that holy warfare to earn the reward of eternal life promised to all the faithful servants of the Redeemer; suggesting that, as a mark of their profession as well as of their Saviour's love, they should wear red crosses on their garments when fighting the battles of their faith.

The warlike spirit of the time was roused by every motive which can touch the heart of man in a rude state of society,—the love of glory, religion, revenge, and of enterprise. Many of the most illustrious princes of the Christian world took up the Cross, and were followed by persons of both sexes, and of all ages, classes, and professions. A vast army poured in from every country, under the most distinguished leaders, of whom the principal were Godfrey, duke of Brabant and Bouillon; Robert of France, the brother of King Philip; and Robert, duke of Normandy, the son of the English monarch. Bohemond too, the chief of the Normans in Apulia, and Raymond, count of Toulouse, led many renowned warriors to Syria.

The tumultuary bands who marched under the standard of the Hermit suffered hardships altogether unknown to modern war. In passing through the plains watered by the Danube, and the hilly countries which lie between that river and the Mediterranean, more than half their number fell victims to disease, famine, and the rage of the barbarians whose lands they infested. But, in spite of these misfortunes, Bohemond laid siege to Antioch in 1097; and on the 15th July, two years after, the ancient and holy city of Jerusalem was taken by assault, with a prodigious slaughter of the garrison. Ten thousand Mohammedans were slain on the site of Solomon's Temple; a greater number was thrown from the tops of houses; and a fearful carnage was committed after all resistance had ceased.

The siege had lasted two months, with various success and a considerable loss of life on either side; and hence arose the savage ferocity which disgraced, on the part of the victors, the last scene of this miserable tragedy. The assailants having endured much from drought, as well as from the sword of the enemy, betook themselves to pious exercises in order to avert the anger of Heaven. The soldiers, completely armed, made a holy procession round the walls. The clergy, with naked feet and bearing images of the Cross, led them in the sacred way. Cries of *Deus id vult*,—God commands it,—rent the air; and the people marched to the melody of hymns and psalms, and not to the sound of drums and trumpets. On the mounts Olivet and Sion, they prayed for assistance in the approaching conflict. The Saracens mocked these expressions of religious feeling, by throwing mud upon crucifixes which they themselves had erected for the purpose; but these insults had only the effect of producing louder shouts of sacred joy from the crusaders. The next morning every thing was prepared for battle; and there was no one who was not ready either to die for Christ, or restore his city to liberty. The night was spent in watching and alarm by both armies. At dawn of day the conflict began which was to determine the fate of the great European expedition, and when noon arrived the issue was still in suspense, or seemed rather to incline in favour of the Mohammedans. The cause of the Western World appeared to totter on the very brink of destruction, and the most valiant among the warriors of the Cross allowed themselves to fear that Heaven had deserted its own people.*

---

* "When the first light brought news of a morning, they on afresh; because they had intercepted a letter tied to the leg of a dove, wherein the Persian emperor promised present succours to the besieged. The Turks cased the outside of their walls with bags of chaff, straw, and such like pliable matter, which conquered the engines of the Christians, by yielding unto them. As for one sturdy

At the moment when all was considered lost, a knight was seen on Mount Olivet, waving his glittering shield as a sign to the soldiers that they should rally and return to the charge. Godfrey and Eustace cried aloud to the army that St George was come to their succour. The spirit of enthusiasm instantly revived, fatigue and pain were no longer felt, the princes led their columns to the breach, and even the women insisted upon sharing the honours of the fight. In the space of an hour the barbacan was broken down, and Godfrey's tower rested against the inner wall. Exchanging the duties of a general for those of a soldier, the Duke of Lorraine fought with his bow : " The Lord guided his hand, and all his arrows pierced the enemy through and through." Near him were Eustace and Baldwin, " like two lions beside another lion." At three o'clock, the hour when the Saviour of the world was crucified, a soldier, named Letoldus of Tournay, leaped upon the fortifications; his brother Engelbert followed, and Godfrey was the third who stood as a conqueror upon the ramparts of Jerusalem. The glorious ensign of the Cross streamed from the walls, and the whole city was soon at the mercy of

---

engine, whose force would not be tamed, they brought two old witches on the walls to enchant it ; but the spirit thereof was too strong for their spells, so that both of them were miserably slain in the place.

" We must not think that the world was at a loss for war-tools before the brood of guns was hatched : It had the battering-ramme, first found out by Epeus at the taking of Troy; the balista, to discharge great stones, invented by the Phenicians ; the catapulta, being a sling of mighty strength, whereof the Syrians were authors; and perchance King Uzziah first made it, for we find him very dexterous and happy in devising such things. And although these bear-whelps were but rude and unshaped at the first, yet art did lick them afterwards, and they got more teeth and sharper nails by degrees ; so that every age set them forth in a new edition, corrected and amended. But these, and many more voluminous engines, are now virtually epitomized in the cannon. And though some say that the finding of guns hath been the losing of many men's lives, yet it will appear that battles now are fought with more expedition, and Victory standeth not so long a neuter, before she express herself on one side or other."—*Fuller's Holy Warre*, p. 41.

the besiegers. The Mussulmans fought for a while, then fled to their temples, and submitted their necks to the sword. The victors, in a document which is still preserved, boasted, that in the Mosque of Omar, whither they pursued the fugitives, they rode in the blood of Saracens up to the knees of their horses.

After the slaughter had terminated, and the soldiers had soothed their minds by certain acts of devotion, the expediency of forming a regular government became manifest to all parties. Godfrey, a hero whose name cannot be too highly honoured, was chosen by the unanimous suffrages of rival warriors to be the first Christian king of Jerusalem. Bohemond, the son of Robert de Guiscard, reigned at Antioch ; Baldwin, the brother of Godfrey, at Edessa ; and the Count of Toulouse at Tripoli. The dominion of the crusaders extended from the confines of Egypt to the Euphrates on the east, and to the acclivities of Mount Taurus on the north ; and several of their principalities lasted nearly two hundred years.

Many attempts have been made to defend the policy and excuse the enormities of the Christian warriors in their enterprise against the Moslem occupants of the Holy Land. These two points ought to be more carefully distinguished than they usually are, whether in the pages of friends or of enemies ; for while the general expediency of a combination of the Christian powers may be supported on good grounds, the cruelty of some of their measures deserves the severest censure. It is remarked by Mr Mills, that the massacre of the Saracens, on the capture of the holy city, did not proceed alone from the inflamed passions of victorious soldiers, but from remorseless fanaticism. Benevolence to Turks, Jews, infidels, and heretics, made no part of Christian ethics in those rude times ; and as the Moslems in their consciences believed it was the will of Heaven that the religion of their Prophet should be propagated by the sword, so their antagonists laboured under a similar delusion that they themselves were the ministers of God's wrath on a disobedient and stiffnecked people. The Latins, on the day after the victory, massacred three hundred men, to whom Tancred and Gaston de Bearn had promised protection, and even given a standard as a pledge of safety. But every engagement was broken, in consequence of the resolution that no pity should be shown to the Mohammedans,—an expedient which was justified in the minds of the invaders, by an apprehension now prevalent amongst them, that their enemy, in conjunction with the Saracens of Egypt, might again reduce the city and recover all the ground they had lost. It was for this reason that the inhabitants of Jerusalem, armed and unarmed, were dragged forth into the public squares, and slain like cattle. Women with children at the breast, boys, and even girls, were slaughtered indiscriminately, and in such numbers, that the streets were covered with dead bodies and mangled limbs. No heart melted into compassion or expanded into benevolence. The stones of the city were ordered to be washed, and a command was issued that this melancholy task should be performed by Moslem slaves. The Count of Toulouse, whose avarice prevailed over his superstition, was loudly condemned for accepting a ransom from a few of the devoted prisoners, whom he sent in safety to Ascalon. So unrelenting, in short, was the passion of revenge among the crusaders, that they set fire to the synagogues of the Jews, many of whom perished in the flames.*

Such conduct merits the deepest execration that moralist or statesman may be pleased to pour upon it. I am nevertheless convinced that, in the peculiar circumstances of the Christian world when Peter the Hermit called its chiefs to arms, a united war against the Mo-

---

* Fuller remarks, that " this second massacre was no slip of an extemporary passion, but a studied and premeditated act. Besides, the execution was merciless, upon sucking children whose not speaking spake for them; and on women whose weakness is a shield to defend them against a valiant man. To conclude, severity, hot in the fourth degree, is little better than poison, and becometh cruelty itself; and this act seemeth to be of the same nature."—*Holy Warre*, p. 41.

hammedan states of Syria was dictated by the soundest political wisdom. The subjects of Omar had already conquered an establishment in Sicily and Spain, and attempted the subjugation of France. Their views were directed towards universal dominion in the West, as well as in the East ; they hoped to witness the triumph of the Crescent in Europe not less certainly than in Asia, and to be able to impose a tribute on the worshippers of Christ, or compel them to relinquish their creed wherever the gospel was professed. Those, therefore, who perceive in the crusades nothing but a mob of armed pilgrims running to rescue a tomb in Palestine, take a very limited view of history. The point in question was not merely the recovery of that sacred building from the hands of infidels, but rather to decide which of the two religions, the Christian or the Mohammedan, should predominate in the world,—the one hostile to civilisation, and only favourable to ignorance, despotism, and slavery ; the other friendly to improvement, learning, and freedom, in all ranks and conditions of life.

It is asserted by Chateaubriand, that whoever reads the address of Pope Urban to the council of Clermont, must be convinced that the leaders in those military enterprises were not actuated by the petty views which have been ascribed to them ; but, on the contrary, that they aspired to save the European continent from a new inundation of barbarians. The spirit of Islamism is conquest and persecution ; the gospel, on the contrary, inculcates only toleration and peace. The Christians, moreover, had endured for several centuries all the oppressions which the fanaticism of the Saracens impelled them to exercise. They had merely endeavoured to interest Charlemagne in their favour ; for neither the conquest of Spain, the invasion of France, the pillage of Greece and the two Sicilies, nor the entire subjugation of Africa, could during the long period of six hundred years rouse them to take any decided step for their own protection. If at last the cries of numberless victims slaughtered in the East, if the progress of the barbarians, who had already reached the gates of Constantinople, awakened them to the necessity of wielding defensive arms, who can say that the cause of the Holy Wars was unjust? Let him who would know the fate of a people subjected to the Mussulman yoke, contemplate Greece. Would those who at this day so loudly exult in the progress of knowledge wish to live under a religion that burned the Alexandrian library, which makes a merit of trampling mankind under foot, and holding literature and the arts in sovereign contempt? The crusades, by weakening the Moslem hordes in the very centre of Asia, prevented Europe from falling a prey to the Turks and Arabs; they did more, they saved her at home from revolutions, with which she was threatened; they suspended intestine wars, by which she was ever and anon desolated; and, finally, they opened an outlet to that excess of population which sooner or later occasions the ruin of nations.*

The administration of Godfrey was gentle and prosperous. He gained a decisive victory over the Vizier of Egypt, who had encamped on the Plains of Ascalon with the view of assisting his Syrian allies to recover Jerusalem from the hands of the Christians. According to the spirit of the age, he joined to the qualities of a brave soldier the profession of an ardent faith and the utmost reverence for the authority of the Church. He refused a precious diadem offered to him by his companions in arms, declaring that he would never wear a crown of gold in the city where the Saviour of the world had worn a crown of thorns. Influenced by the same feeling he was disposed to reject the title of king, and to exercise his office under the name of Defender and Baron of the Holy Sepulchre.

---

* On this interesting subject, see the "Itinéraire" of Chateaubriand, and his "Génie du Christianisme;" the History of England by Sir James Mackintosh, volume first; and Mills' History of the Crusades, volume first, chapter sixth. To these may be added, Dr Robertson's "Historical Disquisition concerning the Knowledge which the Ancients had of India."

Upon the demise of this distinguished commander, which is supposed to have taken place at Jaffa, the government devolved upon his brother Baldwin, who sustained its glory and interests with a steady hand. About the year 1118, he was succeeded on the throne by his nephew, who bore the same name, and who, although sometimes unfortunate, did not tarnish the honour of his family. Melisandra, his eldest daughter, married Foulques of Anjou, and thereby conveyed the kingdom of Jerusalem into the hand of her husband, who enjoyed it ten or twelve years, when he lost his life by a fall from his horse. His son, Baldwin the Third, a youth of a rash temper, and destitute of experience, assumed the sceptre of Jerusalem, which he held twenty years,—a period rendered remarkable by the events of the second crusade, and the rise of various orders of knighthood,—the Hospitallers, Templars, and Cavaliers.

The news from Palestine, that certain reverses had been sustained by the Christians, acted so powerfully on the pious spirit of St Bernard and the troubled conscience of Louis the Seventh, the king of France, as to suggest a second confederation among European princes for the security of the Holy Land. This new apostle of a sacred war was, on many accounts, greatly superior to Peter the Hermit. He was a man of noble birth; possessed learning sufficient to rival the attainments of Abelard, his contemporary; and could speak with a degree of eloquence to which no orator of his age had the boldness to aspire. The French monarch, who had assembled around him a powerful and most splendid army, was joined by the Emperor of Germany, Conrade the Third, whose thousands equalled those of his warlike brother, and whose zeal in the cause of Christendom was not less active.

But the experience of their predecessors, fifty years before, was lost upon these fearless soldiers of the Cross. Without suitable preparation, they encountered the dangers of a long march through hostile countries and sickly climates, the effects of which appeared in the rapid diminution of their numbers, in mutual invectives, and in increasing despair. Not more than a tenth part of the Germans reached the coast of Syria. The French, who had suffered less than their allies, were sooner ready to take the field against the Saracens; and, after proving their arms in a few unimportant skirmishes, they resolved to lay siege to Damascus in concert with the battalions of Conrade. But the evil genius of intrigue defeated their designs. After a fruitless display of a force more than sufficient to have reduced the place, the Christian chiefs withdrew from before the ramparts of the Syrian capital, and fell back upon Jerusalem in sorrow and shame. Conrade soon returned to Europe with the shattered remains of his gallant host; and about a year afterwards his example was imitated by the French king and the greater number of his generals, who were disgusted with the narrow policy on which the war had been conducted.

Baldwin the Third dying without male issue, transmitted the precarious throne of Jerusalem to his brother Amaury, or Almeric; who, after a reign of eleven years, was succeeded by his son, Baldwin the Fourth. The young sovereign being incapable of the duties of government, passed his minority under the wise counsels of Raymond, count of Tripoli, who endeavoured to sustain the weight of kingly power in the midst of very formidable enemies. The name of Noureddin was long terrible to the Christians of Palestine, who had gradually lost their warlike virtues; but they were now about to encounter a still more able, and much more celebrated antagonist, in the person of Saladin, the hero of the Crescent, and one of the most distinguished leaders of that very romantic age.

Baldwin had given his sister Sybilla, widow of William surnamed Longue-Epée, or the Longsword, in marriage to Guy of Lusignan. The grandees of the kingdom, dissatisfied with the choice, divided into parties. The king, dying in 1184, left as his heir Baldwin the Fifth, the son of Sybilla and William just mentioned, a child not more than eight years of age, and who soon afterwards sunk under a constitutional distemper. His mother caused the crown to be conferred on her husband, the ambitious Guy,—a measure which did not allay the jealousy of the nobles who had opposed their union. An alarming dissension prevailed among the barons, some of whom refused to take the oath of allegiance to the new sovereign, and even offered the diadem to Humphrey de Thoron. But the intrigues of Sybilla and the terror of Saladin prevented an open rupture, while events of a more important nature were about to occupy the attention of either party.

The sultan had received from several of the Christian warriors just ground of offence; and, failing to obtain redress from the feeble government of Jerusalem, he took the field in order to chastise with his own hand the more guilty of the aggressors. He encamped near the Lake of Tiberias, where Guy, listening to counsellors who saw not the danger of placing the fortunes of the kingdom on the issue of a single battle, resolved to attack him. For a whole day the engagement was in suspense, and at night the Latins retired to some rocks in the neighbourhood, hoping that they might find a little water to quench their thirst. At the approach of dawn the two armies stood a while gazing upon each other, as if conscious that the fate of the Moslem and the Christian worlds was in their hands. But no sooner did the sun appear than the crusaders raised their war-cry, and the Turks sounded their trumpets and atabals,—a mutual challenge to renew the sanguinary conflict. The bishops and clergy ran through the ranks, cheering the soldiers of the Church. A fragment of the true cross, intrusted to the knights of the Holy Sepulchre, was placed on a hillock, around which the broken squadrons repeatedly rallied, and recovered strength for the combat whereon the interests of their faith were suspended. But the Crescent, supported by more numerous and stronger hands, triumphed on the Plain of Tiberias. The Christians were defeated with great loss; the king, the Master of the Templars, and the Marquis of Montserrat, were taken prisoners; and the piece of holy wood, in which they had put their trust, was snatched from the grasp of the Bishop of Acre.

This victory placed the greater part of Palestine in the power of Saladin, who, upon the whole, used his success with moderation and clemency. The fugitives from every quarter fled to Jerusalem, hoping to escape in that asylum the swords and fetters of the Turks. One hundred thousand persons are said to have been crowded within the walls; but so few were the soldiers, and so feeble was the government of the queen, that the holy city presented no serious obstacle to the progress of the Moslem arms. The Sultan declared his unwillingness to stain with human blood a place which even the followers of the Prophet held in reverence, as having been sanctified by the presence of many inspired individuals. He therefore promised to the people, on condition that they would quietly surrender the city, a supply of money, and lands in the most fertile provinces of Syria.

This offer was rejected, as implying a sacrilegious contract to yield into the hands of infidels the sacred spot where the Saviour of mankind had died. He therefore swore that he would enter their streets sword in hand, and retaliate upon them the dreadful carnage which the Franks had committed in the days of Godfrey. Two weeks were spent in almost incessant fighting, during which the advantage was generally on the side of the assailants. Finding resistance vain, the besieged at length appealed to the clemency of the conqueror. It was stipulated that the military and the nobles should be escorted to Tyre, and that the inhabitants should become slaves, if not ransomed at certain rates to be fixed by the victorious Saladin. Thus, to use the words of the historian, " after four days had been consumed by the miserable inhabitants, in weep-ing over and embracing the Holy Sepulchre and other sacred places, the Latins left the city and passed through the enemy's camp. Children of all ages clung round their mothers, and the strength of their fathers was used in bearing away some little part of their household furniture. In solemn procession, the clergy, the queen, and her retinue of ladies, followed. Saladin advanced to meet them, and his heart melted with compassion when he saw them approach in the attitude of suppliants." The softened warrior uttered some expressions of pity ; and the women, encouraged by his tenderness, declared, that by pronouncing one word he might remove their distress. " Our fortunes and possessions," said they, " you may freely enjoy ; but restore to us our fathers, our husbands, and our brothers. With these dear objects we cannot be entirely miserable. They will take care of us; and that God whom we reverence, and who provides for the birds of the air, will not forget our children." Saladin was a barbarian in nothing but the name. With the most courteous generosity, he released all the prisoners whom the women requested, and loaded them with presents. Nor was this action, so worthy of a gentle and chivalrous knight, the consequence of a merely transient feeling of humanity ; for when he had entered the city of Jerusalem, and heard of the tender care with which the military friars of St John treated their sick countrymen, he allowed ten of their order to remain in the hospital till they could fully complete their work of charity.*

The Mohammedans being once more in possession of the holy walls, took down the great cross from the Church of the Sepulchre, and soiled it with the mire of the streets. They also melted the bells which had summoned the Christians to devotion, and at the same time purified the Mosque of Omar by a copious sprinkling of rose-water. Ascalon, Laodicea, Gabala, Sidon, Nazareth,

---

\* Mills' History of the Crusades, vol. ii. p. 48.

and Bethlehem, opened their gates to the warlike Saladin; who indeed found no town able to resist his arms except Tyre, garrisoned at that period by a body of excellent soldiers under the gallant Conrade. All the inhabitants took arms, and even the women shot arrows from the walls, or assisted in strengthening the fortifications. The Saracens cast immense stones into the place, and attacked it with all the other means in their power; but the spirit of freedom triumphed over the thirst of revenge, and the conqueror of Tiberias was finally compelled to relinquish the siege.

The intelligence that Jerusalem had fallen under the dominion of the Unbelievers created in all parts of Europe a profound sensation of grief and disappointment. The clergy, as on former occasions, preached to all classes the duty and honour of assuming the Cross, and even of dying in the service of the Redeemer, should the sacrifice of life be required at their hands. But the enthusiasm of the eleventh century had now very generally passed away. Every family had to lament the loss of kindred in the field of battle, or in the bonds of a hopeless captivity; and hence the inducements which had crowded the ranks of Godfrey and Conrade were at this time listened to, both in France and England, with comparative indifference.

At length, however, about the year 1190, Philip Augustus, the French king, the Emperor Frederick Barbarossa of Germany, and the celebrated Richard Cœur de Lion, succeeded in raising forces, with the view of wresting once more the Holy Land from the thraldom of the Saracens. Philip received the staff and scrip at St Denys, and Richard at Tours. They joined their armies at Vezelay, the gross amount of which was computed at one hundred thousand, and marched to Lyons in company. There the royal commanders separated; the former pursued the road to Genoa, the latter to Marseilles, the island of Sicily being named as the place of their next meeting.

Among the other fruits of the victory of Tiberias

reaped by the brave Saladin, was the possession of Acre or Ptolemais, one of the most valuable ports on the coast of Syria. The crusaders, aware that they could not maintain their ground in the East without a constant communication with Europe, resolved to recover this city at whatever expense of life or treasure; and with this view they had invested it more than twenty-two months before Richard could carry his reinforcements into Palestine. Upon his arrival an unhappy jealousy arose between him and the King of France, which divided the Christians into two great parties; nor was it until each had attempted with his separate force to ascend the ramparts of Ptolemais, and had even been repulsed with great loss, that they consented to unite their squadrons and act in unison. A reconciliation being effected, it was determined that the one should attack the walls, while the other was employed in guarding the camp from the approaches of Saladin. But the town had already suffered so dreadfully from the length of the siege, now continued nearly two years, that the garrison were disposed to sue for terms. The sultan endeavoured to infuse his own invincible spirit into the minds of his people, and to revive for a moment their languid courage by turning their hopes to Egypt, whence succour was expected. As no aid appeared, the citizens wrung from him permission to capitulate. They were accordingly allowed to purchase their safety by consenting to deliver the city into the hands of the two kings, together with five hundred Christian prisoners who were confined in it. The true cross also was to be restored, with one thousand such captives as might be selected by the allies; it being covenanted, at the same time, that unless the Mussulmans, within forty days, paid to Richard and Philip the sum of two hundred thousand pieces of gold, the inhabitants of Acre should be at the mercy of the conquerors.

It was on the 12th of July 1191 that Ptolemais was recovered by the Europeans; and in the following month Richard,—for the king of France had already turned his face homewards,—gained an important victory over Saladin at Azotus. The progress of Cœur de Lion being no longer disputed, he quickly arrived at Jaffa. That city was now without fortifications, for when the tide of conquest ebbed from the Moslem, their commander gave orders to dismantle all the fortresses in Palestine. It was his policy to keep the invaders constantly in the field, and to exhaust them by incessant marching and sudden attacks. Some time was accordingly lost in restoring the works of this ancient town,—a period which was employed by the enemy in recruiting their ranks, and preparing to contest once more the laurels gained by the conquerors of Azotus.

Richard, still full of confidence, declared to the Saracens that the only way of averting his wrath, was to surrender the kingdom of Jerusalem as it existed in the reign of Baldwin the Fourth. Saladin did not reject this proposal with the disdain which he felt, but made a modification of the terms, by offering to yield all of Palestine that lay between the River Jordan and the Mediterranean. The negotiation lasted some time without farther concession on either side, when at length it became manifest that the Mussulman was not in earnest, but merely sought to derive advantage from the delay which he had the ingenuity to create. Hence the meditated attack on Jerusalem was postponed, and dissension began to prevail in the ranks of Plantagenet. The winter was passed amid privations of every description, which, as they were partly owing to the negligence of the king, gave rise to numerous desertions. The inactive season of the year was occupied in rebuilding the walls of Ascalon,—a task in which the proudest nobles and the most dignified clergy laboured like the meanest of the people. On the return of spring both armies appeared in the field; but as political disturbances in England demanded the presence of Richard, he manifested, for the first time, a greater disposition to negotiate than to fight. He made known to the Sultan that he would be satisfied with the possession of the holy city and of the true cross. But the latter replied, that

Jerusalem was as dear to the Mussulman as to the Christian; and, moreover, that he would never be guilty of conniving at idolatry, by permitting the worship of a piece of wood. Thwarted by the religious prejudices of his enemy, the English commander attempted a different expedient. He proposed a consolidation of the Christian and Mohammedan interests, the establishment of a government at Jerusalem, partly European and partly Asiatic; and this scheme of policy was to be carried into effect by the marriage of Saphadin, the brother of the sultan, with the widow of William, king of Sicily. The Moslem princes would have acceded to these terms; but the union was thought to be so scandalous to religion, that the imans and priests raised a storm of clamour against it; and Richard and Saladin, accordingly, though the most powerful and determined men of their age, were compelled to submit to popular opinion.

In the month of May, therefore, Cœur de Lion began his march towards Jerusalem, with the firm resolution of accomplishing the main object of his armament. The generals and soldiers vowed that they would not leave Palestine until they should have redeemed the Holy Sepulchre. Every thing wore the face of joy when this resolution was announced. Hymns and thanksgivings expressed the general exultation. Terror seized the Mussulmans who were appointed to defend the sacred walls, and even Saladin himself gave way to apprehension for their safety. The Crusaders arrived at Bethlehem; and here the stout mind of Plantagenet first began to vacillate. He avowed his doubts as to the policy of a siege, as his force was not adequate to such a measure, and at the same time to the regular maintenance of his communications with the coast, whence his supplies must be derived. He submitted his difficulties to the Barons of Syria, the Templars, and Hospitallers; declaring his readiness to abide by their decision, whether it should be to advance or to retreat. These officers received information that the Turks had destroyed all the cisterns which were within two miles of the city, at the very moment when they felt that the intolerable heats of summer were already begun; for which reason it was resolved that the attack on Jerusalem should be deferred, and that the army meantime should proceed to some other conquest.

Saladin, aware of the hesitation which had chilled the wonted ardour of his foe, resolved to profit by this turn of affairs, so little to be expected under such a leader. He advanced by forced marches to Jaffa, with the view of reducing it before Richard could send relief. Attacking with his usual vigour, he succeeded in breaking down one of the gates; and such of the inhabitants as could not defend themselves in the great tower, or escape by sea, were put to the sword. Already were the battering-rams prepared to demolish that fortress, when the Patriarch and some French and English knights agreed to become the prisoners of the sultan; fixing at the same time a heavy sum for the ransom of the citizens, if succour did not arrive during the next day. Before the morning, however, the brave Plantagenet reached Jaffa; and so furious was his onset, that the Turks immediately deserted the town; while their army, which was encamped at a little distance, no sooner saw the standard of Richard on the walls than they retreated some miles into the interior.

But the English chieftain, harassed by unfavourable tidings from home, and perplexed by dissensions in his camp, became heartily desirous of peace. Nor was Saladin less willing to grant repose to his country, now exhausted by protracted wars. The two heroes exchanged expressions of mutual esteem; but, as Richard had often avowed his contempt for the vulgar obligation of oaths, they only grasped each other's hands in token of fidelity. A truce was agreed upon for three years and eight months; the fort of Ascalon was dismantled; but Jaffa and Tyre, with the intervening territory, were surrendered to the Europeans. It was provided also that the Christians should be at liberty to perform their pilgrimages to Jerusalem, exempted from the taxes which the Moslem princes were wont to impose.*

Towards the end of the year 1192, Richard the Lion-hearted withdrew from the Holy Land on his way to England,—a journey beset with many perils and adventures, which it is no part of our task to describe. We are told that his valour struck such terror into his enemies, that long after his death, when a horse trembled without any visible cause, the Saracens were accustomed to say that he had seen the ghost of the English prince. In a familiar conversation which Saladin held with the warlike Bishop of Salisbury, he expressed his admiration of the bravery of his rival, but added, that he thought " the skill of the general did not equal the valour of the knight." The courteous prelate replied to this remark, the justice of which, perhaps, he could not question, by assuring the sultan that there were not two such warriors in the world as the English and the Syrian monarchs. Without entering minutely into the comparison of two characters which presented little in common, it must be acknowledged that the courage of the former at the head of his gallant troops prevented many of the evils which had been anticipated from the defeat at Tiberias. Palestine did not, as was apprehended, become a Moslem colony. A portion of the seacoast, too, was preserved for the Christians; while their great enemy was so enfeebled by repeated discomfitures, that fresh hostilities could be safely commenced whenever Europe should again find it expedient to send into the East a renewed host of military adventurers. Richard, besides, gained more honour in Syria than any of the German emperors or French kings who had sought renown in foreign war ; and although a rigid wisdom might censure his conduct as unprofitable to his country, it must be admitted that his actions were in unison with the spirit of the times in which he lived,

---

* Mills' History of the Crusades, vol. ii. p. 129. Michaud, Histoire des Croisades, tome iii. p. 167.

when valour was held more important than the acquisition of wealth, and achievements in the field were esteemed more highly than the most beneficial results of victory.

The sultan did not long survive the departure of his celebrated rival. He died in the year 1193; leaving directions, that on the day of his funeral a shroud should be borne on the point of a spear, and a herald proclaim in a loud voice, " Saladin, the conqueror of Asia, out of all the fruits of his victories carries with him only this piece of linen." The soldiers of this distinguished prince rallied round his brother Saphadin, whom they raised to the throne. Nor did the new monarch disappoint the expectations that were entertained of his wisdom and valour; for by the exertions of military skill, as well as by a sagacious policy, he strengthened the government which was committed to his hands, and was found, at the expiration of the truce, ready to meet the armies of the combined powers of Christendom.

The fourth crusade was called into existence by the active zeal of Pope Celestine the Third, and of Henry the Sixth, the German emperor, who was joined by many of the subordinate princes of Northern Europe. The term of peace fixed by Richard and Saladin had indeed expired; but both Christians and Moslems, exhausted by war and famine, were disposed to lengthen the period of repose, and at all events to abstain from a renewal of their sanguinary conflicts. Nevertheless, when the new champions of the Cross arrived at Acre, all remonstrances against fresh aggression were disregarded. Saphadin, who was informed of their hostile intentions, anticipated them in the field, and before they could advance to Jaffa, he had battered down the fortifications and put thousands of the inhabitants to the sword. A general action, it is true, took place soon afterwards, in which the strength and discipline of the Germans secured the victory; but, when advancing to Jerusalem, the conquerors allowed themselves to be turned aside in order to reduce the insignificant fortress of Thoron, where they met with a repulse so serious as to defeat the main object of the campaign. Factious contentions now disturbed the councils of the Latins; vice and insubordination raged in the camp; and, to crown their miseries, the crusaders were informed that the sultans of Egypt and Syria were concentrating their troops with the view of attacking them. Alarmed at this intelligence, the German princes deserted their posts in the night, and fled to Tyre: the road to which was soon filled with soldiers and baggage in indiscriminate confusion; the feeble relinquishing their property, and the cowardly casting away their arms.

Another battle took place in the neighbourhood of Jaffa, which terminated, as before, to the advantage of the Christians. But the death of the emperor, the chief patron of the expedition, again disconcerted their measures. Many returned to Europe to assist at the election of his successor; while the residue of the army, thrown into a fatal confidence by their late triumphs, were destroyed by a body of Turkish auxiliaries, who surprised them during the revels in which they were commemorating the virtues and abstinence of Saint Martin.

The crown of Palestine meantime, greatly shorn of its lustre, had devolved upon Isabella, daughter of Baldwin and sister to Sybilla. Her third husband, Henry, count of Champagne, was acknowledged as king; and upon his death she was advised to give her hand to Almeric of Lusignan, the brother of Guy who had formerly swayed the sceptre. This union being approved by the clergy and barons, the marriage was celebrated at Acre, where the young couple were proclaimed the sovereigns of Cyprus and Jerusalem.

The repeated failure of the Christian armaments impressed upon the people of Europe a belief, either that the real difficulties of the enterprise had been concealed from them, or that the time fixed in the councils of Providence for the deliverance of the Holy Land had not yet arrived. In such circumstances, it required the authority of the Church and all the power of eloquence, seconded by the performance of numerous miracles, to rouse the slumbering zeal of those who had money to give or arms to use in the service of the Cross. Fulk the preacher, who equalled Peter the Hermit in the ardour of his address and Bernard in oratorical talents, co-operated with the Pope, Innocent the Third, in convincing the several kingdoms under his spiritual dominion of the necessity of a fifth combined effort, in order to expel the infidels from the sacred inheritance.

The voice of religion was again listened to with pious obedience, and a large force was mustered in France and the Low Countries. As, however, the arms of the Christian chiefs on this occasion were not employed against the Saracens, but against their own brethren of the Grecian empire, the object of our work does not require that we should do more than follow their steps to the shores of the Bosphorus. In April 1204, Constantinople fell into their hands, and was subjected to all the horrors and indignity which usually punish the resistance of a strong city. The remains of the fine arts, which the Eastern Church had preserved as consecrated memorials of her triumph over paganism, were destroyed with peculiar industry by the less polished Latins, who were pleased to view with contempt the superior taste of their rivals. The establishment of the crusaders in the capital of the Lower Empire, where they elected a sovereign and formed an administration, was the only result of the fifth expedition against the Moslems. Their dominion lasted fifty-seven years, at the end of which Manuel Paleologus, a descendant of Lascaris, and the son-in-law of the Emperor Alexis, recovered the throne of the Cæsars, and finally expelled the usurpers from the city of Constantine.

The successes of the French against the Greeks had, however, an indirect influence in promoting the welfare of the Christians in Palestine. The Mussulmans were alarmed, and Saphadin gladly concluded a truce for six years; but the country was doomed to be soon deprived of the rare tranquillity afforded by a cessation of arms. Almeric and his wife being dead, Mary, the daughter of Isabella by Conrade of Tyre, was acknowledged queen of Jerusalem; while Hugh de Lusignan, son of Almeric by his first wife, was proclaimed king of Cyprus. There was not at that time in Palestine any powerful nobleman capable of governing the state; on which account the civil and ecclesiastical potentates resolved that Philip Augustus of France should be requested to provide a husband for Mary. The French monarch fixed his eyes on John de Brienne, who was esteemed among the knights of Europe as being equally wise in council and experienced in war.

The hopes inspired by this union raised the pretensions of the Christian community so high, that they refused to prolong the truce which still subsisted between them and the sultan. The latter, therefore, marched an army to the neighbourhood of Tripoli, and threatened hostilities. The young king took the field at the head of a respectable force, and displayed his valour in many a fierce encounter; and though he did not succeed in conquering his foes, he saved his states from the utter annihilation with which they were threatened. He foresaw, however, the approaching ruin of the sacred cause; for he could not fail to observe that, while the Saracens were constantly acquiring new advantages, the Latin barons were embracing every opportunity of returning home. He accordingly wrote to the Pope, that the kingdom of Jerusalem consisted only of two or three towns, and that its fate must already have been determined but for the civil wars which had raged among the sons and successors of Saladin.

His Holiness was not deaf to a remonstrance so just and important. In a circular letter to the sovereigns of Europe, he reminded them that the time was now come when a successful effort might be made to secure possession of Palestine, and that while those who should fight faithfully for God would obtain a crown of glory, such as refused to serve him would be punished everlastingly. He employed, among other arguments, a consideration which has since been often urged by Protestant writers against his own church ; stating, that "the Mohammedan heresy, the Beast foretold by the Spirit, will not live for ever—its age is 666." He concluded with the assurance, that Jesus Christ would condemn them for gross ingratitude and infidelity, if they neglected to march to his succour at a time when he was in danger of being driven from a kingdom he had acquired by his own blood.

The preacher of the next crusade was Robert de Courçon, a man inferior in talents and rank to St Bernard, but whose fanaticism was as fervid as that of the Hermit and Fulk. He invited all to assume the Cross, and enrolled in the sacred militia women, children, the old, the blind, the lame, and even the distempered. The multitude of crusaders, as might be expected, was very great, and the voluntary offerings of money were immense. A council was held in the church of the Lateran, in which the Emperor of Constantinople, the Kings of France, England, Hungary, Jerusalem, Arragon, and other countries, were represented. War against the Saracens was unanimously declared to be the most sacred duty of the Christian world. The usual privileges, dispensations, and indulgences, were granted to the pilgrims ; and the Pope, besides other expenses, contributed thirty thousand pounds.

It was in the year 1216 that the sixth crusade, consisting chiefly of Hungarians and the soldiers of Lower Germany, landed at Acre. The sons of Saphadin were now at the head of affairs in Syria, their father having retired from the fatigues of royalty ; and, although unprepared to oppose so large a host with any prospect of success, they mustered what forces they could collect and advanced to Naplosa, the ancient Shechem and modern Nablous. But the insubordination of the invaders made victory more easy than was anticipated. Destitute of provisions, they wandered over the country, committing the greatest enormities, and suffering from time to time very severe losses from the just indignation of the inhabitants. At length the sovereign of Hungary, disgusted with the campaign, refused to remain any longer in Palestine,—a defection which compelled the King of Jerusalem, the Duke of Austria, and the Master of the Hospitallers, to take up a defensive position on the Plain of Cesarea. The knights of the other military orders, the Templar and Teutonic, seized upon Mount Carmel, which they fortified for the occasion. But their fears were relieved in the spring of the following year by the arrival of a large body of new and most zealous crusaders from the upper parts of Germany. Nearly three hundred vessels sailed from the Rhine, which, after having sustained more than the usual casualties of a voyage in the North Sea, landed on the shore of Syria those martial bands who had assembled in the neighbourhood of the Elbe and the Weser.

For reasons which are not very clearly assigned, but having some reference, it may be conjectured, to the exhausted state of the country, the chiefs of the Crusade came to the resolution of withdrawing their troops from Palestine, and of carrying the war into Egypt. Damietta, not unjustly regarded as the key of that kingdom on the line of the coast, was made the first object of attack; and so vigorous were the approaches of the assailants, that the castle or fortress, which was supposed to command the town, fell into their hands. Meantime a reinforcement from Europe appeared at the mouth of the Nile. Italy sent forth her choicest soldiers, headed by Pelagius and De Courçon, as legates of the Pope. The Counts of Nevers and La Marche, the Archbishop of Bourdeaux, the Bishops of Meaux, Autun, and Paris, led the valiant youth of France; while the English troops were conducted by the Earls of Chester, Arundel, and Salisbury, men celebrated for their heroism and experience in the field.

The tide of success flowed for some time so strongly in favour of the Christians, that the Saracen leaders

were desirous to conclude a peace very advantageous to
their invaders. When the loss of Damietta appeared
inevitable, the Sultan of Syria, Khamel the son of
Saphadin, apprehensive that the enemy would immediately advance against Jerusalem, issued orders to destroy
the fortifications, to prevent its being held by them as a
place of defence. But in the negotiation which was
opened between the contending powers, the Mussulmans
consented to rebuild the walls of the sacred city, and to
liberate all the prisoners in Syria and Egypt. Of the
whole kingdom of Palestine, they proposed to retain
only the castles of Karac and Montereale, as necessary
for the safe passage of pilgrims and merchants in their
intercourse with Mecca. As an equivalent for these
important concessions, they required nothing more than
the instant evacuation of Egypt, and a complete relinquishment of the conquests which had been recently
made in it by the arms of the crusaders.

The Christian chiefs, after a stormy discussion, resolved to reject the terms offered by the allied sultans,
and to prosecute the siege with vigour. The devoted
town, having been invested more than a year and a
half, was at length carried by assault; but so reso-
lute and persevering had been the defence, that of
seventy thousand inhabitants, who were shut up by the
Europeans, only three thousand remained to witness
their triumph.

The Saracens, fatigued with the horrors of war, once
more proposed a treaty on terms similar to those which
were offered before the fall of Damietta. But the
victors, whose wisdom in council was never equal to
their valour in the field of battle, again refused to
conclude a peace. The prevailing party recommended
an immediate attack upon Grand Cairo; anticipating
the reduction of the whole of Egypt, and the final subjection of all the Mohammedan states on the shores of
the Mediterranean. This vision of greatness, however,
soon vanished before the real difficulties of a campaign
on the banks of the Nile. In a few months the leaders

of the expedition found themselves reduced to the necessity of soliciting permission to return into Palestine; consenting to purchase safety by giving up all the acquisitions they had made since the first day that they opened their trenches before Damietta. The Barons of Syria and the military orders retired to Acre, where they held themselves in readiness to sustain an attack from the indignant Moslems; the mass of the volunteers and pilgrims soon afterwards procuring the means of returning into Europe.

Frederick the Second of Germany, who had engaged to lead a strong force into Syria, was so long prevented by domestic cares from fulfilling his promise, that he incurred the resentment of the Pope, who actually pronounced against him a sentence of excommunication.* The emperor at length was induced to marry Violante, the daughter of John de Brienne, and accepted as her dowry the kingdom of Jerusalem. In the year 1228, he arrived at Acre, with the view of making good his pretensions to the sacred diadem,—an object which he finally attained, not less by the connivance of the sultan than by the exertions of his military companions. The son of Saphadin felt that his throne had been rendered insecure by the ambition or treachery of his own kindred, and was therefore much inclined to cultivate an amicable feeling with so powerful a prince as the sovereign of Germany. In pursuance of these views a treaty was signed, providing that for ten years the Christians and Mussulmans were to live on a footing of brotherhood; that Jerusalem, Jaffa, Bethlehem, Nazareth, and their

---

* A curé at Paris, instead of reading the bull from the pulpit in the usual form, said to his parishioners, "You know, my friends, that I am ordered to fulminate an excommunication against Frederick. I know not the motive. All that I know is, that there has been a quarrel between that prince and the Pope. God alone knows who is right. I excommunicate him who has injured the other, and I absolve the sufferer." The emperor sent a present to the preacher, but the Pope and the king blamed this sally: *le mauvais plaisant*—the unhappy wit—was obliged to expiate his fault by a canonical penance.—*Mills' History*, vol. ii. p. 253.

dependencies, were to be restored to the former; that the Holy Sepulchre was likewise to be given up to them; and that the people of both religions might offer up their devotions in that house of prayer, which the one called the Temple of Solomon, and the other the Mosque of Omar. Thus the address or good fortune of Frederick more effectually promoted the object of the Holy Wars than the heroic phrensy of Richard Cœur de Lion; many of the disasters consequent on the battle of Tiberias were wiped away; and the hopes of Europe for a permanent settlement in Asia appeared to be realized.

But the emperor had performed all these services while the stain of excommunication was yet unremoved from his character. The fidelity of the knights, accordingly, whose oaths had a reference to the supremacy of the Church, and the attachment of the clergy, could not be relied upon. Hence, when he went to Jerusalem to be crowned, the Patriarch would not discharge his office; the places of worship were closed; and no religious duties were observed in public during his stay. Frederick repaired to the chapel of the Holy Sepulchre surrounded by his courtiers, and boldly taking the crown from the altar, placed it on his own head. He then issued orders for rebuilding the fortifications of his eastern capital, after which he returned to Acre, whence he almost immediately set sail for Europe.*

---

* The address of the Pope to the fourth Council of Lateran, as translated by Michaud, is not a little striking:—"O vous qui passez dans les chemins, disait Jérusalem par la bouche du Pontife, regardez et voyez si jamais il y eut une douleur semblable à la mienne! Accourez donc tous, ô vous qui me chérissez, pour me délivrer de l'excès de mes misères! Moi, qui étais la reçue de toutes les nations, je suis maintenant asservie au tribut; moi, qui étais remplie de peuple, je suis restée presque seule. Les chemins de Sion sont en deuil, parceque personne ne vient à mes solemnités. Mes ennemis ont écrasé ma tête; tous les lieux saints sont profanés; le saint sépulchre, si rempli d'éclat, est couvert d'opprobre; on adore le fils de la perdition et de l'enfer là où naguères on adorait le fils de Dieu. Les enfants de l'étranger m'accablent d'outrages, et montrant la croix de Jesus, ils me disent:—' *Tu as mis toute ta confiance dans un bois vil; nous verrons si ce bois te sauvera au jour de danger.*' "—*Histoire des Croisades,* tome iii. p. 394.

The peace established between Frederick and the Saracen rulers was not faithfully observed by the latter, some of whom did not consider themselves as bound by its stipulations. The sufferings endured by the Christians of Palestine accordingly called their brethren in Europe once more to arms. A council, held under the auspices of the Pope at Spoleto, decreed that fresh levies should be sent into Asia so soon as the truce with Khamel, the sultan of Damascus, should have expired. Many of the English nobility, inflamed by the love of warlike fame, took the Cross, and prepared to follow the standard of the Earl of Chester, and of Richard, earl of Cornwall, brother to King Henry the Third.

In this pious movement the lords of England were anticipated by those of France, who, in the year 1239, landed in Syria, and prepared to measure lances with the Moslems. News of these warlike proceedings having reached the nephew of Saladin, he forthwith drove the Christians out of Jerusalem, and demolished the tower of David,—a monument which till that time had been regarded as sacred by both parties. The combats which followed, although fought with great bravery on the side of the invaders, terminated generally in favour of the Saracens; and the French accordingly, after losing a great number of their best warriors, were glad to have recourse to terms of peace. The Templars entered into treaty with the Emir of Karac, while the Hospitallers, actuated by jealousy or revenge, preferred the friendship of the Sultan of Egypt.

The following year Richard, the earl of Cornwall, arrived with his levy, hoping to find his allies in possession of all the towns which had been ceded to the Emperor of Germany, and enjoying security in the exercise of their religious rites. His surprise was therefore very great, when he discovered that the principal leaders of the French had already fled from the Plains of Syria; that the knights of the two great orders had sought refuge in negotiation; and, finally, that the conquests of the former Crusaders were once more limited to a few fortresses and a strip of territory on the coast. He marched in the first instance to Jaffa, with the view of concentrating the scattered forces of Europe; but receiving notice, as soon as he arrived, that the Sultan of Egypt, who was then at war with his brother of Damascus, was desirous to cultivate friendly relations, he lent a ready ear to the terms proposed. The Mussulman consented to relinquish Jerusalem, Beritus, Nazareth, Bethlehem, Mount Tabor, and a large portion of the Holy Land, provided the English earl would withdraw his troops and preserve a strict neutrality.

These conditions being ratified by the Egyptian sovereign, the Earl of Cornwall had the satisfaction to see the great object of the crusaders once more accomplished. Palestine again belonged to the Christians. The Hospitallers opened their treasury to rebuild the walls of Jerusalem, while the Patriarch and clergy entered the holy city to re-consecrate the churches. For two years the gospel was the only religion administered in the sacred capital, and the faithful had begun to exult in the permanent subjection of their rivals when a new enemy arose, more formidable to them than even the Saracens.

The victories of Zingis Khan had displaced several nations belonging to the great Tartar family, and among others the Karismians, who continued their retreat southward till they reached the confines of Egypt. The sultan, who perhaps had repented the liberality of his terms to the English, advised the expatriated barbarians to take possession of Palestine. He even sent one of his principal officers and a large body of troops to serve as their guides; upon which, Barbacan, the general of the savage exiles, at the head of twenty thousand cavalry, advanced into the Holy Land. The garrison of Jerusalem, being quite inadequate to its defence, retired, and were followed by many of the inhabitants. The invaders entered it without opposition, sparing neither life nor property, and respecting nothing, whether sacred or profane. At length the Templars and Hospitallers, forgetting their mutual animosities, united their bands to rescue the country from the grasp of such savages. A battle took place, which, after continuing two whole days, ended in the total defeat of the Christians; the Grand Masters of St John and of the Temple being among the slain. Only thirty-three individuals of the latter order, and sixteen of the former, with three Teutonic cavaliers, remained alive, and succeeded in making their way to Acre, the last refuge of the vanquished knights. The Karismians, with their Egyptian allies, after having razed the fortifications of Ascalon and Tiberias, encamped on the seacoast, laid waste the surrounding territory, and slew or carried into bondage every Frank who fell into their hands. Nor was it till the year 1247 that the Syrians and Mamlouks, insulted by this northern horde, attacked them near Damascus, slew their chief, and compelled the remainder to retrace their steps to the borders of the Caspian Lake.

The intelligence did not fail to reach Europe that the members of the Church in Palestine had been put to death or dispersed by the northern shepherds. Innocent the Fourth suggested the expediency of another crusade, and even summoned all his faithful children to take arms. He wrote to Henry the Third, king of England, urging him to press on his subjects the necessity of punishing the Karismians. But the spirit of crusading was more active in France than in any other country of the West, and it revived in all the vigour of its chivalrous piety in the reign of Louis the Ninth. Agreeably to the superstition of the times, he had vowed, whilst afflicted by a severe illness, that in case of recovery he would travel to the Holy Land. The Cross was likewise taken by the three royal brothers, the Counts of Artois, Poictiers, and Anjou, by the Duke of Burgundy, the Countess of Flanders and her two sons, together with many other knights of high degree.

But it was not till 1249 that the soldiers of Louis

were mustered, and his ships prepared for sea ; the former amounting to fifty thousand, while his vessels of all descriptions exceeded eighteen hundred. They set sail for Egypt ; a storm separated the fleet ; but the royal division, in which were nearly three thousand knights and their men-at-arms, arrived in the neighbourhood of Damietta. On the second day the king ordered the disembarkation ; he himself leaped into the water; his warriors followed him to the shore ; upon which the Saracens, panic-struck at their boldness and determination, made but a slight show of defence, and fled into the interior. Although the town was now better prepared for a siege than it was at that period when it defied the arms of the crusaders during eighteen months, yet the garrison were pleased to seek safety in the fleetness of their horses. Louis fixed his residence in the city ; a Christian government was established ; and the clergy, as they were wont on such occasions, proceeded to purify the mosques.

Towards the close of the season, after being joined by a body of English volunteers, the French monarch resolved to march to Cairo and attack the sultan in the heart of his kingdom. But the floods of the Nile, and the intersection of the country by numerous canals, occasioned a second time the loss of a brave army. Famine and disease, too, aided the sword of the enemy, till at length the victors of Damietta were compelled to sue for a peace which they could no longer obtain. A retreat was ordered ; but those who attempted to escape by the river were taken prisoners, and the fate of such as proceeded by land was equally disastrous. While they were occupied in constructing a bridge over a canal, the Saracens entered the camp and murdered the sick. The valiant king, though oppressed with the general calamity of disease, boldly sustained the shock of the enemy, throwing himself into the midst of their ranks, resolved to perish rather than desert his troops. One of his attendants succeeded at length in drawing him from the presence of the foe, and conducted him to a village, where he sank under his wounds and fatigue into a state of utter insensibility. In this miserable condition he was overtaken by the Moslems, who announced to him that he was their captive. One of his brothers, the gallant Artois, had already fallen in battle; but the two others, Anjou and Poictiers, with all the nobility, fell into the hands of the enemy.

The sultan did not abuse his victory, nor seek to impose upon Louis terms which a sovereign could not grant without forfeiting his honour. He agreed to accept a sum equivalent to five hundred thousand livres for the deliverance of the army, and the town of Damietta as a ransom for the royal person. Peace was to continue ten years between the Mussulmans and the Christians; while the Franks were to be restored to those privileges in the kingdom of Jerusalem which they had enjoyed previous to the recent invasion of the French. The repose which succeeded this treaty was interrupted by the murder of the sultan, who fell a victim to the jealousy of the Mamlouks; but, after a few acts of hostility too insignificant to be recorded, the emirs renewed, with certain modifications, the basis of the agreement on which the peace was established. Louis himself made a narrow escape from the sanguinary intrigues of those military slaves who had imbrued their hands in the blood of their own master. They declared that, as they had committed a sin by destroying their prince, whom, by their law, they ought to have guarded as the apple of their eye, their religion would be violated if they suffered a Christian king to live. But the other chiefs, more honourable than the Mamlouks, disdained to commit a crime under any such pretext; and the French monarch, accordingly, was allowed to accompany the poor remains of his army to the citadel of Acre.

It has been remarked, that the expedition of St Louis into Egypt resembles in many respects the war carried on in that country thirty years before. In both cases the Christian armies were encamped near the entrance of the Ashmoun canal, beyond which they could not advance ; and the surrender of Damietta in each instance was the price of safety. The errors of the Cardinal Pelagius seem not to have been recollected by the French king, who, in fact, trode in his steps with a fatal blindness, and ended by paying a still severer penalty.

A gleam of hope arose in the minds of the crusaders from finding the rulers of Egypt and of Syria engaged in a furious war. The Mamlouks even condescended to solicit the co-operation of Louis, and agreed to purchase it by remitting one-half of the ransom which still remained unpaid. They farther consented to deliver up Jerusalem itself, and also the youthful captives taken on the banks of the Nile, whom they had compelled to embrace the Mussulman faith. But before the Franks could appear in the field, the interposition of the caliph had restored peace to the contending parties, both of whom immediately resumed their wonted dislike to the European invaders.

The infidels, however, at this period did not pursue their schemes of conquest with the vigour and ability which distinguished the movements of Noureddin, and more especially of Saladin, his renowned successor. They might have swept the feeble and exhausted Christians from the shores of Palestine ; but they merely ravaged the country round Acre, and then proceeded to Sidon, in the strong castle of which Louis and his army had taken refuge. The blood and property of the citizens satisfied the barbarians, who departed without trying the valour of the soldiers who occupied the garrison.

The death of Queen Blanche, the mother of the king, and regent during his absence, afforded him a good apology for leaving the country, of which he had long been tired. The Patriarch and Barons of the Holy Land offered him their humble thanks for the honour he had bestowed upon their cause, and for the benefits which he had conferred upon themselves individually. Louis, sensible that he had gathered no laurels in Palestine, and that the interests of the Church were even in a more hopeless condition than when he landed at Damietta, listened to their address with mingled emotions of shame and regret, and forthwith prepared himself for his voyage homewards.*

Thus terminated that expedition, of which, says a French author, the commencement filled all Christian states with joy, and which, in the end, plunged all the West into mourning. The king arrived at Vincennes on the 5th of September 1254, accompanied by a crowd collected from all quarters. The more they forgot his reverses, the more bitterly he called to mind the fate of his brave companions, whom he had left in the mud of Egypt or on the sands of Palestine; and the melancholy which he showed in his countenance formed a striking contrast to the public congratulation on the return of a beloved prince. His first care, says the historian, was to go to St Denys, to prostrate himself at the feet of the apostles of France; the next day he made his entrance into the capital, preceded by the clergy, the nobility, and the people. He still wore the cross upon his shoulder; the sight of which, by recalling the motives of his long absence, inspired the fear that he had not abandoned the enterprise of the crusade.†

The misfortunes sustained in the field were greatly increased by the dissensions which prevailed among the military orders after the departure of Louis. The Templars and Hospitallers, especially, never forgot their

---

* " On se rappelait alors les vertus dont il avait donné l'exemple, et surtout sa bonté envers les habitants de la Palestine, qu'il avait traités comme ses propres sujets. Les uns exprimaient leur reconnaissance par de vives acclamations, les autres par une morne silence; tout le peuple qu'affligeait son départ, le proclamait *le père des Chrétiens*, et conjurait le Ciel de répandre ses bénédictions sur la famille du vertueux monarque et sur le royaume de France. Louis montrait sur son visage qu'il partageait les regrets des Chrétiens de la Terre-Sainte; il leur addressait des paroles consolantes, leur donnait d'utiles conseils, se reprochait de n'avoir fait assez pour leur cause, et témoignait le vif désir qu'un jour Dieu le jugeât digne d'achever l'ouvrage de leur délivrance."—*Michaud, Histoire des Croisades*, tome iv. p. 299.

† Michaud, tome iv. p. 302.

jealousies except when engaged in battle with the Mussulmans; for, in every interval of peace, they mutually gratified their arrogance and contempt by wrangling on points of precedency and professional reputation. At length an appeal to arms was made, with the view of determining which of these kindred associations should stand highest as soldiers in the estimation of Europe. The Knights of St John gained the victory; and so bloody was the conflict, that no quarter was granted, and hardly a single Templar escaped alive.

But these unseemly disputes were soon drowned amid the shouts of a more formidable warfare waged against Palestine by the Mamlouk sovereign of Egypt, the sanguinary and bigoted Bibars. His troops demolished the churches of Nazareth and Mount Tabor; after which they advanced to the gates of Acre, inflicting the most horrid cruelties upon the unprotected inhabitants. Sephouri and Azotus were taken by storm, or yielded upon terms. At the reduction of the former, it was agreed that the knights and garrison, amounting in all to six hundred men, should be conducted to the nearest Christian town. But no sooner was the sultan put in possession of the fortress than he violated the conditions of surrender, and left the knights only a few hours to determine on the alternative of death or conversion to Islamism. The prior and two Franciscan monks succeeded by their exhortations in fixing the faith of the religious cavaliers; and hence, at the time appointed for the declaration of their choice, they unanimously avowed their resolution to die rather than incur the dishonour of apostasy. The decree for the slaughter of the Templars was pronounced and executed; while the three preachers of martyrdom, as if responsible for the conduct of their countrymen, were flayed alive.

A large Christian state had been formed at Antioch, in alliance with the kingdom of Jerusalem. Bibars, after reducing Jaffa and the castle of Beaufort, marched his fierce soldiers against the capital of Syria, and soon added it to the number of his conquests. Forty thousand believers were on this melancholy occasion put to the sword, and not fewer than one hundred thousand were led into captivity. The barbarian, indeed, avowed the fell purpose of exterminating throughout the East all who professed the gospel; extending the terror of death or the ascendency of the Koran from the Nile to the mountains of Armenia. But his progress was stopped by the intelligence which reached him in Palestine, that the King of Cyprus had resolved to interpose his arms in behalf of the Holy Land, and was about to make a descent on the coast at the head of a large force collected from various nations. Bibars returned to Cairo, fitted out a fleet for the conquest of that island, and intended, during the absence of its sovereign, to annex it permanently to the dominions of Egypt. But his ships were lost in a tempest; his military character suffered from the failure of the enterprise; his power was weakened; and he ceased to be any longer the scourge and dread of the Christian world.

Before the atrocities of this Mamlouk chief were made known in Europe, the people of the West had made preparations for the ninth crusade. Louis was not able to conceal from himself, that his first expedition to the Holy Land had brought more shame on France than benefit to the common cause. Nay, he was not without fear, that his personal reputation was in some degree tarnished by the fatal result of his attack on Egypt, so unwisely and rashly conducted. The Pope favoured his inclination for a new attempt; and accordingly, in a general meeting of the higher clergy and nobles, held at Paris in 1268, the king exhorted his people to avenge the wrongs which Christ had so long suffered at the hands of the unbelieving Moslems.

In England a similar spirit had long prevailed among the priesthood and the great body of the commons; but Henry the Third, taught by experience that the late crusades had only weakened the friends and strengthened the enemies of true religion, refused to countenance this popular folly at the time when Louis first assumed the

Cross. On the present occasion, however, he permitted his son Edward, with the Earls of Warwick and Pembroke, to receive the holy ensign, and to join the sovereign of France in his renewed attempt to plant the emblem of the faith on the walls of Jerusalem.

It was not till the spring of 1270 that St Louis spread his sails the second time for the Holy Land. The feelings of religious and military ardour which animated the heart of this pious monarch were diffused through the sixty thousand soldiers who followed his banners. He could count too, among his leaders, the descendants of those gallant chiefs, the Lords of Brittany, of Flanders, and Champagne, who in former generations had distinguished themselves in fighting the battles of the Church. But notwithstanding such promising appearances, this proud armament took the sea under an evil omen. The fleet was driven into Sardinia; and there a great and unfortunate change was made in the plan of operations. Instead of proceeding to Palestine, it was resolved that the troops should be landed in the neighbourhood of Tunis, to assist the Christians in extending their faith in opposition to the disciples of the Koran. Success, indeed, crowned the first efforts of the invaders; Carthage fell into their hands; and more splendid conquests seemed to invite their progress into the heart of the Mohammedan nations of Northern Africa. But a pestilential disease, the scourge of those burning shores, soon spread its ravages among their ranks. Louis, the main support of the expedition, was stricken with the fatal sickness, and died, leaving his army, which had accomplished nothing, to prosecute the war, or to return with sullied standards into their native country.*

---

\* It was during the siege of Tunis that Louis died. "Our Edward would needs have had the town beaten down, and all put to the sword; thinking the foulest quarter too fair for them. Their goods (because got by robbery) he would have sacrificed as an anathema to God, and burnt to ashes: his own share he execrated, and caused it to be burnt, forbidding the English to save any thing of it; because that coals stolen out of that fire would sooner burn

Prince Edward, who condemned the vacillating conduct of his allies, had already passed from Africa into Sicily, where he spent the following winter. In the early part of the year 1271, he set sail for Acre, where he landed at the head of only one thousand men; but so high was his reputation among the Latins of Palestine, that he soon found his army increased sevenfold, and eager to be employed in the redemption of the sacred territory. He led them, in the first place, against Nazareth, which did not long resist the vigour of his attack; and, almost immediately afterwards, he surprised a large body of Turkish soldiers, whom he cut in pieces. The Moslems imagined that another Cœur de Lion had been sent from England to scourge them into discipline, or to shake the foundation of their power in Syria. Edward was brave and skilful as a warrior, and owed his success not less to his able dispositions than to his personal courage. But he was cruel and lavish of human blood. The barbarities which disgraced the triumphs of the first crusade were repeated on a smaller scale at Nazareth, where the prince put the whole garrison to death, and subjected the inhabitants to unnecessary suffering.

The resentment of the Governor of Jaffa is said to have pointed the dagger which was aimed at the heart of the English prince by the hand of an assassin. This wretch, as the bearer of letters, was admitted into the chamber of Edward, who, not suspecting treachery, received several severe wounds before he could dash the assailant to the floor and despatch him with his sword.

---

their houses than warm their hands. It troubled not the consciences of other princes to enrich themselves herewith, but they glutted themselves with the stolen honie which they found in this hive of drones: and which was worse, now their bellies were full, they would go to bed; return home, and goe no farther. Yea, the young King of France, called Philip the Bold, was fearful to prosecute his journey to Palestine; whereas Prince Edward struck his breast, and swore, that though all his friends forsook him, yet he would enter Ptolemais though but only with Fowin his horse-keeper. By which speech he incensed the English to go on with him."— *Fuller's Holy Warre*, p. 217.

But as the weapon used by the Saracen had been steeped in poison, the life of his intended victim was for some hours in imminent danger. The chivalrous fiction of that romantic age has ascribed his recovery to the kind offices of one of that sex whose generous affections are seldom chilled by the calculations of selfishness. His wife, Eleanora, is said to have sucked the poison from his wound, at the hazard of instant death to herself,—a story which, having received the sanction of the learned Camden, has not unfrequently been held as an indisputable fact. The more authentic edition of the narrative attributes the restoration of his health to the usual means employed by surgical skill, aided by the resources of a strong mind and a vigorous constitution.*

It soon became manifest, that the valour and ability of the prince, unsupported by an adequate force, could make no lasting impression upon the Moslem power in Syria. Accordingly, after having spent fourteen months in Acre, he listened to proposals for peace made by the ruler of Egypt, who, being engaged in war with the Saracens, whom he had displaced, was eager to terminate hostilities with the English. A suspension of arms, to continue ten years, was formally signed by the two chiefs; whereupon the Mamlouk withdrew his troops from Palestine, and Edward embarked for his native country.

The loss and discomfiture which for more than a hundred years had concluded every attempt to regain the

---

* " It is storied how Eleanor, his lady, sucked all the poison out of his wounds, without doing any harm to herself. So sovereign a remedy is a woman's tongue anointed with the virtue of loving affection! Pity it is that so pretty a story should not be true (with all the miracles in love's legends), and sure he shall get himself no credit who undertaketh to confute a passage so sounding to the honour of the sex. Yet can it not stand with what others have written."

" The Admirall of Joppa, hearing of his recoverie, utterly disavowed that he had any hand in the treachery; as none will willingly father unsucceeding villany. True it is he was truly sorrowfull; whether because Edward was so bad, or no worse wounded, He knoweth that knoweth hearts. Some wholly acquit him herein, and conceive this mischief proceeded from Simon earl of Montfort's hatred to our prince."—*Fuller's Holy Warre*, p. 220.

Holy Land, did not yet extinguish the hope of final success in the hearts of the clergy and sovereigns of the West. Gregory the Ninth, who himself had served in the Christian armies of Syria, exerted all the means in his power to equip another expedition against the enemies of the faith. The small republics of Italy, which found a ready employment for their shipping in transporting troops to Palestine, were the first to embrace the cause recommended by their spiritual ruler. The king of France seemed to favour the enterprise, and advanced money on the mortgage of certain estates within his dominions belonging to the Templars; Charles of Anjou followed the example of his royal relation; and Michael Palæologus, the emperor of the East, announced his willingness to take arms against the ambitious sultan, who already threatened the independence of Greece. A council held at Lyons in 1274 sanctioned the obligations of a crusade, and imposed upon the Church and other Estates such taxes as appeared sufficient to carry it to a successful issue. But the death of the Pope dissolved the coalition, and all preparations for renewing the war were immediately laid aside,—never to be resumed.

The Franks in Palestine, now left to their own resources, ought to have cultivated peace, and more especially to have abstained from positive and direct aggression. Their conduct, however, was not marked by such abstinence or wisdom. On the contrary, by attacking certain Mohammedan merchants, they provoked the anger of the sultan, who swore by God and the Prophet that he would avenge the wrong. A war, fatal to the Christian interests, was the immediate consequence. Their fortresses were rapidly demolished; and at length, in the year 1289, the city of Tripoli, the principal appanage of the kingdom of Jerusalem, was taken, its houses were consumed by fire, its works dismantled, and its inhabitants massacred, or sold into slavery.

Acre now remained the sole possession of the Latins, in the country where their sovereignty had been acknowledged during the lapse of nearly two centuries. A short peace granted to Henry the Second of Cyprus, the nominal king of the Holy Land, postponed its fate and the utter abolition of Christian authority in Syria a few years longer. Within its walls were crowded the wretched remains of those principalities which had been won by the valour of European soldiers. A reinforcement of unprincipled Italians only added to the disorder which already prevailed in the town, and increased the number of offences by which they were daily accumulating upon their heads the vengeance of the fanatical Mamlouks, who longed for an opportunity to attack them.

At length, in the month of April 1291, a force which has been estimated at more than 200,000 men, issued from Egypt, and encamped on the Plain of Acre. Most of the inhabitants made their escape by sea from the horrors of the impending siege; the defence of the place being intrusted to about twelve thousand good soldiers, belonging chiefly to the several orders of religious knighthood. The command was offered to the Grand Master of the Templars, who, being prevailed upon to accept, discharged its duties with firmness and military skill. But the enemy were not inferior in valour, and their numbers were irresistible. Prodigies of bravery were displayed on both sides; the assailants threw themselves, with desperate resolution, into the breach, from whence they were repeatedly driven back at the point of the sword, or hurled headlong into the ditch. But the sultan was prodigal of blood, and had vowed to humble the Nazarenes who dared to dispute his authority. The walls, accordingly, after having been several times lost and won, were at length finally occupied by the united Tartars and Mamlouks; and the Crescent was at that moment elevated to a place which it has continued to occupy during the greater part of five centuries. Struck with terror, the few small towns, which till this period had been allotted to the Christians, surrendered at the first summons, and saw their inhabitants doomed either to death or to a painful captivity. In one word, the Holy Land, which since the days of Godfrey had cost to

Christendom so much anxiety, blood, and treasure, was now lost; the sacred walls of Jerusalem were abandoned to infidels; and henceforth the disciple of Christ was doomed to purchase permission to visit the interesting scenes consecrated by the events recorded in the gospel.

The titular crown of Palestine was worn for the last time by Hugh the Great, the descendant of Hugh, king of Cyprus, and Alice, who was the daughter of Mary and of John de Brienne. At a later period this empty honour was claimed by the house of Sicily, in right of Charles, count of Anjou and brother of Louis IX., who was thought to unite in his own person the issue of the king of Cyprus and of the Princess Mary, the daughter of Frederick, sovereign of Antioch. The Knights of St John of Jerusalem, afterwards denominated Knights of Rhodes and Malta, and the Teutonic Knights, the conquerors of the north of Europe and founders of the kingdom of Prussia, are now the only remains of those crusaders who struck terror into Africa and Asia, and seized the thrones of Jerusalem, Cyprus, and Constantinople.

Although no expedition from the Christian states reached the Holy Land after the close of the thirteenth century, the fire which had so long warmed the hearts of the crusaders was not entirely extinguished in several parts of Europe. Edward the First of England, for example, still cherished the hope of opening the gates of Jerusalem, or of leaving his bones in the sacred dust of Palestine. A similar feeling animated the monarch of France; while the Pope, who derived manifold advantages from the prosecution of such wars, summoned councils, issued pastoral letters, and employed preachers, as in the days that were passed. But dissensions at home during the first half of the fourteenth century, and the general conviction of hopelessness which had seized the public mind respecting all armaments against the Moslems, occasioned the failure of every attempt to unite once more the powers of Christendom in the common cause.

In the following century, the ascendency of the Turks,

not only in the East, but on the banks of the Danube and the northern shores of the Mediterranean, compelled the people of Europe to act on the defensive. The fall of the Grecian empire, too, rendered the intercourse with Syria at once more difficult and dangerous. Egypt in like manner was shut against the Christians, being subjected to the same yoke which pressed so heavily on the western parts of Asia. Hence, during more than two centuries, a cloud hung over the affairs of Palestine, which we in vain attempt to penetrate. Suffice it to remark, that it remained subject to the Mamlouk sultans of Egypt till the year 1382, when they were dispossessed by a body of Circassians, who invaded and overran the country. Upon the expulsion of these barbarians, it acknowledged again the government of Cairo, under which it continued until the period of the more formidable irruption of the Mogul Tartars, led by the celebrated Tamerlane. At his death the Holy Land was once more annexed to Egypt as a province; but in 1516, Selim the Ninth, emperor of the Othman Turks, carried his victorious arms from the Euphrates to the Libyan Desert, involving in one general conquest all the intervening states. More than three hundred years have that people exercised a dominion over the land of Judea, varied only by intervals of rebellion on the part of governors who wished to assert their independence, or by wars among the different pashas, who, in defiance of the supreme authority, have from time to time quarrelled about its spoils.

From the period at which the crusaders were expelled from Syria down to the middle of the last century, we are chiefly indebted for our knowledge of the Holy Land to the pilgrims whom religious motives induced to brave all the perils and extortions to which Franks were exposed under the Turkish government. The faith of the Christians survived their arms at Jerusalem, and was found within the sacred walls long after every European soldier had disappeared. The Jacobite, Armenian, and Abyssinian believers, were allowed to cling to those memorials of redemption which have at all times given so great an interest to the metropolis of Palestine; and occasionally a member of the Latin church had the good fortune to enter the gates of the city in disguise, and was permitted to offer up his prayers at the side of the Holy Sepulchre. In 1432, when La Broquiere undertook his pilgrimage into the East, there were only two French monks in Jerusalem, who, as he relates, were held in the most cruel thraldom.

The increasing intercourse between the Turks at Constantinople and the governments of Europe, gradually produced a more tolerant spirit among the former, and paved the way for a lasting accommodation in favour of the Christians in Palestine. We find, accordingly, that in the year 1507, when Baumgarten travelled in Syria, there was at Jerusalem a monastery of Franciscans, who possessed influence sufficient to secure his personal safety, and even to provide for his comfort under their own roof. At a somewhat later period, the Moslem rulers began to consider the reception of pilgrims as a regular source of revenue; selling their protection at a high price, and even creating dangers in order to render that protection indispensable. The Christians, meanwhile, rose by degrees from the state of depression and contumely into which they had been sunk by the conquerors of the Grecian empire. They were allowed to nominate patriarchs for the due administration of ecclesiastical affairs, and to practise all the rites of their religion, provided they did not insult the established faith,—a condition of things which, with such changes as have been from time to time occasioned by foreign war or by the temper of individual governors, has continued to the present day.

As the civil history of Palestine for three centuries is nothing more than a relation of the broils, the insurrections, the massacres, and changes of dynasty, which have periodically shaken the Turkish empire in Europe as well as in Asia, we willingly pass over it, as we thereby only refrain from a tedious recapitulation of names and dates, which could not have the slightest interest for any class of readers. At the close of the eighteenth century, however, its affairs assumed a new importance. Napoleon Bonaparte, whose views of dominion were limited only by the bounds of the civilized world, imagined that, by the conquest of Egypt and Syria, he should open up for himself a path into the remoter provinces of the Asiatic continent, and perhaps establish his power on either bank of the Ganges.

It was in the spring of 1799 that the French general, who had been informed of certain preparations against him in the pashalic of Acre, resolved to cross the desert which divides Egypt from Palestine at the head of ten thousand chosen men. El Arish soon fell into his hands, the garrison of which were permitted to retire on condition that they should not serve again during the war. Gaza likewise yielded without much opposition to the overwhelming force by which it was attacked. Jaffa set the first example of a vigorous resistance; the slaughter was tremendous; and Bonaparte, to intimidate other towns from showing a similar spirit, gave it up to plunder and the other excesses of an enraged soldiery. A more melancholy scene followed,—the massacre of nearly four thousand prisoners who had laid down their arms. Napoleon alleged, that these were the same individuals who had given their parole at El Arish, and had violated their faith by appearing against him in the fortress which had just fallen. Under this pretext he commanded them all to be put to death, and thereby brought a stain upon his reputation, which no casuistry on the part of his admirers, and no considerations of expediency, military or political, will ever remove.*

---

* The motives for the massacre of Jaffa are stated by Bourrienne in so impartial a manner, that we are inclined to believe he has given a true transcript of his master's mind. " Bonaparte sent his aides-de-camp, Beauharnois and Croisier, to appease as far as possible the fury of the soldiery, to examine what passed, and to report. They learned that a numerous detachment of the garrison had retired into a strong position, where large buildings surrounded a courtyard. This court they entered, displaying the scarfs which marked

Acre, so frequently mentioned in the history of the crusades, was again doomed to receive a fatal celebrity from a most sanguinary and protracted siege. Achmet Djezzar, the pasha of that division of Palestine which stretches from the borders of Egypt to the Gulf of Sidon, had thrown himself into this fortress with a considerable army, determined to defend it to the last extremity. After failing in an attempt to bribe this Mussulman chief, Bonaparte made preparations for the attack with his usual skill and activity ; resolving to carry the place by assault before the Turkish government could send certain supplies of food and ammunition, which he knew were expected by the besieged. But his design was

---

their rank. The Albanians and Arnauts, composing nearly the entire of these refugees, cried out from the windows that they wished to surrender, on condition their lives were spared ; if not, threatening to fire upon the officers and to defend themselves to the last extremity. The young men conceived they ought, and had power, to accede to the demand, in opposition to the sentence of death pronounced against the garrison of every place taken by assault. I was walking with General Bonaparte before his tent when these prisoners, in two columns, amounting to about four thousand men, were marched into the camp. When he beheld the mass of men arrive, and before seeing the aides-de-camp, he turned to me with an expression of consternation ' What would they have me to do with these ? Have I provisions to feed them ; ships to transport them either to Egypt or France ? How the devil could they play me this trick ?' The two aides-de-camp, on their arrival and explanations, received the strongest reprimands. To their defence, namely, that they were alone amid numerous enemies, and that he had recommended to them to appease the slaughter, he replied in the sternest tone, ' Yes, without doubt, the slaughter of women, children, old men, the peaceable inhabitants, but not of armed soldiers : you ought to have braved death, and not brought these to me. What would you have me do with them ?'—But the evil was done. Four thousand men were there—their fate must be determined. The prisoners were made to sit down, huddled together before the tents, their hands being bound behind them. A gloomy rage was depicted in every lineament. A council was held in the general's tent," &c.

On the third day an order was issued that the prisoners should be shot,—an order which was literally executed on four thousand men. " The atrocious crime," says M. Bourrienne, " makes me yet shudder when I think of it, as when it passed before me. All that can be imagined of fearful on this day of blood would fall short of the reality !"—*Memoirs*, vol. i. p. 156.

frustrated by the presence of a British squadron under Sir Sidney Smith, who, in the first instance, captured a convoy of guns and stores forwarded from Egypt, and then employed them against him, by erecting batteries on shore. Notwithstanding these inauspicious circumstances, Napoleon opened his trenches on the 18th of March, in the firm conviction that the Turkish garrison could not long resist the fury of his onset and the skill of his engineers. " On that little town," said he to one of his generals, as they were standing together on an eminence which still bears the name of Richard Cœur de Lion, " on that little town depends the fate of the East. Behold the key of Constantinople or of India !"

At the end of ten days a breach was effected, by which the French made their first attempt to reduce the towers of Acre. Their assault was conducted with so much firmness and spirit, that for a moment the garrison was overpowered, and the town seemed lost. The pasha, renowned for his personal courage, threw himself into the thickest body of the combatants, and at length, by strength of hand and the most heroic example, rallied his troops, and drove the enemy from the walls. The loss of the French was great, and the disappointment of their leader extreme. Napoleon was deeply mortified when he saw his finest regiments pursued to their lines by English sailors and undisciplined Turks, who even proceeded to destroy their intrenchments.

Bourrienne relates, that during the assault of the 8th of May more than two hundred men penetrated into the city. Already the shout of victory was raised ; but the breach, taken in flank by the Turks, could not be entered with sufficient promptitude, and the party was left without support. The streets were barricaded ; the very women were running about throwing dust into the air, and exciting the inhabitants by cries and howling ; all contributed to render unavailing this short occupation by a handful of men, who, finding themselves alone, regained the breach by a retrograde movement ; but not before many had fallen.

The want of proper means for forming a siege, and perhaps the contempt which he entertained for barbarians, occasioned a great deficiency in the works raised before Acre. Bonaparte was not ignorant of the disadvantages under which his men laboured from the cause now assigned; and it was principally for this reason that he trusted more to the bayonet than to the mortar or cannon. He repeated his assaults day after day, till the ditch was filled with dead and wounded soldiers. His grenadiers at length felt greater horror at walking over the bodies of their comrades than at encountering the tremendous discharges of large and small shot to which they had fallen victims.

On the 21st of May, after sixty days of ineffectual labour under a burning sun, Napoleon ordered a last assault on the obstinate garrison of Ptolemais, which had barred his path to the accomplishment of the most splendid conquests. This attempt was not less fruitless than those which had preceded it, and was attended with the loss of many brave warriors. A fleet was at hand to reinforce Djezzar with men and arms; the French, on the contrary, were perishing under the plague which had already found its way into their ranks, and were besides constantly threatened by swarms of Arabs and Mamlouks, who had assembled in the neighbouring mountains. His failure in this effort, accordingly, dictated the necessity of a speedy retreat towards Egypt, where his affairs continued to enjoy some degree of prosperity, and in the magazines of which he might still find the means of restoring the health and vigour of his troops.

The siege of Acre, says the biographer of Bonaparte, cost nearly three thousand men, including the killed, and such as died of the plague and their wounds. Had there been less precipitation in the attack, and had the advances been conducted according to the rules of art, the town, says he, could not have held out three days; and one assault such as that of the 8th of May would have sufficed. But he admits that it would have been wiser in their situation, destitute as they were of heavy artillery and provisions, while the place was plentifully supplied and in active communication with the English and Ottoman fleets, not to have undertaken the siege at all. In the bulletins, he adds, always so veracious, the loss of the French is estimated at five hundred killed and a thousand wounded; while that of the enemy is augmented to fifteen thousand. These documents are doubtless singular materials for history,—certainly not because they are true. Bonaparte, however, attached the greatest importance to these narratives, which were always drawn up or corrected by himself.*

The reader may not be displeased to consider the motives which induced Napoleon to persevere so long in the siege of Acre. " I see that this paltry town has cost me many men, and occupies much time; but things have gone too far not to risk a last effort. If we succeed, it is to be hoped we shall find in that place the treasures of the pasha, and arms for three hundred thousand men. I will raise and arm the whole of Syria, which is already greatly exasperated by the cruelty of Djezzar, for whose fall you have seen people supplicate Heaven at every assault. I advance upon Damascus and Aleppo; I recruit my army by marching into every country where discontent prevails; I announce to the people the abolition of slavery, and of the tyrannical government of the pashas; I arrive at Constantinople with armed masses; I overturn the dominion of the Mussulman; I found in the East a new and mighty empire, which shall fix my position with posterity; and perhaps I return to Paris by Adrianople or Vienna, having annihilated the house of Austria."†

Whatever accuracy there may be in these reminiscences, there is no doubt that Napoleon frequently remarked in reference to Acre, " the fate of the East is in that place." Nor was this observation made at random; for had the French subdued Djezzar and buried

---

* Memoirs of Napoleon Bonaparte, vol. i. p. 163.    † Ibid. p. 165.

his army in the ruins of the fortress, the whole of the Syrian provinces would have submitted to their dominion. He expected besides a cordial reception from the Druses, those warlike and semi-barbarous tribes who inhabit the valleys of Libanus, and who, like all the other subjects of the Ottoman government, had felt the pressure of the pasha's tyranny. His eyes were likewise turned towards the Jews, who in every commotion which affects Palestine are accustomed to look for the indications of that happy change destined, in the eye of their faith, to restore the kingdom to Israel in the latter days. It was not indeed till a period somewhat more recent that he openly extended his protection to the descendants of Abraham; but it is not improbable that the notion had occurred to him during his Eastern campaigns, of employing them for the purpose of establishing an independent sovereignty in that country, devoted to his ulterior views beyond the Euphrates.

During the siege of Acre, the several detachments of the French army stationed in Galilee were attacked by a powerful Mussulman force which had assembled in the adjoining mountains. Junot, who was induced to risk an engagement near Nazareth, would have been cut in pieces by the Mamlouk cavalry, had not Bonaparte hastened to his assistance. Allusion has already been made to the masterly conduct of Kleber, who, at the head of a few hundred men, kept the field a whole day against an overwhelming mass of horsemen that attacked his party near Mount Tabor. On this occasion, too, the speedy aid of Napoleon secured a victory, and scattered the enemy's troops over the face of the desert. But he found, upon his return to the trenches, that the same men, whose columns dissipated like smoke before his battalions on the plain, were extremely formidable behind an armed wall; and that all the skill of his engineers and the bravery of his veterans were of no avail, when opposed by the savage courage of Turks directed by European officers and supported by English seamen.

The sufferings which the French endured in their retreat across the desert were very great, and afforded constant exercise for the self-possession and equanimity of their leader. "A fearful journey," says one of their number, "was yet before us. Some of the wounded were carried in litters, and the rest on camels and mules. A devouring thirst, a total want of water, an excessive heat, a fatiguing march among scorching sand-hills, demoralized the men: a most cruel selfishness, the most unfeeling indifference, took place of every generous or humane sentiment. I have seen thrown from the litters officers with amputated limbs, whose conveyance had been ordered, and who had themselves given money as a recompense for the fatigue. I have beheld, abandoned among the wheat-fields, soldiers who had lost their legs or arms, wounded men, and patients supposed to be affected with the plague. Our march was lighted up by torches, kindled for the purpose of setting on fire towns, hamlets, and the rich crops with which the earth was covered. The whole country was in flames. It seemed as if we found a solace in this extent of mischief for our own reverses and sufferings. We were surrounded only by the dying, by plunderers, by incendiaries. Wretched beings at the point of death, thrown by the wayside, continued to call with feeble voice, 'I have not the plague, I am but wounded;' and to convince those that passed, they might be seen tearing open their real wounds, or inflicting new ones. Nobody believed them. It was the interest of all not to believe. Comrades would say, 'He is done for now; his march is over;' then pass on, look to themselves, and feel satisfied. The sun, in all his splendour under that beautiful sky, was obscured by the smoke of continual conflagrations. We had the sea on our right: on our left and behind us lay the desert which we had made; before were the sufferings and privations that awaited us."\*

For some time after the departure of the French, no

---

\* Memoirs of Napoleon Bonaparte, vol. i. p. 168.

event occurred to give any interest to the history of Palestine. The Mussulman instantly resumed his power, which for a time he appeared determined to exercise with a strong hand and with little forbearance towards the Franks, from the terror of whose arms he had just escaped. But the ascendency of Europe, as a great assemblage of Christian States, checked the intolerance of the Turk, and imposed upon him the obligations of a more liberal policy. Hence it may be confidently asserted, that although the members of the Greek and Latin Churches in Syria were severely taxed they were not persecuted. They were compelled to pay heavily for the privilege of exercising the rites of their worship, and of enjoying that freedom of conscience which is the natural inheritance of every human being; but their property was held sacred, and their personal security was not endangered, provided they had the prudence to rest satisfied with a simple connivance, or bare permission, in things relating to their faith.

The state of the Holy Land may indeed be known with sufficient accuracy from the topographical description which we have given in a former chapter. With regard, again, to the civil government of the country, it has been remarked that, the pashas being very frequently changed, and often at war with each other, while the jurisdiction of the magistrates in cities was so undefined, and the hereditary or assumed rights of the sheiks of particular districts were so various, it was extremely difficult to discover any settled rule by which the administration could be conducted. The whole Turkish empire, indeed, has the appearance of being so precariously balanced, that the slightest movement within, or from without, seems likely to overturn it. Every where is seen absolute power stretched beyond the limits of all apparent control, but finding, nevertheless, a counteracting principle in that extreme degree of acuteness to which the instinct of self-preservation is sharpened by the constant apprehension of injury. Hence springs that conflict between force and fraud, not always visible but always operating, which characterizes society in all despotic countries.

In the minute subdivision of power, which in all cases partakes of the arbitrary nature of the supreme government, the traveller is often reminded of patriarchal times; when there were found judges and even kings exercising a separate dominion, at the distance of a short journey from one another. As an instance of this I may mention, that on the road from Jerusalem to Sannour, by way of Nablous, there are no fewer than three governors of cities, all of whom claim the honours of independent sovereigns; for, although they acknowledge a nominal superiority in the Pasha of Damascus, they exclude his jurisdiction in all cases where he does not enforce his authority at the head of his troops. The same affectation of independence descends to the sheiks of villages, who, aware of the uncertain tenure by which their masters remain in office, are disposed to treat their orders with contempt. Like them, too, they turn to their personal advantage the power of imposition and extortion which belongs to every one who is clothed with official rank in Syria. They sell justice and protection; and, in this market as in all others, he who offers the best price is certain to obtain the largest share of the commodity.*

But since the year 1832 a remarkable change has been brought to pass in the political relations as well as the internal government of Palestine. Abdallah, the pasha of Acre, having given offence to his master at Constantinople, was indebted to the Viceroy of Egypt for reconciliation and the continuance of his delegated power. He soon, however, so far forgot this obligation as to afford an asylum to the discontented subjects of Mohammed Ali, and even receive them into his service. Irritated at this ungrateful conduct, and not unwilling perhaps to have so good a pretext for war, the Egyptian

---

* See Jowett's Christian Researches in Syria and the Holy Land, p. 315.

pasha sent his son Ibrahim at the head of a powerful army to attack Abdallah in his own province. As the sultan had not been consulted in these proceedings by either of his lieutenants, he no sooner heard that Acre was besieged than he issued a firman from his capital commanding both of them to resume the attitude of peace. Positive orders were given to Mohammed to withdraw his troops instantly from Syria, and commissioners were despatched to enforce the injunctions of the divan. But these instructions were not regarded by the belligerent parties; and the Porte, accordingly, doubting the fidelity of his great vassal, directed armies to march and fleets to be prepared, in order to punish him as a rebel. The viceroy treated these menaces with contempt, and in defiance of them proceeded to complete his plans for chastising his turbulent neighbour, as well as for extending the limits of his own authority.

The Egyptian army, which amounted to nearly fifty thousand men, had immediately upon entering the Syrian territory, taken with little difficulty the important towns of Gaza, Jaffa, and Caiffa. But Acre, where Abdallah commanded in person, made so strong a defence as to resist successfully during several months all the efforts of the invader by sea and land. The pasha had hoped that relief would be sent by the supreme government, and therefore though the town was reduced to a heap of ruins, he would not consent to surrender it. A Turkish force, indeed, under a leader named Osman, had advanced to Tripoli, who, however, upon hearing that a part of the enemy's troops were moving to attack him, took to a hasty flight, leaving his camp, ammunition, artillery, and provisions. This attempt to support him having failed, the governor of Acre found it necessary to accept terms of accommodation and admit the enemy,—an event which took place in the month of May 1832.

Having by this achievement provoked the utmost resentment of the Porte, the viceroy, without any pretence towards duty or submission, resolved to set his power at defiance, and conquer the whole of Syria. His son, accordingly, having refreshed his troops and received reinforcements, left Acre on the 8th June, and marched directly upon Damascus. He arrived before it on the 14th, and found a considerable body of infantry and cavalry under its walls; but the terror of his name rendered the conflict of short duration. The Turks fled at the first charge; the governor and principal authorities immediately followed the example of the soldiers, and the Egyptian army took possession of the city. After a short interval of repose the victor continued his march through the pashalic of Damascus towards that of Aleppo. On the banks of the Orontes, near a village called Homs, an effort was made to check his progress by an army which he estimated at 20,000, under the command of the pasha, having with him several officers of the same rank who had been expelled from their several governments by the approach of the conquerors. The chief of Aleppo commenced the engagement with great spirit; but finding his undisciplined followers unable to keep the field against the veteran battalions of his adversary, he retired with considerable loss in men as well as of his cannon, tents, and provisions.

When Ibrahim had arrived at Antioch he received notice that a force amounting to 36,000 of all arms, under Hussein Pasha, was posted at Beilan to guard the passes which lead through Mount Taurus. Although the position was very strong, he resolved to hazard an attack; being desirous to conduct his victorious army into Caramania, where he was certain the sultan would listen to such terms as he might think fit to propose for the settlement of affairs in Syria and Egypt. The result fully answered his expectation. At the head of his artillery he silenced the batteries opposed to him, and then carried the heights by main force. Hussein was obliged to give way, after seeing his army dispersed rather than subdued, but was unable after the battle to collect more than one-third of his imposing armament.

This victory gave to Ibrahim the power of crossing

that vast barrier which proves the natural defence of the Turkish empire on its eastern border. The last efforts of the sultan were therefore put forth to stop his farther progress. An army of about sixty thousand men was drawn together under the command of the grand vizier himself, who immediately advanced in search of his antagonist. The hostile lines encountered each other on the 21st December 1832, when a conflict which lasted six hours terminated in the utter defeat of the imperial general. The loss on both sides was very great ; but the vizier, who was wounded and taken prisoner, saw himself, towards the close of the day, entirely destitute of an army, most of the survivors among his men having either fled or joined the invaders. The triumph of Koniah seemed to place Constantinople in the hand of Ibrahim, and the effects might have proved fatal to the Ottoman sovereignty, had not Russia interposed her good offices in its behalf.

Although the Egyptian prince found it expedient to withdraw his victorious bands from Caramania, and to relinquish all the advantages he had gained westward of Mount Taurus, he was allowed to retain, in name of the viceroy his father, all his conquests in Syria and Palestine. Being free from all the stronger prejudices of religion and nationality, the government of Cairo has extended much favour towards Europeans, whose learning and arts are held in the highest esteem. At Damascus, for example, where formerly an English consul was not allowed to enter, the Christians now enjoy the fullest protection. The civic authority is administered by a liberal and enlightened man, who, on account of these qualities, was selected for the office by Mohammed Ali : and at Jerusalem there is no longer to be dreaded the tyranny of a bigoted commander, who thought himself entitled to treat all believers in the gospel as contemptible miscreants. The depredations so generally practised in other days by the lawless Bedouins are now suppressed or greatly checked ; and as a proof of this statement it is only necessary to refer to the fact already mentioned, that Abou-Goosh, the celebrated robber, who used to infest the road from Jaffa to Jerusalem, has been deprived of power by command of Ibrahim Pasha. In the course of a few years, travelling in the Holy Land will be as safe and commodious as it now is on the banks of the Nile.*

This chapter would not be complete were we to omit all allusion to the Jews, the ancient inhabitants of Palestine. Their number, according to a statement lately published in Germany, amounts to between three and four millions, scattered over the face of the whole earth, but still maintaining the same laws which their ancestors received from their inspired legislator more than three thousand years ago. In Europe there are nearly two millions, enjoying different degrees of political privilege, according to the spirit of the several governments; in Asia, the estimate exceeds seven hundred thousand; in Africa, more than half a million; and in America, about ten thousand. It is supposed, however, on good grounds, that the Jewish population on both sides of Mount Taurus is considerably greater than is here given, and that their gross number does not fall much short of five millions.†

In Palestine, of late years, they have greatly increased. It is said that not fewer than ten thousand inhabit Saphet and Jerusalem; and that in their worship they still sing those pathetic hymns which their manifold tribulations have inspired; bewailing amid the ruins of their ancient capital the fallen city and the desolate tribes. In Persia one of them addressed a Christian missionary in these affecting words:—" I have travelled far; the Jews are every where princes in comparison with those in the land of Iran. Heavy is our captivity, heavy is our burden, heavy is our slavery; anxiously we wait for redemption."

History, says an eloquent writer, is the record of the

---

* Hogg's Damascus, vol. i p. 150; and vol. ii. p. 23. Annual Register for the years 1832, 1833.

† Weimar Geographical Ephemerides; and History of the Jews, vol. iii. p. 410.

past; it presumes not to raise the mysterious veil which the Almighty has spread over the future. The destinies of this wonderful people, as of all mankind, are in the hands of the all-wise Ruler of the universe : his decrees will certainly be accomplished; his truth, his goodness, and his wisdom, will be clearly vindicated. This, however, we may venture to assert, that true religion will advance with the dissemination of sound and useful knowledge. The more enlightened the Jew becomes, the more incredible will it appear to him that the gracious Father of the whole human race intended an exclusive faith, a creed confined to one family, to be permanent; and the more evident also will it appear to him that a religion, which embraces within the sphere of its benevolence all the kindreds and languages of the earth, is alone adapted to an improved and civilized age.*

We presume not to expound the signs of the times, nor to see farther than we are necessarily led by the course of events; but it is impossible not to be struck with the aspect of that grandest of all moral phenomena which is suspended upon the history and actual condition of the sons of Jacob. At this moment they are nearly as numerous as when David swayed the sceptre of the Twelve Tribes; their expectations are the same, their longings are the same; and on whatever part of the earth's surface they have their abode, their eyes and their faith are all pointed in the same direction,—to the land of their fathers, and the holy city where they worshipped. Though rejected by God and persecuted by man, they have not once, during eighteen hundred long years, ceased to repose confidence in the promises made by Jehovah to the founders of their nation; and although the heart has often been sick, and the spirit faint, they have never relinquished the hope of that bright reversion in the latter days, which is once more to establish the Lord's house on the top of the mountains, and to make Jerusalem the glory of the whole world.

---

* History of the Jews, vol. iii. p. 418.

## CHAPTER IX.

### *The Natural History of Palestine.*

Travellers too much neglect Natural History—Maundrell, Hasselquist, Clarke—GEOLOGY—Syrian Chain—Libanus—Calcareous Rocks—Granite—Trap—Volcanic Remains—Earthquakes and Volcanic Eruptions in Syria and Southern Italy—Chalk—Marine Exuvia—Precious Stones—METEOROLOGY—Climate of Palestine—Winds—Thunder—Clouds—Waterspouts—Ignis Fatuus—ZOOLOGY—Scripture Animals—The Hart—The Roebuck—Fallow-deer—Wild-goat—Pygarg—Wild-ox—Chamois—Unicorn—Wild-ass—Wild-goats of the Rock—Saphan, or Coney—Mouse—Porcupine—Jerboa—Mole—Bat—BIRDS—Eagle—Ossifrage—Ospray—Vulture—Kite—Raven—Owl—Night-hawk—Cuckoo—Hawk—Little Owl—Cormorant—Great Owl—Swan—Pelican—Gier Eagle—Stork—Heron—Lapwing—Hoopoe—AMPHIBIA AND REPTILES—Serpents known to the Hebrews—Ephe—Chephir—Acshub—Pethen—Tzeboa—Tzimmaon—Tzepho—Kippos—Shephiphon—Shachal—Saraph, the Flying-serpent—Cockatrice Eggs—The Scorpion—Sea-monsters, or Seals—FRUITS AND PLANTS—Vegetable Productions of Palestine—The Fig-tree—Palm—Olive—Cedars of Libanus—Wild-grapes—Balsam of Aaron—Thorn of Christ.

EVERY one who writes on the Holy Land has occasion to regret that travellers in general have paid so little attention to its geological structure and natural productions. Maundrell, it is true, was not entirely destitute of physical science; but the few remarks which he makes are extremely vague and unconnected, and, not being expressed in the language of system, throw very little light on the researches of the natural philosopher or the geologist. Hasselquist had more professional learning, and has accordingly contributed, more than any of his predecessors, to our acquaintance with Palestine, viewed in its relations to the animal, the vegetable, and the mineral kingdoms. Still the reader of his Voyages and Travels in the Levant cannot fail to perceive, that some of the branches of knowledge, which are now cultivated with the greatest care, were in his day very little improved; and more especially, that they were extremely deficient in accuracy of description and distinctness of arrangement. Dr Clarke's observations are perhaps more scientific than those of the Swedish naturalist just named, and particularly in the departments of mineralogy and geology, to which he had devoted a large share of his attention. But even in his works we look in vain for a satisfactory treatise on the mountain-rocks of Syria; on the geognostic formation of that interesting part of Western Asia; or on the fossil treasures which its strata are understood to envelop. We are therefore reduced to the necessity of collecting from various authors, belonging to different countries and successive ages, the scattered notices which appear in their works, and of arranging them according to a plan most likely to suit the comprehension of the common reader.

### SECTION I.—GEOLOGY.

At first view it would appear that the ridges of Palestine are all a ramification of Mount Taurus. But the proper Syrian chain begins on the south of Antioch, at the huge peak of Casius, which shoots up to the heavens its tapering summit, covered with thick forests. The same chain, under various names, follows the direction of the eastern shore of the Mediterranean, at no greater distance, generally speaking, than twenty-four miles from its waters. Mount Libanus forms its most elevated point. At length it is divided into two branches, of which the one looks westward to the sea, the other, which bounds the plain of Damascus, verges in the direction of the desert and the banks of the Euphrates. Hermon, whose lofty top condenses the moisture of the atmosphere, and gives rise to the dews so much celebrated in the Sacred Writings, stands between Baalbec and the capital of Syria. The latter ridge received from the Greeks the denomination of Anti-Libanus,—a name unknown among the natives, and which, being employed somewhat arbitrarily by historians and topographers, has occasioned considerable obscurity in their writings.

The hills in this district are composed of a calcareous rock, which has a whitish colour, is extremely hard, and rings in the ear when smartly struck with a hammer. The same description applies to the masses that surround Jerusalem, which on the one hand stretch to the river Jordan, and on the other extend to the plain of Acre and Jaffa. Like all limestone strata, they present a great number of caverns, to which, as places of retreat, frequent allusion is made in the books of Samuel and of the Kings. There is one near Damascus, capable of containing four thousand men; and it must have been in a similar recess that David and his followers encountered their unhappy sovereign when pursued by him on the hills of the wild-goats.

The mountains that skirt the Valley of the Dead Sea present granite and those other rocks which, according to the system of Werner, characterize the oldest or primitive formation. Mount Sinai is a member of the same group, and exhibits mineral qualities of a similar nature, extending to a certain distance on both sides of the Arabian Gulf. It is probable that this region, at a remote epoch, was the theatre of immense volcanoes, the effects of which may still be traced along the banks of the Lower Jordan, and more especially on the lake itself. The warm baths at Tabaria show that the same cause still exists, although much restricted in its operation,—an inference which is amply confirmed by the lavas, the bitumen, and pumice, which continue to be thrown ashore by the waves.

Syria and Palestine, says Mr Lyell, abound in volcanic appearances, and very extensive areas have been shaken at different periods, with great destruction of cities and loss of life. Continual mention is made in history of the ravages committed by earthquakes in Sidon, Tyre,

Berytus, Laodicea, and Antioch, as also in the island of Cyprus. The country around the Dead Sea appears evidently, from the accounts of modern travellers, to be volcanic. A district near Smyrna, in Asia Minor, was termed by the Greeks Katakekaumene, or the Burnt, where there is a large arid territory without trees and with a cindery soil.

The same author has collected some interesting observations on the "periodical alternation of earthquakes in Syria and Southern Italy." It has been remarked by Von Hoff that, from the commencement of the thirteenth to the latter half of the seventeenth century, there was an almost entire cessation of earthquakes in Syria and Judea; and during this interval of quiescence, the Archipelago, together with part of the adjacent coast of Lesser Asia, as also Southern Italy and Sicily, suffered greatly from that cause,—volcanic eruptions being at the same period unusually frequent in the same regions. A more extended comparison, also, of the history of the subterranean convulsions of these tracts seems to confirm the opinion that a violent crisis of commotion never visits both at the same time. It is impossible for us to declare, as yet, whether this phenomenon is constant in this and other regions, because we can rarely trace back a connected series of events farther than a few centuries; but it is well known that where numerous cones are clustered together within a small area, two of them are never in violent eruption at once. If the action of one becomes very great for a century or more, the others assume the appearance of spent volcanoes. It is therefore not improbable that separate provinces of the same great range of volcanic fires may hold a relation to one deep-seated focus, analogous to that which the apertures of a small group bear to some more superficial rent or cavity. Thus, for example, we may conjecture that at a comparatively small distance from the surface Ischia and Vesuvius mutually communicate with certain fissures, and that each affords relief alternately to elastic fluids and lava there generated. So we may suppose Southern Italy and Syria to be connected at a much greater depth with a lower part of the very same system of fissures; in which case any obstruction occurring in one duct may have the effect of causing almost all the vapours and melted matter to be forced up the other, and if they cannot get vent, they may be the cause of violent earthquakes.*

I have already alluded to that great volcanic convulsion mentioned in the nineteenth chapter of Genesis, which, interrupting the course of the river Jordan, converted into a lake the fertile plain occupied by the cities of Adma, Zeboim, Sodom and Gomorrah, and reduced all the valley southward to the condition of a sandy waste.†

Dr Clarke remarks that in the neighbourhood of Cana there are several basaltic appearances. The extremities of columns, prismatically formed, penetrate the surface of the soil, so as to render the path very rough and unpleasant. These marks of regular or of irregular crystallization generally denote, according to his opinion, the vicinity of water lying beneath their level. The traveller having passed over a series of successive plains, resembling in their gradation the order of a staircase, observes, as he descends to the inferior stratum upon which the water rests, that crystallization has taken place, and then the prismatic configuration is commonly denoted basaltic. Such an appearance, therefore, in the approach to the Lake of Tiberias is only a parallel to similar phenomena exhibited by rocks near the lakes of Locarno and Bolsenna in Italy, by those of the Wener Lake in Sweden, by the bed of the Rhine near Cologne in Germany, by the Valley of Ronca in the territory of Verona, by the Pont de Bridon in the State of Venice, and by numerous other examples in the same country. A corresponding effect is produced on a small scale on the southern declivity of Arthur Seat, at Edinburgh, near the spot where the hill overhangs the Lake of Duddingstone; and numerous other instances are known to occur in the islands which

---

\* Principles of Geology, book ii. part ii. chap. i.
† See page 211. Burckhardt's Travels in Syria, preface, p. vi.

lie between the coast of Ireland and Norway, as well as in Spain, Portugal, Arabia, and India.

When these huge crystals have obtained a certain regularity of structure, the form is often hexagonal, or six-sided, resembling particular kinds of spar and the emerald. Patrin, during his travels in the deserts of Oriental Tartary, discovered when breaking the Asiatic emerald, if fresh taken from the matrix, not only the same alternate concave and convex fractures which sometimes characterize the horizontal fissures of basaltic pillars, but also the concentric layers which denote concretionary formation. It is hardly possible to have a more striking proof of coincidence, resulting from similarity of structure, in two substances otherwise remarkably distinguished from each other. At present geological science cannot pronounce more distinctly concerning an appearance in nature which, perhaps, exhibits nothing more than the common process of crystallization upon a larger scale than has usually excited attention. Suffice it to remark, that such a phenomenon is very frequent in the vicinity of very ancient lakes, in the bed of all considerable rivers, or by the borders of the ocean.*

In a country where there are so many traces of volcanic action, the rocks of the lower levels cannot fail to bear marks of their origin. Hasselquist relates, that the hill of Tiberias, out of which issues the fountain whence the baths are supplied, consists of a black and brittle sulphurous stone, which is only to be found in large masses in that neighbourhood, though it is commonly met with in rolled specimens on the shores of the Dead Sea, and in other parts of the great Valley of the Jordan. The sediment deposited by the water is also black, as thick as paste, smells strongly of sulphur, and is covered with two skins or cuticles, of which the lower is of a fine dark-green, and the uppermost of a light rusty colour. At the mouth of the outlet, where the stream formed little cascades over the stones, the first cuticle alone was found, and so much resembled a conferva, that one might have taken it for a vegetable

---

* See Clarke's Travels, vol. iv. p. 191.

production; but nearer the river, where the current became stagnant, both skins were visible, the yellow on the surface, and under it the green.\*

There are observed, in the same hollow, small portions of quartz incrusted with an impure salt, and nodules of clay extremely compact. Near the edge of the valley there lie scattered on the sand considerable portions of flinty slate; and amid the common clay, which forms the basis of the soil, are perpendicular layers of a lamellated brown argil, assuming, as it were, the slaty structure. Dr Clarke noticed among the pebbles near the Lake of Tiberias pieces of a porous rock resembling the substance called toadstone in England; its cavities were filled with zeolite. Native gold was likewise found there; but the quantity was so small as not to draw from the travellers a suitable degree of attention.

The vale of the Asphaltites is farther remarkable for a species of limestone called the fetid, the smell of which, as its name imports, is extremely offensive. It is still manufactured in the East into amulets, and worn as a specific against the plague; and that a similar superstition existed with regard to this stone in very early ages is rendered manifest by the circumstance, that charms made of the same substance were found in the subterranean chambers under the pyramids of Sakhara in Upper Egypt. The cause of the fetid effluvia emitted from this rock, when partially decomposed by means of friction, is now known to be connected with the presence of sulphuretted hydrogen. All bituminous limestone, however, does not possess this property. It is not uncommon in the calcareous beds called in England black marble, but it is by no means their characteristic quality. The fragments obtained in the valley of the Jordan have this savour in a high degree; and it is admitted that the oriental limestone is more highly impregnated with hydro-sulphuret than any hitherto found in Europe.†

According to Dr Shaw, the upper strata of rocks on the hills along the coast are composed of a soft chalky

---

\* Hasselquist's Voyages and Travels, p. 284.
† Clarke's Travels, vol. iv. pp. 223, 307.

substance, including a great variety of corals, shells, and other marine exuviæ. Upon the Castravan mountains, near Beirout, there is a singular bed, consisting likewise of a whitish stone, but of the slate-kind, which unfolds in every flake of it a great number and variety of fishes. These, for the most part, lie exceedingly flat and compressed, like the fossil specimens of fern; yet are, at the same time, so well preserved, that the smallest lineaments and fibres of their fins, scales, and other specific properties of structure, are easily distinguished. Among these were some individuals of the squilla tribe, which, though one of the tenderest of the crustaceous family, had not suffered the least injury from pressure or friction. The heights of Carmel, too, present similar phenomena. In the chalky beds which surround its summit are gathered numerous hollow flints, lined in the inside with a variety of sparry matter, and having some resemblance to petrified fruit. These are commonly bestowed upon pilgrims, not only as curiosities, but as antidotes against several distempers. Those which bear a likeness to the olive, usually denominated "lapides judaici," are looked upon, when dissolved in the juice of lemons, as an approved medicine for curing the stone and gravel,—a specific, we may presume, which, after the fashion of many others, operates upon the body through the power of the imagination.*

The miserable condition of ignorance and neglect into which every thing connected with industry has fallen under the Turkish government, prevents us from obtaining any information in regard to the mineral stores of that country, "whose stones are iron, and out of whose hills thou mayest dig brass." Volney indeed relates, that ores of the former metal abound in the mountains of Kesraoun and of the Druses, in other words, in the extensive range of which Libanus is the principal member. Every summer the inhabitants work those mines, which are simply ochreous. There is a

* Travels or Observations relating to several Parts of Barbary and the Levant, vol. ii. p. 153.

vague report in the district, that there was anciently a vein of copper near Aleppo ; but it must have been long since abandoned. It was also mentioned to the traveller, when among the Druses, that a mineral was discovered which produced both lead and silver; though, as such a discovery would have ruined the whole district by attracting the attention of the Turks, they made haste to destroy every vestige of it. A similar feeling prevails respecting precious stones,—that branch of mineralogy which first gains the attention of a rude people. From the geological character of the Syrian mountains, there is no doubt that Palestine might boast of the topaz, the emerald, the chrysoberyl, several varieties of rock-crystal, and also of the finer jaspers. The Sacred Writings prove that the Jews were acquainted with a considerable variety of ornamental stones, as may be seen in the description of the mystical city in the book of Revelation, of which " the twelve gates were twelve pearls." But the present inhabitants of Canaan, regardless of the natural wealth with which the hills and the valleys abound, trust to violence for the means of luxury, and to the most unprincipled extortion and robbery for their accustomed revenue. From them, therefore, neither knowledge nor elegance can ever be expected to receive any attention.

### SECTION II.—METEOROLOGY.

Under this head we include the usual properties of the atmosphere which minister to health and vegetation, for it has been justly remarked that Syria has three climates. The summits of Libanus, for instance, covered with snow, diffuse a salubrious coolness in the interior ; the flat situations, on the contrary, especially those which stretch along the line of the coast, are constantly subjected to heat, accompanied with great humidity ; while the adjoining plains of the desert are scorched by the rays of a burning sun. The seasons and the productions undergo a corresponding variation. In the mountains the months of spring and summer very nearly coincide with those in the southern parts of Europe; and the winter, which lasts from November to March, is sharp and rigorous. No year passes without snow, which often covers the surface of the ground to the depth of several feet during a continuance of many weeks. The spring and autumn are agreeable, and the summer by no means oppressive. But in the plains, on the other hand, as soon as the sun has passed the equator, a sudden transition takes place to an overpowering heat, which continues till October. To compensate for this, the winter is so temperate that orange-trees, dates, bananas, and other delicate fruits, grow every where in the open field. Hence, we need hardly observe that a journey of a few hours carries the traveller through a succession of seasons, and allows him a choice of climate; varying from the mild temperature of France to the blood-heat of India, or the pinching cold of Russia.

The winds in Palestine, as in all countries which approach the tropics, are periodical, and governed in no small degree by the course of the sun. About the autumnal equinox, the north-west begins to blow with frequency and strength, rendering the air dry, clear, and sharp; and it is remarkable that on the seacoast it causes the headach, like the north-east wind in Egypt. We may farther observe that it usually blows three days successively, like the south and south-east at the other equinox. It continues to prevail till November, that is, about fifty days, when it is followed by the west and south-west, called by the Arabs, " the fathers of rain." In March arise the pernicious winds from the southern quarter, with the same circumstances as in Egypt; but they become feebler as we advance towards the north, and are much more supportable in the mountains than in the low country. Their duration at each return varies from twenty-four hours to three days. The easterly winds, which come next in order, continue till June, when they are commonly succeeded by an inconstant breeze from the north. At this season the wind shifts through all the points every day, passing with the sun from east to south, and from south to west, to return by the north and recommence the same circuit. At this time, too, a local wind, called the land-breeze, prevails along the coast during the night; it springs up after sunset, lasts till the appearance of the solar orb in the morning, and extends only a few leagues to sea.

Travellers have observed that thunder, in the low lands of Palestine as well as in Egypt, is more common during the winter than in summer; while in the mountains, it is more frequent in the latter season, and very seldom heard in the former. In both these countries it happens oftenest in the rainy months, or about the time of the equinoxes, especially the autumnal; and it is farther remarkable that it never comes from the land-side, but always from the sea. These storms, too, generally speaking, take place either in the evening or morning, and rarely in the middle of the day. They are accompanied with violent showers of rain, and sometimes of uncommonly large hail, which, soon covering the face of the country with stagnant water, give rise to a copious evaporation.

The phenomenon alluded to by the prophet Elijah is still found to diversify the aspect of the eastern sky. Volney remarks, that clouds are sometimes seen to dissolve and disperse like smoke; while on other occasions they form in an instant, and from a small speck increase to a prodigious size. This is particularly observable at the summit of Lebanon; and mariners have usually found that the appearance of a cloud on this peak is an infallible presage of a westerly wind, one of the precursors of rain in the climate of Judea.*

Waterspouts are not unfrequent along the shores of Syria, and more especially in the neighbourhood of Mount Carmel. Those observed by Dr Shaw appeared to be so many cylinders of water falling down from the clouds; though by the reflection, it might be, of these descending columns, or from the actual dropping of the fluid contained in them, they would sometimes, says he, appear at a distance to be sucked up from the sea. The theory of waterspouts in the present day does in fact

---

* Travels or Observations, vol. ii. p. 135.

admit the supposition here referred to; that the air, being rarefied by particular causes, has its equilibrium restored by the elevation of the water, on the same principle that mercury rises in the barometer, or the contents of a well in a common pump. But the opinions of the learned traveller on this subject are extremely loose and unscientific, and are only valuable in our times as marking a certain stage in the progress of meteorological inquiry.

The same author has recorded a fact which we have not observed in the pages of any other tourist. In travelling by night, in the beginning of April, through the valleys of Mount Ephraim, he was attended for more than an hour by an *ignis fatuus* that displayed itself in a variety of extraordinary appearances. It was sometimes globular, and sometimes pointed like the flame of a candle; then it spread so as to involve the whole company in its pale inoffensive light; after which it contracted and suddenly disappeared. But in less than a minute it would begin again to exert itself as at other times, running along from one place to another with great swiftness, like a train of gunpowder set on fire; or else it would expand over more than two or three acres of the adjacent mountains, discovering every shrub and tree that grew upon them. The atmosphere from the beginning of the evening had been remarkably thick and hazy, and the dew, as felt upon the bridles, was unusually clammy and unctuous. In such weather similar luminous bodies are observed skipping about the masts and yards of ships, and are called by the mariners *corpusanse*, a corruption of the *cuerpo santo*, or sacred body, of the Spaniards. The same were the Castor and Pollux of the ancients. Some writers have attempted to account for these phenomena, particularly for the *ignis fatuus*, by supposing it to be occasioned by successive swarms of flying glow-worms, or other insects of the same nature. But, as Dr Shaw observes, not to perceive or feel any of these insects, even when the light which they produce spreads itself around us, should induce us to explain both this appearance and the other on the received principle that they are actually meteors, or a species of natural phosphorus.*

### SECTION III.—ZOOLOGY.

In this article we shall confine our attention to such animals as are mentioned in Holy Scripture; our object being restricted to an elucidation of the natural history of Palestine as it presents itself to the common reader, and not according to the arrangement which might be required by the rules of science.

In the fourteenth chapter of Deuteronomy, where a distinction is made between the clean and the unclean, or those which might be eaten and such as were prohibited, we find in the former class the ox, the sheep, the goat, the hart, the roebuck, the fallow-deer, the wild-goat, the pygarg, the wild-ox, and the chamois. As to the three first, being domesticated animals which are common in all countries, we shall not waste time by exhibiting any description. The next in order, the "hart," is also quite familiar; but every scholar knows that the Hebrew term *Aïl* is so vague in its import, that it has been understood to signify a tree as well as a quadruped. Thus the fine expression in the forty-ninth chapter of Genesis, uttered by Jacob in reference to one of his children, " Naphtali is a hind let loose; he giveth goodly words," has been translated by Bochart, Houbigant, and others, in these terms, " Naphtali is a spreading tree, giving out beautiful branches." The meaning of the Patriarch unquestionably was, that the tribe about to descend from his son would be active and powerful, enjoying at once unrestrained freedom and abundance of food. It might be expressed thus: Naphtali is a deer roaming at liberty, he shooteth forth noble branches, or majestic antlers; his residence shall be in a beautiful woodland country; and, as Moses also predicted, " he shall be filled with the blessings of the Lord."

The *roebuck*, or tzebi of the Hebrews, is regarded by Dr Shaw as the gazelle or antelope, a beautiful creature,

---

\* Travels through Syria and Egypt, vol. i. p. 313.

which is very common all over Syria, the Holy Land, Egypt, and Barbary. It is known among Greek naturalists by the name of *dorcas*, from an allusion to its fine eyes, the brilliancy and liveliness of which have passed into a proverb in all eastern countries. The damsel whose name was Tabitha, which is by interpretation Dorcas, might be so called from this particular feature. The antelope likewise is in great esteem among the Orientals for food, having a very sweet musky taste, which is highly agreeable to their palates; and therefore the tzebi might well be received as one of the dainties at Solomon's table.\* If then, says the author just quoted, we lay all these circumstances together, they will appear to be much more applicable to the gazelle or antelope, which is a quadruped well known and gregarious, than to the roe, which was either not known at all, or was at least extremely rare in those countries.

The *fallow-deer*, or yachmur of the Bible, is received among commentators as the *wild-beeve*,—an animal equal in size to the stag or red-deer, to which it bears some resemblance. It frequents the solitary parts of Judea and the surrounding countries, and, like the antelope, is every where gregarious. Its flesh is also very sweet and nourishing, and was frequently seen at the tables of kings.

The *wild-goat*, or akko, mentioned in Deuteronomy, is not held sufficiently specific by naturalists, who imagine that it must be identified with another animal called by the Seventy *tragelaphus*, literally the goat-deer. The horns of this species, which are furrowed and wrinkled as in the goat-kind, are a foot or fifteen inches long, and bend over the back, though they are shorter and more crooked than those of the ibex or steinbuck. It is not unfrequently known by the more familiar name of *lerwee*.

Considerable obscurity hangs over the natural history of the *pygarg*, the characteristics of which have not hitherto been well determined. The word itself, it has been remarked, seems to denote a creature whose hinder parts are of a white colour. Such, says Dr Shaw, is the *lidmee*, which is shaped exactly like the common ante-

---
\* 1 Kings, iv. 23.

lope, with which it agrees in colour and in the shape of its horns ; only that in the lidmee they are of twice the length, as the animal itself is of twice the size.

The sixth species is the *wild-ox*, or thau of the Mosaical catalogue, which has generally been rendered the *oryx*. Now this animal is admitted to be of the goat-species, with the hair growing forward, or towards the head. It is farther described to be of the size of a beeve, and to be likewise a fierce creature, contrary to what is observed of the goat or deer kind ; which, unless they are irritated and highly provoked, are all of them of a shy and timorous nature. The only quadruped that we are acquainted with, to which these marks will apply, is the buffalo, well known in Egypt and in various parts of Western Asia. It may be so far reckoned of the goat-kind, as the horns are not smooth and even as in the beeve, but rough and wrinkled as in the former. It is besides nearly the same as the common beeve, and therefore agrees to this extent with the description of Herodotus. It is also a sullen, spiteful animal, being often known to pursue the unwary, especially if clad in scarlet. For these reasons the buffalo may not improperly be taken for the thau or oryx, whereof we have had hitherto little account.*

The *chamois*, or zomer of the ancient Jews, has by different authors been described as the camelopard or giraffe. The Syriac version renders the original term into one which signifies the mountain-goat, and in this respect coincides with our common translation of the Scriptures ; though it is extremely doubtful whether, in the days of Moses, the chamois or the ibex was to be found in any district of Palestine. Dr Shaw holds the opinion that the zomer must have been the giraffe ; for though it was a rare animal, and not known in Europe before the dictatorship of Julius Cæsar, it might, he thinks, have been common enough in Egypt, as it was a native of Ethiopia, the adjoining country. It may therefore be presumed, says he, that the Israelites, during their long residence in the land of the Pharaohs, were

---

* Shaw's Travels, vol. ii. p. 280.

not only well acquainted with it, but might at different times have tasted its flesh.

This inference is rejected, with some show of reason, by the editor of Calmet's Dictionary, who remarks, it is very unlikely that the giraffe, being a native of the torrid zone and attached to hot countries, should be so abundant in Judea as to be made an article of food. The same argument applies to the chamois, which, as it inhabits the highest mountains, and seeks the most elevated spots, where snow and ice prevail, to shelter it from the heat of summer, was probably unknown to the people of Israel. Hence it still remains doubtful to what class of animals the zomer of Moses should be attached, though in our opinion the balance of authorities seems to incline in favour of a small species of goat which browsed in the hill-country of Syria.

The *unicorn*, or reem, mentioned in the book of Job, has given similar occasion to a variety of opinion. Parkhurst imagines that by this term is meant the wild-bull, for it is evidently an animal of great strength, and possessed of horns. Mr Scott, in his Commentary on the Bible, adopts the same view, and reminds his reader that the bulls of Bashan described by the Psalmist are by the same inspired writer denominated reems. Other expounders of Sacred Writ maintain, that the creature alluded to by the Patriarch of Uz can have been no other than the double-horned rhinoceros.[*]

The *wild-ass*, or para, celebrated by the same ancient author, is generally understood to be the onager, an animal which is to this day highly prized in Persia and the deserts of Tartary, as being fitter for the saddle than the finest breed of horses. It has nothing of the dullness or stupidity of the common ass; is extremely beautiful; and, when properly trained, is docile and tractable in no common degree. It was this more valuable kind of ass that Saul was in search of when he was chosen by the prophet to discharge the duties of royalty. "Who hath sent out the wild-ass free? or who hath loosed the bands of the wild-ass? Whose house I have made the wilder-

---

[*] Job, xxxix. 9, 10, 11, 12.

ness, and the barren land his dwellings. He scorneth the multitude of the city, neither regardeth he the crying of the driver. The range of the mountains is his pasture, and he searcheth after every green thing."*

The "wild-goats of the rock," described in the chapter just quoted, are supposed to be the same as the ibex or bouquetin. This animal is larger than the tame goat, but resembles it much in form. The head is small in proportion to the body, with the muzzle thick and compressed, and a little arched. The eyes are large and round, and have much fire and brilliancy. The horns are so majestic, that when fully grown they occasionally weigh sixteen or eighteen pounds. He feeds during the night in the highest woods; but the sun no sooner begins to gild the summits, than he quits the woody region, and mounts, feeding in his progress, till he has reached the most considerable heights. The female shows much attachment to her young, and even defends it against eagles, wolves, and other enemies. She takes refuge in some cavern, and, presenting her head at the entrance, resolutely opposes the assailants. Hence the allusion to this affectionate creature in the book of Proverbs: "Let thy wife be as the loving hind and the pleasant roe."

The saphan of the Bible is usually translated *coney*. " The high hills are a refuge for the wild-goats, and the rocks for the conies." But it is now believed that the ashkoko, an animal mentioned by Bruce, presents properties which accord much better with the description of the saphan given in different parts of the Old Testament, than the coney, hare, or rabbit. This curious creature, we are told by that traveller, is found in Ethiopia, in the caverns of the rocks, or under great stones. It does not burrow or make holes like the rat or rabbit, nature having interdicted this practice by furnishing it with feet, the toes of which are perfectly round, and of a soft, pulpy, tender substance: the fleshy part of them projects beyond the nails, which are rather sharp, very similar to a man's nails ill-grown, and appear given to it rather for the defence of its soft toes, than

---
* Job, xxxix. 5, 6, 7, 8.

for any active use in digging, to which they are by no means adapted.*

A learned writer, who has considered this subject with great attention, gives as the result of his inquiry, that the saphan of the ancient Hebrews, rendered "coney" in the English Bible, is a very different animal; that it has a nearer resemblance to the hedgehog, the bear, the mouse, the jerboa, or the marmot, though it is not any of these. It is the webro of the Arabians, the daman-Israel of Shaw, the ashkoko of Bruce, and clipdass of the Dutch.†

The prophet Isaiah, in recording the idolatrous and profane habits of his countrymen, mentions the " eating of swine's flesh, and the abomination, and the *mouse*." This is supposed to be the jerboa, an animal common in the East, about the size of a rat, and which uses only its hind-legs. There can be little doubt that this is the creature alluded to by the Hebrew legislator when he said, " whatsoever goeth upon its *paws*, among all manner of beasts that go on all four, those are unclean unto you." Hasselquist tells us that the jerboa, or leaping-rat as he calls it, moves only by leaps and jumps. When he stops he brings his feet close under his belly, and rests on the juncture of his leg. He uses, when eating, his fore-paws, like other animals of his kind. He sleeps by day and is in motion during the night. He eats corn and grains of sesamum. Though he does not fear man, he is not easily tamed; for which reason he must be kept in a cage.

The *porcupine*, or kephad, is spoken of in the writings of Isaiah under the denomination of the bittern. " I will make Babylon a possession for the bittern and pools of water." In another chapter, the inspired author associates the kephad with the pelican, with the yanshaph or ardea-ibis, and with oreb, or the raven-kind; and hence a considerable difficulty has arisen with regard to the class of animals in which it ought to be ranked. Bochart had no doubt that the porcupine was in the

---

* Appendix to Bruce's Travels, p. 139.
† See an article in the sixth volume of the Wernerian Memoirs by the late Professor Scott of St Andrews, "On the Animal called Saphan in the Hebrew Scriptures."

mind of the prophet when he wrote the description of the Assyrian capital wasted and abandoned. This creature is a native of the hottest climates of Africa and India, and yet can live and multiply in milder latitudes. It is now found in Spain, and in the Apennines near Rome. Pliny asserts that the porcupine, like the bear, hides itself in winter. In a Memoir on Babylon, by the late Mr Rich, it is stated that great quantities of porcupine-quills were found on the spot; and that in most of the cavities are numbers of bats and owls.

The mole and the bat are reckoned among the unclean animals forbidden to the Jews by their Divine lawgiver. The latter is distinctly included under the following description : " Every creeping thing that flieth shall be unclean to you ; they shall not be eaten." The legs of the bat appear to be absolutely different from those of all other animals, and indeed they are directed, and even formed, in a very particular manner. In order to advance, he raises both his front-legs at once, and places them at a small distance forward ; at the same time the thumb of each foot points outward, and the creature catches with the claw at any thing which it can lay hold of; then he stretches behind him his two hind-legs, so that the five toes of each foot are also directed backward : he supports himself on the sole of this foot, and secures himself by means of the claws on his toes; then he raises his body on the front-legs, and throws himself forward by folding the upper arm on the fore-arm, which motion is assisted by the extension of the hind-legs, which also push the body forward. This gait, though heavy, because the body falls to the ground at every step, is yet sometimes pretty quick, when the feet can readily meet with good holding-places ; but when the claw of the front-foot meets with any thing loose, the exertion is inefficient.*

---

* Daubenton. Calmet, vol. iv. p. 645. See also Shaw, Hasselquist, and Bochart.

## SECTION IV.—BIRDS.

In the writings of Moses the winged tribes are divided into three classes, according as they occupy the air, the land, or the water.

### BIRDS OF THE AIR.

| English Translation. | Probable Species. |
|---|---|
| Eagle, | Eagle. |
| Ossifrage, | Vulture. |
| Ospray, | Black Eagle. |
| Vulture, | Hawk. |
| Kite, | Kite. |
| Raven, | Raven. |

### LAND BIRDS.

| | |
|---|---|
| Owl, | Ostrich. |
| Night-hawk, | Night-owl. |
| Cuckoo, | Saf-saf. |
| Hawk, | Ancient Ibis. |

### WATER BIRDS.

| | |
|---|---|
| Little Owl, | Sea-gull. |
| Cormorant, | Cormorant. |
| Great Owl, | Ibis Ardea. |
| Swan, | Wild-goose. |
| Pelican, | Pelican. |
| Gier Eagle, | Alcyone. |
| Stork, | Stork. |
| Heron, | Long Neck. |
| Lapwing, | Hoopoe. |

These are the unclean birds, according to the Mosaical arrangement and the views of the English translators. But it must not be concealed, that the attainments of the latter in ornithology were not particularly accurate; and, as a proof of this, we may mention a fact obvious to the youngest student of Oriental languages, that the same Hebrew words in Leviticus and Deuteronomy are not always rendered by the same term in our tongue. For example, the vulture of the former book is in the latter called the glede; and there are many similar variations, in different parts of the Old Testament, with regard to the others.

The *swan*, or tinshemet of the Hebrews, is a very doubtful bird. The Seventy render it by *porphyrion*, which signifies a purple hen, a water-fowl well known in the East. Dr Geddes observes, that the root or etymon of the term *tinshemet* denotes *breathing* or *respiring*,—a description which is supposed to point to a well-known quality in the swan, that of being able to respire a long time with its bill and neck under water, and even plunged in mud. Parkhurst thinks the conjecture of Michaelis not improbable, namely, "that it is the goose, which every one knows is remarkable for its manner of breathing out or hissing when provoked." The latter writer observes, " what makes me conjecture this is, that the Chaldee interpreters who in Leviticus render it *obija*, do not use this word in Deuteronomy, but substitute the ' white kak,' which, according to Buxtorf, denotes the goose." Norden mentions a goose of the Nile whose plumage is extremely beautiful. The flesh is of an exquisite aromatic taste, smells of ginger, and has a great deal of flavour. Can this be the Hebrew *tinshemet*, and the *porphyrion* of the Seventy?

Again, it is conjectured by modern naturalists that the heron should be included among storks. Commentators, it is true, are quite at a loss in regard to the precise import of the original term *anapha*, and some of them, accordingly, leave it altogether untranslated. It is not improbable that the Longneck mentioned by Dr Shaw may be the animal alluded to by the sacred lawgiver. This bird is of the bittern-kind, somewhat less than the lapwing. The neck, the breast, and the belly, are of a light yellow colour, while the back and upper part of the wings are jet-black. The tail is short; the feathers of the neck are long, and streaked with white or a pale yellow. The bill, which is three inches long, is green, and in form like that of the stork; and the legs, which are short and slender, are of the same colour. In walking and searching for food, it throws out its neck seven or eight inches; whence the Arabs call it Boo-onk, or Longneck.[*]

The *hoopoe* is thought to be pretty well ascertained; yet we might suppose that a bird which frequents water more than the European variety does, would not have been misplaced if inserted at the close of the list given above. The accuracy of the inspired writer, however,

---

[*] Calmet's Dictionary, vol. iv. p. 659.

in treating this part of the subject, has been generally extolled,—a precision which, there is no doubt, will hereafter lead to the most satisfactory conclusions in determining the several species he enumerates. All these birds being fish-eaters, no distinction is afforded as arising from diversity of food; but the Hebrew naturalist begins with those which inhabit the sea and its rocky cliffs, the gannet and the cormorant; then he proceeds to the marsh-birds, the bitterns; then to the river and lake birds, the pelican, the king-fisher, or the shagarag; then the stork, which is a bird of passage, lives on land as well as on water, and feeds on frogs and insects no less than on fish; then to another, which probably is a bird of passage also, because it is mentioned the last in the catalogue. The hoopoe is certainly migratory, feeds less on fish than any of the former kinds, and has, in fact, no great relation to the water.

It was objected by Michaelis that the *chasidah* of the Hebrews could not be the stork, because the latter bird does not usually roost on trees; and yet it is asserted in the hundred-and-fourth Psalm that the fir-trees are a dwelling for the stork. But Doubdan, who had no hypothesis to maintain, relates that he saw storks resting on trees between Cana and Nazareth; and Dr Shaw says expressly, the storks breed plentifully in Barbary; and that fir-trees, and other trees when these are wanting, are their usual retreat. It is therefore probable that this bird conforms its manners to circumstances; that wherever it obtains rest, security, and accommodation, there it resides, whether in a ruin or a forest. So that on the whole we need not hesitate, merely because the European stork seldom inhabits trees, to admit that it is the chasidah of the Sacred Scriptures.

We purposely abstain from the description of such birds as are common to Palestine and to the climates of Europe. The ostrich, no doubt, is peculiar to the deserts of Syria and of Arabia, and might therefore demand a more minute delineation than is consistent with our limits. Suffice it to mention, that it is one of the largest and most remarkable of the feathered tribes, and has been celebrated from the most remote antiquity by many fabulous writers, who ascribe to it qualities more wonderful than even those which it actually possesses. Its height is estimated at seven or eight feet, and in swiftness it surpasses every other animal. That it is gregarious no naturalist any longer doubts, being generally seen in large troops at a great distance from the habitations of man. The egg is about three pounds in weight, and in the warmer countries of the East is usually hatched by the rays of the sun alone; though in less heated regions the bird is observed to practise incubation.

The same remarks might be applied to the pelican, whose solitary life as an inhabitant of the desert is occasionally referred to in the Sacred Writings. It appears, however, to be migratory, whence we may conclude that it is also gregarious, and does not always remain alone. In their motion through the air, the pelicans imitate the procedure of the wild-goose, and form their van into an acute angle. When of full age, the male is superior in size to the swan, weighs twenty-five pounds, and from wing to wing extends not less than fifteen feet. The upper mandible is flat and broad, and hooked at the end; the lower mandible has appended to it a very dilatable bag, reaching eight or nine inches down the neck, and large enough to contain several quarts of water. Its food is fish; in diving for which it sometimes descends from a great height. When it has filled its pouch, it flies to some convenient point of a rock, where it swallows its prey at leisure. The vulgar notion, that the female pelican feeds her young with blood from her breast, has arisen from the use of the bag just described, which she opens from time to time to discharge a supply of fish or water for their nourishment.

### SECTION V.—AMPHIBIA AND REPTILES.

In the book of Deuteronomy there is an allusion made to a destructive creature, in the following terms: —" Their wine is the poison of *dragons* and the cruel venom of asps." It is thought that the gecko is the animal contemplated in this description, it being acknowledged by all naturalists to contain a mortal poison. Nature in this instance, says Buffon, appears to act against herself: in a lizard, whose species is but too prolific, she exalts a corrosive liquid to such a degree as to carry death and dissolution into all living substances which it may happen to penetrate. This deadly reptile has some resemblance to the chameleon; his head, almost triangular, is big in proportion to his body; the eyes are very large, the tongue is flat, covered with small scales, and the end is rounded; the teeth are sharp, and so strong that, according to Bontius, they are able to make an impression even on steel. The gecko is almost entirely covered with large warts, more or less rising; the under part of the thigh is furnished with a row of tubercles, raised and grooved. The feet are remarkable for oval scales, somewhat hollowed in the middle, as large as the under surface of the toes themselves, and regularly disposed over one another, like slates on a roof. The usual colour of this animal is a clear green, spotted with brilliant red. It inhabits the crevices of half-rotten trees as well as humid places: it is sometimes met with in houses, where it occasions great alarm, and where every exertion is made to destroy it speedily. Bontius writes, that the bite is so venomous that, if the part affected be not cut away or burned, death ensues in a few hours.

Calmet enumerates eleven kinds of serpents as known to the Hebrews, the names of which are as follow:—

1. Ephe, the viper.
2. Chephir, a sort of aspick.
3. Acshub, the aspick.
4. Pethen, a similar reptile.
5. Tzeboa, speckled serpent.
6. Tzimmaon.
7. Tzepho, or Tzephoni, a basilisk.
8. Kippos, the acontias.
9. Shephiphon, the cerastes.
10. Shachal, the black serpent.
11. Saraph, a flying serpent.

The first of these is remarkable for its quick and penetrating poison; it is about two feet long, and as thick as a man's arm, beautifully spotted with yellow and brown, and sprinkled over with blackish specks, similar to those of the horn-nosed snake. It has a wide mouth, by which it inhales a great quantity of air, and, when fully inflated, ejects it with such violence as to be heard at a considerable distance.

The *shachal*, or black serpent, is described by Forskall as being wholly of that colour, a cubit in length, and as thick as a finger. Its bite is not incurable, but the wound swells severely; the application of a ligature prevents the venom from spreading; or certain plants, as the caper, may be employed to relieve it. Mr Jackson describes a black serpent of much more terrific powers. It is about seven or eight feet long, with a small head, which, when about to assail any object, it frequently expands to four times its ordinary size. It is the only one that will attack travellers; in doing which it coils itself up, and darts to a great distance by the elasticity of its body and tail. The wound inflicted by the bite is small, but the surrounding part immediately turns black, which colour soon pervades the whole body, and the sufferer expires.

But, viewed in connexion with Scripture, the most interesting in the list given in the preceding page is that which stands the seventh in order. Speaking of the happy time revealed by the prophetical spirit, Isaiah remarks that " the sucking child shall play on the hole of the asp, and the weaned child shall put his hand on the cockatrice' den." The editor of Calmet's Dictionary imagines that the naja, or cobra di capello, is the serpent here alluded to by the holy penman, and which is known to possess the most energetic poison. We cannot, indeed, discover positively whether it lays eggs; but the evidence for that fact is presumptive, because all serpents issue from eggs; and the only difference between the oviparous and viviparous is, that in the former the eggs are laid before the fœtus is mature, in the latter the fœtus bursts the egg while yet in the womb of its mother.

If the egg be broken, the little serpent is found rolled up in a spiral form. It appears motionless during some time; but if the term of its exclusion be near, it opens its jaws, inhales at several respirations the air of the atmosphere, its lungs fill, it stretches itself, and, moved by this impetus, it begins to crawl.

The eggs of this reptile have probably given occasion to a fable, which says that cocks can lay eggs, but that these always produce serpents; and that though the cock does not hatch them, the warmth of the sand and atmosphere answers the purposes of incubation. The eggs of the tzepho, of which she lays eighteen or twenty, are equal to those of a pigeon, while those of the great boa are not more than two or three inches in length. As an instance that the eggs of poisonous serpents do not always burst in the body of the female, we may mention the cerastes, which, we are assured, lays in the sand at least four or five, resembling in size those of a dove.

On the grounds now explained, we may understand the language of the prophet Isaiah, who says of the wicked that "they hatch cockatrice' eggs; he that eateth of their eggs dieth, and that which is crushed breaketh forth into a viper." The reptile here alluded to under the name of cockatrice is the tzepho or tzephoni; which, we find, lays eggs so similar to those of poultry, as to be mistaken and eaten for them. Labat farther relates that he crushed some eggs of a large serpent, and found several young in each egg; which were no sooner freed from the shell than they coiled themselves into the attitude of attack, and were ready to spring on whatever came in their way.

In the forty-ninth chapter of Genesis we find the remarkable prediction uttered by Jacob in reference to Dan, that he "shall be a serpent by the way, an adder in the path, that biteth the horse-heels." The original term here is shephiphon, and is understood by several authors to denote the cerastes, a very poisonous kind of viper, distinguished by having horns. This animal, we are informed by Mr Bruce, moves with great rapidity, and in all directions, forward, backward, and sidewise. When he wishes to surprise any one who is too far from him, he creeps with his side towards the person, and his head averted, till, judging his distance, he turns round and springs upon him. " I saw one of them at Cairo crawl up the side of a box in which there were many, and there lie still as if hiding himself, till one of the people who brought him to us came near him ; and though in a very disadvantageous posture, sticking as it were perpendicularly to the side of the box, he leaped nearly the distance of three feet, and fastened between the man's forefinger and thumb, so as to bring the blood. The fellow showed no signs of either pain or fear ; and we kept him with us full four hours, without applying any sort of remedy, or his seeming inclined to do so."

The Arabs name this serpent siff, siphon, or suphon, which seems not very far distant from the root of the Hebrew word siffifon or shephiphon. It is called by the Orientals the *lier in wait*,—an appellation which agrees with the manners of the cerastes. Pliny says, that it hides its whole body in the sand, leaving only its horns exposed, which, being like grains of barley in appearance, attract birds within its reach, so as to become an easy prey. From these circumstances we see, more distinctly, the propriety of the allusion made by the Patriarch to the insidious policy which was to characterize the descendants of Dan in the later periods of their history.

There is mention made in Holy Scripture of the fiery flying serpent, a creature about whose existence and qualities naturalists have entertained a considerable difference of opinion. It is now generally admitted, that, in Guinea, Java, and other countries, where there is at once great heat and a marshy soil, there exists a species of these animals, which have the power of moving in the air, or at least of passing from tree to tree. Niebuhr relates, that at Bazra, also, " there is a sort of serpents, called *heie sursurie*. They commonly live on dates ; and as it would be troublesome to them to come down one high tree and creep up another, they hang by the tail to the branch of one, and, by swinging that about, take advantage of its motion to leap to that of a second. These the modern Arabs call flying serpents,—*heie thiâre.* I do not know whether the ancient Arabs were acquainted with any other kind of flying serpent."*

Near Batavia there are certain flying snakes, or dragons as they are sometimes called. They have four legs, a long tail, and their skin speckled with many spots; their wings are not unlike those of a bat, which they move in flying, but otherwise keep them almost unperceived, close to the body. They fly nimbly, but cannot hold out long; so that they only shift from tree to tree at about twenty or thirty yards' distance. On the outside of the throat are two bladders, which, being extended when they fly, serve them instead of a sail.†

The *scorpion*, or okrab of the Hebrews, has also been invested by Oriental naturalists with the power of flying. Lucian tells us that there are two kinds of scorpions, one residing on the ground, large, having claws, and many articulations at the tail; the other flies in the air, and has inferior wings like locusts, beetles, and bats. In tropical climates the scorpion is a foot in length. No animal in the creation seems endowed with such an irascible nature. When caught, they exert their utmost rage against the glass which contains them; will attempt to sting a stick when put near them; will, without provocation, wound other animals confined with them; and are the cruelest enemies to each other. Maupertuis put a hundred of them together in the same glass; instantly they vented their rage in mutual destruction, universal carnage! In a few days only fourteen remained, which had killed and devoured all the others. It is even asserted, that when in extremity or despair the scorpion will destroy itself. Well might Moses mention this animal as one of the dangers of the howling wilderness! They are still very numerous in the desert between Syria and Egypt. Dr Clarke tells us that one of the

---

* See Calmet, vol. iv. p. 688.
† Churchill's Voyages, vol. ii. p. 296.

privates of the British army, who had received a wound from one of them, lost the upper joint of his forefinger before it could be healed. The author of the Revelation considers them as emblematic of the evils which issue from the bottomless pit. " And there came out of the smoke locusts upon the earth; and unto them was given power, as the scorpions of the earth have power. And they had tails like unto scorpions; and there were stings in their tails: and their power was to hurt men five months."*

We ought not to be surprised that the translators of the English Bible were occasionally at a loss to distinguish the genera and species of the several animals mentioned in the Sacred Writings; for even at the present day, when we possess infinitely higher advantages in point of natural knowledge, we cannot precisely determine even the class or order to which some of them belong. We have an example of this obscurity in the fourth chapter of the book of Lamentations, where it is said that " even the sea-monsters draw out the breast, they give suck to their young ones." The original expression, tannin, appears applicable to those amphibious animals that haunt the banks of rivers and the shores of the sea, and was probably used by the prophet with a reference to the seal species, which suckle their young in the manner described in his pathetic elegy.

It is true that it is used in Genesis in connexion with the epithet large, and is therefore not improperly rendered " great whales." Hence it has been concluded, that the word tannin may comprehend the class of lizards from the eft to the crocodile, provided they be amphibious; also the seal, the manati, the morse, and even the whale, if he came ashore; but as whales remain constantly in the deep, they seem to be more correctly ascribed to the class of fishes. Moreover, whether the people of Syria had any knowledge of the whale-kinds, strictly so called, is a point which deserves

---

* Revelation, ix. 3, 10.

inquiry before it be admitted as certain. At all events, it is manifest that the tannin of the Scripture must have indicated an animal which has many properties common to the seal; for it not only applies the breast to its young, but has the power of exerting its voice in a mournful tone. The prophet Micah says, " I will make a wailing like the tanninim," a phrase which, in our translation, is unhappily rendered " dragons." It has also the faculty of suspending respiration, or of drawing in a quantity of breath and of emitting it with violence. " The wild asses," says Jeremiah, " stand upon the high places; they puff out the breath like the tanninim (here again translated dragons); their eyes fail because there is no grass." On the whole, remarks the editor of Calmet, we may consider the Hebrew *tahash* as being decidedly a seal; but *tannin* as including creatures resident both on land and in water, or, in other words, the amphibia.*

### SECTION VI.—FRUITS AND PLANTS.

It has been remarked that, if the advantages of nature were duly seconded by the efforts of human skill, we might in the space of twenty leagues bring together in Syria the vegetable riches of the most distant countries. Besides wheat, rye, barley, beans, and the cotton-plant, which are cultivated every where, there are several objects of utility or pleasure, peculiar to different localities. Palestine, for example, abounds in sesamum, which affords oil; and in dhoura, similar to that of Egypt. Maize thrives in the light soil of Baalbec, and rice is cultivated with success along the marsh of Hoolé. Within these twenty-five years sugar-canes have been introduced into the gardens of Saida and Beirout, which are not inferior to those of the Delta. Indigo grows without culture on the banks of the Jordan, and only requires a little care to secure a good quality. The hills of Latakie produce tobacco, which creates a com-

---

* Calmet's Dictionary, vol. iv. p. 696.

mercial intercourse with Damietta and Cairo. This crop is at present cultivated in all the mountains. The white mulberry forms the riches of the Druses, by the beautiful silks which are obtained from it; and the vine, raised on poles or creeping along the ground, furnishes red and white wines equal to those of Bourdeaux. Jaffa boasts of her lemons and water-melons; Gaza possesses both the dates of Mecca and the pomegranates of Algiers. Tripoli has oranges which might vie with those of Malta; Beirout has figs like Marseilles, and bananas like St Domingo. Aleppo is unequalled for pistachio-nuts; and Damascus possesses all the fruits of Europe; inasmuch as apples, plums, and peaches, grow with equal facility on her rocky soil. Niebuhr is of opinion that the Arabian coffee-shrub might be cultivated in Palestine.*

The *fig-tree*, the *palm*, and the *olive*, are characteristic of the Holy Land, and therefore deserve our more particular attention. In regard to the first, the earliest fruit produced, which is usually ripe in June, is called the boccore; the later, or proper fig, being rarely fit to be gathered before the month of August. The name of these last is the kermez, or kermouse. They constitute the article which passes through the hands of the merchant, after being either preserved in the common way or made up into cakes. They continue a long time on the tree before they fall off; whereas the boccore drop as soon as they are ripe, and according to the beautiful allusion of the prophet Nahum, " fall into the mouth of the eater upon being shaken."

The *palm* must at one time have been common in Palestine, though at present it fails to attract attention either on account of number or of beauty. In several coins of Vespasian, as well as of his son Titus, the land of Judea is typified by a disconsolate woman sitting under one of these trees. Jericho, which was formerly distinguished as the " city of palms," can still boast a few of them, because, besides the advantage of a sandy soil and a warm climate, it commands a plentiful supply of water,

---

* Malte-Brun, vol. ii. p. 130.

an element absolutely indispensable to their growth. At Jerusalem, Shechem, and other places to the northward of the capital, not more than two or three of them are ever seen together; and even these, as their fruit rarely comes to maturity, are of no farther service than, like the palm-tree of Deborah, to shade the council of the sheiks, or to supply the branches, which, as in ancient days, may still be required for religious processions.*

The *olive* no longer holds the place which it once occupied in the estimation of the inhabitants of Palestine. The wretched government under which they exist has rooted out all the seeds of industry, by rendering the absence of wealth the only security against oppression. But in those places where it continues to be cultivated, it affords ample proof to establish the accuracy of the inspired writer, who denominated Palestine a land of oil-olive and honey.

The *cedars of Libanus*, as is stated in a former chapter, still maintain their ancient reputation for beauty and stature; while the mountain-forests whereon they grow, are diversified by a thousand elegant plants, which dispute with them the possession of the lofty ridges. Here the astragalus tragacanthoides displays its clusters of purple flowers; and the primrose, the amaryllis, the white and the orange lily, mingle their brilliant hues with the verdure of the birch-leaved cherry. Even the snow of the highest peaks is skirted by shrubs possessing the most splendid colours. The coolness, humidity, and good quality of the soil, support an uninterrupted vegetation; and the bounties of nature in those elevated regions are still protected by the spirit of liberty.

Hasselquist is of opinion that the *wild-grapes* mentioned by the prophet Isaiah must be the hoary nightshade, or solanum incanum, because it is common in Egypt, Palestine, and Syria. The Arabs call it wolf-grapes, as, from its shrubby stalk, it has some resem-

---

* Shaw's Travels, vol. ii. p. 152. See also Dr Harris's "Dictionary of the Natural History of the Bible," London edition of 1833, a work replete with the most valuable information.

blance to a vine. But the sacred writer could not have found a weed more opposite to the vine than this, or more suitable to the purpose which he had in view, for it is extremely pernicious to that plant, and is rooted out wherever it appears. " Wherefore," exclaims the holy seer, " when I looked that my vineyard should bring forth grapes, brought it forth poisonous night-shade ?"*

The author just named describes the "Balsam of Aaron" as a very fine oil, which emits no scent or smell, and is very proper for preparing odoriferous ointments. It is obtained from a tree called behen, which grows in Mount Sinai and Upper Egypt, and, it is presumed, in certain parts of the Holy Land. Travellers assert that it is the very perfume with which the ancient high-priest of the Jews, with whose name it is connected, was wont to anoint his beard, and which the Psalmist extols so much on account of its mollifying qualities,—the emblem of domestic harmony and brotherly love.

There still exists a thorn in Palestine known among botanists by the name of the " spina Christi," or thorn of Christ, and supposed to be the shrub which afforded the crown worn by our Saviour before his crucifixion. It must have been very fit for the purpose, for it has many small sharp prickles, well adapted to give pain ; and as the leaves greatly resemble those of ivy, it is not improbable that the enemies of the Messiah chose it from its similarity to the plant with which emperors and generals were accustomed to be crowned ; and hence that there might be calumny, insult, and derision, meditated in the very act of punishment.†

---

* Isaiah, v. 4. † Voyages and Travels in the Levant, p. 288.

# INDEX.

## A.

Aaron, Balsam of, described, page 394.

Abdallah, pasha of Acre, offends the Sultan, 356. Is attacked by the Viceroy of Egypt, 357.

Abdi, Wilderness of, contains extensive ruins, 210.

Abdomim, the place of blood, 228.

Abraham, the place of his interment, 209.

Acre recovered by the Christian warriors, 317. Finally taken by the Tartars and Mamlouks, 344. Besieged by Bonaparte, 349. Its importance in his eyes, 352, 353. Is taken by Ibrahim Pasha, 357.

Adma, one of the cities of the Plain, 366.

Adrian, Emperor, rebuilds Jerusalem, 24.

Agrippa, Herod, obtains the government of all Palestine, 98; his sudden death, 99.

Alcimus assumes the title of high priest under the Syrians, 88.

Aldersey, Laurence, account of his voyage to Syria, 136.

Aleppo, copper found in the neighbourhood, 370.

Amaury or Almeric becomes king of Jerusalem, 312.

Amphibia, peculiar to Palestine, described, 384.

Anti-Libanus, a term unknown among the ancients, 364.

Antioch besieged by Bohemond, 304.

Antiochus Epiphanes, his severities towards the Jews, 86.

Antipas, Herod, deprived of his tetrarchy, 98.

Antipater made procurator of Judea, 92.

Aphaca, a village among the heights of Lebanon, celebrated for a temple of Venus, 286.

Arabs, resemblance of the Hebrews to them, 60.

Archelaus succeeds his father Herod, 96.

Arculfus visits Jerusalem, 133.

Aristobulus subdued by the Romans, 92.

Arthur Seat, geological features of, 366.

Arvieux, his remarks on the preference of a pastoral life, 59.

Assyria, always desirous to obtain possession of Palestine, 71.

## B.

Baalbec, supposed to be the ancient Baal-gad, 281. Its ruins described, 283.

Bahar Loth, or Dead Sea, 214.

Baldwin succeeds Godfrey as king, 311.

Bankes, Mr, his description of festival at Bethlehem, 199.

Barcochab the impostor, 296.

Baumgarten, Martin de, is rudely treated by the Saracens, 136.

Beilan, great victory gained there by Ibrahim Pasha, 358.

Beirout, remarkable for fossil remains, 369.

Belus, the river, celebrated for its red colour, and for art of making glass, 292.

Bernard, St, preaches in favour of crusade, 311.

Bertrandon de la Broquière visits Jerusalem, 135.

Beth-amareen, village of, mentioned, 243.

Bethany, the village of, 195.

Bethesda, Pool of, the remains still visible, 184.

Bethlehem, the scenery around described, 195; the church of, 197.

Bethulia, held by Knights of Jerusalem, 207; identified with the Herodium, 208.

Bibars, Sultan of Egypt, attacks the Christians, 338. Reduces Antioch, 339.

Bitumen, large quantities of, 219.

Bonaparte invades Syria, 348. Attacks Acre, but is repulsed, 349-351.

Bouldesell, William de, travels into Palestine, 134.

Breidenbach, journeys to Holy Land, 135.

## C.

Calendar, Jewish, divided into civil and ecclesiastical, 119.

Calvary, the cleft in the rock, 165.
ana of Galilee, now Kefer Kenna, 277. The house where the marriage was celebrated, 278.
Canaan, its ancient and modern divisions, 37-40.
Capernaum, now called Talhewm, or Tel Hoom, 256. Formerly a place of some importance, 257.
Caramania, entered by Ibrahim at the head of his army, 358.
Carmel, Mount, the predicted curse fallen upon it, 292. The heights of, present some striking fossil remains, 369.
Castravan mountains contain a singular bed of whitish stone, 369.
Celestine III., Pope, originates the fourth crusade, 322.
Chasidah, or stork, described, 383.
Chateaubriand, his account of Jerusalem, 145.
Cheron, his work on Palestine, 138.
Clarke, Dr, his description of Jerusalem, 147. His opinions disputed, 186. His scientific observations praised, 363.
Climate, variety of, in Palestine, 370, 371.
Colleges, Levitical, fountains of national literature, 117.
Conrade III. joins the crusaders, 311.
Constantine orders a church to be built over the tomb of Christ, 25.
Cornwall, Richard Earl of, gains successes in Holy Land, 332.
Courçon, Robert de, preaches up a holy war, 326.
Crusaders take Jerusalem, 306. Their policy considered, 309.

D.

Damascus, the Pasha of, his power described, 356. The city taken by Ibrahim, 358. English consul admitted, 359.
Damietta taken by crusaders, 327. Surrendered to Saracens, 336.
Dan, the position of the town so named, 280.
Darkness identified with Evil Spirit, 113.
David, King, his conduct to Nabal, 61. His skill as a warrior, 72. Takes Jerusalem, and makes it the metropolis of Palestine, 73. Builds a suburb on Mount Zion, ib. Defeats the Philistines, ib. Makes preparations for building the temple, and leaves a flourishing kingdom to his son, 74.
Days, division of among the Hebrews, 120.

Dead Sea described, 210-221.
Dedication, feast of, mentioned, 127.
Dier el Akmar, a scene in Libanus, 288.
Diocesarea, the ancient Zippor, and modern Sephouri, 289.
Doubdan, his work on Palestine, 138.
Druses, inhabitants of Libanus, 270. Bonaparte expected aid from them, 353.

E.

Earthquakes frequent in the Syrian provinces, 364. Their periodical occurrence in Syria and southern Italy, 365.
Easter, mode of celebrating the feast at Jerusalem, 163.
Ebal, the mount so named, 237.
Edward, Prince of Wales, joins Louis IX. in a crusade, 340. His exploits and wound, 341. Concludes a peace and returns home, 342.
El Aksa, a Turkish house of prayer at Jerusalem, 157.
Elders of Tribes among the Hebrews, 58. They demand a king, 71.
El Gaur, valley of, 35.
Elijah, the phenomenon of the small cloud, 372.
Elizabeth, her vault or chapel, 205.
El Zowar or El Ghor mentioned, 211.
Emerald, peculiarities of the Asiatic variety, 367.
Esdraëlon, the grand Plain of, described, 270.
Eusebius, his measurement of Jerusalem, 191.
Ezra joins Nehemiah and Zerubbabel in conducting Judah and Benjamin to their own land, 84.

F.

Felix, his violence and fraud, 101.
Festus, his mild government in Judea, 101.
Fig-tree, its varieties and seasons, 392.
Flagellation, Pillar of, 164.
Florus, his avarice and cruelty condemned, 101.
Foulques of Anjou becomes King of Jerusalem, 311.
Frederick Barbarossa, the Emperor, enters the Holy Land, 316.
Frederick the Second of Germany makes peace with the Saracens, 330.
Freebooters, common to Hebrews and Arabs, 60. The life of a robber not deemed disreputable, 61.

# INDEX.

French, their dreadful sufferings in Syria, 354.
Fulk, the preacher of fifth crusade, 324.

## G.

Galilee, richness of its soil, 34. Sea of, described, 256.
Gallus, Cestius, repulsed under the walls of Jerusalem, 102.
Gamala, the remains of, 253. Supposed by Dr Seetzen to be Gadara, 254. Great appearances of ancient opulence, 255.
Gecko, a poisonous reptile, described, 385.
Geology, a sketch of it as applied to Western Syria, 363.
Georgewitz, Bartholomeo, his work on the Holy Land, 136.
Geraza, or Djerash, the ruins pointed out, 245-248. Supposed to be the Gergasha of the Hebrews, 248.
Gerizim Mount, a heathen temple built on it, 238.
Gethsemane, Garden of, 189.
Gilboa, the mountains of, described, 269.
Gilead, the land of, described, 244.
Goat, the wild variety of Palestine, 375.
Godfrey takes Jerusalem, 306. He is made first Christian king of it, 307.
Gold, a native variety found near Tiberias, 368.
Gomorrah, its ruin ascribed to a volcanic eruption, 366.
Gonzales, his travels in the Holy Land, 138.
Grotto of Nativity, 198.

## H.

Halley, Dr, his opinions respecting the Dead Sea, 217.
Hart, the Aïl of Scripture, mentioned, 374.
Hasselquist, his acquirements as a naturalist, 362.
Hebrews, all agriculturists or shepherds, 62. Their wealth consisted in camels, kine, sheep, and goats, 64.
Hebron, or El Hhalil, the burialplace of the Patriarchs, 208.
Hecatæus, his opinion as to the extent of Jewish territory, 45.
Helena, Empress, builds churches in the Holy Land, 26.
Henniker, Sir F., his travels in Palestine and Egypt, 139. His narrow escape, 228.
Henry VI. the German Emperor, goes to Holy Land, 322.

Heraclius, the Emperor, expelled Persians from Syria, 301.
Hermon, Mount, its dews celebrated in Scripture, 363.
Herod the Great invested with the charge of Galilee, 92. He erects several forts and citadels, 94. Rebuilds the temple of Jerusalem, and dies four years before the common era of Christianity, 95.
High Places permitted by Samuel, 121.
Hinnom, the vale of, at the foot of Mount Zion, 192.
Holy Sepulchre described, 160.
Homs, battle of, gained by Ibrahim Pasha, 358.
Hoopoe, an aquatic bird, 382.

## I.

Ibrahim Pasha suppresses bands of robbers, 360. Attacks Abdallah, the pasha of Acre, 357. Compels him to accept terms of accommodation, ib. He takes possession of Damascus, 358. Gains an important victory at Homs, ib. Defeats Hussein Pasha at Beilan, ib.
Ignis Fatuus, a singular variety, 373.
Indigo, grows naturally in Palestine, 391.
Innocent III. suggests fifth crusade, 324.
Iron found in Mount Lebanon, 369.
Isabella, queen of Jerusalem, 323.
Islamism, rise of, 302.
Israelites enjoyed a real equality, having no degraded class, 114.

## J.

Jacob, his well described, 237, 241.
Jaffa relieved by Richard, 320.
Jehoiakim threatened by Nebuchadnezzar, 80.
Jehoshaphat, valley of, 179.
Jennin, the village of, 244. Anciently called Ginoa, ib.
Jephthah, the fate of his daughter annually lamented, 128.
Jerboa, supposed to be the Saphan of Scripture, 379.
Jeremiah, the prison of, 233.
Jericho, a poor village, sacked by Vespasian, and rebuilt by Adrian, 222. The position of it fixed by Josephus, 223.
Jeroboam revolts from the house of David, 78; and establishes the emblems of an idolatrous faith, 79.
Jerusalem, its situation and holy

places—called Ælia Capitolina, 25. Sacked by Nebuzar-adan, 81, 83. Is taken by Pompey, 91. Description of, 146, 152. Modern manners and inhabitants, 230. Repaired by Romans, 296. Is sacked by the Persians, 301. Taken by the Crusaders under Godfrey, 306. Reduced by Saladin, 315.

Jews, origin of, 18. Importance of their history, 20-22. Extent of their territory, 46. Their insurrections, 96. Their miserable condition in modern times, 232. Indulgence shown to them, 298. Their number throughout the world, 360. Affecting complaint of, ib. They continue to cherish their ancient hopes, 361.

John, St, his convent described, 204.

Jordan, the wilderness of, 212-214. The river, its dimensions, and quality of the water, 221. The fountains of, 280.

Joshua, his counsel to Hebrew people, 42.

Judas the Gaulonite, the opinions of his followers, 100.

Judea reduced to a Roman province, dependent on the prefecture of Syria, 96.

Judges, Hebrew, compared to Carthaginian Suffetes, 54. Character of, 69.

Julian favours the Jews, and attempts to rebuild the temple, 299.

Junot risks a battle near Nazareth, 353.

### K.

Kedron, the brook of this name, 190.

Kefer Kenna, the ancient Cana, 277.

Khamel, Sultan of Damascus, makes peace with Crusaders, 329.

King's Dale described, 180.

Kings, Sepulchres of the, 185, 234, 235.

Kleber, General, his masterly conduct, 353.

Koniah, great victory gained by Ibrahim, 359.

Koran, remarkable copy of, 159.

### L.

Land, extent of, given to Hebrew families, 47. Redemption of, 48.

Latin Christians severely taxed in Palestine, 355.

Law, book of, long neglected, 116.

Learning of Hebrews, 103. Its various branches, 104.

Leban or Lebonah, a village near Jerusalem, 236.

Lebanon, the mountains composed of calcareous rock, and are full of caverns, 364.

Levi, tribe of, separated for special purposes, 64. Their maintenance, duties, and towns, 66. Described as a literary noblesse, 68.

Libanus, cedars of, 287.

Light identified with Good Spirit, 113.

Longinus, Cassius, made Prefect of Syria, 100.

Louis VII. engages in a crusade, 311.

Louis IX. leads a force to Palestine, 333. He takes Damietta, 334. He returns to France, 337. Embarks again for Syria, 340. He dies at Carthage, ib.

Lyell, Mr, his opinions stated, 364.

### M.

Maccabees, account of their zeal and courage in the war with the Grecian Kings of Syria, 88.

Maimonides, his opinion on courts of justice, 57.

Malte-Brun, his opinion as to the fate of Sodom, 215.

Mariamne, wife of Herod the Great, cruelly murdered, 93.

Mariti, the Abbé, quoted, 216, 217, 227.

Meteorology of Syrian provinces, 370.

Michaelis, his description of the tribe of Levi, 68. His opinion of the engulphed cities at the Dead Sea, 214.

Military service, obligation of Hebrews to, 49.

Milton, his description of the Mountain of Temptation, 227.

Mohammed, viceroy of Egypt, defies the power of the Sultan, 357. Is commanded to withdraw his armies from Syria, ib. Resolves to conquer the whole of that country, 358.

Mole, this animal reckoned among unclean things, 380.

Months, Jewish, explained, 119.

Moses anticipated regal government, and gave rules for the conduct of the king, 72.

### N.

Nablous, the ancient Shechem, 239.

Nativity, the Grotto of, at Bethlehem, 198.

# INDEX. 399

Nau, Father, his notions respecting the Lake Asphaltites, 216.
Nazareth, the modern Nassera, its interesting antiquities, 271. Its magnificent church, 277.
Nebuchadnezzar threatens the kingdom of Judah under Jehoiakim, 80.
Nehemiah aids Zerubbabel in restoring Judah and Benjamin, 84.

## O.

Offence, Mount of, origin of the name, 181.
Okrab, or scorpion, delineated, 389.
Olive, this plant now neglected, 393.
Olives, Mount of, commands the best view of Jerusalem, 152.
Omar, mosque of, the St Peter's of Turkey, 153. Described by Dr Richardson, 153, 154. His victorious career, 302.
Oryx, or wild-ox, described, 376.
Osman Pasha leads a Turkish force to support Abdallah of Acre, 357.

## P.

Palestine, dimensions and boundaries of, 17-35. Its present aspect, 28. Fertility of, 30. Annexed to Egypt as a province, 346. Natural history of, 362.
Passover, feast of, rules for its observance, 122.
Pastoral life preferred by the people of the East, 59.
Pelican, the solitary bird mentioned in Scripture, 384.
Pentecost, feast of, object explained, 124.
Persians invade Judea under their general Carnsia, 300. They sack Jerusalem, 301.
Peter, St, his house shown at Tiberias, or Tabaria, 261.
Peter the Hermit, his zeal and success, 303, 304.
Philip Augustus, king of France, engages in the third crusade, 316.
Plants found in Syrian provinces, 391.
Poetry, Hebrew, excellence of, 129.
Pompey takes Jerusalem, 91. Penetrates into the Holy of Holies, 92.
Precipitation, Mount of, near the town of Nazareth, 274.
Prophecy, meaning of the term in Scripture, 105.
Prophets, Schools of, 104. The studies pursued in them, ib.
Prophets, Great and Less, 110. The studies in which they were engaged, 111.

Pygarg, or lidmee of the Bible, 375.

## Q.

Quarantina, the mountain so called, 226.
Quirinius made Prefect of Syria, 97; called Cyrenius in St Luke's Gospel, ib.

## R.

Rachel, the tomb of, described, 196.
Rahbah, the village of, 224.
Redemption of land, 48. Of houses, 49.
Reem, or unicorn, described, 377.
Regal government anticipated by Moses, 72.
Rehoboam, his despotism, 78.
Richard Cœur de Lion becomes a crusader, 316. Defeats Saladin at Azotus, 318. Relieves Jaffa, 320. Returns to England, 321.
Richardson, Dr, his description of Holy Sepulchre, 160-162.
Roebuck, or tzebi, described, 374.
Russia interposes in behalf of Turkey, 359.

## S.

Saladin, the Sultan, opposes the Crusaders, 312. Defeats the Christians at Tiberias, 314. He takes Jerusalem, 315. Is repulsed before Tyre, 316. His remark on the character of Richard, 321. His death and funeral, 322.
Samaritans, their submission to Antiochus, 87.
Santa Saba delineated, 211.
Saphadin, Sultan, encounters the crusaders, 322.
Saphan, or coney, described, 378.
Saphet, still has a university, 279.
Saul consults the soothsayer, 106. He is chosen king, 72. His character, history, and death, ib.
Science little known among Hebrews, 118.
Scriptures, Hebrew, striking sublimity of, 112.
Sebaste, the modern name of Samaria, 242. The town described, 243.
Seetzen, Dr, his description of the country beyond Jordan, 245.
Serpent, the fiery flying, 388.
Sharon, plain of, described, 143.
Shechem or Nablous, remarkable for ancient copies of, the Samaritan Pentateuch, 240.
Shechinah, lost during captivity, 85.
Sheiks, their dishonest character, 356.

Shephiphon, or cerastes, a kind of viper, 387.
Siloam, Pool of, noticed, 178.
Simeon, the Tower of, 195.
Sinai, Mount, its geological relations described, 364.
Smith, Sir Sidney, mentioned, 280.
Sodom, apples of, 220. Its destruction ascribed to an earthquake, 366.
Solomon succeeds his father David, 74. His traffic with foreign nations, ib. Disregards the leading principles of the Hebrew constitution, 75. Founds Tadmor, ib. The advantages of this city for trade, 77. His books, 111. His acquirements in natural knowledge, 118. His Pools noticed, 202.
Spina Christi, or thorn of Christ, mentioned, 394.
Suffetes of Carthage compared to Hebrew Judges, 54.
Synagogues, origin of, 121.

T.

"Table of Christ" described, 275.
Tadmor founded by Solomon, 75. Its numerous advantages as a trading city, 77.
Tannin, an amphibious animal, 390.
Tekoa, the village of, mentioned, 206.
Territory, extent of Jewish, 46.
Theocracy established among Hebrews, 53.
Thunder in Palestine more common in winter than in summer, 372.
Tiberias, a town on the sea of Galilee, built by Herod Antipas, or by Tiberius, 258. Supposed to be the Chinneroth of the Hebrews, 261. Still celebrated for its warm baths, 263. Famed for its ancient university, 264.
Tor or Tabor, the mount of, 265.
Tribes, independence of, 48. Constitution of, including heads and princes, 50, 51.
Trumpets, feast of, explained, 125, 126.
Tudela, Benjamin of, his Travels, 303.
Turks acquire ascendency in Syria, and threaten Europe, 345, 346.
Compelled to adopt a more liberal policy, 355.
Turpentine, Valley of, 144.

U.

Unction, stone of, 166.
Urban, Pope, countenances the crusaders, 304.
Urim and Thummim ceased with the desolation of Jerusalem, 85.

V.

Vespasian establishes a garrison on Mount Sion, 295.
Via Dolorosa described, 177.
Virgin, Fountain of the, 179.
Vizier defeated at Koniah by Ibrahim, son of the Viceroy of Egypt, 359.
Volcanoes in various parts of Palestine, at Tiberias, and in the valley of the Dead Sea, 364.
Volney quoted, 140, 202, 369.

W.

Water of Dead Sea, its specific gravity, 217.
Waterspouts common in Syria, 372.
Werner, his geological system mentioned, 364.
Willibald, travels to Jerusalem, 133.
Winds, the prevailing ones in Palestine, 371.
Writing not generally known among the Hebrews in early times, 118.

Z.

Zabulon, vale of, described, 291.
Zingis Khan displaces Karismians, who invade Palestine, 332.
Zeboim destroyed by a great volcanic eruption, 366.
Zedekiah revolts against the King of Babylon, 81. His defeat and captivity, ib.
Zelophedad, the case of his daughters considered, 127.
Zerubbabel employed in restoring captives, 84.
Zippor, the modern Sephouri, 289. Its ruins, 290.
Zomer, an animal known to the ancient Jews, 376.
Zoology of Palestine described, 374.

THE END.